MATRIARCH

MATRIARCH

A Memoir

TINA KNOWLES

WITH KEVIN CARR O'LEARY

ONE WORLD   NEW YORK

One World
An imprint of Random House
A Division of Penguin Random House LLC
1745 Broadway, New York, NY 10019
oneworldlit.com
randomhousebooks.com
penguinrandomhouse.com

Library of Congress Cataloging-in-Publication Data
Names: Knowles, Tina, author.
Title: Matriarch : a memoir / Tina Knowles.
Description: First edition. | New York, NY : One World, 2025.
Identifiers: LCCN 2024060350 (print) | LCCN 2024060351 (ebook) |
ISBN 9780593597408 (hardcover) | ISBN 9780593597415 (ebook)
Subjects: LCSH: Beyoncé, 1981- | Knowles, Tina, 1954- |
Singers—United States—Biography. | Mothers of celebrities—Biography. |
LCGFT: Biographies. | Autobiographies.
Classification: LCC ML420.K675 K56 2025 (print) | LCC ML420.K675 (ebook) |
DDC 782.42164092 [B]—dc23/eng/20241223
LC record available at https://lccn.loc.gov/2024060350
LC ebook record available at https://lccn.loc.gov/2024060351

Printed in the United States of America on acid-free paper

9 8 7 6 5 4 3 2 1

First Edition

Illustrations by Camila Pinheiro
Book design by Elizabeth Rendfleisch

The authorized representative in the EU for product safety and compliance is Penguin Random House Ireland, Morrison Chambers, 32 Nassau Street, Dublin D02 YH68, Ireland. https://eu-contact.penguin.ie.

To my mother,
Agnes Derouen Buyince,
who taught me by example.
The very best parts of me came from you.

To my daughters,
who became my friends:
Solange, Beyoncé, Kelly, Angie—
you are my crew, my tribe, my ride-or-dies.
What would I do without you?

To all the women out there
who are the Matriarchs of their families.

I am the mother of the world. All these children are mine. Anybody let me love 'em, they're mine. Those that don't let me love 'em, then I love 'em anyhow.

—Willie Mae Ford Smith (the mother of gospel music), *I Dream a World*

CONTENTS

ACT THREE: A WOMAN   337

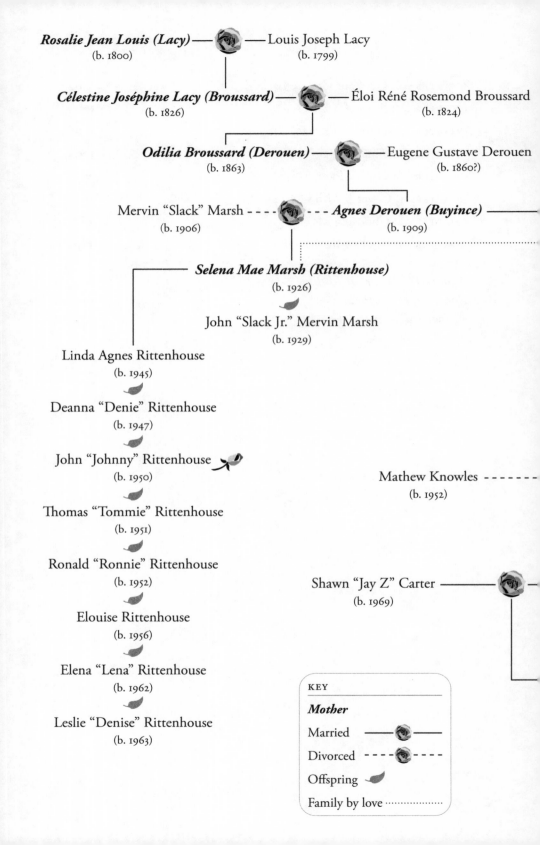

Rosalie Jean Louis (Lacy) — Louis Joseph Lacy
(b. 1800)   (b. 1799)

Célestine Joséphine Lacy (Broussard) — Éloi Réné Rosemond Broussard
(b. 1826)   (b. 1824)

Odilia Broussard (Derouen) — Eugene Gustave Derouen
(b. 1863)   (b. 1860?)

Mervin "Slack" Marsh ----- **Agnes Derouen (Buyince)**
(b. 1906)   (b. 1909)

Selena Mae Marsh (Rittenhouse)
(b. 1926)

John "Slack Jr." Mervin Marsh
(b. 1929)

Linda Agnes Rittenhouse
(b. 1945)

Deanna "Denie" Rittenhouse
(b. 1947)

John "Johnny" Rittenhouse
(b. 1950)

Mathew Knowles -------
(b. 1952)

Thomas "Tommie" Rittenhouse
(b. 1951)

Ronald "Ronnie" Rittenhouse
(b. 1952)

Shawn "Jay Z" Carter
(b. 1969)

Elouise Rittenhouse
(b. 1956)

Elena "Lena" Rittenhouse
(b. 1962)

Leslie "Denise" Rittenhouse
(b. 1963)

KEY

Mother

Married — 🌹 —

Divorced ---- 🌹 ----

Offspring 🍃

Family by love ·············

The Mother Tree

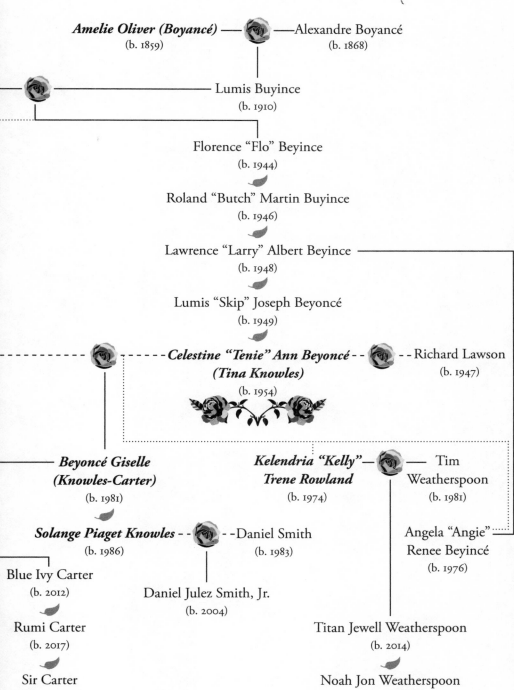

Amelie Oliver (Boyancé) — Alexandre Boyancé
(b. 1859)   (b. 1868)

Lumis Buyince
(b. 1910)

Florence "Flo" Beyince
(b. 1944)

Roland "Butch" Martin Buyince
(b. 1946)

Lawrence "Larry" Albert Beyince
(b. 1948)

Lumis "Skip" Joseph Beyoncé
(b. 1949)

**Celestine "Tenie" Ann Beyoncé
(Tina Knowles)**
(b. 1954)

Richard Lawson
(b. 1947)

**Beyoncé Giselle
(Knowles-Carter)**
(b. 1981)

**Kelendria "Kelly"
Trene Rowland**
(b. 1974)

Tim
Weatherspoon
(b. 1981)

Solange Piaget Knowles - - Daniel Smith
(b. 1986)   (b. 1983)

Angela "Angie"
Renee Beyincé
(b. 1976)

Blue Ivy Carter
(b. 2012)

Daniel Julez Smith, Jr.
(b. 2004)

Rumi Carter
(b. 2017)

Sir Carter
(b. 2017)

Titan Jewell Weatherspoon
(b. 2014)

Noah Jon Weatherspoon
(b. 2021)

UNDER THE PECAN TREE

December 1958

LATER, A DAUGHTER will miss the sound of her mother calling her name.

You can't convince her of this when she is young. Not while that voice is so plentiful in the air. She hears her mother say her name over and over, whether as a command to pay attention or a plea to know her worth; a sigh of maternal love or a warning to be cautious.

She cannot understand in those moments what she would someday trade to hear that voice again.

"TENIE."

I was four years old and in a dream. The kind where the sequins my mama had sewn onto a Sunday dress became diamonds to be plucked and passed out to only the best friends. Or one where we discovered the Pleasure Pier amusement park on Galveston Beach was running free rides with all the five-cent sodas we could drink. That kind of dream. And now, here was my mama, calling me home just as it was getting good.

"Teeenie." She said my name louder now, the accent of my mother's childhood Creole smoothed out but still there. Agnes Derouen Buyince had polished her soft voice to a pleasing shine on her way to the sixth grade, as far as school went for a Black girl back where she grew up in Louisiana.

Before I opened my eyes, the first thing I noticed was that our house was warm. In Galveston—well, in any poor house—when you went to bed in winter all the heat was shut off. Old houses like ours didn't have heating anyway, just a space heater. Even here on the island off the Gulf Coast of Texas, the nights could get down to freezing.

A warm house in the morning meant my mama was well. Ever since she had me, the last of her seven babies at age forty-four, my mother had been sickly. She would go into John Sealy, a charity hospital in Galveston, at least twice a year with heart ailments that seemed tied to her constant worrying. Her health problems weren't made up or exaggerated, rather something scary that lurked in the background like a phantom, waiting. I was always fearful of when they would come back. When my mother was home, she would get up before everybody else in the family, around five in the morning, to light the heater. If she was staying in the hospital, my father or one of us kids would have to get up to coax the heater to life. We never did it early enough like her, and the rest of the day it would feel like we were catching up to the chill that stayed two steps ahead. But this day, I knew she was fine, and we were warm.

We had this little two-bedroom home with seven people living in it: My three older brothers, Larry, Butch, and Skip, slept in one bedroom, and my mom and dad built a partition wall in their bedroom to give my older sister Flo her own space. My bed was kind of floating out in the middle of that room.

In that bed, too cozy to move, I heard my mother in the kitchen fixing breakfast. My parents were big on us all eating together. I could smell the homemade bread toasting in the stove, her pecan pancakes on the griddle, and the sausages my three brothers would wolf down before school.

I closed that one eye again, then remembered it was now December. Each morning I woke up one day closer to Christmas, which also meant one day closer to my fifth birthday in January. That got me off the bed, the padded feet of my all-in-one pajamas hitting the floor. I slid on those footy pajamas, pretending I was an ice skater on the worn wood floor to the kitchen. Everyone was already at the table, of course. Everyone always got up before me. My big sister Flo was fourteen and all business getting ready for school—I was born on her tenth birthday, and her party was canceled when my mom went to the hospital to have me. "She came into the world screwing my life up," Flo would say. Butch was twelve, his good looks and gift of gab causing a stir wherever he went, boys already hating him as much as girls loved him. Quiet, brilliant Larry was ten, reading the newspaper that my mother also read front to back. Skip was making some corny joke to try to get our father laughing, a nine-year-old who had already mastered dad jokes. It was tough to get a laugh out of my daddy—Lumis Buyince was so handsome that he had worked hard to seem gruff. I would always sit on his lap and try to hug on him. He might let you hug him a couple of times and then you'd hear in his thick Creole accent, "*Okay! That's enough. Get goin'. Go on now.*" We would giggle at how uncomfortable our affection made him.

Sounds like a lot of people, but our house was quiet. My parents were older, closing in on fifty years old and already grandparents whose two oldest kids had moved out long before I showed up. They were tired, and I *was* tiring. I'm pretty sure I had ADHD, but people didn't know what that was. So they just called you *bad*. My nickname at first was Dennis the Menace, after the little comic about a mischievous boy that ran in the *Galveston Daily News*. But the name that stuck was Badass Tenie B.

Tenie was short for Celestine Ann, which didn't suit me because people didn't say it right. You say it like "Celeste-een," but I would get "Sell-isteen" or worse, "Sulluh-steen." The *B* was for my last name, Beyoncé, and the Badass was for everything I did. I never hurt anyone, I just moved quicker than I could think. God had given my mother, the most cautious woman I would ever know, a girl without fear. Or, my mom might have said, any kind of sense. So Badass Tenie B was a good fit.

My sister and brothers didn't want to be bothered with a hyper four-year-old, and their real lives happened out of sight with their friends at school. When they left for the school day and my dad drove to work at the docks, it was only my mother and me. By the time they all were out the door, she had already been to the seven o'clock mass that she went to every single day at Holy Rosary Catholic Church across the street. Then she'd start her seamstress work. Sewing. That was her profession, and her mother was a seamstress before her.

My mother had a gift for making the most beautiful masterpieces from remnants. When you went to the fabric store in Galveston, remnants were the ends of the expensive bolts of fabric. If it had once cost something outlandish, maybe six dollars a yard, now it could be yours for fifty cents. There might have been a half of a yard left, certainly enough for a little girl's dress, and they would durn near just give the fabric to you. Mama was a beader, taking tiny seed pearls and meticulously sewing each millimeter bead into a dress or jacket, one by one, to make a work of art.

But before any of that work started in those early winter days like this one, we picked pecans. This was the harvest time for the pecan tree in our backyard, when my mother would go out every morning after breakfast to fill a bag. She would make pecan pralines, or press them into the pastries of pies, or hand them to the boys to crack and eat fresh to keep them busy and fed. We always had pecans, and I don't know when I realized it was because they were free.

"Come on, Tenie," my mama said, grabbing the large brown burlap bag to head out to the yard. I followed in my pajamas outside, attempting cartwheels behind her.

The pecan tree was huge, beautiful with a rounded canopy of branches. I skipped around its scaly gray-brown trunk, pretending to have a ribbon as I stretched out the opening lines of "Maybe" by the Chantels. "Maybe, if I cry every night, you'll come back to me. . . ." Whirling, I looked up at the tree's sturdy branches, strong enough to hold even the bigger boys. My brother Larry had built a bench high in the branches, and that plank of wood was my throne, the yard my kingdom, and my mother our queenly matriarch.

My mama saw me looking up, and she knew I was about to climb. But she needed me on the ground, where the pecans were. Earlier in the season, she might need to send the boys out with a stick to shake the tree for an avalanche of pecans to collect, but now they fell freely. You just had to beat the birds to them.

To keep me grounded, she told me stories from our family history. "Now, Tenie," she would say, lassoing my focus before launching into some tale about my grandmother, or a story from early in her marriage to my daddy.

As she talked, I picked up pecans. All the while, I did somersaults and cartwheels, or spun in place until I fell back, holding on to the earth that might throw me off. But I *listened*. I listened to every single word my mother told me. These people, my people—my ancestors and my parents when they were young—were characters in a long drama that I was now a part of. Their struggles were not mine, but their lessons could be. This was my inheritance, these stories that people had done their best to erase or degrade to keep us from passing them down. So that we wouldn't know our history and ourselves.

Just like she did in her work as a seamstress, my mother could take the stories of lives that might have been discarded or lost, some precious scrap of information, and weave it into the tapestry of her storytelling as something precious and unique. Sometimes all we had were names, but even names held multitudes, and mother to daughter, each had kept a word going. We would not be lost.

I could ask my mother anything under the pecan tree. And that December morning I did have a question. The night before, I'd sat at the kitchen table next to Larry as he wrote his name at the top of his homework. I said I wanted to practice my own name, so he let me borrow his pencil and said each letter for me. When we got to my last name, Larry thought for a second. "Yours is different, Tenie," he said. He reminded me that all of us kids had different spellings of our parents' last name, Buyince. There was Beyincé, Boyance, and mine, Beyoncé.

Now in the yard, I placed my hands on the ground and tried to do a handstand, leaning against the tree as I formed the question. "Mama, our names . . ." I said, looking at her upside down, as she bent to the grass. "You know, it's all those different spellings."

I talked as if maybe she had never noticed. As if she'd gone to the store and carelessly brought home a mismatched set of last names.

"That's what they put on your birth certificate," my mother said, focusing on the pecans.

I tumbled over, kicking my feet in the air as if that would slow my fall. "Why didn't you make them fix it?" I asked, sitting up again. "Fight and say it's not right?"

"I did one time," my mama said, not looking at me. "The first time."

"So what happened?" I pressed, stern now. I picked up a pecan and wasn't sure I even wanted to give it to her to put in the bag.

"I was told, 'Be happy that you're getting a birth certificate.' Because, at one time, Black people didn't even get birth certificates."

There was a hurt in my mother's voice, and she picked up pecans quicker, as if they might run off. "What's a birth . . ." I'd already forgotten the word.

"*Certificate,* Tenie," she said. "It says what your name is."

"Well, I want to change my name," I said. I held that pecan tight between my thumb and forefinger.

"You can't change your name," she said. "Your name is beautiful. Celestine Ann Beyoncé."

It was music when my mother said it, but I wouldn't budge. "I hate this name," I said. "Nobody can say Celestine." I mimicked the ugly zombie-voice pronunciation I often heard: "Sulluh-steen."

She laughed, coming closer to me with the bag, still keeping a hand low to the ground for pecans. "What would you rather your name be?"

"Something easy," I said, finally dropping the pecan in the bag. "Plain. Linda Smith."

"You are Celestine," she said, smiling. She squatted to push the hair off my face and pull leaves off my pajama legs. "Like my sister and my grandmother."

My mother's sister had died as a baby, and she was named for her grandmother—my great-grandmother—Célestine Joséphine Lacy, who had lived to be almost a hundred. Gone long before my mother gave me their name. "She was very pretty," my mother said, "like you." She caught herself and stood up as she added her usual line: "But pretty is as pretty does, Tenie."

And there under the pecan tree, as she did countless times, that day my mother told me stories of the mothers and daughters that went before me. The house of Derouen, her maiden name, a matrilineal line as worthy of memorization as the bloodlines of the mythological Greek gods I would learn later. I am the daughter of Agnes, who was Odilia's daughter, who was Célestine's, who was Rosalie's. My mom did not have the details found in the records of modern historians and genealogists. She had what had been passed down to her, which was, above all, the knowledge that these mothers held on to their daughters against all odds.

Rosalie, born around 1800, had been enslaved all her life in Louisiana when she had her daughter Célestine on a June day in 1826. My mother told me her great-grandmother Rosalie called her Célestine "Tine," pronouncing her nickname just like mine. At a time when

Black families were considered property and routinely ripped apart, they managed to stay together. There was a close call, when the newly widowed woman who enslaved the mother and daughter in Louisiana said she was scaling down and only needed six out of the twenty-nine people she held in captivity and forced labor. The rest would be farmed out for her relatives, their fates unknown. But Rosalie held on to her Tine, and they were part of that six that stayed.

Célestine became a mother herself as a teenager, giving birth to two sons. Her children's biological father was the widow's white grandson, Éloi Réné Broussard, who was about two years older than Célestine. And then, in 1853, the widow who had enslaved them died, and all of her "property" was presented for public auction. Three generations of my family—Rosalie, Célestine, and her two children—were placed on a block to be sold individually.

I type those words, say them aloud, and I feel that fear and rage in my blood, the trauma passed down through my DNA.

Éloi Réné Broussard came forward at the auction. A receipt shows he paid $1705 in cash for Célestine and her two children. *His* children. A relative of the widow put down money for Rosalie's life, and she was taken from her daughter and grandchildren. I don't know if they ever saw each other again.

Célestine and the children moved into Éloi's house, where he had a white wife and his three daughters. He and Célestine would have ten more children, and she would live in his house for fifty years. She named her first daughter Rosalie after the mother taken from her, and then she had Odilia, my mother's mother.

Éloi was my great-grandfather. With all its awful complexity, that is who he was. Éloi acknowledged paternity of all of his children with Célestine and donated a small bit of land and livestock to her before his death in 1904. The way it's been presented to me, Éloi acknowledging that he was the father of her children gave Tine some degree of security, even before the Civil War. There was a portrait commissioned of her at some point, which I'm told speaks to her standing. I know it shows her beauty.

But under the pecan tree, what mattered was this: Célestine was enslaved, and she became *free*. And she got her kids free. They stayed together.

These stories under the pecan tree nourished my soul, and part of that was my mother making sure that I knew what an honor it was to be Black. Once I was wearing a T-shirt that read "100% BLACK" while I was out buying groceries.

"You better take that off," a Black man I was walking by said, peppering the insult with a certain familiarity to soften the blow. "You're no hundred percent." I knew this was about my skin being light.

Stopping in my tracks, I turned to him. "Brother," I said, "I'm the Blackest woman you'll ever meet."

From my first breath, I was told, shown, and embraced into knowing that it is an honor to be a Black person. My mother saw to that, making sure I carry all these mothers with me. Rosalie, who had Célestine, who had Odilia, who had Agnes, who had me, who had Beyoncé and Solange. This is not simply about a bloodline. I watched my mama mother children who were not hers by birth. I have mothered children, like my daughters Kelly and Angie, who are as much my daughters as if I carried them. We all have this power to be matriarchs, to be women of the sacred practice of nurturing, guiding, protecting—foreseeing and remembering. The matriarch's wisdom is ancient, for she is filled with the most enduring, ferocious love.

When my oldest daughter was born, my mother had just died, and it was inconceivable to me that she would not be there to show *me* how to be a mother. I wanted my mother to be the one to tell my daughter these stories of all the mothers that overcame incredible odds to be with each other. My firstborn daughter looks so much like my mom, more like her than me. But that is genetics—how would I pass on our *spirit*? That unspoken knowing? The pride of our history?

So my first gift to my daughter would be my name, Beyoncé. It didn't matter how it was spelled when it was given to me, it was our name. Our history. The most valuable possession I had, and it was now mine to give. I've kept a word going.

ACT ONE

A Daughter

CHAPTER I

BADASS TENIE B

June 1959

I was three steps out the door by the time my mama realized I'd pulled my disappearing act again. She'd turned her head in the kitchen, and I was running out the house to my sister Selena's.

"You need to let me comb your hair," my mother called from the door. "And brush your teeth!"

"Okay, Mama," I said, aiming to fall between pleasing and pleading as I kept my pace. I could not stop. A perfect summer day—like this one at age five—could last you forever if you started it early enough.

"Or else I'm not gonna let you go over there, Tenie," she said, her voice farther from me now. She would not get louder than that, I knew. She had what people on the island called a "sweet demeaneh" and I could outrun the sound of her disapproval even if it followed me on the breeze off the water behind me.

In Galveston, the wind off the Gulf is a constant reminder that you are on an island. The city is a skinny strip of beach town two miles off the coast of Texas. Now the wind was at my back, and the gray pavement of the lane was already warmed by the morning Texas sun. I was barefoot, which was the only way to live in June. Wearing shoes just meant keeping track of them when you took them off at Galveston Beach or climbed a tree. And Selena's house wasn't more than a slim eighth of a block around the corner. Otherwise, my overprotective, fearful mother would never have let me go on my own.

When you're little, you don't know how small your world is. Mine was contained in my neighborhood, and the four points of my compass were set: There was the east and west daily back-and-forth between my house and Selena's. Then Holy Rosary Catholic Church to the north, so close we could see into my siblings' Catholic school directly from our front door. And just a few blocks south was the small strip of segregated beach that we were allowed onto. They took thirty miles of coastline and only allowed us access to three blocks' worth of sand and water between 29th Street and 32nd Street. As kids on the tiny island of Galveston, our lives centered around that bit of beach—but I still loved being at Selena's house best of all.

My oldest sister, Selena, was twenty-seven years old when I was born, and she and her husband, John, had eight kids by the time she was thirty. My nieces and nephews were closer in age to me than my siblings, and they were my very best friends.

I ran faster in the lane, racing with myself as I passed the little houses tucked tight next to each other. I spotted a yellow buttercup in the grass I had not seen yesterday, but by the time I had decided to stop to pick it, my legs had kept moving until I found myself at the steps to the little porch of Selena's duplex without the flower. This happened all the time—my body moving and my brain catching up.

Now I could finally stand still, and my heart beat so fast from the run, like a tiny bird fluttering in my skinny chest. Not fluttering, more like hurling itself against the cage of my ribs, trying to escape. Sometimes that heart felt like it was leading me, making me run faster, outrunning boys with my long legs. And me, always following it, never going as fast as it wanted. A heart threatening to burst out and fly away from any tether—me, my family, Galveston.

I gave myself a second to calm down outside Selena's house. It looked big, but they only lived in the downstairs of the duplex and had no yard to really speak of. Suddenly, I moved, trying to jump the first two steps of her porch like the big kids did. A high jump in my mind, a prize I was always chasing as the baby of the family. I fell just short, having to do the stutter-step compromise of taking two steps like a normal five-year-old. *Next time,* I told myself, marching through the open door to my sister's house, a finish line into the living room.

Immediately the music of all that life in Selena's house enveloped me, excited me, held me. The sounds of her three sons and five daughters: Deanne, Linda, Leslie, Elouise, and Elena, Tommie, and of course

Ronnie and Johnny. Don't try to keep track of all of them—even Selena couldn't.

And there she was, my big sister, turning to see me as she exhaled the smoke of a cigarette. The way Selena Mae Rittenhouse smoked her Salem Menthols was something out of a movie, the two manicured fingers holding the cigarette, rolling the smoke around her tongue and then blowing it out as a glamorous verdict on any situation. You could not meet my sister and not think of the word "spitfire"—a spark taking the trim shape of a woman who swore by the power of dark red lipstick and wearing a girdle and sleeping in a bra to stay tight through having all those kids.

Selena, who her kids called M'dear, kept her house as streamlined, occasionally doling out a "get your stuff together because we don't have time for that," to keep everyone in line. Her husband was a trucker, often doing long drives as she did her seamstress work while looking after the kids. You can't be so tender when you have eight stair-step kids—it would be hard to be soft and still keep ahold of things, so she was no-nonsense in a sisterly way. I was starting to realize that everyone in the neighborhood saw her as the big sister they wished they had, and as I put my arm around her waist as a greeting, I had the sense to be grateful that this beautiful, funny woman was mine.

Deanne—Denie—turned the radio up and grabbed Elouise to twirl a circle around me. They were dancing to Jackie Wilson, "Mr. Excitement," singing "Lonely Teardrops." Galveston was a radio town. I did a quick dip with them as the beat dropped on Jackie's second "say you will," but then I kept walking through the house.

I was looking, of course, for Johnny.

I homed in on him standing outside on the side staircase, the sunlight falling on his face. Johnny's head was slightly bowed, always looking like he was listening to—or for—something only he could hear. My nephew Johnny was nine, four years older than me, and he was my very best friend. If you ask me what my earliest memory is of him, you might as well ask me about how I knew I needed air to breathe or water to drink. Johnny was just *there*. My mother put our inseparable closeness less delicately: "When Johnny farts, you gotta be there to catch it."

Now we smiled at each other, best friends reunited, and I was at the door to him when his brother Ronnie jumped into the doorway to scare me. I jumped back just as fast.

"I got you!" Ronnie yelled. "I got you, Tenie. I saw you coming. Didn't I, Johnny? And I said, 'Oh, I'm gonna get her.' Right?"

I rolled my eyes in the way my mother said might freeze someday and moved to stand on the balls of my feet. At five I was already taller than seven-year-old Ronnie—but back then I was taller than every-body. I knew Ronnie could not *stand* that I was taller because he was such a competitive athlete about everything. I raised my chin to look down my nose at him.

"You didn't *get* me," I said.

"I did scare you, Tenie," Ronnie said. "Your face!"

I pulled back a hand, ready for another of our knock-down, drag-out fights. Once a week Ronnie and I would have to have at least one—real fistfights, always squaring off. But Johnny cut in.

"It *was* funny, Tenie," said Johnny, his soft voice conspiratorial, try-ing to get me to see the humor. And maybe it was funny, I thought, but only because Johnny said so. I unclenched my fist to push my hair behind my ear, then faked going left to do a twirl to the right around Ronnie, a half-turn pirouette to stand next to Johnny. So close to him that my left foot almost stepped on his right one.

Ronnie reached down to pick up a ball, pretending I hadn't just fooled him. "We're gonna play kickball in the lane."

"I think we should go to the beach," I said.

"Naw, kickball," Ronnie said. But that's how it was with me and Ronnie. I would say the sky was blue and he would say the sky is *not blue*. The sky would be anything *but* blue.

I shrugged a no and Ronnie got on his tiptoes. "Tenie, why do you have to try to be a boss?"

"I'm not *trying* to be a boss," I said. "I am the boss."

Johnny laughed. Ronnie didn't. "We'll decide on the way," Johnny said, and that meant we would end up doing whatever he wanted to do. Because, really, *Johnny* was the boss, and we all knew it. Even at nine years old, he ran everything. Now he walked from the back steps into the house, stopping only to give a wiggle with the girls to the end of "Little Bitty Pretty One." Without a word, our whole crew, almost all my nieces and nephews, walked in step with Johnny out the front door.

Outside we moved the singular way children do, crisscrossing and meandering. Some of us marched backwards if we had to, just to keep a conversation, falling and laughing. I saw the buttercup flower again and stopped now to pick it. I breathed in the flower's scent and resisted the urge to smear the yellow on someone's face or chin. Instead, I tucked it over Johnny's ear, and we smiled at each other.

Johnny's presence could calm me and that careless heart that always led me into trouble before I really knew what I was doing. The heart that made adults call me "bad." Badass Tenie B wasn't ever mean— I tended to be the victim of every wrong impulse I said yes to. I would literally play with fire, drawn to it because its unpredictable nature seemed to temporarily drown out mine. Seeing a small flame, beautiful as it glowed, made me feel calm.

In houses like mine, you would have to light your stove with a match. When my dad was at work and my mom left me with my older siblings, I would sometimes go in the kitchen and turn the gas on, then wait a few seconds to put the match on it so the fire would go *whoosh*. A fireball that disappeared as fast as it came, as pretty as anything I'd ever seen.

One day I said to myself, "Oh, I'm gonna get a big one." I let the gas go long, and then when I lit the match the flame was so ferocious the force of it sent me clear under the kitchen table in the middle of the floor. Knocked me *out*.

I came to as my brothers Skip and Larry entered. "She's dead," Larry said, as nonchalant as you please because he knew I was fine. He probably saw me fluttering my eyes to peek at them, the way little kids do. I was mad he was so easygoing about my death, but I kept my eyes closed because I needed all the sympathy I could get to keep from getting in trouble.

"Yep," said Skip. "What do we do with her?"

"Just get her feet and let's go put her in the trash can" was Larry's answer. They picked me up and started carrying me, so I started screaming, "No, I am not dead!" I had the nerve to be mad at them when my parents came home and the boys told on me. "They were gonna throw me out!" I yelled.

Dad moved the matches, but even that seemed like a challenge to take on. Competitive Ronnie and I were together in this. We'd light the toilet paper on fire in the bathtub, watching it burn and turn like a snake. Ronnie made everything a test of my will. He would only have to say the words "bet you . . ." and I would be ready for whatever dare. "Bet you won't jump off that porch." I'd be Superman. "Bet you can't beat me in a real fight." I'd be Miss Golden Gloves. "Bet you won't start a fire." A cranky old neighbor had left his ratty work boots out, and the dare was that I wouldn't light them on fire. I went and got those matches my daddy thought he hid, along with some paper to put in the boots to get a good fire going. We loved the colors.

Johnny challenged me in a different way. While Ronnie helped me find stunts to briefly release the energy, Johnny was a place where I could put all that energy into looking after someone. Protecting him. Because as powerful as Johnny was in the family, with nothing happening without his stamp of approval, he could be instantly fragile in Galveston, which was the whole world. In a second, the place we loved could become a hardass little town. Johnny was obviously gay by the time he was three they say, and I had never known him to hide that light. Selena filled him with such love and had him so confident that he never hid who he was. But he would be called things, and adults, strangers, would sometimes eavesdrop on our conversations and grimace at his freedom, or raise an eyebrow at his loud, free laugh. They would shoot him a look, menacing and judgmental, and I would give it back magnified.

Johnny would listen to my stories, my explanation for how I skinned my knee or how I got sick trying to see if breathing underwater would turn me into a real mermaid. He'd shake his head. "Lucille Ball," he called me, even that young, the "Lu" sung high as he laughed at my latest predicament. In Johnny, all that energy I had, all those big feelings, found a focus. It was my honor to be his protector. To give him the flower that he tucked behind his ear.

Now we all walked, loose-limbed and free. Our two houses always moved through Galveston as one family. "Seventeen kids if you see one," people would say, all of us already standing out because we were so well dressed thanks to my mother and Selena's seamstress work. "Sharp" was the word people used to describe our tribe, and that was the standard for our family's culture. My mother beaded all my dresses into masterpieces, and Selena's kids all had beautiful clothes that were expertly maintained. If you messed with us, we could take you out, but the skirt would be ironed. When you were on the ground, you could admire the perfect hem of my nephew's pants, with a crease like the edge of a penknife. Our fashion wasn't about what other people thought of us, however—it was our first understanding of art. A celebration of beauty, of detail, of design.

We slowed down, as we always did, by the Stanfords'—another family with eight kids. Then those children would start to trickle out and join us.

"The beach?" I suggested to Johnny, though I knew he would say no. Johnny didn't love the beach the way I did.

"Let's go to your house," he said, which I also knew he would say. Us kids always gathered at my house, because we had the yard we all thought was huge. My mother made sure that our yard was where everyone wanted to be. Anything to keep us in her sights and reach, as she was always worried something would happen to us.

Her secret weapon was S&H Green Stamps. These were part of a rewards program at grocery stores, where you received a certain amount of green postage-like stamps with your purchase. You licked the back of them to place them in a Sperry & Hutchinson stamp book, and when it was full, you would then be able to redeem the stamps toward items in the S&H catalog, the *Ideabook*. Most people would get household items, say, a blender or a set of dishes. But my mother held out for the big game: a Ping-Pong table, sets for badminton and croquet, and one of our biggest gets, a swing set. Do you know how revolutionary it was to bring a swing set to a poor neighborhood with that many kids? It was like an amusement park in our backyard, with everything centered around the pecan tree. And under my mother's eye.

You were supposed to spend money to get the stamps, which we didn't really do. I figured out a way around that. Ronnie, Johnny, and I would wrangle a few kids and we would sit right outside the grocery store. "Okay, now look sad," I would tell them, and you never saw such a dejected bunch. Elbows on our knees, fists holding up our cheeks, waiting for our mark. And like a fish on a line, there one would be, coming out of the store. Men acted as if they'd never shopped in their lives, holding the stamps out like they would actually lose something by pocketing them. The best were the women who wanted to act like they were above collecting the stamps. But they sure would walk out holding them to show they'd spent enough to earn that many.

"What a cute family," a woman would say.

I'd look up, trying to seem like we'd never heard that before. Us? Cute? If you say so, ma'am.

Then they'd say the magic words: "You want my stamps?"

We'd rise to our feet, like no one had ever paid us such a kindness. "Yes," I would say, gratitude making me breathless in my performance.

"Thank you so much," Johnny would say, somehow keeping a straight face. We would really work it. The little grifters. Then we'd watch them walk away, smug with their public display of affluence, and we would sit right back down to wait for the next mark.

We were playing poor, none of us knowing we were actually *very* poor. Some of that comes from living in a neighborhood with so many people in the same boat—you don't have people to feel less than in comparison. My parents made it seem like it was our choice to be thrifty. When they said "We can't afford that" in response to some want or need, it seemed like it was a decision about what was worth putting our money toward, never lack.

My father worked as a longshoreman, which was probably the highest-paying job for a Black man in Galveston. In all of Texas, probably. Longshoremen could really provide for their families, but my father was blind in his right eye and deaf in that ear. When I overheard people asking my mother or older siblings what happened to my daddy—nobody ever asked *him*—they referred to "the accident" back in Louisiana. No one would tell me more until later. What I did know was that his impairment meant he was only cleared to move small crates from ships, using manual labor. There weren't many light loads, so even though he was a hard worker and made a lot of money in a day's work—as much as a man doing another job might make in a week—he might only work that one day for a few weeks.

My daddy also liked to drink, and he made up for not touching alcohol all week by getting real familiar with it every Friday and Saturday. Our mama used to send my older sister Flo to be there when Daddy got his check to cash it with him and take most of it home while he went out.

He was a weekend alcoholic, and Saturdays were the worst. My father had become an unofficial barber for all the longshoremen, who lined up at his porch Saturday afternoons to pay for his haircuts. Starting at twelve noon they would have beer out there, and that would continue until he left with people to go find more. Then my mom would be standing in the screen door early in the morning when she thought I was asleep, nagging the hell out of him about going out drinking. How irresponsible he was staying "out all night." It would be midnight and for years I thought staying out until twelve meant you stayed out all night. I hated hearing that and blamed her for their struggles because I *loved* my daddy. He was so handsome and kind, my hero. As she whisper-hissed at him, I thought, *My mama just wanna take his money from him.* How many times did I confront her the next morning? Saying, "*You* should be stronger to just stop him from doing it if it bothers you so much."

I didn't understand that my mother probably made more than him as a seamstress, since, a lot of the time, my daddy was on what they called Pennies. It was a sort of unemployment, thirty-five dollars a week with seven people in the house and my mama always sharing our food with people. Then at church with my parents—because no matter how drunk my daddy got Saturday night, that man went to church every single Sunday—I would watch my mother put a dollar, sometimes three, in the collection plate and get so mad at her. "Mama, why can't we afford anything I want, and you're just putting all this money into church? How you gonna put in a whole dollar?" Because to me— to *us*—a dollar was a *lot*.

"Tenie, this *is* how we make it," she said, pointing to the collection plate as it moved along. "*This* is how we don't go hungry. It's called tithing. God provides for us because we give back."

I shook my head, watching that money leaving us.

"Tenie, one day you're gonna understand that this is how I'm able to stretch this money." God had to be stretching that dollar to no end.

But on that June day, as we arrived at my yard with all the kids we'd collected on the way from Selena's, how could I *not* feel rich? People I loved scattered about, pairing off and grouping. Some on the swing set, a few starting to play badminton as Ronnie tried to order kids into teams. My brother Skip came out to show us how to really play table tennis, with Larry putting his engineer mind to explaining the vital importance of angles to your serves.

My mom poked her head out, and I watched as kids each took note, calling out "Tenie Mama!" to tell her something or find some reason to seek her nurturing. A shoelace to be tied, a drink of water to be asked for. She was known as Tenie Mama in the neighborhood for all the times the kids said, "Tenie's mama is taking us to the beach." Or "I'm gonna ask Tenie's mama." I felt pride thinking that she was an extension of me. As children, and even as we grow into adults, our mothers become synonymous with *us*. They exist for our needs. Many of us think *we* give them life, rather than understanding the truth that we owe our existence to them.

All the kids in the yard felt that way, because when you were with Tenie Mama, you were Agnes's child. She looked after every one of us, finding stuff for us to do together. Any activity that was free she found out about because she read every word of that newspaper. If there wasn't a free concert, there was always the beach. In December, she helped kids gather acorns from all the oaks in Galveston because there was a flower shop that would pay five dollars per bushel, and my mama split the cash fairly so we could all buy Christmas presents. On the weekends all summer, she would walk me and the neighborhood children down to the beach, packing hot dogs for each child and five-cent sodas she bought on sale at the store. Our next-door neighbor Miss Russell would also give us her "commodities"—government cheese, butter, and Spam—and Mama would stretch that to pack sandwiches to feed everyone. Mary Russell was our surrogate grandmother, so chatty from loneliness after outliving all her people that you had to walk fast by her house, or you'd hear "C'mere now" from her porch and be trapped. We guessed she was almost a hundred because she told us she was born a slave in Brazoria County. Orphaned or taken, she didn't know her own birthdate, growing up picking cotton and cutting cordwood. We later found out Miss Russell was estimated to be born in 1870. Though slavery ended on paper in 1863, notice of emancipation came to Texas's enslaved people of Galveston two and a half years late—the first Juneteenth of 1865. Who knows how long it took for word of newfound freedom to make it to a little girl living on a plantation.

As the kids all followed my mother and the fried Spam and cheese sandwiches, courtesy of Miss Russell, they would collect more and more friends on the way to the beach, not even knocking on doors— just yelling out in yards, "Tenie Mama's taking us." My mother always figured out ways to make what she had become enough. Dividing attention, food, money—all that care—into equal parts. The algebra of motherhood.

On these trips, my mother would remind us all of the limits placed on us. White people had segregated the beach, and only allowed Black people access to a strip of three blocks. That small space was book-ended by the Pleasure Pier amusement park to the left, if you were looking at the water, and the in-town beach to the right. We could go on the Ferris wheel and merry-go-round of the Pleasure Pier along with the white people, but it was only as an equal opportunity to spend our money there. They made a fortune off that place. The in-town beach, however, was considered the "real" beach, and we weren't to step a toe on it.

If you went past that beach, three or four miles down to the right, there was a part of West Beach that we could be on. The whites found its rocks and grit distasteful and had unofficially abandoned it to us. But you had to drive down there, not walk, and you had better not get out of your car on the boulevard. Not till you got down the hill onto West Beach—then you could do what you wanted to do.

My mother drilled these and many other rules for survival into us. One of the many cruelties of racism is that mothers are made to be the guards of their children, enforcing rules that were designed to limit them. Constantly telling them what they cannot do for fear that if they don't remember the box they were put in, they will be hurt or killed.

She was not wrong. A few years later, my brothers—Larry, Skip, and Butch—would be at the beach riding bikes on the boulevard. They were in junior high and high school, playing with two friends of theirs. They rode their bikes half a block into the white area, probably one following the other. They later said they didn't realize where they were.

Some white teenagers slowed their car, then stopped. They called my brothers the n-word to get their attention and started shooting them up with BB guns. They aimed for faces, Larry getting the most BBs in his face, head, and neck. BBs get under your skin—embed themselves in—and the pain was unbearable. My brothers came home, bloody and injured, trying to pull the BBs out of themselves. My dad was at work, and my mother asked a neighbor to drive her with them to the hospital.

All for half a block of space. Had these teenagers just driven back and forth, hunting us? Did they have these spaces only to guard them? To not even enjoy themselves but keep us from having them? With all the energy put into preventing Black people from doing things, what did they have that did *not* involve us?

Before my brothers got shot up, I didn't have the capacity to understand this pressure on my mother as she took care of all these kids. To simply go to the beach and keep all these Black children alive, some her children and grandchildren, some entrusted to her for the day.

But she kept doing this for us. And on days when it was gloomy or cold, my mother might let us all ride the free ferry across to Bolivar Peninsula and back. This was the way to Louisiana, where she was from. Out on the water that rocked and soothed us, she'd hand us day-old bread to feed the seagulls, each kid jostling another to give them more. "This is our own boat," she would tell us.

The ferry had cars, and I'd see them drive off while we turned around to get the next one back. I would watch them, wondering where some of the people were going. Galveston was a resort town, so it could be anywhere. I had a child's understanding of life and geography, but this was the very beginning of realizing how small my world was, and how big the world out there might be.

That impulse to see what was outside Galveston grew until I thought about it all the time, even that June day, surrounded by all this love in my yard. *What would it be like,* I thought, *to go and keep going?*

Johnny touched my arm. His fingers splayed on my forearm just for a second, and he turned to the pecan tree in the middle of our yard. He'd said something I had not heard, but we didn't need words. I followed him as he climbed up the tree so we could sit on that bench in the tree together. Without a word spoken, we turned to each other and began clapping our hands together, falling into the game-songs that generations of Black girls, and some boys, have passed down to each other. I can't remember which one we started with that day, but I do know that if Johnny were right here next to me this instant, we could raise our hands to each other and fall right back into that handclap rhythm.

My heart stayed in that rhythm, content for now. *This* was abundance. A game-song with my best friend, a swing set bought on stamps, bulk-packed hot dogs, five-cent sodas, our own boat, and bread for the birds. We shared what we had, and we felt like we had it to give. My family was on Pennies, but we were living like millionaires.

CHAPTER 2

GALVESTON

July 1959

THAT SUMMER, THE price of my older sister Flo being able to go downtown to meet her friends was that my mother made her take me. A fifteen-year-old girl could only get into so much trouble when saddled with a five-year-old. Flo took the bargain, but a smile was not part of the deal. My sister was determined to act as if I were not there.

It took work to miss me. The skirts our mama made us flared, mine more so since I twirled as I walked, which meant that I wasn't generally watching what was in front of me. When I tripped, which I always did, Flo kept right on walking. Her three friends seemed to worry more about me getting lost than she did, but about an hour into walking around downtown, I figured out Flo's trick. Instead of looking back and having to acknowledge her little sister acting the fool, she would briefly linger at one of the windows of the shops, take note of my safety in its reflection, and keep on.

If you haven't been yet, Galveston looked a lot like New Orleans, but with all that beautiful architecture laid out in a more orderly grid of numbered streets. "Downtown" was north of Broadway, going west up from 20th Street to 25th. The Black business district of Galveston was also north of Broadway, going west from 25th Street. Galveston had a history of moneymaking and was notable in the South for Black entrepreneurship—we owned and operated our own stores, as if For Us By Us were a city. We had our own grocery stores, restaurants, and theaters. When relatives came from out of town, certain things about

Galveston would stick with them, and they would bring them up again and again. Things I took for granted shocked them, like having a Black-run filling station.

We had one movie theater we were allowed into, the white-owned George Washington Carver Theater, which was run-down, but it showed the movies that had us in them. They had recently premiered *Imitation of Life* and it's where I saw *Porgy and Bess,* which I was obsessed with. I loved musicals and the idea that you could take any troubles and make them beautiful by putting them to song. Every year the Carver theater made a big deal of rerunning *Stormy Weather* with Lena Horne and *Carmen Jones* with Dorothy Dandridge. I would walk out of the theater feeling taller, as if to accommodate the soul that had grown to fit the leading ladies' examples. I fantasized about them coming to Galveston on the entertainment circuit and saying, "Tenie, come with us."

I have never been naïve—I know people laugh when I call Galveston progressive, but I cannot overstate the importance of the city to our culture. The island had a long history as one of America's main natural ports and capitals of trade—on par with New York City—and was at one point the second- or third-richest city in all of the United States, depending on who you asked. Galveston was the most profitable cotton port on the Gulf, and all the cotton grown in Texas went through the city as it was sold to the world. And the shame of it is that Galveston was once one of the largest ports for the slave trafficking of human beings across the Atlantic. Cuba, only eight hundred miles away, was a major hub in the buying and selling of enslaved people kidnapped from Africa, and Galveston was their first stop in the United States before being trafficked to other cities in the South.

All that money in Galveston made it the Southern Wall Street. This was how much Texas prioritized Galveston: It was the first city in the state to have a bank, then a post office, and then the first in the state to get telephones and electricity in homes. For us, Galveston was home to Texas's first public high school for Black children, Central High, and the first Black public library in the entire nation. Black intellectuals—the talented tenth that W. E. B. Du Bois talked about—came from all over Texas and the rest of the country to Galveston to teach Black children at Central High. Galveston had money, but we also had all that pride, all that excellence centered in one place.

The storm of 1900—a hurricane that remains the deadliest natural disaster in U.S. history—destroyed Galveston and killed at least eight thousand people. They built the seawall to stop the next flood, but the banks fled. Imagine New York City never recovering from 9/11. The mafia moved in, making it a bootlegging and gambling oasis for thousands of tourists—Las Vegas before Las Vegas. The city had lots of clubs and restaurants, and even as a kid I could see why so many people came here. This quaint beautiful place by the water with gorgeous architecture.

And then you went to the Black areas and there was so much poverty there. By design, Galveston contained the Black neighborhood on Northside, the area above Broadway. That's where the two housing projects were, meant to cluster us. When my family came from Louisiana, it was important to my father that we not live in that area. We lived in a poor, working-class neighborhood too, but my father believed the projects were created to continue cycles of poverty. Later, when I befriended kids who lived there, I would go and *love* being there. To my eyes, they had beautiful apartments, and we had holes in our floors.

I told my parents how fun it was there, and my dad cut me off. "I don't want you over there," he said, in the Creole accent that I now thought made him sound so country. "I don't want you over in the projects."

"Why?" I asked, exasperated. "They're living better than *us*. They got a nicer house than we do. You're around here thinking you're better than . . ."

"I got three boys," he said. "I got to protect my boys. I don't want them going over there, so you're not either." My father was buying into a sort of respectability politics, and he was also worried about his kids. But all I thought was that he was missing what was in front of his face: *Oh,* I thought, *he thinks we're living better and we're not at all.*

That was later for me, though I know that when I was five, teenage Flo was having those same conversations with my parents. She was a sophomore at Central High, and to a teenager like Flo, Downtown was the big deal. She loved fashion, and everyone in the family knew the story about her running away from home as a little girl because she didn't like the clothes our mama put her in. She'd made it four doors down to a neighbor's house, leaning on the door and saying, "Don't let

Agnes in! Don't let Agnes in!" Even then, so little but conspiratorial with adults in referring to our mother by her name. Mama would have had a fit if she heard one of us call her Agnes, but choosing outfits was serious stuff to Flo. Now, I was starting to like fashion too, and Downtown was where all the stores were. The three big ones were McCrory's, Woolworth's, and Kress. They were dime stores—and they were popping.

The stores had lunch counters, the best burgers and shakes in town. You couldn't eat inside, only white people could, but there would be a window, usually at the rear, where we could order. Then we'd take the food and bring it to a bench and eat there. I didn't know yet that was our only choice—I was still learning the boundaries and walls set on me by segregation. I thought it was only natural to eat outside. But Flo knew. Students her age in 1959 would do personal acts of rebellion. Like one time drinking from the Whites Only fountain instead of the one marked Colored. A friend of Flo's had used the white bathroom at one of the department stores, just to see it.

After lunch, Flo and I went to the fancier shops with her friends, getting an eye on the trends and thinking about what we could ask our mom to make. We were watched by the shopkeepers, but I didn't notice then. Flo and I waited on a corner for a bus to go back to our neighborhood. Her friends simply walked home to where they lived in Northside.

The bus was still new for me, and I admired how Flo knew all the nuances of waiting for one like a grown-up: the expectant looks down the street; the smoothing of the skirt. She was practicing to be an adult, and I tried mirroring her until, to her embarrassment, the excitement of seeing the bus coming made me bounce and shout. She muttered something at me but took my hand as we got on. The front of the bus was empty, save for one white woman sitting with her purse in her lap, a slash of purple lipstick on her mouth. I watched her watch Flo.

When I slowed to sit in one of the many open seats up front, Flo gripped my hand harder to lead me to the crowded back of the bus. There were so many people crammed there that it was standing room only. It was only when she and I made it to the back that the driver started moving the bus again. He was white, and I didn't know then that only white men were allowed to be bus drivers.

The bus lurched forward. I didn't get why we were standing

crammed in with all these people. When we tilted a little on a turn, Flo let go of my hand to steady herself. I was free.

I walked to the front of the bus. Marched with all the sense of a five-year-old who knew everything. "Tenie," ordered Flo, but I didn't look back. I took a seat and looked out the window.

I heard a chorus behind me. Tuts and sighs, murmured half-sentences. This wasn't only annoying Flo, this was upsetting people. Just me sitting in a seat. I didn't know why they were tripping. This was the life, watching Galveston go by. And if they didn't know better, well, let Flo and everyone else stand in the back like a fool.

Flo was suddenly standing beside me. "Tenie. Come."

I didn't even look at her. Instead, I knelt on the seat to get a better view out the window. Now *my* window. Flo grabbed my arm and pulled me hard, the way only a big sister knows how. "Ow!" I said, exaggerating as only a little sister knows how.

A voice boomed sharp: *"You had better not do that to her."* It was the white woman. There was spittle on the purple of her lip, clashing with the reddening of her face. "Her mother would *fire* you if she knew that you were doing this."

She thought Flo was my babysitter. My sister had rich brown skin and green eyes. I, on the other hand, had blond-looking hair in candy curls. The woman mistook me for white. Worthy of her protection.

"Her mama is *my* mama," Flo said, quickly and with an exasperated defiance that would echo through our lives.

The woman's face twisted, confused, and then she looked at me as if I'd reneged on some deal. Sold her something I did not own. That face, the snarl of it, froze me.

Flo grabbed me by my hair. *"Tenie. Move."* She dragged me to the back of the bus and the choir of tutting people shaking their heads, grimacing in judgment. I had upset things, but they were also annoyed with Flo for allowing me to.

I said something mean to her, about her hurting me. This girl of fifteen left to watch a naïve five-year-old sister. Flo looked at me, and there was a flash of something on her face. Her eyes were wide open, and I wasn't sure if she was going to cry or hit me. But she looked away.

The white woman kept turning back and then craning her neck forward to get the driver's attention. He didn't look back, keeping on his route the whole time. I don't even know if he noticed.

This was the status quo, and it was exactly what Galveston's politicians hoped would remain. When local officials had to stand up and be asked by some reporter about the protests around the South, they would say some variation of, "Oh, we don't have that kind of racial tension in Galveston. Our Negroes are happy. They've got good jobs, and they like it as it is. Peaceful."

CHAPTER 3

WEEKS ISLAND

August 1959

THERE WERE NINE of us crammed into my daddy's car, and it was past midnight as we got to the only road leading onto Weeks Island. Every summer, we'd take a trip to where my parents were from. The thickness and quickness of my parents' Louisiana accents made their old home one word for me in my mind: *Weeksalund.*

The drive from Galveston took six hours, me riding the whole way on somebody's lap. As the youngest, I had moved all over the car, ending now in the front on Flo's lap. Flo was squeezed between our daddy to my left and our mama to my right, then my aunt Lydia open-mouthed snoring on the wide-open passenger window. In the back were my three brothers and a cousin. It would always be at least one of our cousins with us on these drives back to Weeks Island.

Daddy always made us leave late in the day to beat the heat, driving all the way with the windows down. Each visit, he insisted on surprising his brothers back home, even if it was one or two in the morning when we finally got there.

"Next time, can we just let them know we coming?" Flo asked my daddy, mid-conversation in her mind but now letting us in. "'Cause this is always embarrassing." Flo was fifteen, so everything was an embarrassment, but I thought she had a point.

"No, that's our way," my daddy said, driving slower now that we were almost there. "This is our tradition."

Flo sighed in that way she had about her and shifted me off her lap to my mama's. I noticed she brushed the invisible crumbs of me off the cotton of her dress. I had a flash of little-sister anger but was too tired to do anything more than breathe out a huff. In previous visits, I'd always arrived asleep in pajamas, carried from the car out cold on a shoulder straight to a blanket on a floor or a corner of a bed. Dead to the world until I awoke to see my cousins staring at me, this stranger who'd crash-landed in the night from Planet Texas.

I had napped here and there with the rhythm of the road, but now I was determined to stay awake. I looked to the backseat and saw my brothers were just as wide-eyed and vigilant in this darkness. Weeks Island was another world from Galveston. We had life at night. Even if all the locals went to bed, you could drive by the tourists, their faces lit by the floodlights of downtown, or see the moon shining low over the Gulf. Here, even the moon seemed farther away, and my daddy's headlights could only cut through just enough of the inky-black night to not run off the road on a curve. Every turn seemed to have another oak or cypress looming over us. Spanish moss hanging from trees like rags, roots exposed as gnarled fingers of hands waiting to snatch me from the car.

Daddy had turned the radio off, so all we heard was the crunch of the tires on the white seashell-gravel road and the hissing of the insects. Or was it snakes? When I'd sat in the back the first part of the trip, my brothers had filled my head with the scariness of Weeks Island. Banana spiders in webs that would catch you, curled up water moccasins lurking in puddles after rain, and alligators gliding free in the bayou that formed a marshy fence around the land, isolating it off from the rest of the Louisiana coast.

Was this what was bothering my mother? I was used to the comfort of her lap, but as soon as we reached the island, she'd become tense. This had been her home, and my daddy moved here when he was a kid after his mother died. I placed my head back on my mama's shoulder, hoping to ease her nerves. I had started to learn that I could be brave if I thought someone else was scared.

We drove up a hill to Aunt Mandy's house. This was my mother's sister, older than her by a few years. The house was dark but came alive when we knocked. My uncle left to go house to house and collect members of my parents' families, saying that Agnes and Lumis had come home. The women started frying chicken, and the front door stayed open as more grown-ups kept coming over, each one hugging my parents, rating my brothers' height, and leaning down to my face to ask me, "Now who's this?" My cousins, dragged from their beds and houses, had the same question, these sleepy-eyed, one-bit-awake kids glowering at us like we'd interrupted the best sleep of their lives.

My mama's family was glad to see her, but it was my father's brothers who seemed overjoyed to have Boo come home. That was Daddy's nickname as the baby of the family. It was better than his other nickname, which was "the runt." And he did seem younger now in the presence of his brothers. They were all so tall, taller even than my dad, and I kept moving out of the way of knees and feet as my relatives rushed to him. I looked up as these brothers hugged, then pulled back with a pause, then roughly pulled him in again. My father, who would say a gruff and final "Okay" whenever us kids hugged on him, let himself be embraced by his family.

Each uncle did the same thing when they got there: hugging Boo and then pretending not to look at his right eye. They talked too loud to him at first, overcompensating, knowing he was deaf in that ear too.

They'd seen him only a few times since the accident here at Weeks Island, the day that changed everything, and they still needed to get their bearings.

"You can see driving okay at night?"

"Oh sure," said my daddy, moving quickly to distract them.

"You gettin' on okay?"

"Fo' sho'."

A pot fell in the kitchen, empty and no harm done. But it made a loud bang through the small house and my mother jumped in place, then shrank. I saw her eyes scan the room, doing a quick accounting of the whereabouts of each child. My father looked at her, then away.

My mother smiled, one of the ones you could only tell was put on if you'd studied her close for five years straight like I had. She didn't sit back down but moved over to me to place an appraising hand on my shoulder. "You're tired," she said.

"No, I'm not," I lied. People had started to sit down, eating the chicken and drinking. I wanted to stay in the action. I moved toward my mother to get her to sit down, softly herding her the way only kids can do. If she stood any longer, I knew she would be pushing me to some corner of the house to sleep. She sat back on the couch, and I climbed into her lap to keep us there. I wanted to be with the grown-ups. I wanted to know what they knew.

My Aunt Mandy was talking, which I think was her way of breathing she did it so much. She would visit Galveston sometimes, and I loved the music of her talking. The asides and confidences of an adult who knew all the good stories. My mother told me the family history meant to raise me right, and Mandy was there to give the more colorful stories in-between.

There in the living room, it did not take long for everyone to get to talking about the accident at the salt mine. The explosion. Now I understand how close it seemed to them, even a decade gone by. It was a story they all played a part in, something they were still making sense of.

The memories they shared that night were ones I already knew parts of. My mom was the storyteller, and with my daddy you had to just pull the family history out of him. But what happened at the mine was the one story my daddy would tell. Because he was still pissed. He would die pissed at that salt place for running my family out of Louisiana.

EVERYONE AT WEEKS ISLAND HAD BEEN FILLED WITH THE FEAR OF one day being made to leave it. It wasn't that it was paradise, it was a place where you did what you were told as you lived out your days working at the salt mine, the one job on the island. And here sat my mama and daddy, living reminders to every relative of what could happen if you stepped out of line. Even hell can seem like paradise if it's the home you're made to leave.

The entire island had been a slave colony in the 1800s, a two-thousand-acre sugar plantation worked by enslaved Black men, women, and children. The plantation's owner was a white man named David Weeks, and while the family business appeared to be sugar, it was really slavery. Reading his family's collected letters now, you see an obsession with preventing their captives from running away. The island's isolation made escape especially difficult, the moat of alligators waiting for anyone fleeing from their little kingdom, which David's son William F. Weeks inherited. William's letters continually return to the two hundred enslaved people he called "nigs," and how he could maximize his profit from their labor as the Southern economy faced the Civil War. By 1860, nearly *half* of the entire population of Louisiana was enslaved people. In 1863, the presence of Union troops in Louisiana scared William, who feared the army taking enslaved people from plantation owners, so he briefly trafficked his captives with him to Texas to hire them out for profit. People named in inventory lists— like Lucretia, Judah, Ellen, and Spencer—could be "rented," as he put it. "Men at $25 per month, women at $20, girls & boys at $15," William writes, "this amt is to be paid in good cotton ready for market at eight cent per pound." Humans were bartered for the cotton they picked because the Confederacy's currency—the Greybacks they started printing in 1861—were by then worthless bills of credit not backed by any asset.

William returned to take over Weeks Island again after the war, taking advantage of Louisiana enacting the new Black Codes of other Southern states. The Black Codes created more forced work, ordering that "freed" people sign yearly *"labor contracts"* for extremely low wages with the same people who used to consider them property. They were trapped again, living in the same terrible conditions.

Eventually, it was discovered that underneath all the green of Weeks Island was something even more valuable than sugar: a giant salt dome. William's heirs—rich from the work of enslaved people—sold the land. Over the years, various salt companies took a turn at managing the enterprise—and the people who served it.

When my family lived there, the salt company owned the entire island, from the mine itself to every one of the workers' homes, plus the general store, and the separate churches and barber shops for the white and Black villagers. *Everything.* The Black population of Weeks Island rented concrete homes, with life so regimented that if yellow paint was supplied to each family on a Friday there was an understanding that every house would be painted that yellow when the village manager drove through Monday. There were no elections, so law and order meant the deputy sheriff was also the salt mill supervisor, and the justice of the peace and village constable worked at the plant. Everyone had a role at the mine, and most had started work at an early age. A first job might have you picking out the dark lumps from the salt at age eleven, then sewing the sacks for the salt as a teenager. Maybe work up to be a loader or a crane operator, a job you'd have for decades. Education at Weeks Island, if you got any, stopped at junior high. Kids were given the option of taking a bus thirty-four miles to the Black high school in New Iberia. And then back.

Who could do that? So, at the start of the 1940s, my daddy was paid nine dollars a week working at the mine. Four hundred and sixty-eight dollars a year at around thirty years old.

My daddy had moved to Weeks Island young, bouncing from a brother or sister after his mother died. I was never clear how much school my father attended as a motherless child working in return for a home. One of the places he landed was next door to my mom's parents. My maternal grandfather, Eugene Derouen, worked as a salt sweeper at the mine, raising sixteen children—mostly daughters—with my grandmother Odilia. My mother was Odilia's last child. And like me, she was a surprise baby in her mother's mid-forties.

I picture my parents as teens, Lumis and Agnes. He had a crush on her, of course, the most beautiful of the many Derouen girls. She wasn't just striking—early on she showed a gift for *creating* beauty. As the youngest of the family, most of the chores were already seen to. So she would create work, pressing her sisters' hair or picking wildflowers to arrange them in a glass just so. But of her talents, sewing was her crowning glory. She started young, making her sisters' clothes and adding her flair to anything ordinary.

Seeing Lumis in the neighborhood, was Agnes aware that he thought she was beautiful? I don't know. I do know that at fifteen years old she only had eyes for another guy who'd grown up on the island: Mervin "Slack" Marsh, who had left and gone to Texas, then came back in his fancy car to sweep her off her feet. Nineteen and nearly as handsome as she was beautiful, Slack plucked her like one of those flowers and ran her off to Galveston. Slack loved her as a *girl,* but he had different ideas about the duties of a *wife*. He would get so mad at her for not knowing how to cook or clean to his expectations—what good was making the table look nice when the food was burnt and flavorless? He said he was holding up his end, making good money as a longshoreman at the wharf. But her? Nothing she tried was right.

The marriage was destructive to her physically and mentally. She became pregnant, and when she was about three months along, she found out that her mother had died at Weeks Island. She was heartbroken, but then, soon after she turned seventeen, she gave birth to a baby girl: my oldest sister, Selena Mae.

Having a baby in the house only made Slack point out more short-comings. Slack sent word back home that he needed my mother's twenty-six-year-old sister, Lydia, to come from Weeks Island to teach my mother how to cook and clean. Lydia, who snored all the way on our drive to Weeks Island. Growing up, Lydia was considered country even for Weeks Island, never abandoning her Creole for English as so many other people did. So her name was always pronounced "Leeedja," the *E*'s going down like a slide, and the *ja* a quick uppercut. And Lydia, this country girl, *loved* Galveston. She couldn't be happier to leave Weeks Island, and quickly got herself a boyfriend—saying "buwahfrien" in her Creole accent, laughing at this found luck of a new life away from Weeks Island.

But my mother grew more miserable as her marriage got more toxic. When she got pregnant again, she felt even more trapped. My mama had her second child, Slack Jr., on a hot August day in 1929. Now she had two kids and she'd just turned twenty.

It was on a night some months after the new baby arrived that Slack pushed things too far. For the first time in her life, my mother stood up to Slack. This change so shocked him that he put her out.

Worse, she could only take the baby. He said she had to leave Selena.

My sister was three years old, four at most. Aunt Lydia stayed, promising to care for Selena, and my mother, devastated and lost, re-turned to her family home at Weeks Island. Slack kept Selena from my mother for a year. My mama made each of those days sound like its own year.

Sometime after Slack finally sent Selena to my mother, my mama started up with my daddy. He'd grown handsome, with a sharpness to his chin that fit the quiet way he carried himself. Looks-wise, he could have been mistaken for Slack's brother, except Daddy was always de-pendable. He liked to drink on the weekends even then with his broth-ers, but it was harmless stuff.

Even before they were married, after Slack got around to granting my mother a divorce, my dad raised both of her children as if they were his. And they became his. They had Slack's last name, but it was just the way my family carried themselves.

They waited a long time to have more kids, but by 1947, my parents had two more: my sister Flo, who was three, and my brother Butch, who was around one year old and had started walking. Selena and Slack Jr. were twenty and seventeen, starting their own lives. In the late summer of that year, my mother learned she was pregnant. I know my mother worried how they would make it, and I also know the answer that her singular faith gave her: God would provide.

Now, in the living room with all my relatives, people traded facts and details back and forth about the day that changed everything. They'd all been involved, because all my daddy's older brothers worked at the mine. Seniority set your pecking order for the company, so as the baby of the family my father had one of the worst jobs: dynamiting. For this, his yearly salary was $468. The company was always expanding the mine, and they used explosives to break up the salt rock. My daddy and another man would go way in, deep into the very edges of the mine. There were two crews, because the white people didn't work with Black people, and the Black people, of course, had the most dangerous jobs. And dynamiting was the riskiest of them all.

It was three o'clock when my daddy and the other man who handled the dynamite went down the white-rock tunnel to the newest part of the mine. The two made their way down farther and farther, through a tunnel into the depths and then—

Boom.

An explosion. A stick of dynamite went off prematurely. The blast hit one whole side of my daddy—a spray of explosive and rock salt searing into his right eye and blowing out his eardrum.

The tunnel behind them caved in, and boulders came down on the other man, trapping his legs. The lights they carried went out, and the two of them were sealed in their pitch-black tomb.

My daddy's nine brothers heard the explosion where they were on the surface of the mine. "We were begging management," said one of my uncles. "You know, 'Please let us dig through, because they might be alive.' And the company says, 'No. There's no way they could survive that blast. They're dead.'"

The mine's policy was that it was too dangerous to dig for people— Black or white—and start moving stuff not knowing what else was going to fall. But my daddy's brothers were freaking out because this was their baby brother. This was Boo.

Management sent everybody home. Whenever they had an explosion or a cave-in, whatever time it happened, they called it "knocking off early." Blew the whistle and cleared the place. I don't know who came up with the plan, probably Uncle Alec, who was close to my daddy in age and spirit. But my uncles all made the motions of leaving, then waited until everybody got out.

They hopped the fence and started up their digging equipment to go find him. "They kept going," my daddy said. "And then there they were."

My uncles moved the boulder off the man's legs to pull him out. He'd gone into shock and passed out. My father was too weak to walk himself, so his brothers carried him and the man out. They raced them to the hospital that took Black people, which was a little bit north of the island.

A doctor told my daddy his eye was too damaged to ever see out of it again, and he wouldn't get his hearing back on his right side either. The other guy my uncles saved went into the operating room, and a surgeon said he hoped the man would be able to keep one of the legs.

They were all still at the hospital when management showed up with the police, who also worked for the company. Every single one of the brothers was fired, including my father and the one-legged man still in the operating room. They said my uncles had disobeyed company orders and stolen the equipment.

The police made a show of arresting the two oldest brothers, the most senior miners in the family, for using the company equipment. They called them "the ringleaders" and said it was for "breaking and entering."

I don't know who finally told my mother. I picture her at home, this woman of faith who still lived with a constant dread of something terrible happening. Pregnant, and then there's this knock at the door, someone telling her my daddy had nearly died and was out of a job. Which at Weeks Island was as good as dead anyway.

DADDY STARTED TELLING THE STORY.

The man had come unannounced to my parents' house shortly

after my daddy got home from the hospital. He was white, from a ways north, and said he wanted to talk to my daddy about how being part of a union would have made things different. The first time they talked, my father simply listened to his pitch. He used "we" a lot. "We," he said, had heard my daddy was fired and the guy who needed a wheelchair was also out with no benefits. "We," he said again, wanted my daddy to help organize a play for the salt miners to unionize.

"If you were part of a union, they couldn't do this to you," said the man. "You're half blind and half deaf and all out of luck. What kinda bargain is that?"

My daddy was pissed enough to be interested. The company had realized losing ten brothers affected productivity and they hired the five senior brothers back. Now the younger brothers were mad at the older ones, calling them sellouts. And the big brothers thought the younger ones didn't appreciate that they had families to support. The company had divided the family, and my daddy wasn't sure how long they would let him stay at Weeks Island.

The first threat was left at my parents' house a couple of days after the union man approached him. All the note said was STOP TALKING. My daddy knew people got killed over union stuff, but he couldn't imagine something like that happening at Weeks Island. So he kept talking to the man, and then brought his brothers to come meet with the guy. By the end, they all said, "We want to sign up for the union."

Word spread to the wrong people.

My parents were home at night, sitting in a living room that was identical to the cookie-cutter one we all sat in as he told the story. They had been listening to the radio, a gospel station out of New Orleans. The signal coming in was just strong enough to cross the Gulf waters. Flo and Butch, four and one, were asleep in the bedroom.

Suddenly, a Molotov cocktail broke the glass of the front window. The bottle shattered on the floor in front of them. *Whoosh.* The gasoline took flame as it spread all over the living room. The fire was everywhere.

My parents managed to get to my brother and sister, grabbing the children and nothing else to flee the burning home. My father said he stood outside, watching everything they'd worked for turn to ashes.

My mother pulled his arm, telling him to run. A cousin had a car.

He would drive them where they needed to go. With all this union stuff, she said they were not safe to even see the sun rise in Louisiana.

"I'm getting my kids out of here," my mother said. "We're leaving."

"To go *where?*" asked my father.

But she was already running, pregnant and carrying both children to her cousin's house. There was nowhere to go except the last place on earth she wanted to go back to.

Galveston.

MY MOTHER'S PLAN WAS TO GO TO HER SISTER LYDIA'S. GET TO Galveston and then figure it out—anything to get safely off of Weeks Island. By then, Lydia had married that boyfriend, but when they got to Galveston, probably at about two o'clock in the morning, her "house" was one room in a rooming house. And here came my mama with two kids and a husband. Not only was it against the rules of the place, Lydia said, they simply didn't have room.

"Go to him," Lydia said to my mother in her Creole. She didn't need to say his name. "Same house."

Slack. My mother's ex-husband who she hadn't spoken to in years. Who she *hated.* He was the only person they had left to turn to. I picture her standing there holding Butch, and my daddy holding Flo. All they had in life and nowhere for them to sleep. She did what she had to do, and she would see what Slack would do.

The outside of the house was unchanged since he'd put her out. She rang the bell.

Slack answered the door in his pajamas, holding the door open a crack and squinting at this pitiful scene. His ex-wife Agnes, who he could not stand, was huddled there with two kids flanking her. Behind her, with a protective hand on her shoulder, was Lumis, who he knew from when he was a kid. Lumis, who had raised his children.

"We have nowhere else to go," my mama said.

There was a long pause, and no matter how many times I heard about that moment, I felt the destiny of my family in the balance.

Slack opened the door wider. And he told them to come in.

"Stay as long as you need," he said.

He let them in. For me, there is the miracle of mercy here, on both parts. My mother's willingness to be humble, and maybe Slack's hope that this would be the start of his redemption. Each choosing to do the hard thing.

Slack's new wife helped them get settled in for the night. I have lost track which one he was on, so don't go thinking he's a saint. Slack had been a womanizer, and he would always be very gruff, but he was becoming kinder with age.

My mother woke up early in the house she had once fled. She got up and helped the new Mrs. Marsh with breakfast. Slack reminded them that he meant it when he said they could stay as long as they needed. Days turned into weeks, and they ended up staying there a couple of months as they rebuilt their lives.

I asked my mother once, much later, "How did you feel being in that house?"

She answered quick. "I felt horrible," she said, as if she'd been waiting to be asked. "I didn't want to be there. It made me sick to my stomach because I had hated every single day I was there the first time, and I hated every single day after. But—" She trailed off. Shrugged. Busied her hands. "Him and your daddy, they got along real well," she said, a touch rueful. "He liked your daddy."

Slack did. The two men, who looked so much alike they could have been brothers, became close friends. Slack owed my daddy for treating his kids as his own; my father owed Slack for taking in his family. Slack pulled off a miracle getting my dad a job. Not just a job, but a union job as a longshoreman in the local. As my daddy couldn't hear in one ear and couldn't see out of one eye, there were rules that disqualified him from being a longshoreman loading ships. But Slack got my daddy in the local and stuck his neck out for him. He would load and unload the smaller crates that required manual labor. My daddy shouldn't have been able to get that work, but that shows you the camaraderie between all those Black men in the union working together. Slack took a risk helping him, but any one of those men could have told on my daddy and had him ousted.

There weren't many light loads, and that was why we were *so* poor. But it was something, and the kind of something you could build a life on. My mother found a house they could afford. It was really beat up, but Mama went in and painted it, wallpapered it up, shined every surface she could. She found some seeds, starting with roses, and planted a garden.

My mother had my brother Larry in March, then Skip the following year, and then five years after that, the big surprise of me, their last baby. My oldest sister, Selena, and her husband, John, moved into a house around the corner, and Slack Jr. started working as a longshoreman in Galveston with both his daddies.

Mama made a home for us out of nothing. She nursed her roses and made it nice. That was just her way.

Now, in this bright living room in the dark of Weeks Island, I had leaned back in the safety of my mother's arms. She lifted me up, and I was carried—in her arms and in their story—to sleep.

I WOKE ON THE CORNER OF A BED TO TWO OF MY GIRL COUSINS staring at me. Sisters, tall and small. I remembered them from last night, but who was who I could not tell you.

"Do you want to walk around with us?" Tall and Small asked.

"What do you guys do here?" I asked.

"Walk around" was the short answer from Tall, as if there was something wrong with me.

"Oh," I said. "Yeah, okay. I can walk around. Let me ask my mama."

I don't think I ever asked my mama's permission for anything back then, but I wanted to see if there was a better offer first. The older boys had already left to explore the edge of the bayou, probably to get eaten by alligators and never be seen again. Flo was talking to an older girl cousin about something, but then hushed when I walked toward them.

I found my mother sitting in the sun outside with her needle and thread, a neat pile of clothes next to her that she had already mended for family. The air was so thick here, and Weeks Island didn't have a breeze like the one off the water at home. I imagined growing up here like she did, and I curled my lip at the thought. I'd often thought about what it would be like to live somewhere far away from Galveston. But not here. Sometimes you have to leave your home to know it's home.

"I'm *glad* you moved to Galveston," I said as a greeting.

She didn't answer, just raised her eyebrows and returned her attention to a tear she was mending. "Good morning, Tenie."

"Good morning, Mama," I said. "They wanna walk around."

"Who's they?"

I pointed at Tall and Small. When you are five, nobody expects you to remember names. My mama nodded and got up to go get me three nickels. "Tenie," she said, "I want you to listen to your cousins today, okay? Weeks Island is not your home. This is somebody else's home."

Tall and Small walked me out the door and we moved down the hill of houses toward what they called town. The homes were all the exact same size, and super close together, boxes set in ordered rows. From where we walked, you could see where all this order ended, the lush green of the trees and swamp pushed to the straight-lined edges of a salt mine town.

The cousins were about ten and eight, both sharp and funny, teasing each other about playing tour guide to me without being mean. When we got to a cement-lined pool of water in the center of town, they each laughed when Small said "This is the pond," like it was a big sightseeing thing. Nearby, I spotted a little corner store and I thought of those nickels my mama gave me. Maybe there'd be ice cream. Ice cream was its own activity anywhere you went. In Galveston, Miss Sims owned the corner store we all went to. She had the best ice cream, the cones we kids would parade around with like prizes before they melted in the Galveston sun. We'd see how Weeks Island's rated.

I made a beeline for the shop, the girls following me. I saw some white kids go in before me, and Tall and Small stopped just as I was getting ready to walk in the store.

"We can't go in there now," Small said as I reached for the door. She looked at me like I was out of my mind. I gave that same look back.

"Tenie, you can't go in there while white kids are in there," Tall said.

"Why?"

"You *can't*," Small said. "You gotta wait till they come out."

But they were taking *so* long. "They can't *stop* you from going in a store," I said, reaching for the door to push it open. "I don't *want* to wait—"

I was one step inside. The lady working at the counter hissed, "You need to go back outside."

I froze, more scared of the venom in the voice than understanding what she was telling me to do.

Outside, my cousins called my name behind me. The two white kids had penny candy in their hands. They looked over at me confused.

The lady placed her palms on the counter. "Go. Back. Outside," she said.

I walked out, too surprised to cry or fully react. I started saying something to the girls.

"Shut up," one said, each word a sharp blow to knock sense in me. "You're not gonna get *us* in trouble."

"Okay." Quiet. Making myself small at age five.

We walked home quickly, them using a secret language of sisters: quick looks, eyerolls, and shakes of the head. Whatever they agreed to in those moments was set, because as soon as we got back to their house they went right to their mother.

"We're not taking Tenie with us anymore," said Small.

"'Cause she just got a big mouth," said Tall. My aunt Mandy and my mother looked at me.

"I'm not . . ." I trailed off. Not *what*? I didn't know. Not whatever that woman thought I was. Not whatever those kids with the candy thought I was. Not even what my cousins thought I was.

I thought my mother would fix it, but she sided with my cousins. "Y'all can't come down here and make things bad for them."

It wasn't until visiting Weeks Island that I felt confronted by racism. The first time it was targeted so directly at me that the behavior didn't have to be explained. Now, I was clear enough to connect the dots: There were rules. I could reel them off: the bus, the beach, and the one that said if you were walking on the sidewalk and a white person was walking by, you had to step off the sidewalk into the street. How many rules did I know, but not even know that I knew? And what did I not know that could hurt me at a place like Weeks Island?

Butch came into the house, leading my brothers behind him. He already looked like a country kid, talking Louisiana after one morning there. They'd seen five water moccasins, including one Skip almost stepped on in a murky dip in the gravel road. It had hissed and they ran. But my mother cut their story off, quizzing my brothers about where else they'd been and what they did. They answered like they'd been accused of doing something wrong.

She wasn't afraid of snakes. It was people who terrified her. We were only four years on from the murder of Emmett Till, the fourteen-year-old Chicago child who like so many kids was visiting relatives in the South. Three days into visiting family in Mississippi, he went to a corner grocery store, just like me. He bought chewing gum; I wanted ice cream. My brother Butch would be fourteen soon. What did Emmett Till "do"? Look someone in the eye? We weren't from the North like him, but we went to the grocery store all the time with white people in Galveston, the way he did in Chicago.

All of us, Emmett Till too, had gone back in time and place, visiting the family we came from. But when you went to these little towns, all of a sudden you had to change who *you* were. I saw my cousins as "trained," and I didn't see why they didn't see anything wrong with waiting outside a store. I didn't understand then that it was survival.

"You don't know what could happen," Mama told us, though she seemed to be talking to herself. "You have to be more careful."

My mother's hands went down to her sides, then up toward her chest. I felt a tightening in my own. Like when you're in water too deep and you lift your chin over the waterline. Start to tread water to stop your body from panicking. I'd always *witnessed* my mother's anxiety, heard it and seen it, but this was the beginning of me *feeling* that fear. Worse, it felt natural, like it had been there all along, passed down to me with all her trauma. Waiting to activate inside me.

I DON'T REMEMBER HOW MANY DAYS WE STAYED THAT VISIT. I couldn't wait to get back to Galveston and counted the hours like stamps to trade in for a day closer to home. I was collecting anecdotes too, country stories to tell Johnny when I got back.

Butch was in heaven the whole time, the Creole Kid, grabbing branches above him to steady his gait along the swamp to climb into an uncle's tiny little boat. He wanted to stay in Louisiana, said it over and over, and I saw something in my parents when he said that. I couldn't tell if they wished they could stay too, or if they simply wanted him to have what they'd had. A simple life out here, even if surrounded by the dangers of snakes and people. This land itself was his birthright, where his soul felt at home. Didn't he deserve this? Didn't my parents?

My cousins got over the trouble they said I caused and started talking to me again. I stayed closer to my aunt Mandy's house—and closer to her. She was funny, and while my mother told stories to explain things, she told them for the fun of it. The first time I heard the words "shacking up" was from her, and it was about my parents living together before my mother's divorce was finally granted. My mother got bashful, but it was okay because it was Aunt Mandy poking fun. "Saint Agnes," Mandy joked, and I laughed too, then my mother.

"They had a whole thing before you showed up," Aunt Mandy said. "You know your mama and daddy used to sing at the Canteen?"

"Really?" I asked. I knew my mother had a beautiful voice, but only from singing while she worked or hymns sung at church. It was her tune I followed as I sang to myself. But my daddy? I'd never heard him sing in his life. "What's the Canteen?"

"The bar," said Mandy. "Your daddy could really sing."

"It was a club," my mother said quickly. "Like a nightclub."

The Canteen was the little dance place on the island. I realized I'd seen the building on the walk with my cousins. "In front of people?" I asked.

They both laughed. "Yes," my mother said.

"They were good," said Mandy, who never humored a person in her life. "They were real good."

"Well, what happened?" I asked.

My mama shrugged. "That's all over, Tenie."

CHAPTER 4

HOLY ROSARY

September 1959

I CLUTCHED THE PENCIL my mother gave me and smoothed the skirt of my uniform. The white collar of the shirt was starched to a height that it grazed my chin if I moved too fast. I had a short criss-cross tie, dark like the sweater vest I wore. It was scratchy but it felt important with its embroidered badge reading HOLY ROSARY. A badge I was proud to wear after years of watching my siblings go across the street to school.

My mother had let me try on my school uniform once, determined that I keep it perfect for this moment, my first day of kindergarten. The first sign of trouble was the scowl on Sister Fidelis. She was Black, like all the other nuns at Holy Rosary Catholic School, and certainly the oldest of all of them, at least eighty to my five-year-old eyes. I bet she had been the first sign of trouble at Holy Rosary for generations of kids. Short and squat, her voluminous black habit swirled around her with every move, her wrinkled face framed in white, then hooded in the darkness of her cloak. Sister Fidelis had the longest set of rosary beads I'd ever seen, holstered loose around her waist like a gun at the ready. I don't know what I had pictured in my excitement about my first day of school, but this was boot camp, and she was our drill sergeant.

Sister Fidelis had us line up outside before letting us go in. She said that from now on, once we heard the bell, we were to enter the classroom in silence. Girls first, then boys, and we were to sit in the rows alphabetically by last name. She stalked the line of kids, her habit swirling around her, making her even more domineering as she grabbed us by the chin to turn our whole body in the proper direction. "Silence," she said, over and over. For all I knew, Sister Fidelis might have been one of the original nuns from 1886, when Holy Rosary was established as the first Catholic school for Black children in all of Texas. The nuns had also been the first Black sisters to teach in Texas.

My mother insisted I get there early, even though it was right across the street from our house. I watched my classmates arrive, driven by dads on the way to work or with moms coming off the bus, wearing smart nurses' uniforms or carrying the lunches they would eat in teachers' lounges. These children, I would learn, were the sons and daughters of Galveston's Black middle class—professors, accountants, nurses, and teachers—who thought a Catholic private school was a better fit than the public schools, George W. Carver Elementary on the west side or Booker T. Washington to the east. I had no concept of class— I was just looking for familiar faces from the neighborhood and realized that none of these people lived around me.

Holy Rosary already felt like home because we practically lived in the church attached. My mama went to mass every day, but we were there every Sunday, and extra during Lent and Holy Week. I'd keep my brothers company while they cleaned the schoolyard of trash, or tag along with my mother when she brought over choir robes she'd made—

"Silence!" Sister Fidelis commanded again, derailing any child's train of thought. She looked up as the bell rang once. "In," she said, pushing one child and then another into the classroom. We found our seats quickly, and as I sat at my desk, I thought, *This is school.* I watched Sister Fidelis write her name on the board, her back to us as she engaged in the beautiful swirl of her script. I was admiring the high swoop of her *L* when she suddenly froze and threw the chalk down.

"Who is talking?" she screamed. I hadn't heard anything. Maybe a murmur. Not me.

And then this boy next to me that I'd never met pointed at *me.* And so, reflexively, I pointed right back at him.

Sister Fidelis marched to where we were, the swirl of her black cloak grazing desks as she passed. She grabbed each of us by an ear, yanking hard to get us to our feet. Still gripping our ears, she dragged us both up to the front of the room. There was a stick on her desk, waiting for just this moment. A wooden stick with two holes in it.

"Put your hands out," she said.

The boy immediately put his behind his back. He looked terrified. And I realize now he was so frightened because he knew what was coming. But no adult had ever hit me before. My parents had never spanked me, let alone hit me with a stick.

So I held out my hands.

Sister Fidelis turned to the boy, boring holes in him with the fire in her squinted eyes. Then he put his hands out too and winced in advance. The boy leaned back, seeming to bring his self as far away from what was happening as he possibly could.

Sister Fidelis brought the stick down on my open palms, and I was stunned by the pain. I went to pull them away, but Sister grabbed both my wrists quick with her left hand, making hooks of her pointer finger and thumb. The two holes in the stick made a shrill whistle in the air as she brought it down again, the warning before the lightning of pain. I think now how practiced she was at inflicting hurt on children. That she knew just how to grab the wrists to keep the palms spread out.

"I said *silence*," she intoned on the last one, releasing my wrists. It was the boy's turn, and as Sister shifted her attention to him, my head turned to the door. My shirt collar now felt tight. The sweater hot and confining.

Oh, I don't like this, I said to myself. And I ran right out that classroom door, out to the schoolyard, and across the street to my house. My mother would fix this.

I burst through the front door. *"Mama,"* I yelled, ripping the sweater off. I couldn't describe what happened—I didn't even know the words—and held out my hands to show her. Hoping that alone would help heal the stinging. "I don't like this," I said again, my feet dancing in an involuntary step to stop the pain. "I don't . . ." I said, softer now. "I don't . . . I don't want to go."

My mother looked at my hands. She knew exactly what happened. Now she would protect me. She would march over there and God better grade nuns on a curve because Sister Fidelis was going to need all the help she could get from above when my mother got to her. All the stuff she did for the church, all the yardwork she made my brothers do for them, all the times my daddy would drive somebody from Holy Rosary to wherever they needed to go. Kiss that goodbye.

When my mother said nothing, and picked up my sweater, I thought she didn't understand how serious I was. "I'm not going back there," I said.

"Well, it's not a choice," she said.

I was confused. My parents didn't spoil me or indulge me. I was an impetuous, hyper kid, and they reined that in with a clear structure of right and wrong, then letting me learn my lessons on my own. And part of that sureness was that they would stand up for me when someone did something to me. Protect me.

"Mama," I said, as she pulled the sweater over my head.

"Tenie," she answered, finality to her voice as she straightened the collar. She went to the mirror and adjusted her own dress. Made sure she also looked perfect as she walked out the door. "Come," she said.

I'd believed that she would always protect me. And with each step back to the Holy Rosary door, I thought she would prove me right. But she didn't. My heart beat against my chest now, up high in my throat as Sister Fidelis came to the door with a look of contempt for both of us.

"Celestine," she said, pronouncing it "Sulluh-steen" as she always would. My mother did not correct her. Or tell her to never lay hands on her child again. In fact, she made me apologize to Sister for running away, and then she turned back to the house. My mama did not turn to see me again. I waited for at least that, but it didn't come.

Alone with me outside the classroom, Sister Fidelis leaned down so that her face was even with mine. This short ancient woman and a tall little girl. "If only you knew," she said. And then, unable to resist whatever mean devil whispered on the dark expanse of her slumped shoulder, Sister said plainly: "You don't belong here."

"I HEAR THEY GET THEIR HEADS SHAVED BALD WHEN THEY BECOME nuns." This was Marlene, waiting to double Dutch at recess. In those first weeks, Marlene was considered the expert on Sister Fidelis because her mother was taught by her, and she said Sister had no patience then either.

"I wonder if they cut off their hair or the boobs first?" said Patricia, who we called Tricia, finishing her turn with a hop. That was the other theory—that when girls entered the sisterhood to become nuns, they cut off their boobs.

"Oh my God," I said, "I can't believe they do that." I couldn't even imagine them ever having lives before they became nuns. They were these shapeless figures floating the halls with their hands clasped in front of them, telling you to your face that they knew what was in your mind. We kids were all together in this, and I was fortunate to make friends now that I was navigating the world for the first time without all the other kids in my family. I was a girls' girl early, and maybe there was a feeling that I took the heat from Sister Fidelis in a way that allowed them a little breathing room.

The pattern had continued over those weeks, though Sister Fidelis never hit me again. I think I made such a big deal of it that they knew I wasn't a little kid that was gonna take the hitting. So they got more creative—making me kneel in a corner or sending me to stand in the sun with books up over my head. Sister Fidelis would single me out for punishment, along with another boy, Glen, whose father was a barber. It was always something with him and me, and they picked on him so much that it was the first time I pitied another kid. It was an awful feeling because I recognized it in the way other kids sometimes looked at me. Sister Fidelis ensured the whole class could see us when she made me and the boy go stand in the sun.

I tried to talk to Glen under that sun, anything to distract myself from my arms shaking. But he was afraid. "We can say we were praying," I said. But he was afraid, and I gave up.

Each time I was punished, I would run, out that door and racing home to my mother. For the first time, the girl who was always running *to* some place began running away from something.

"Mama, what's 'vain'?"

I was crying on our doorstep. She had learned not to even let me in the house when I ran home from school. Sister Fidelis had just called me that.

"That you think you're cute," my mother said, buttoning her coat to bring me back.

Oh, I thought, deciding I never wanted people to think that I thought I was cute. It would be safer to let them know that I knew I wasn't cute. Better yet, just show them that I knew I wasn't worthy. Then they wouldn't have to try so hard to convince me.

My mom perfected that turnaround of taking me back to school when I ran away. When I looked up at her to get her to understand, she looked so sad and scared.

Did I think something would change in my mother? Actually, yes. I honestly thought each time that my mother would be redeemed by taking action. That her love for me would take over, and whatever control the nuns and the church had over her would take its rightful place second to me. I tried to get my father to help me—he couldn't stand the nuns, and he would have me come to run the errands with them as he chauffeured them around. He'd let me sit in the front seat next to him, and he acted as if they were invisible. I told myself he was showing them that I was under his protection.

My mom went to mass at seven in the morning, seven days a week, 365 days a year. Only missing it if she was in the hospital, and even then, she had us bring her prayer book and rosary beads to her. Our families went every Sunday, all mingled close in our usual spots. Our family took up five or six rows. Beside us was my mom's first husband, Slack, and by then we had all taken to calling him Big Pop. His wife—Aunt Terry to us—and their kids were like my brothers and sisters: Andre, Brandon, and Steve, the youngest boy, and Sharon, the baby. My sister Selena—always the conduit joining us as family—would bring all eight of her kids. I would sit next to my nephew Johnny, unless my mother decided we needed to be separated. There was so much ritual involved, and it was exhausting to a little kid.

In a Catholic mass, there is Holy Communion every time, and it's the most important aspect of the faith. It manages to be both the bedrock and the summit of what is believed—what everyone is really there for. You go up to the altar and take the wafer, the Eucharist, as a sign of mutual adoration between you and God. He is present in the wafer, and you are worthy to take Him with you out into the world. If you are not worthy to receive communion in life, you will not be part of the everlasting covenant in death.

"Take this, all of you, and eat it," the priest would say, holding up a wafer. "This is my body which will be given up for you."

Not all of us. I would kneel with my mother as everyone else went up to take communion. Kids had to be seven or eight before they were considered worthy of a first communion, so I was always jealous that Flo and my older brothers could go. They came solemnly back up the aisle like seen-it-all models on a runway, looking so grown.

"You can go up," I told my mother one Sunday that fall. I thought it looked babyish that she stayed with me. I didn't need babysitting at church.

"No, I can't," she whispered.

"Yes, you can," I said. I had a child's view of this. Of course, this was all about me.

"No, Tenie, I'm not allowed."

"Why?"

"Shh."

I did *not* shh. I turned to her. "What do you mean you're not allowed?"

"Tenie, if you don't—" she whispered. "Later."

I held her to it later, when she and I went for a walk. In an age-appropriate way, my mama told me that because she had been divorced, the Church said she wasn't able to receive communion. It was a hard rule.

This woman, the most devout Catholic in there, kneeling in prayer as she was considered unworthy of what everyone else was going up to the altar to share in. Meanwhile, she had to watch her ex-husband, Big Pop—who had had several wives—go up and take communion with no problem. Not to mention my daddy, who embarrassed us reeking with the after-smell of all that alcohol from the night before. And you know he could curse up a storm. Not hurting anybody, but compared to Saint Agnes? Who did so much for Holy Rosary?

I felt that anger later, but at five, I just saw her getting the same message that Sister Fidelis said to my face: We didn't belong.

SISTER FIDELIS WAS HINTING AT SOME SECRET THE NUNS KNEW about me that I didn't. It was at the tip of her forked tongue, even when handing a penmanship paper back to me. "If you only knew," she'd say, "you'd be very grateful to be here."

I *was* different from the other kids. On Mondays they would talk about how they spent a whole Saturday at the Pleasure Pier, and one boy bragged he ate so much candy he threw up. They seemed to hear "no" less often. They didn't hear "We can't afford that." I was a little jealous, but mostly it was that I became conscious of something I couldn't square. How did we have the best dresses of anybody in

Galveston, and how was I going to this private school, and yet we never had any money to do things?

The truth was that my parents were basically indentured servants to Holy Rosary, bartering work in exchange for tuition for me and my siblings. That's why my father was a chauffeur at the nuns' beck and call. Why my mother sewed every stitch in that place, both the church and the school. And why my brothers cleared each scrap on the asphalt of that yard. It was such a sacrifice to work and humble themselves so their kids and grandkids could get an education.

Still, my family was useful to them. On Fridays we would crown a statue of the Blessed Virgin Mary. They picked one girl, and at the end of the school day she would put on a white dress and this little mantilla, and get to feel like a bride, walking to the statue holding the flower crown. The whole school would be watching, singing "Mary We Crown Thee with Blossoms Today."

On a Wednesday, I saw Sister Fidelis talking to a nun for a few minutes, and then the nun came to me. "You have a white dress?" she asked. The voice was sweet, surprising.

"I don't know," I said, "but my mom will make one."

I went home vibrating, and my mom noticed that happy energy she'd missed. We went right to the fabric store, and she went through the white remnants of bridal fabrics until she found the perfect ends to make something beautiful. This was the excitement of my *life*. I watched her get to work that night, and she continued all day Thursday. When the nuns were cold to me that afternoon, I thought, *I know I am lovable. I know you don't* really *hate me, or else you wouldn't let me crown the Blessed Virgin Mary tomorrow.*

My mother put so many finishing touches on it until it was ready for Friday. "Oh Tenie," she said when I tried it on. She was right, it was her masterpiece. She had put all the love and longing of her life into creating something worthy of the occasion. Worthy of their grace.

I went to school carrying the dress to change in to for the ceremony later that day. "Good," Sister Fidelis said when she saw it. She called the other nun in. She held the dress up, and I could feel the class move forward to look.

Then she brought the dress over and held it up to Linda Kendeson. "Linda," said the nun. "You will crown Mary today."

Now, Linda was a very sweet girl, and she had recently suffered a horrible tragedy. Her mom had died suddenly, but we never talked about it in class. She was out, and then she was back. We were told to be nice to her, but not to talk about it.

I wanted Linda to be happy, but I didn't understand what was happening. Linda didn't either, but her uncertain smile was enough for Sister Fidelis to justify what she had done to me.

"I don't want her to have my dress," I said, louder than I thought it would come out.

"Oh, look at you," Sister Fidelis said. "There you go." She looked at the other nun, who nodded, as if this was the exact confirmation they needed. "You're the most selfish little girl. You have all these beautiful dresses, and this little girl has lost her mother. You're just mean. You've got a bad spirit."

I cried, more for shame now than disappointment. I did not wait for recess to run home. When I told my mom, I saw something small in her break a little too, but only for a moment. She sat me on the couch, hugging me and positioning me so I couldn't see her face. "Well, Tenie, you do have all those beautiful dresses," she said. "*And* you have your mom." She hugged me closer. "Linda doesn't have all that stuff, and she doesn't have a mom. So you should be kind. Let her wear the dress."

"It's my dress."

"Then give her *your* dress. Because we can make you another dress. We can't make another you or another me, and we can't make another Linda's mom. You have this to give her."

I would like to tell you that I nodded and felt the serenity of the Blessed Virgin Mary as I agreed. I would be lying. I still didn't want to give Linda the dress, and I didn't see why I had to. I felt the shame of being a mean little kid. A good girl would just give Linda the dress. A bad girl would be as mad as I was.

"Mama," I said, "you should come to the school and make sure I get my dress back."

She did walk me over, and when she brought me to Sister Fidelis, she not only told her that it was fine for Linda to use the dress, she said Linda could *keep* the dress.

"Can you let Tenie do it next week?" asked my mother.

"We'll let her one day," Sister Fidelis said, making a promise she would not keep. As my mom walked back, her shoulders slumped, I turned but didn't know where to look, and my eyes fell on Sister Fidelis's fingers rubbing one of her rosary beads like it was her last coin. She leaned slightly to my ear. "We're going to break that rebellious spirit in you."

That day, I watched Linda Kendeson in the dress my mother made for me, bright as a light marching to the statue of the Blessed Virgin Mary. Watching her, I felt something I didn't expect. I realized I was happy for her; proud that my sacrifice brought her this moment of joy.

A lesson was deeply ingrained right then: It made me feel so good to give up things that were very important to me.

CHAPTER 5

CLAIMING OUR POWER

WHEN I TOLD Johnny about my troubles at school, he seemed to get it on a deeper level than the rest of the family. Not just because he knew what Sister Fidelis was capable of—he understood on a basic level what it was to be constantly shown outside our family you don't fit in. He continued calling me "Lucy," after Lucille Ball, who was always getting herself into trouble on *I Love Lucy*. Sometimes he would mutter it, pulling leaves from my hair after I did fifteen somersaults to show I could, or yell it as he quickened his cool walk to catch me when I'd shimmied too far out on a branch and needed to be caught.

After I turned six in January, we all readied for Johnny to turn ten March 10. Double digits. There was something about him turning ten that made my brothers anxious for him. He was as confident as he'd always been, and no one in our family had urged him to "act" less gay. Back then, the word thrown around was "sissy," but I never heard anyone call Johnny that. Nobody disrespected him, and I believe that started because his mama didn't disrespect him. And my mama didn't. They embraced him for who he was, as much as they had language for it back in that time.

But my brothers knew the world of boys in middle school and were afraid of what might happen to Johnny. They were superstar athletes, and they found their social standing in sports. It was in the way boys talked to each other—or didn't talk—just walking to a court and picking up a basketball game. Trash talk that they didn't carry off the court.

Seeing my brothers play reminded me of how Johnny and I communicated. A glance and your eye followed where you were supposed to look; you see an opening, you go for it. With Johnny and me, it was opportunities for conversation and laughter, or noticing something beautiful; with them it was making a pass to score a point or show off the powers their bodies were growing into.

So with the best of intentions, my three brothers and Johnny's brothers Tommie and Ronnie decided they were going to make Johnny play basketball. He went along with it, going to the court at Holy Rosary, just them with me tagging along. I sat cross-legged on the edge, watching.

He was trying, running around in his natural way, not putting on some butch act. When he would shoot the ball, he'd groan a loud *"oooh"* with the effort. Sounding somewhere between Lena Horne and himself. He used humor to hold on to his dignity.

"Man up, Johnny," Skip said. "Man up!"

"Get the ball and shoot it," Ronnie said.

They had never talked to him like this, but this was their language of the court. That was the culture, and they had convinced themselves that Johnny had to learn it, too.

"Man up," someone said, dismissive and exasperated, the way they would say to a friend in the game. But this was Johnny. He looked down for a second, and quietly said, more to himself than the boys, "I don't like this at all."

That was it. I jumped up like I was saving someone from a train, as dramatic as could be. "Leave him *alone*," I cried, the heroine rescuing her wounded matinee prince. "He don't wanna play that."

"Lucy," he said to me, exasperated. And I laughed. They didn't. I was Johnny's protector, but the boys thought they were protecting him too. Behind Johnny, a cute boy walked up to the court. Johnny followed my eye to him. He was older, somebody's cousin, and gave my brothers the expectant look of someone looking for a game. Without a word, he joined in, taking Johnny's place, and they fell into playing pickup.

Johnny and I went home to my mother, and I immediately started in on how they made Johnny play when he didn't want to. "They were making fun of him."

"Were they, Johnny?" she asked.

"No," he said. "Not really. I just don't like basketball."

My mom took a beat. "Johnny," she said, "how you can—" She stopped. "Here. Come." She waved her hand toward her sewing table and let him take her chair and pulled one chair over for herself. This was her "fixer" mode, the quick, efficient movements she made when taking on a project.

"Johnny, if you make clothes for people? They will adore you. They're not going to make fun of you." She also knew what bullies at school could do, and she knew he needed armor. She took his hands and guided him along the path of a stitch. "I know you have an imagination," she said. "And I know you know what's nice. You make clothes for them? They will do anything for you."

She taught him how to sew, and his mother, Selena, provided a daily master class. Sewing was the gateway to so many things for him, allowing him to create the clothes he had in his head. The vision was there, and he made the most exquisite pieces from a young age. He entered the sixties wearing the wildest fashions, making them first for the family and then for others who would stop us on the street and ask, "Where'd you buy that?" And yes, his skills *did* make people adore him. The coolest guys came to him to make clothes for them, paying him in cash, but also with their protection. Nobody ever called him names, and he would enter his teen years safe, which is all my mother, his grandmother, wanted for him.

And yet . . . I see how limited that hope was. She couldn't dream for him beyond survival. Because she didn't just teach him sewing: This was her way, and I didn't know it at the time, of earning love. In her effort to keep us safe, she taught us we were only as loved as we made people feel, and the only way to prove our worth was to show our value to others.

Knowing how to sew gave us opportunities and security, but in the end, it was still bartering. My mother would teach me so much, but this was another lesson it would take me almost my whole life to unlearn.

ON MARCH 10, 1960, THE NIGHT OF JOHNNY'S TENTH BIRTHDAY, Flo went to the school dance at Central High. We all knew our school—it was always called "our school" no matter how old you were—was as good as Ball High, the white public school, and in some ways better. Whatever deficits the school had in funding compared to the white school, Central made up for it in the quality of its faculty. For one, the school principal, Dr. L. A. Morgan, had a PhD, and the teachers at Central fought hard to get those coveted spots and stay there. There was a rigorous curriculum at a college academic level. And unlike Ball High, Central won state championships in football, baseball, basketball, and track. Flo, a sophomore, was a majorette, making her a minor celebrity at every parade and game. I couldn't wait to be a Central Bearcat like my sister.

This was not an average school dance. With everyone in attendance on the eve of spring break, Kelton Sams, a Central junior, could see to the finishing touches of organizing the start of a nonviolent protest the next day at the Woolworth's lunch counter in downtown Galveston. A month before, college students started a movement of sit-ins at lunch counters in the South, beginning with students at the historically Black North Carolina Agricultural and Technical College. Over the course of three months, this movement would spread to fifty-five cities with college students risking their lives with sit-ins to change history.

Flo's classmates wanted to stand up to this humiliation in Galveston. Kelton arranged for a select group of Central High students to meet the next day at the F. W. Woolworth's at Market Street downtown. Their money was good enough for every other part of Woolworth's— why not the lunch counter? When they sat down and requested service, the waitress called them the n-word and said she wasn't serving them. Management shut down the restaurant, and even removed the seats that were *near* the lunch counter. More and more classmates came, and with school out, Central High students heard about it on the radio and filled the lunch counters around town—McCrory's, Walgreens, Kress. My sister Flo participated in the sit-ins, which the *Galveston Daily News* deemed an invasion of "Negro sitdowners." Maybe to calm Galveston, there was talk in the paper that many Negroes were seen at gas stations, filling up for the drive back to Houston. They might have wanted to dismiss them as outside agitators, but this was Galveston's youth, kids like Kelton and Flo. And after weeks of commitment from those young people, in April Woolworth's caved along with the other businesses running lunch counters, making Galveston the first city in the South to desegregate the act of eating a burger in peace.

My mother knew the stakes and forbade my sister to do any more sit-ins. In September, Flo heard about a planned action at the new Dairy Queen at 26th Street and Broadway that afternoon. They had built a window in the back, assuming we would accept the status quo. Kelton Sams was organizing it, and he said he felt there was a strong chance that this time the students would be arrested.

I don't know how my mother suspected my sister was up to something. Saint Agnes heard everything—she was passive, but she was the original helicopter parent. "You better not go down there," she said several times. She was well aware that factions of Galveston's white establishment saw the lunch counter victory as a score that needed to be settled in blood.

When Flo didn't answer, my mother hatched a plan to stick her with me, a pesky first grader who would come back and tell everything. "Tenie is going with you today," she said. "Tenie, don't let your sister go." Flo still said nothing, until my mother finally put herself right in her face. *"Don't go,"* she said.

Flo took me outside and turned to me. "I'm going," she said.

This was the choice she gave me. I could stay or I could go with her. I took her hand.

We met up with a group of her friends and headed to Dairy Queen. It was already a scene. Kelton Sams had had some classmates buy burgers at the window in the back, but then go inside to sit down. More and more people came to take seats. The franchise owner went ballistic and called the cops to arrest everyone for loitering.

What I recall comes to me now in flashes: I remember the cops being there, and them taking one of the girls we came with. I saw about ten kids on the ground, handcuffed with their hands behind their backs. Some were sitting, some were lying down.

A cop reached for Flo and had her by the arm. I immediately started crying—fake crying—screaming, "Please don't take my sister." I was so angry, but some instinct told me to make as much of a sobbing, snotty six-year-old nuisance of myself that the cops wouldn't want me. I did a tug-of-war with the cop over Flo, until he relented, acting disgusted. I pulled Flo to me, half climbing her, half pulling her down to me—really playing it to the hilt. He bent to our faces and yelled in a harsh hot-breathed tone, *"Go home now!"*

We left. Thirteen young people were arrested. Loitering charges were dismissed by a judge weeks later, but even after that, the *Galveston Daily News* listed each high schooler's full name and home address. All for the crime of buying a hamburger.

I promised Flo over and over as we walked the whole way home that I wouldn't tell. But as soon as I got in the house, this was me: "She went to that sit-in you told her not to go to!" My mom was so mad at Flo. "Not only did you jeopardize *you,* they could have taken Tenie to jail."

My sister couldn't stand me anyway, and now you know why. I was always telling on her. Even when what she was doing was right.

THE RUMOR STARTED NEAR THE END OF A SCHOOL DAY. THIS KID Lee came over to Tricia and me, barely able to talk from telling this story all over. He'd heard from God knows where. A nun was whaling on a fourth grader with a ruler, and he'd grabbed it from her. "He called her a *bitch!*"

"*No,*" I said. It was unfathomable. To grab the ruler and call one of the sisters that word? You would burn on the spot. It was terrible, it was awful, it was . . . the best thing we had ever heard.

My dad's car was in the driveway, and I knew he was supposed to be working that day. I thought my mama must be sick again and I walked a little faster. But they were both there in the living room. It was something serious, because my mother looked hollowed out, close to falling over right there on that couch. My dad exhaled the smoke of his Winston like he was punching the air.

"What all is going on?" I asked.

"Tenie, leave us alone for a bit," said my mother.

They still said nothing, and I wandered to my room to change. Skip was in the boys' bedroom, still in his uniform. He usually took it off the first chance he got.

"Skip, did you—"

He turned to look at me, and he looked pretty good for someone whose soul was damned for eternity. Skip said he was in class working out a joke in his head. It made him laugh, real soft, but Sister heard him and made him come to the front of the room. She had him face the class, stood behind him, and she pulled his pants down.

"In front of everybody?" I asked.

"Everybody," he said, his eyes wide. "So she starts hittin' me with the ruler. And I didn't know what to do because I wanted to pull my pants up, but she wouldn't let me. So I grabbed the ruler."

"And you really called her a bitch?"

"Yeah."

I looked at him closer, thinking maybe I could tell if he was damned now. But he looked proud. "Tenie," he said. "Everybody applauded."

I didn't care if Skip was damned to hell. I was with those kids cheering for him on the way down, and I was with *him*. He'd stood up for all of us.

My parents were at his door. We were all going to go over to church to meet with Father. The nuns had decided Skip had a devil in him and the priest had to get it out. My mother repeated what they said, believing every word and clinging to this idea that Satan was to blame. Not her son. Not the nuns who hurt us and drove him to it.

My parents took me too, and we slow-marched over to Holy Rosary like we were going to an execution. Father prayed over him, casting out the demons as the nuns knelt, murmuring in scowling solidarity. The sisters wouldn't talk to us, looking away until Father poured holy water over Skip's head. The demon was exorcised, or my family had been humiliated enough—either way, they seemed pleased.

My mother acted as if this was the worst day in her life, and maybe it was to her. But Skip's reward was at Holy Rosary, where he was a hero at the school. He never wanted for anything—other students let him skip any line and the younger kids made way for him in the hall.

The nuns got their revenge in a million different ways. I started shrinking more and more at Holy Rosary, getting through each day until I had stacked enough to make a week, then a month, then years. I stopped running away, because it only made it feel worse when my mom wouldn't stand up for me. For first grade, I was able to escape the nuns and have a "regular" teacher at the school. But then in second grade it was back to the nuns. They continued to single me out, the longshoreman's daughter privileged to sit with the children of people with big jobs.

I began to dream of witches. Me in my school uniform, and the witches circling me, taunting me about how stupid I was. So dumb that I could not see that all along they had been hiding in the black habits of nuns. Pretending to be women of God to lure foolish girls to hell. In the dreams, I was cut off from my family, but sometimes they were there. They could see what was happening but did nothing to help me. I would spend years dreaming of the witches and even more undoing the lessons taught a girl who would become a woman who was never enough.

CHILDREN CAN BECOME MALLEABLE, BUT THEY CAN BREAK. IN THE fourth grade, they planned a big program for November, and my mother was asked to make all the costumes for the girls, of course, and she found the prettiest red and black for them.

"Make up a Spanish dance for the program," a nun told me after school. She picked two girls to be the lead dancers and left, so I got to work teaching them the moves. I was suddenly a little choreographer, talking to them the way I would my nieces.

"One, two, cha-cha-cha," I intoned, doing the sidesteps and movements of the skirts. And we were really getting it. We gripped the edges of our uniforms, lifting them at the knee to swish the skirt to the rhythm of the music we created.

Two nuns came back in, and one slammed the door. We froze. "Oh, *you*," one yelled. The one who told me to do the cha-cha. "You're . . . you're such a *nasty* girl! Why are you teaching them to raise your dresses up?"

"Hunh?" I was confused. The two nuns came at us, taking me first by the wrist and grabbing one of the girls to pull us both into the cloakroom. They left the other girl outside. They made me and the other girl turn and raise our dresses up, which showed our underwear. And they began to hit us with sticks. This felt shameful, the trauma more twisted than I'd previously had at Holy Rosary.

The nuns, starting with Sister Fidelis, had failed. They couldn't break my spirit. When it was close, when even my mother weighed it down with her good intentions, something would show me to hold on: Johnny would try basketball and be brave enough to quit; Skip would grab the ruler that beat him; Flo would reach out her hand to take me to the sit-in. I would say, "Enough."

Not long after I made a declaration to my parents: I was done with Holy Rosary. The school went through eighth grade. I couldn't imagine four more years of this life.

"I'm not going back there next year," I said.

"Oh yes you are," my mother said quick.

"I'ma start running away again," I said, flat. "And actually, I don't think *any* of us should go to that school." Johnny was almost done there, but there were still my nieces and nephews in other grades. It wouldn't be enough for me to escape alone.

It was over. I would start public school in September—all of us in the family would. The next time a nun looked me in the eye and said, "You don't belong here," I answered quickly and firmly in my head: *I belong anywhere I want to be.*

CHAPTER 6

DREAMING WITHIN THE LINES

August 1964

M Y MOTHER DIRECTED the whole thing from her hospital bed, telling my brothers Larry and Skip exactly where the forms were. "They're going to want Tenie's report card from Holy Rosary—just bring all of 'em—and her birth certificate, okay?"

She had been in John Sealy Hospital a few days, no sign of getting better. They'd put off registering me for the fifth grade at Booker T. Washington as far as they could. It was making my mom anxious, and anything that made her anxious made her sicker. I wanted her home, not only because I missed her, but I wanted to miss being at that hospital. Too many hours I'd spent looking through the same months-old copy of *Ebony* somebody left, reading and rereading a cover story on Sidney Poitier hitchhiking north to New York to become an actor.

Larry interrupted my mother talking and my reading. "Why can't Daddy go?" He was starting his junior year at Central High—too smart to deal with fifth-grade business.

"No," my mama said. "This is what I do. And you go for me." She decided we should go home now to get the forms and bring them over to the school. "Put them in a nice envelope, Larry. You're in charge of them." Her eyes looked me over. "Tenie, when you go home, put on the yellow dress. With the eyelets at the collar. Skip, you put on a nice shirt."

"Okay, Mama," we both said. But Larry noticed that my dress

was blue when we left the house for Booker T. Washington. I could have worn a pink tutu and Skip wouldn't have noticed, but Larry did everything by the book. "Mama said the yellow one."

"I like this one," I said.

"Why'd I put on this shirt then?" asked Skip. He was starting ninth-grade middle school, more comfortable now in a basketball or football uniform than the itch of school collars.

"'Cause you did," I said, "I don't know." I had a bigger plan any-way and got right to it. "Larry, when we get there my name is Tina, okay?"

"Tenie, no."

"Just tell them I'm Tina Beyoncé," I said. That was the new name I'd come up with, because I hated being called Celestine with a passion. I'd prayed on being able to change it, and asked God to find some way. Now, God made it so it would be just us kids regis-tering. How was I going to put my mama through the trouble of being in the hospital and not do right by her and God by taking this opportunity?

"Sulluh-steen," Skip joked, purposely saying it wrong like everyone else.

"Who's that?" I asked. "I don't know her. She doesn't sound like anyone I *want* to know."

"I don't know a Tina," Skip said.

"Oh, that's me," I said. "You can call me Tenie, but everyone else can call me Tina."

"You can call yourself whatever," said Larry, "but they're gonna use what's on the birth certificate, Tenie. They have to."

"Well, *you* don't have to give it to them."

Larry didn't answer. He had that engineer's mind: Step one, put the forms in the envelope. Step two, present the forms. Step three, enroll your sister to complete the task.

"Please," I said to Larry. "Please, just help me do this."

The three of us got quiet as we entered Booker T. Washington, the elementary school for us on the east side. Schools were still segre-gated in Galveston, ten years after *Brown v. Board of Education,* the Supreme Court decision calling segregation in public schools uncon-stitutional. When states simply said no, the following year the Supreme Court issued a clarification with *Brown II,* saying they had to desegregate schools "with all deliberate speed." Translation: when-ever's good for you. Which explains how, even though both me and the *Brown v. Board of Ed.* decision were now ten years old, when it came to school desegregation, Galveston could justify taking its sweet time.

The school had that clean, empty feel they get right before the year starts. The main office was right by the entrance, and we got to the door as a mom was leaving with a boy about my age. The woman at the desk looked behind us as we walked in. "Where's the child's mother?"

"Our mom is in the hospital," Larry said.

The woman's demeanor immediately softened. "Oh, I'm sorry. I can help you." I realize now how we looked, these cute kids standing there trying to do the business of mothers. She pulled a form out of a drawer to feed it into her typewriter. "Let's see, okay," she said, turning the wheel. I looked at Larry as she lined up the paper. I silently mouthed to him *please*.

"Child's name?"

I kept my eyes on Larry as he looked at her, then at me. I saw his mind calculating, weighing the two paths. He cleared his throat.

"Well," he said to me. "Tell her your name."

"I'm Tina Beyoncé," I said, an exhale after years of holding my breath. "Tina spelled like Tina," I added. I only had to spell out my last name. I was free. Skip's mouth dropped open, but he said nothing. I had never loved my brothers more.

We'd gone through the rest of the form when she asked for the birth certificate and report cards. *Shoot,* I thought.

"Uh, we'll have to bring it to you later," Larry said, the envelope behind his back. "I'm sorry. I forgot."

"Our mama's in the hospital," I repeated, seeing how that worked so well the first time.

"She . . . she knows, Tenie," said Larry. "Tina."

I gave the woman the pitiful look I used to give people to get the S&H stamps. She melted all over again. "We can't really—" She said, "Well, you know what?" She was having a back-and-forth conversation with herself. "It's fine in this case. This is fine. We can enroll her, just bring it in when you can."

By the time I brought in that paperwork, it didn't matter what it said. Everybody at school knew me as Tina Beyoncé. My mom came home, and I was extra nice to her for the trouble I'd caused her with my answered prayer. With the help of God and my brothers, I had claimed my own name.

THIS WAS GOING TO BE WHEN I GOT IT, I JUST KNEW IT. SMACKED or simply brought down a peg, but it was coming.

I had been at school a week, and my fifth-grade teacher Miss Olivier asked me to stay behind while the other kids went to recess. She had been so nice to me, and it was the first time in my whole life in school that I was the teacher's pet. The nuns who had taught me were mean as hell, but they did give me a head start on my learning. Back at Holy Rosary, they never let you pronounce "door" as "do'" or "flo'" instead of "floor." Punishment for poor diction was swift. We also had access to better books and learning materials. Not only was I more advanced in math and reading than my classmates, but when the woman registered me without seeing my report cards, she placed me in the D group of students. These were kids who needed extra help.

"Tina," Miss Olivier started. I braced myself as she looked as if she was searching for the words. "You are *so* smart."

No teacher had ever said anything positive to me before. When a teacher believes in you, that can sustain you for an entire lifetime. It can create a new foundation, and everything that went before can become fertilizer to grow on.

I waited for the take-back. It didn't come.

"Okay, you can go," she said with a smile.

When I came back from recess, Miss Olivier handed me a note to bring to another teacher, Miss Barrow. Teachers used to send notes to each other using kids as carrier pigeons. Do you know I always read the notes? It felt like top-secret info but it was usually about lunch or covering a break. This one said: "As much of a delight as this child Tina is to have in my class, she is running circles around these kids. She needs to be in an A or B group—can you take her on?"

I handed Miss Olivier's note to Miss Barrow, doing a poor job of acting like I didn't know what it said. I eyed all the kids, who were looking at the new kid. Miss Barrow read the note, and wrote in pretty script at the bottom, *Yes.*

That note and that yes changed my life. Not because I joined Miss Barrow's B class or was sent on some academic trajectory that I might have missed. My life changed because sitting in the middle of that classroom was Vernell Jackson.

Cute and bow-legged, which was really the thing to be then, Vernell had a smile that was so good she didn't just give it away. She was more likely to smile at something she'd said herself. I'd actually sat with her on one of those first days in the cafeteria. I'd only earned a close-lipped smile that time, but I remembered her because she was loud and bois- terous, greeting people as they walked by. I was so quiet; I admired that comfort in owning her space.

Vernell and I didn't talk much that first week in my new class. I got to Friday holding my own, but still not knowing anybody. I was at lunch, once again sitting at a table of random people who didn't object when I brought my tray over.

I was drinking my milk when this girl came up to me with three girls flanking her. "Just so you know, Mary Elizabeth is going to fight you after school." The talker rocked back and forth with the air of a boxing promoter. Don King in box braids.

"Me?"

"Yeah," she said, pulling this pretty girl to her side. "Tell her."

"I'm gonna fight you," the girl murmured.

"I don't know you."

"I know you?" She said it like a question, and grimaced when Little Don King slapped her back.

"Yeah," said Don King. "She does. This is my cousin and she's gonna kick your ass."

"So, you're Mary Elizabeth and you wanna fight me?" I asked the girl.

Don King snorted. "Yes, are you dumb?"

"No," I said. "But I asked *her*." I mean, I was ready to fight who- ever.

"Then meet us after school," she said. "Miss Sims's."

Miss Sims ran a corner store on 30th Street we all grew up going to, selling every sweet and staying none-too-sweet herself—grouchy as anything. I'd always been a junkie for Miss Sims's store anyway, and my go-to at the shop was the Jack's cookies Johnny and I would get two-for-a-nickel. She was known for her hand-packed ice cream, but that was for summer. Now, Miss Sims was the meeting place of Booker T. Washington School's social life, because most people walked down M Street and turned right at her store on 30th. There were a lot of spinsters on that street, and they were the window audiences to all the goings-on. Nosy, mean old gossips who knew the soap opera of kids' lives. And there was lots to see because all the fights happened right there.

I wasn't scared of Mary Elizabeth. I was still Badass Tenie B and had no worries about a fight. *I know I'ma beat her ass,* I thought, *I just don't know who she is.* You like to know why you're punching back. But I walked toward Miss Sims's at three o'clock, quietly stretching out my fingers and pulling my hair back.

There were about twenty or thirty kids already gathered when I got outside Miss Sims's. The little fight promoter was getting people riled up and directed me to stand opposite Mary Elizabeth. The poor thing was trying her best prizefighter swagger, bobbing to keep eye contact with me as I took in the whole crazy scene. It was only me on one side, thirty kids spoiling for a fight on the other. Those spinsters were all at the window, ready to see me go down like the *Hindenburg.*

I was just getting resigned to being alone, hoping that once I beat Mary Elizabeth there wouldn't be a round two or three with her friends, when someone came up from behind and stood next to me. It was Vernell from class.

"What are y'all doing?" Vernell asked me and the crowd, her loud voice commanding attention.

"She just came to fight me, and I don't know why," I said, more to Mary Elizabeth than Vernell.

"So you don't want to fight?" the promoter asked me for the crowd to hear. "You're scared?"

"I'm not backing out," I said.

"You're *not* gonna fight," Vernell told me. "Mary Elizabeth is a punk. She don't want to fight you." But she whispered to me in a tone that pumped me up too. "Look at her, she's scared. They think you're soft. You're nobody's soft, I can tell that."

The promoter moved quick, taking a rock and drawing a line in the dirt between me and Mary Elizabeth. "*Step over that line!*" she dared me.

"Okay," I said, taking a huge step. Vernell laughed. I was ready for the actual fight, but it turned out there was more to the ritual. The promoter then placed a chip on Mary Elizabeth's left shoulder. "Knock that off her shoulder!" Mary Elizabeth narrowed her eyes at me, her hands already in fists. Vernell gave a "suit yourself" shrug.

"Okay, whatever," I said again. I raised my left hand to slap the chip away and was clenching my right fist to knock her out when—

Whoosh. Someone big grabbed me from behind with one arm and started carrying me away! "Okay, Tenie," he said.

It was Skip. He was walking back from middle school and saw me standing up against thirty kids. I started kicking and fighting *him,* doing my best "Hold me back!" act that I wanted to fight. But even as I struggled, I was relieved. Vernell laughed, and the last thing I saw of that crowd as Skip carried me off was her big smile beaming at me.

"What are you doing?" he asked.

"I was about to beat that girl."

"Who?"

"I couldn't tell you," I said.

Vernell explained it to me when she walked home with me the next day. "Mary Elizabeth is soft, and she doesn't want to be soft," said Vernell. "These kinds of girls, they think if you bully someone you get your reputation. And you're this cute new girl who they think is soft."

I instinctively deflected the compliment. "*You're* real cute," I said.

"I know," Vernell said, as if the joy of being her still tickled her. "I am, aren't I?" We laughed, as we did every day when we walked home together, turning at Miss Sims's, where she went right, and I went left.

EVERY MAY, MY FATHER MADE A SHOW OF HATING THE ATTENTION that came with his birthday. "It's his own fault," I told Johnny, who was helping set up a yard to make it special for the party. "The grumpier he gets about it, the funnier it is, and people keep doing the most."

I had a little radio, and Johnny and I absently moved our arms to "Stop! In the Name of Love." There was such an elegance and fun to being with Johnny. He had one of the outfits he was becoming famous in town for making, his signature patchwork of polyester made from remnants, just like my mama taught him. But he was a genius at fifteen—my mama aimed for beauty and Selena achieved incredible style with their sewing, and Johnny aimed for an artistic statement. We'd watch a movie and he'd get excited about someone in lime or Kelly green, and then he would find that color remnant, but do it in a satin flare pant, before bell bottoms were even a thing. Or a maxi coat that you could hardly wear because people kept stopping you to ask where you got it.

Just fifteen years old, Johnny had a great job as a waiter at a fancy hotel and they had him managing people already. He said it was because he was so used to managing us. "Those people are easy," he said. "I've been in the trenches with you all. The trenches!" It was a Friday, and we were starting my daddy's birthday gathering on the early side to accommodate Johnny's work schedule. That was how it was with Johnny. Even Christmas, when the hotel would close the kitchen at two in the afternoon, we all simply waited until four o'clock. Nobody would eat until he got there. We thought about it, talked about it, cursed the hotel that gave him that good paycheck, but we all waited for Johnny. He'd come in and start playing music and everybody would dance before we even sat to eat. The whole mood of the house would change.

"What are you gonna do with all that money?" we'd tease Johnny.

"Buy M'Dear a fur coat," he'd say. And Selena would smile, take a beautiful drag on her Salem Menthol, looking like she was already wearing one. Soon enough she would be, when Johnny walked into Eiband's department store—the Bergdorf of Galveston—and put a fox-fur stole on layaway. He paid for that fur for a year, and it would be legendary in our family. "Selena has a *real* fur coat," we'd all whisper so she could hear, her feet not touching the ground.

It wasn't any use buying a big birthday gift like that for my daddy—he liked cash. That was the running joke in my family. Because each and every birthday, Christmas, Father's Day, everybody would give him cards and he would make a show of opening the card and shaking it to see if money came out. Nobody really had money to buy gifts, so you might put a few dollars in there, maybe a five. He'd toss the card behind him without so much as reading it, then count the cash. Whoever gave him the money would tell him what to do with it.

"Get you a pack of cigarettes." "Oh, go buy you some chocolate-covered cherries." "That's for a six-pack of beer."

The gruffer he got, the more people wanted to give him cards to get the laugh, but it always bugged me. I'd say, "Daddy, you're so rude—you should read the card!" and I became part of the act. "Go off," he'd say to me. "Mind your own business." And then people would laugh more. "Yeah, Tenie. Mind your business."

I was sensitive about it because I'd always been one for making cards, and if I had a piece of paper as a little kid, I'd end up drawing hearts on it and try to spell out "I love you." My mama would make a big old fuss over reading them, even counting the hearts, but my daddy would kind of look at the note quick and throw it on the table.

Sure enough, at the party my daddy did his act after dinner, shaking out the cards. He was turning fifty-five, which seemed old to me when I was eleven, so I'd written him a real gushy poem. And I watched him shake out my card and toss it behind him. People looked at me, waiting for me to do my part of objecting. But I didn't want to be part of the joke if it was on me.

One of my nephews then got a big hand for giving him a five. I slinked out of the yard and into the house. Flo was in the kitchen, making faces at having to clean even though no one really asked her to. Sometimes Flo would get frustrated at something and take it elsewhere. Now I was doing that too.

"I know he's not really that gruff," I said. "But it's so rude."

Flo didn't answer, and acted like washing the dinner forks to have them for cake was a job of the most importance. I started drying and stacking them.

"I mean, I don't have money, but he just tossed my card and didn't even read the poem."

"Girl, *please*," she said, as brusque as anything. "Daddy can't read or write."

I turned to look at Flo, not sure if she was kidding. She wasn't. She said it like I should know. And sharp, like I was dumb for not knowing. Our daddy being able to read was one more fantasy her annoying little sister had made up in her head. I did feel foolish, and it gave me that familiar feeling of needing to run. I turned my head as if I'd heard my name, then made a show of drying one last fork. I turned and walked out the front door to sit on the porch.

Daddy couldn't read? I sat in shock, watching a neighbor walking by like the world was still turning. Mrs. James. My mother would have called to her, invited her to come to the yard. "Have a lemonade." I was not my mother, who saw to everything. How had I not figured out my daddy couldn't read? No matter how many forms I'd seen him bring home from work and hand to my mother to sign or fill out. My mother, so on top of everything that it seemed natural. This woman we all depended on, figuring out every bill, summing up every news article that might matter.

Mrs. James waved at me, and I waved back. "Nice night," she said, nodding to the sound of the music coming from the yard. Probably Johnny, in charge of the music, had turned up Junior Walker's "Shot-gun." If I didn't invite Mrs. James to join us, she would tell people we were playing loud music. But I just answered, "It is," and tried to smile. Did *she* know this thing about my daddy? Who in town knew? How late was I?

Of course, it was Flo who told me. My big sister understood the world and each one of its boundaries before I did: We had to sit in the back of the bus. We were supposed to get a good job and stay in Galveston. Our daddy couldn't read or write. She had to drag me by the hair through all these understandings I was supposed to have fig-ured out by now on my own. I'd been clueless, no matter how many times he squinted, taking off his glasses to rub the bridge of his nose like he was suddenly too tired to make sense of whatever was in front of him. The shaking of the cards he was given so he could toss them away unread.

This last realization, going back my whole life, made my stomach turn over in shame. Not that he couldn't read, but that I'd given him so many opportunities to feel ashamed that he couldn't read. Handing him these love notes. "Oh, he's so grumpy," I'd say when he threw the note on the table, until I believed it.

Which came first, his trouble saying "I love you" back, or his need to hide not being able to read? He was never a warm, fuzzy person, because it had to have been such a scary and sad life for him. Had he even gone to school at all? I'd seen Weeks Island, and I knew how he'd been farmed out to siblings once his mama died. When he was doing all that work, who was seeing to him going to school?

Who was reading to him, sounding out the letters until he could too?

I got up and went to the yard, doing my classic walk-quick-before-my-mind-caught-up thing. People were dancing to the rhythms Johnny set. My father was done opening cards now, but still in his chair with the money counted, holding court in his grumpy way. Before I was aware of what I was doing, I had put my arms around him. I felt so bad for everything.

He pulled back after a two-count beat, made a sound like a wince. "Okay," he said. That was always the sign to let go. I didn't.

"Go on," he told me, but loud so it was part of the bit for everyone. "Get."

Instead, I told him what was in the card. "I love you," I said. "I have the best daddy in the world."

"Okay, Tenie," he said, slightly softer, but not too soft. "Now get."

BY THAT SUMMER OF 1965, WHEN LARRY ENDED JUNIOR YEAR AND Butch graduated, the world outside Galveston looked different than it had when I enrolled in fifth grade in September. President Johnson had won the election as "the peace candidate" in November, but now there was talk of the draft expanding as the war in Vietnam only got bigger. That year, Black Americans filled over 30 percent of the ground troops in Vietnam, while our population as a minority in the United States was only 12 percent. More telling, we were almost a quarter of the U.S. Army's casualties. We saw combat more and died more—no wonder Dr. King called it "a white man's war, a Black man's fight."

Butch enlisted in the Air Force early, which might have saved him from having to go to Southeast Asia, and instead he was stationed in San Antonio. The family drove out to see him, and other than Weeks Island, that was my first trip out of Galveston. We stayed in a motel one night, one with a dirty little swimming pool that I thought was amazing. Butch showed us around, and was so sweet, his good looks now backed by a new confidence. *This could be you,* I said to my eleven-year-old self. Someday I could give my family a tour of the life I built for myself.

The following summer, when Larry graduated in 1966, the Johnson administration even offered students the Selective Service College Qualification Test, an SAT of sorts to see if college freshmen were smart enough to earn the deferment from the draft. There was this feeling that a generation of boys would become men in order to be taken and killed by lottery.

My parents couldn't understand one of the kids going to college in the hope of something, but going to school to stay away from harm? Leaving home to survive? *That* they understood. They'd left Louisiana with only the clothes on their backs, starting over with nothing. These were the stakes that my parents could understand. Now they were all for college. And so, my brilliant brother Larry, who could have gone anywhere, went to Galveston Junior College.

I ENTERED MIDDLE SCHOOL THAT FALL OF 1966, JUST AS SKIP WAS entering his junior year. Even Skip was leaving me, though not really.

Someone from Ball High, the white high school, recruited him to leave Central and go there for his junior year. To slow down the change brought by the 1964 Civil Rights Act, many schools limited integration plans by adopting the "Freedom of Choice" plan, which said students over fifteen years old could *choose* to individually integrate schools. This allowed Ball High to slowly let in certain Black kids, and as a star athlete, Skip would be valuable to them.

"Freedom of Choice" certainly wasn't reciprocal—no white family was sending their child to Central. But Skip took the bait.

"I don't know what he's thinking," I told my best girlfriend Vernell. "I bet it's all just a bunch of well-trained Negroes there." That's what we called the kids who went out of their way to be pleasing to white people to get ahead.

"Oh, let him," she said. "It's a nice campus. Their books don't have missing pages. They go on trips."

"So?" I said, though she had a point. Vernell cared more about academics than I did. She was a girly girl who loved school—the example my mother always pointed to when I, her tomboy, showed up at home with dirty socks and leaves in my hair from climbing a tree.

"And he's going to have more opportunities there," Vernell added.

"They only want him there to make their football team look good. That's all they'll want any of us for. They won't want a nobody like *me*, I'll tell you that."

"Oh, I don't know, Tina," Vernell said. I thought she was going to say I wasn't a nobody, but she kept going. "Maybe it's just not a bad thing at all. You can't make him be a Bearcat at Central. He's a Tor at Ball High."

And he didn't mind it. It pained me that he never complained.

Until they almost killed him.

CHAPTER 7

HELLHOUNDS ON
OUR TRAIL

October 1967

"I DON'T THINK YOU should go," my mother told Skip the night of the party. He was getting ready in front of the mirror before picking up his girlfriend. "I just don't think you should go."

My mother's concern about the world outside our windows was a constant hum now. It was spring, and I was thirteen to Skip's seventeen. He politely kissed the top of her head and named the kids who had invited him. White kids, but ones from the football team who Skip was close to. "Trust me," he said. "It's fine."

He had earned this. Skip was the straightest arrow, who never drank or smoked cigarettes. My mother seemed dramatic as usual, and, just as usual, I placed a barrier between me and her. I was so afraid of her fear, and how it could sometimes take over me when I let it get too close.

Now I picture Skip at the party with his girlfriend. The sweetness of him in that six-three frame. Some guys at the party slipped something in his drink. This was a thing then, to make a joke out of loosening up the straight-edge guy. He didn't slur at first, he just said crazy stuff that made them all laugh. Then he got a little stumbly and his girlfriend got scared.

"Let's go," she said, holding Skip's arm, though if he fell he would take her down with him. Skip couldn't drive in the state he was in, and she couldn't drive period. In whatever logic she had in an emergency like that, she called two cabs. One to take her home, and one to take him home.

They loaded Skip into the backseat of the cab, and she gave the driver our address. It was such a tiny thing: We lived on N $^1/_2$ Street, and the driver took Skip to N Street. The same number, but that house was Miss Patrick's.

I picture my sweet brother taking deep breaths in the car, feeling bad that he wasn't able to make jokes for the driver. This was his thing—making people laugh. And I see him getting out at the wrong house and not realizing. Staggering up to the porch alone and being too disoriented to figure out what to do. Miss Patrick was an old woman who was very nice, and she had a couch on her porch. When you walked by, she would wave, and we would nod in shared kindness.

Skip fell onto the couch outside Miss Patrick's, passing out on his side. Miss Patrick heard a noise outside and looked out the window. With Skip's face turned away from her, she could only see the fairness of my brother's skin in the moonlight. She immediately called the police. "It's a white man on my porch," she said.

Galveston was a resort town. White people came and got drunk, ending up in places. You called the cops, and they slept it off. They'd have an interesting story to bring back home, while it was business as usual to us and the cops.

But when the white cop arrived, he saw he was not dealing with another white man. This was a Black guy, a big one. Young. My sweet brother.

Miss Patrick opened the door slightly to keep watch. She saw the cop, a little guy, pull out his billy club, and looked again at the man sleeping on her porch. What would make him do this about a white man? Looking closer, she immediately began to speak.

"Oh no, that's Skippy," she said. Her voice minimizing, sweet, pleasing. "He's a good boy. That's not like him. Let me call his mom. They can come get him."

She kept talking, and the cop cut her off. "No," he said, louder and tougher for himself and everyone in the world. He was a little guy. "*No*. He's under arrest."

Miss Patrick had already run inside and dialed my sister Selena as the cop took the billy club, placing it under my brother's chin to wake him. It's like every situation where Black men are provoked into "resisting" by being hurt. He pushed Skip's head back hard with the club, and my brother woke up.

Instinctively, Skip hopped up and tried to grab the billy club to pull it away. The cop smacked him with the club and jumped back, scared. My brother was even stronger because of whatever they'd slipped him, and this little guy couldn't do anything with him. He pulled a gun on Skip and called for backup.

After Miss Patrick called her, Selena called my house and sent her kids down the lane they shared. Ronnie arrived first, sprinting track-star fast. He saw the cop aiming the gun at Skip, who was furious. Ronnie tried to reason with them both and as he talked, about six more police cars arrived. Cops jumped out of barely stopped cars, already aiming their guns at Skip. They got closer to him, dragging him onto the ground facedown. They cuffed him and stood over him.

That's what I saw when my mom and I got there, her in her night-gown and me in my cotton pajamas. My dad was one step behind, buttoning his shirt. Skip was disoriented, the cops shouting at him on the ground as he kept saying he didn't do anything.

More family arrived, and we were a chorus around the scene. Miss Patrick, overcome, kept saying my brother's name over and over to prove to the cops she knew him and didn't want this. My father, speaking in the calm man-to-man voice to people that he knew might not see him or his son as men. And my mother, quietest, and most fright-ened of all, begging for Skip's life.

They got him up and started moving him to a police car. We knew that once he was taken, anything could and would happen to him. It was long talked about in the community that cops took us to the beach and let us loose only to shoot us and say we resisted or ran away.

There was one Black police officer in the group, and when every white cop ignored her, my mother focused on him. "Please," she said, crying so much her sweet voice was thick. She sank to her knees before this cop. "Please don't let them kill my son." She said it over and over, a sobbing prayer. "Please don't let them kill my son."

The Black cop would not look at her. He would not acknowledge my mother's existence or anything that they shared in common.

My mother was still on her knees as each car took off in a squeal of tires but no sirens and no lights. She changed the mantra of her prayer to one of grief. "They're gonna kill my son," and then, over and over so I worried she too would die: "They are *killing* my son."

WE ARRIVED AT THE STATION TO FIND BARELY ANYONE THERE. The police, who had left so fast in their cars, should have beaten us there.

In silence, we stood waiting in the station. Five minutes became ten. Fifteen, then forty long minutes. We were sure Skip was at the beach. Was he alive in this moment? And now in this one? Had they killed him yet? I was so close to Skip that I thought maybe I would know. I did not.

And then a single police car arrived but no one got out. Someone in the station made us all leave. We didn't know if Skip was dead in that car or what had happened. They did not let us see him or his body.

For the rest of that night, my mother led us in prayer.

The next morning, we received a call that Skip was being let out of jail. We all went, not sure what we would find. There was Skip. Standing. Beaten, but standing. His shirt was covered in dried blood, which mostly seemed to come from a gash they gave him in his head. They'd fractured one of his ribs. His eye was swollen so shut I didn't know how it would ever open again.

Skip told us they'd taken him to the beach, and they beat him so bad. The cliché is that he was never the same, and it's true. None of us were. We tried. Well, my mother couldn't fake it. But Skip made his jokes. My father tried to hide when his mind wandered back to that night, but I could see it. I was afraid of how vulnerable I felt, and I wrapped that fear in anger to protect it. I didn't look for trouble, but I would be ready if it returned.

We never had a chance to move on even if we could have. After that, the police began targeting my family for harassment. They focused on my dad, stopping him for traffic things. My sister Flo had become a nurse at John Sealy Hospital and worked the three-to-eleven shift. He would pick her up from work, and the red and blue would light up behind him. They hounded us all for years, maybe trying to goad us into doing something. To prove they were right about us. That what they did to Skip was justified. Or maybe they were simply having fun.

This one story was happening all over the place, indicative of what families like ours endured and continue to endure all over. It reminds me of the enslaved people who escaped Weeks Island and the vagrancy laws that ensured their arrest and then continued enslavement. The slave catchers on the loose.

CHAPTER 8

LADIES AND GENTLEMEN, THE VELTONES

January 1968

H ARRIET WAS LATE for rehearsal again. Sorry, *Harrette*. She had insisted on changing her name when we formed our singing group, the Veltones. That was about as much effort as she put into the previous year of us being a trio.

"I think we should just start without her," I told Gail. We were on my porch, where we always did rehearsals, a tape machine at the ready. My finger hovered over the Play button on the Delfonics' "La-La Means I Love You." We had the song down, but really needed to focus on the choreography before the eighth-grade talent show.

"Maybe give her five more minutes," she said. "We can do more warm-ups." Gail DuPree was the other member of the group. A wiz with arranging all the harmonies, she really had the ear for what would sound good. And that was three girls, not two with one showing up whenever. The problem was Harrette's boyfriend. As much as I was obsessed with the group—rehearsing every day, turning my front porch into a stage, making all the dresses, saving up to buy music—she was obsessed with her boyfriend. He liked it fine when she was singing for him, but when he saw everyone looking at her onstage at Central Middle School? He got jealous and found ways to keep her from performing. I didn't understand why anyone would give up something you loved for a boy, but Harrette would say that's because I'd never been in love. She knew that would bug me.

Our audiences *were* growing. We had made a small name for ourselves in Galveston on the talent show circuit. Enough of a name that show announcers stopped mistakenly introducing us as the Belltones. But now the Veltones had a lot more competition. Overnight, after the Supremes and the Temptations hosted their own variety show in the December 9 *Laugh-In* time slot on NBC, girl groups and boy groups were the craze at Black schools across the country. I thought I was Diana Ross.

The Veltones were known for our style, which I cared about as much as the harmonies. My mama helped me make all our dresses, and I would visualize our performances, seeing what would work when we contrasted looks or made them cohesive. We didn't just do girl songs—we liked re-creating the sound of Smokey Robinson singing with the Miracles. The quiet-storm slow songs that made the audience feel like grown folks, hugging on each other.

And here came our third girl, Harrette, an inch behind her boyfriend as they walked to the house. It turned out she was late even for her last day as a Veltone. She was leaving the group, she told us, to spend more time with her boyfriend. They made this big show of a kiss while Gail and I rolled our eyes. Then they kept walking, in search of something else for him to be jealous of.

"We don't need her," I told Gail, maybe loud enough that Harriet could hear. She was just Harriet to me now that she wasn't a Veltone.

"Yeah, but we need *somebody*," said Gail. She sat down on the porch swing, so I did too. Gail was right—a duo didn't have the draw of a girl group. "Somebody who can really sing," she added.

"Well, *we* can sing," I said. It was true. If we had settled for simply looking the part, we would have been the Velvettes, but we were the Veltones because of our harmonies. Still, image was part of it, and I had that ability to see the big picture of us onstage. In my mind, I removed Harriet, leaving Gail, who had a cute little figure, and me, super skinny and tall. I knew what was missing.

"You know," I said, "round here guys like those really curvy girls."

Gail looked down at the two of us and laughed.

"You're plenty fine, Gail," I said. "But we need a thicker, fine girl."

My best friend Vernell looked the part. She had a deep speaking voice, and we thought the harmonies would be just amazing. Vernell was so excited when we put her in the group.

"So here's how it goes," I told Vernell at her first rehearsal. "We play the song loud in the beginning, so people recognize it, okay? But then we turn the music down, so we sing into the mic over the vocals." That was the way we all did it before they came out with tapes of only the instrumentals. This also meant our dresses had to be really something special, with all these people staring at you for maybe twenty or thirty whole seconds before we even sang a word. That made the addition of Vernell so important.

There was just one problem: We practiced with Vernell for five days and she never could sing a lick. Plus, she'd change keys on you so many times in one song, she could be a locksmith. We got it so all she had to do was one "woo" harmony, but hers was a flat, hollowed-out bass of a creature feature. "The Bible says 'make a joyful noise,'" she would say. "It don't matter if you can sing or not if it's a joyful noise."

"It's some noise," I whispered to Gail.

"You brought her here," Gail told me, "so you need to tell her it's not working out." I was going *through* it because Vernell had been so excited, but she ended up doing it herself.

"I quit," she said after her one last attempt at an "aah" nearly made us fall over. "I just wanted to wear the costume anyway."

She kept the look as a peace offering, but I made a new costume quickly for our next candidate, Polly. Pauletta was the girlfriend of my nephew Tommie, Selena's son. We actually called him Preach for preacher since he was always so goody-two-shoes and religious. When we did funerals for insects or whatever, he would always preach a sermon. We all thought he was going to be a priest, but he met Polly and that changed. Polly was so cute she could have met the Apostle Paul on the road to Damascus and he might have changed his mind back too.

Right on the first note, she could really harmonize. And Gail and I couldn't stop telling her how great she was.

I probably needed someone to tell *me* that. One of the reasons I loved pop music was the stakes: Everything mattered in getting someone to love you. The good songs were about longing and devotion—unrequited maybe, but never uncertain. But *I* was, and I felt alone in this city of curvy fine girls who were all getting boyfriends. Harriet was right about me never being in real love. First off, I was in middle school and taller than all the boys, and that was not good. Guys wanted girls they could tilt their heads to kiss, with big legs they longed to touch. Everybody only wanted to be my friend, and I had that little sister energy. I just wasn't *considered*.

We were right about Polly. She was what our group needed, and instead of limiting us, her boyfriend Tommie became a sort of manager for the Veltones, hyping us up and taking our photos. Now when we went to a school or union hall for a competition, it was Tommie who would look for the place for us to get ready. It could make a girls' bathroom seem like a dressing room. We were doing really well, working our way through the talent show circuit, looking the part of success in the red mini prints paired with high-heel boots.

There was one afternoon at rehearsal that I realized I had found my passion. I wanted to be an entertainer for the rest of my life. I was too shy to tell anyone else that I even had aspirations for anything. Certainly never said, "That's what I'm gonna be." But I spoke it to the girls: "We're gonna be discovered and get a record deal."

CHANGE DROVE UP IN A RED STINGRAY CONVERTIBLE AND AN asymmetrical haircut. Lydia was twenty-one and dating my brother Larry, and I was obsessed with her. She was always dressed to the nines, making every look work, and one day she decided to show me, this fourteen-year-old, a bit of what life was like in Houston. "I was just trying to get in good with the family," Lydia would admit to me later, after I told her she was the mentor who changed my life.

The spring evening goes like this: I wait for Lydia on the porch because I don't want her to come in and visit with my parents. I want it to be like the movies I love, where the hero girl answers this call to adventure when it rolls up. I hear the jangle-guitar of her radio before I see her, playing Jimi Hendrix as loud as it would go.

We take off for Houston, her grabbing the radio dial to careen through the stations, not settling until she finds a song she likes. When she does, she gasps like she's found a friend who gets her. The soundtrack set, Lydia asks me what I like to do. "I sing," I find myself saying. She turns in her seat to look at me, and nods as if she had a feeling. *I look like a singer,* I think. *She can tell.*

She tells me the plan is to go to dinner—"this place I like"—and then see Alvin Ailey after. I don't know who that is, but I nod. "Your money's no good in Houston," she says. "Please don't even think about money."

When we park the Stingray at the restaurant, I feel that bird in my heart fluttering. It's up now in my head, and I stand taller to make room for it as we walk in. The first thing I notice is that the restaurant has tablecloths. Later, Lydia will tell me this was a chain restaurant, "kind of like an Applebee's." It's the nicest restaurant I have been in. I am terrified to do something wrong, so I mirror everything Lydia does.

After dinner, she hurries us to a theater and we take our seats. The Alvin Ailey American Dance Theater, based in New York City, is touring. I read the program like I will be quizzed, and I don't know what to expect from titles like "Revelations," "Blues Suite," and "Reflections in D." It says Ailey was born in Rogers, Texas, a square-mile town north of Houston. I try to keep reading the program, but the audience has me spellbound.

"They're just so classy," I say to Lydia. I don't have another word. They are dressed well, arriving in the nice cars I saw out there. In Galveston, I see the one Black doctor and the one Black dentist, but here is an audience full of them. It isn't so much that they are affluent, but that they are the type of people who use that money to see modern dance on a Friday night.

And now I am sitting among them. *I would like this life,* I think.

Even that falls away when the curtain rises. Everything I think I know is swept away by "Revelations," which is *so* rooted in Texas and yet transcendent. Beginning in the muted colors of tan and light brown fabric, the dancers move to the music of church gospel, the grief and fear of my parents right there as if Ailey walked alongside them at Weeks Island. The show moves to the light blues and whites of the life I knew in Galveston—the clouds and whitecap waves of the sky and Gulf, and the Easter dresses of those who would gather to be seen at the seawall. And then the red lights and black cloths as a lone dancer runs to "Sinner Man," somehow capturing exactly how I felt at Holy Rosary. Ailey finishes the work with the joy and the freedom and redemption of "Rocka My Soul in the Bosom of Abraham."

Sitting there, I see what art can do. The specific moments Alvin Ailey drew upon from his life seem to match with mine. I look around at that audience again, and they all have that same shiny-eyed look of recognition. When you see art that sees you. I am changed.

I can barely talk when the lights come up. I feel like I am coming out of a good dream, awake now, and I thank Lydia for taking me. I do not stop thanking her until she drops me off in front of my house. I do not stop thanking her for the rest of my life.

My home doesn't seem smaller when I walk through the front door and my world in Galveston doesn't seem shabby. It just seems like the beginning of my story, not something to shed or deny, but something to draw from, the way Alvin Ailey did. He took Rogers, Texas, with him, and when the time came, I would take Galveston with me.

Because I know now I have to leave.

As summer started, I had the biggest crush on Robert Fulton and would stare at him like he owed me money. He was two years older than me, and I looked for him everywhere but school, which he was constantly skipping. I'd thought about cutting class and tried to get Vernell in on it. "And do what?" she asked me. "All that trouble to walk around this town? Nope." This was why Vernell got straight A's.

It was so bad I unloaded on my mom in the kitchen. "Nobody ever likes me," I said. "I really like this boy, but really Mama, I just want *a* boyfriend. Not any, but, okay, like *any*."

My mother sat down at the table. "You go to church," she said.

"Oh God, Mama, this isn't about—"

"No, you go to church with me, and you pray. This boy's gonna like you."

Skip came in, interrupting us. The coaches at Ball High told him he had to gain weight over the summer before his senior year, and they wanted him eating round the clock, especially at night. Two scrambled eggs, two Blue Ribbon Texas sausages with pork and beef and everything but the kitchen sink in them. Round that off with two pieces of toast with butter and jelly from corner to corner, and a big glass of milk at ten o'clock at night.

My mom got to cooking, and I got to smelling that food. "Put some on for me, Mama," I said. I matched Skip almost bite for bite and went to bed so full I slept like a chubby angel. The next morning my mother got me up for seven o'clock mass. "You want this boy to like you or not?" she asked when I rolled over. I did, so I got up, went to church, and lit that candle for my love life.

"You watch," she said, nodding approvingly.

For the rest of the summer, I ate all those delicious high-fat foods with Skip late into the night. Gradually, I noticed Skip and I were gaining weight; he with the muscle of all-day practice, and me starting to fill out and get the curves I wanted so bad. I was still too thin, but I began to get boobs and hips. All of a sudden, people *saw* me.

In September, I went to the Down Beat with Johnny. It was an all-ages club down at West Beach, set up with an open-air deck. Robert Fulton was there, and he not only noticed me, he danced with me. We started dating, and my miracle story became one of my mother's biggest church recruitment stories. "You know, she prayed for that boyfriend," she would tell anyone and everyone. "And look at her—she can't get rid of him! *It's better than voodoo!*"

My mother was right about me not being able to get rid of Robert. He was great, but I kind of wanted to be two girls: one who had a boyfriend and one who could continue to devote all her spare time to rehearsing with the Veltones. When it came down to it, my work ethic won out. I saw Robert around my Veltones schedule, which probably made it seem like I was playing hard to get, but I was really serious about singing.

I made our costumes with my mother, bouncing ideas off each other. Hers were practical, mine about getting buzz going. One of my favorites was this dress I thought was so genius: I saved up to buy patent-leather knee-high boots, two pairs of blue and two pairs of white. We each wore a white boot and blue one, and I made the mini-dresses blue on the side of the white boot, and white on the side of the blue boot. Everybody went crazy over it.

It felt like things were really happening for us, but then Polly's aunt kept giving us trouble about it taking so much time away from home. Her aunt was always tough on her, but we all understood she had a hard life. Polly's mom had died, and it fell to her unmarried sister to take in a bunch of kids. She was very strict and didn't want Polly to do anything but stay home and take care of her siblings. No exceptions, and now that included rehearsals.

"Then we'll do the rehearsals at your house," I said.

"Yeah, but I gotta babysit," said Polly.

"I can babysit," I said.

"Me too," said Gail. "Tell that baby to sit and watch us sing."

So the Veltones moved headquarters from my porch to Polly's aunt's house in the projects, singing for kids and soothing a baby as we danced. It was simply what we had to do to keep the group together.

It was worth it, and we made it to a big talent show in Houston. We won and stayed to take a bunch of pictures. So many that we kept pushing back the return to Galveston. Polly's aunt got really mad when Tommie brought her home so late.

After that night, Polly's aunt wouldn't even let her compete in any more shows. The Veltones could practice—meaning, keep babysitting the kids—but we couldn't perform. It made no sense. There was a show coming up in Houston where we knew there would be talent scouts. Gail confessed that she thought it was getting to be a lot of work, and she wanted to spend more time with her boyfriend. Tommie and Polly would eventually marry too. But the Veltones were over, just on the edge of being discovered.

When I told my parents what happened, they accepted the end of the Veltones like it was a hobby. I was so confused because my parents had been so supportive of the group. My father made himself our chauffeur, driving us whenever practice went late, taking us to and from competitions and shows. My mother could not have done more for the group, spending money they did not have to help me make costumes, attending every single performance, always finding some way to individually boot us up.

"But I want to be a singer," I said now, my voice falling between a kid dreaming and a young adult setting a goal. I didn't say "I'm gonna be a singer"—I said I *wanted* to.

"You can always sing."

"No, like for my life," I said. "A *singer* singer."

"Oh girl," said my mother. "Do you see any singers in Galveston?"

"Well, they wouldn't be *here*."

"Baby, I wish you could go be a singer, and I would do anything for you to do that," my mom said. "But you got to be realistic." Her life couldn't allow for that risk—she did what she could to get through each week. She continued, "If you finish high school and you get a good job, like at the post office or at the hospital—"

"What do you mean, *if* I finish school?"

"Tenie, you are a very attractive girl. I mean, some man would be so happy to take care of you."

"How 'bout I wanna take care of me? Myself," I said. "'Cause I do.

I want to be the one who takes care of me." I was just as surprised by my growing anger as she was. She thought she'd acknowledged a gift. All those years of telling me that it's what's inside that counts, and the truth was that if you were *pretty enough,* that was *enough.* "What are you saying?" I asked. "I should just plan on getting married?"

"You want too much, Tenie," she said. "You could settle down and get married here in Galveston."

I didn't know how to answer that. My mother had always said things like, "You need to learn how to sew 'cause you'll never be broke." Now that I was cute, my security could simply come from a man.

"I think I could be a singer," I said again, softer this time. Unsure.

My mother gathered a lifetime of good intentions to say, "I don't want you to be disappointed." She was trying to protect me from being beaten down by life. My parents, who would have done anything to make my dreams come true, didn't know how to safely support that dream of being a singer.

In reality, *I* didn't know how to be a singer without Gail and Polly. I gave Gail my blessing to leave the group and assured Polly it was not her fault. The Veltones never even got a farewell concert.

FOOTBALL WAS GOING TO BE SKIP'S CHANCE TO GET OUT OF Galveston. He was doing well at Ball High, despite my misgivings about him even being there and my mother's fears that he would always be a target at a white school. As a football player, his skill and his size didn't make him exempt from racism, but they offered him some privilege of protection. The guidance counselors had helped him through college scholarship applications with boilerplate letters from boosters that made him and every other player sound like the second coming of Texas football. My parents, who went to every single one of his games, were thrilled. This was a blessing they could not have dreamed of, but there it was.

I came home one night from being out with Johnny. Skip was at the kitchen table. My parents stopped talking when I walked in, so I knew it was bad. Skip looked lost, the world closing in around him.

His girlfriend was pregnant. From my room, I could hear my parents. "You gotta do the right thing," my dad said. "This girl is going to have a baby, and you gotta marry her." Skip would have to stay in

Galveston, all the different lives he might have had evaporating before his and our eyes. They were Christian people and they thought they were doing the good Christian thing. Other families might have chosen potential fame and fortune—even their opportunity—and hoped to send a check if the girl was lucky, but not them. Unable to sleep that night, I went to the kitchen and found my parents still at the table, crying about Skip.

This was not the first time a Ball High football player had gotten a girl pregnant, but it had to have been their first Black player. I imagine the conversation, that assurance behind closed doors that this was about a Black girl in trouble. The machine went into action. A booster talked to some alumni, calls were made, and they got Skip a good job at Pennzoil in Galveston.

The marriage did not work out. People that young change, even with the permanency of a baby girl, and then another soon after. I thought that Skip could have played football professionally and become famous as an exceptional kicker. It was hard to watch that door close—and to see my parents become even more afraid to risk anything on a dream for me, too.

CHAPTER 9

AN EDUCATION IN LIBERATION

September 1968

F OR US KIDS in Galveston, at least the Black kids, the 1968 closing of Central High School was as monumental as the 1900 storm that wiped out the city. Galveston was finally forced to comply with a May order from the Supreme Court, declaring that students needed to go to the school that was closest to them starting September 1968. If white families living closer to Central than Ball High worried about sending their children to a Black school, they didn't have to. Central High was simply closed down, turned into a junior high. We would trade our culture and history to be treated like second-class citizens at Ball High.

As I started ninth grade, the people who would have been my teachers at Central scrounged for jobs at Ball High. Someone who had a high-ranking administrative position at Central would have to audition for a lower-rung job. There were some good white teachers and allies among the students at Ball High, but the majority of the white kids did *not* want us there. I certainly didn't want to be there, but there were those "well-trained Negroes" who were flattered into complicity by the white administration, tasked with quieting us uppity folks. They were safe, "articulate."

"Why are you so angry?" they would ask me. Because I *was,* and that would get me listing off the reasons. All the programs we had at Central—record-setting scholastic clubs and a theater group that got Galveston to the statewide drama championships—gone. "They get to keep all the people in the band," I'd say, "all the cheerleaders, and we have to act a certain way to be part of anything." If you were a Bearcat cheerleader, you'd be lucky to even be considered to try out for a spot as a Tor. What Ball High wanted was our athletes. At games, we would sometimes break into Central's Bearcat chants, feeling nostalgia even as *teenagers*. They cracked down on that quickly, sending out the well-trained ambassadors. "Okay," one said to me, "we're at Ball now."

"I'm still a Bearcat," I said.

"But they had to integrate," the ambassador said.

"Guess what, it's okay to integrate—I understand that," I said. "I don't understand why we couldn't have just wiped the whole thing out and started the New School or whatever. Make it an integrated situation where everybody has to try out and do their best?"

He shrugged, but there was no explaining to him the grief I felt when all he saw was opportunity. My lifelong dream of being a Bearcat was stolen. I couldn't wait to go to Central and be a majorette like my sister. To march at all the Black events in town. To have the connections of all those Black businesses and members of the vibrant PTA who used Central as a meeting place to inspire the next generation. There weren't a lot of people who were conscious, but we found each other. A group of people, led by a young man named Michael Merritt, created a sort of Black student union. To Ball High's credit, I will say that they allowed us to develop a Black studies program. Michael knew a lot about the Black Panthers, which I had become obsessed with. I was inspired by their free breakfast program, and the engagement of female members like Ericka Huggins and Elaine Brown, who would become leaders. (Years later, I would also have the opportunity to tell Elaine Brown how much she meant to me when she had dinner at my home.)

There was a white kid at Ball High who helped Michael produce an event in the auditorium for Black History Month, showcasing the leaders of the Black liberation movement with us playing roles. I got Angela Davis, mainly because I had a big old afro, which I had been growing out to perfection.

At the end we all raised a fist to say, "Black Power." It felt right, but it did not sit right with the administration. They were on board with the program, but they were specifically not happy with the Black Power sign. They couldn't see that celebrating the beauty and power of being Black wasn't immediately anti-white. "It's not even about you," I said.

"It's about *us*." But one of the ways racism works is erasure. They didn't want us to know our history because they were afraid of our futures.

I GRIPPED MY STOMACH, TRYING TO BREATHE THROUGH THE NAUSEA.

It was about six in the morning and my father and I were in the emergency room of John Sealy Hospital, a place I knew well by age fourteen. Not just on account of my mother, but with so many kids in the family—well over a dozen if there was one—every week someone was at the emergency room. John Sealy was a charity hospital because it was a teaching hospital, part of the University of Texas Medical Branch, the largest single industry on the island. They turned out some of the best doctors, but as a patient you were a guinea pig.

Flo worked there as a nurse, but that got us no special treatment. They took you when they took you. You could spend all day there waiting, and I'd been there enough to see the treatment of Black and white patients blur as they made poor white families wait too. The ones who I had seen wait the longest were the Hispanic people.

My father and I had arrived at the emergency room before dawn, unable to wait any longer. I'd been sick in the night, a vomiting that would not go away. He took me on his own because my mother was in bed recovering from being sick with one of her heart things.

My father's accent made it difficult for people at John Sealy to understand him—and easy to dismiss. When he took my mother, no matter what shape she was in, she would somehow do the talking. But this time I could barely speak, and the intake person, who had seen us so many times, just pointed to the waiting area. We sat for hours, watching people get taken before us as I continually shifted in my seat, contorting my body to try to calm the nausea. I was cold, which I now know was from a fever.

A man came, a doctor from his white coat, but he didn't introduce himself to my father. Certainly not me. He might have said, "Follow me." He might have just waved me up with a hand.

I *do* remember that when my father rose to go with me, the man put up a hand. A command to stay. Three more white people—more white coats on two men and a woman—joined this doctor as he walked ahead of me to a triage ward where they drew a curtain around the bed.

As I described my symptoms the lead doctor asked me point blank: "Could you be pregnant?"

"No," I said. I was a ninth grader who'd never had sex. "I've never had . . ." I didn't even want to say sex in front of them, but they didn't seem to be listening anyway. They did a fast examination, him talking to them as if I weren't there. He was their teacher.

"Well, come here with us," he said, and he walked me toward a closed door. Inside the exam room, which they all filed into, there was a hospital bed with metal stirrups. I'd never seen anything like this.

They handed me a gown and told me to strip and get on the bed. I was confused, but I did as told, turning this way and that to cover myself with the gown as I removed my shirt and pants. I left my underwear, which annoyed the doctor once I was on the bed.

"You have to take those off," he said.

"No, I don't want to," I said.

He was stern. "There's other people that we can go help." A threat. I was so sick that I didn't know what to do. I took off my underwear, and then he grabbed my feet to lock each ankle into the stirrup.

As the main doctor started a pelvic exam, I started to cry, saying "no." I begged them to stop—the pain was awful, the humiliation worse. The other doctors leaned in to watch. The doctor did not stop or show any bit of concern, and they acted as if I were some experiment. I begged them to stop, and they did not.

The doctor used a speculum on me, cold and hard, and he broke my hymen. I started to bleed.

I didn't know why I was bleeding. *Oh my God, something is wrong with me. I'm gonna die.* Something had changed in all of them, even the main doctor. They got quiet, and the doctor spoke softer. They realized, *Oh shit, she wasn't lying.* But I read their guilt, their shame at what they'd done, and their realization that I was very ill.

They moved quickly then, hurrying up to get me out of there. They were suddenly much kinder, but never explained what they had done and why I was bleeding. One student handed me a towel to wash up but would not look at me. They said it was an intestinal virus that would pass, then they fled. I had been just another Black girl lying to cover a pregnancy or STD, and now suddenly, and probably temporarily, I was transformed from a guinea pig to a fourteen-year-old human.

Dressed but now colder than ever, I walked out to my father, still crying. I told him what happened.

At home I went straight to the bathroom, and I could hear my father talking to my mother. "They took Tenie in there and they did a test and uh, Tenie said she was bleeding."

"Well," my mother asked my daddy quickly, "do you think she was pregnant?"

"No," my father said. *"Hell no."*

Right then, a wall closed between me and my mother. I had been violated, but her immediate assumption was that I had been lying to her about sex.

I was so confused about the bleeding that I called my sister Flo. She told me I'd never had sex and that was why I bled. I repeated to Flo what our mom said, how she didn't believe me. "I hate her," I admitted, all the powerlessness I felt in the exam room now focused and landing square on her. I couldn't see her fear and need to protect me, I only saw shame. "I am done with her."

But Flo, a nurse at John Sealy, was more concerned that I had an invasive vaginal exam without my consent or, as a minor, my father's permission. I had seen Flo mad, but not like this. She called the hospital, and the excuse was that they didn't think my father spoke English and they were simply trying to help me. Flo told my parents the full story, pointing out that it had to have been obvious they would break my hymen and knew what they were doing. "You could sue them," she said to them. "They did an illegal thing."

My father was so angry, but my mother reverted to her usual reaction: "We can't win against them." She told Flo, "You don't want them mad at you, this is your job," and forbade my father to get involved. Making it worse, I soon developed jaundice and my eyes became slightly yellow. This time, my mother took me to the hospital. It turned out the doctors had been so busy torturing me—assuming this Black girl was pregnant or had a sexually transmitted disease—that they missed that I had viral hepatitis.

My mother felt the chill between us, but I never talked to her about what happened, or what I had heard her say. This was worse to me than her not standing up to the nuns at Holy Rosary. I saw her as weak, unable and unwilling to protect me.

I was more determined now. In three years, when I was a senior, I would graduate and leave Galveston. I would leave her.

THAT SUMMER, I GOT A JOB IN THE GIFT SHOP AT SEA-ARAMA Marineworld, one of the big tourist attractions in Galveston. Sea-Arama was a newish water park with aspirations to be an aquatic Disney World but was still country enough to have alligator wrestling shows. I'd ride my bike to work down there every weekend, and then every day in summer. You knew you were getting close when the chlorine from the pools hit your nostrils, clearing out your sinuses.

I worked with my friend Vernette, who was older than me by a few years, and not to be confused with Vernell. While Vernell was a straight-A student from the projects, Vernette was middle class with a real proper upspeak from living in a white neighborhood. And like everybody in that time, she loved to smoke weed. I didn't mind the weed thing. I just had never smoked.

Vernette called me "square," which I'd never been accused of in my life, so I took a puff off hers. When I decided it wasn't working, I smoked more and found it didn't agree with me. I ended up so paranoid I ran home to my mom. When she opened the door, I accidentally belched smoke right in her face.

After that, I wasn't interested, but Vernette gave me a lesson in rolling a joint. This way, her circle of friends would know I wasn't a narc. So from then on, I would roll everybody's joints, and they were too busy marveling to notice I wasn't smoking. Ask around: My joints became legendary.

My mother was afraid of exactly this kind of trouble and forbade me to go to any teen parties or events for people my age. There was a teen club around the corner called the Psychedelic Shack. I tried to reason with my mother to let me go. "But it's so close!"

"Something is gonna happen and they're always fighting there," my mother would say.

"Yeah, but all my friends are going. Everybody's going. I'm the only person that can't go."

"I don't care about them, I'm talking about you," she said.

"Y'all need to find something to *do*," I said. I'd turned sixteen, an age when everything my parents did irritated me. Since they were older, they had a lot of time, and I thought my mother had nothing else to do but be in my business. "Why don't you trust me?"

She didn't answer, which to me was an answer. She didn't. When we were out together, she would spot a man's eyes looking me over. I wasn't dressing for them or for attention—Johnny and I made clothes that we loved. When I was sixteen, I wore all these midriff tops with low hip-hugger pants. I felt free in them, beautiful.

That was fine with my mother until the world would intrude and notice me. She would take note of men looking at me before I did, so it seemed out of nowhere when she'd suddenly say, "Why do you always have to have your stomach out? And why do you wear your dresses so short? We need to go home so you can put some clothes on and cover up." She only meant to protect me, but I saw it as shame.

"You're no better than the gossips by Miss Sims's," I said to her once.

That hit her, because she disliked them as much as I did. They were the women who sat on the porches by Miss Sims's candy store, which was Johnny's and my main drag considering how much we still loved candy. As we'd grown up, they'd gone from monitoring our kid behavior to forecasting our downfalls. They were always stage-whispering about Johnny being gay, loud enough so we could hear. They resented that he didn't hide the feminine dips of his voice, and maybe more, that he didn't pay a price for it. The same way he bought his mama a fur coat. Didn't he know we were supposed to be poor and act like it? Wasn't he supposed to be hiding who he was?

When I filled out, I became a new character in their little soap opera. "That Tenie, she's gonna be pregnant by the time she's . . ." The woman raised her voice to call to me. "Tenie, how old are you?"

"Sixteen," I yelled.

"Coming up then," the woman said. We just rolled our eyes, but me and Johnny got our revenge one night when we gave them a show. I wanted ice cream real bad, and I put a pillow under my shirt to look pregnant. I made a real look of it as we walked by, holding my back like it ached as Johnny pretended to be furious.

"Now, I told you not to mess with that boy!" he yelled, pretending to beat on me. We were trying not to laugh because we could see them running their walkers to the window to look.

"Oh, you beat me so bad," I yelled. "Please, Johnny, we're family."

We laughed about that for weeks, but then it got too real: My best girlfriend Vernell found out she was pregnant.

The father was this drummer in the school band who was so handsome—chocolate and had a gold tooth, always chewing the Doublemint gum that made his breath smell so good. He used to walk around with his drumsticks, twirling them and beating on anything to make sure we all knew he was a drummer. She was deeply in love with him, but he had other girls having babies for him, too. Vernell, the straight-A student, ended up finishing school at night school. I had friends who were fast girls, and I loved them for who they were, but Vernell was not fast. Her getting pregnant shocked me, but it terrified my mother, who thought that if her example of the "good girl" could get pregnant, then her impetuous daughter was next.

"Mama, I'm not even thinking about sex," I assured her. "No, I just want to go dance with Johnny and be free." She would let me go out, but only with my sister Selena and Johnny.

I was more clear with them. "I'm not doing any screwing," I told Selena and Johnny flat out. "I ain't getting caught up in this little town. I don't want no serious relationship, and I don't want nothin' that's gonna keep me in Galveston. I'm getting the hell out of here."

CHAPTER 10

BEFORE I LET GO

January 1971

My mother didn't want me around guys my age, but every Friday night she let Selena take me and Johnny to the Session. It was a music night at the ILA Hall, my father's longshoremen's union hall; a little ballroom type of thing where you could really dance, and live acts used to come through. You got bands on the way up or the way down—that perfect middle—like the Stylistics and the Chi-Lites, and one of our favorite groups, Archie Bell & The Drells singing "Tighten Up." You'd be up close and personal with the bands, because the room only really fit thirty tables with a small stage.

Johnny and I would work all week on our outfits and our dance routines. We were really good, and honestly, they should have paid us because we'd get that place going. My mom associated the hall with my daddy's work, and I was in good hands with Selena. But there were *grown* men there. And if she had any clue how many of those grown ass men tried to hit on me, she would have been way more terrified of the Session than the Psychedelic Shack.

I was also protected with Selena and Johnny, who was twenty and had grown into being a handsome man, with his mustache and hair a little long in the back. We would pay the five dollars to get "the setup" at our table, which was a bucket of ice, some paper cups, and a couple of Cokes and 7 Ups. The Session was BYOB—Bring Your Own Bottle—and Selena would bring some rum to mix with the Cokes just for her. Johnny and I were mostly dancing. When the Chi-Lites came through, I got a table up close because I had the biggest crush on the two lead singers, Eugene and Robert. After the show, this guy came to the table and handed me a note. "Eugene wants to meet you backstage." I showed it to Johnny, and we were up as quick as you can ask, "Have you seen her?" Selena let us go back there without her, trusting our judgment, so we went to meet everybody. I had so many questions about what it was like to tour, and where they were going next.

"We're heading out tomorrow," Eugene said. "Come and have breakfast with us before we go." Johnny kind of chuckled because we knew what that meant. Poor Eugene was sweet and had no idea I was so young—I looked twenty-one.

I stayed so cool, trying to sound adult and aloof. "No, I have to be at work very early in the morning." This was a lie and never mind that it was Friday night. Johnny looked at me, bemused.

"We should go then, Tina," Johnny said. "You know, *the office*."

"Yes," I said, gravely. "It was nice to meet you." We hightailed it out of there before I completely lost my nerve, because Eugene was a grown man. Probably as old as thirty!

Selena laughed about all that as Johnny drove us home. She went inside while Johnny and I sat in the car to talk. I was seeing Galveston differently now; I was taking inventory of what I would miss. Friday nights with Johnny were at the top of the list. I was scared to leave him, but I was also scared to leave him *alone*.

I knew he was already really lonely, even with me there. Everybody loved Johnny, and they would hang out with him, but who knew Johnny the way I did? He didn't have any gay friends, and I knew it was because all the gay people were scared to even be seen together. I saw people get ridiculed and harassed enough times to not be naïve.

"What about you?" I asked. I'd asked a variation of this so many times now. If I was out there turning away Chi-Lites, didn't he deserve the opportunity to at least be asked?

"What *about* me?" he answered.

"Johnny, you're too old not to have a boyfriend."

He put his head back and laughed. A loud one that filled the car. "You're gonna find me one?"

"I don't know," I said. "But we need to do something."

"Okay, Miss Fix-It," he said. "All this 'we' stuff."

"Yes, we." Then I paused. "You think I'm really Miss Fix-It?" I wasn't sure how I felt about that.

"Well, you try to be. You're always looking for who needs saving."

"I don't think you need saving, Johnny. But you do need company." And I was determined to help him find it.

I WAS SHARING THE CLASS MICROSCOPE WITH JERRY IN BIOLOGY, taking our turn studying slides of cell cultures. Jerry was my lab partner—a great big white guy and really flamboyant. He wasn't ashamed about it, but he got harassed at school. I loved Jerry, so I knew I could ask him a real question.

"Where do y'all go?"

He looked up from the microscope and put an elbow on the counter to lean. I continued, knowing he knew what I meant. "Like, to have fun. Where do y'all meet each other?"

"Oh, the Kon Tiki." He said it so nonchalant. Like it wasn't an Open Sesame magic word.

"What's the Kon Tiki?"

"It's a bar," he said. "There's dancing seven nights a week. It's so much fun."

I tore off a piece of my science paper. "I'm gonna need that address, Jerry. I promise it's safe with me."

That Friday, I sneaked off with Johnny, telling my mama we were going to the Session with Selena, but he and I crossed Broadway to get to the Kon Tiki. It was nondescript, and I realized I had probably walked by here so many times.

Johnny stood outside, and I grabbed the door to open it for him. "After you," I said. The bar was dark, but welcoming, with beautiful colored lights and tropical island decor. The dance floor was packed, people losing it to the Isley Brothers' "It's Your Thing." But I was only looking at Johnny.

He was so *happy*. It was otherworldly to watch this discovery happen as we walked around the Kon Tiki. He would grab my arm in just the right code so that I would look to see someone we knew who was in the closet. I was so young, and I didn't know where to look for fear I'd make anyone think I was judging them.

So when this girl came up and asked me to dance, I immediately said yes. I squeezed Johnny's arm. "Meet people," I said, and ran off with this girl to the center of the floor. We danced through song after song—from "I Want You Back" to Sly's "Family Affair" and then the throwback of "Ain't No Mountain High Enough." Even when I closed my eyes, I could feel the joy and the abandon of everyone dancing. The bassline moving through us, the drums anchoring us to the beat, the people singing along to lyrics that suddenly seemed so perfect. I opened my eyes to see a group of Black men hugging each other as a new song came on, like this was *theirs*. When I'd danced with Johnny, I had always felt the stakes—of course we danced to impress people around us, but it was also something sacred that felt personal to us in that exact moment of time and rhythm. We were *stars*. We wouldn't have put so much work and planning into our private performances if it didn't matter. But I didn't realize that until I saw so much of it shared in community here. This was joy—Black queer joy—*claimed,* not for survival or resilience or even defiance, but for the fullness of joy. We were *all* stars.

It was only a few songs in when I looked down and saw all these little lights all over the floor, flashing on and off to the beat of the music. "Oooh!" I told the girl. "The lights are so pretty."

She laughed, but I was transfixed. This was before disco was mainstream, so I had never seen a floor like that. I finally stopped dancing and told the girl I wanted to check on my friend. Johnny was waiting for me, beaming. "Did you see what was on the dance floor, Tenie?"

"Oh yeah, those pretty lights," I said. "So cool."

"Yeah, but did you see what the lights were?"

I looked back and squinted.

"It's penises," he said. Sure enough, there they were. We cracked up laughing. The club was famous for its colored silhouettes of penises. The Kon Tiki had been burned down in its previous home, and I guess they put that dance floor in so there'd be no confusion on whether or not they were scared.

After that first night, Johnny went to the Kon Tiki without me and found his people there. He took me to a drag show there, both of our first times seeing one, and I was all in. Here was this amazing culture that managed to be underground in Galveston, so I didn't tell anybody, and Johnny didn't either. It was hard, because I thought the world should know more about this. But it wasn't mine to share.

Johnny befriended the drag queens, who recognized a genius costume maker. He started making them costumes, and he became the go-to person to really put a look together. Showstopper beauty with the detail work that Agnes and his mother, Selena, taught him. By then, Johnny had enough money from working that when Selena's upstairs neighbors moved out, he took over the rent on the second floor of the duplex. The two floors shared those stairs on the side, and you could be in Selena's and enjoy the parade of Johnny's visitors coming for glamour.

Selena's husband, Johnny's dad, would be scratching his head all the time watching people coming and going. The drag queens would come down transformed, looking beautiful in full makeup and wigs, wearing the gowns that Johnny made for them. "Tenie, you know, them boys went up there," he said, "but they ain't never come down. Just those girls." We laughed a long time about that one.

I started helping Johnny do hair and makeup up there, too. 'Cause more often than not, I would look at one of his clients and think, *I could do this really good.* I'd have a vision, and Johnny and I would style the wigs together as we played music and told jokes. I loved that moment in the mirror when somebody's transformation happened, but the person was catching up. There was this glint of recognition in their eyes. You've made them look extraordinary, but somehow also brought out their true essence. I realized I liked to make people *feel* beautiful, so they could see that they *are* beautiful.

As I readied for my senior year, I began to count the months to when I would graduate and leave Galveston. I didn't know where I was going, but now that I knew Johnny had his people to draw from and grow with, I needed to find mine.

THE COPS WOULD HAVE BEEN VERY HAPPY TO RUN ME OUT OF town.

On a summer night, I was part of a bunch of happy teenagers tumbling out of the Martini movie theater, the hi-hat of Isaac Hayes's theme song to *Shaft* still playing in our hearts. Down now from our spot in the balcony, all us kids were gathered outside the theater, and I was with my friend Vanessa. Vernell and I had taken her under our wing at Ball High, when Vernell told off some girls who were scaring Vanessa every day, really bullying her. "Stop it," Vernell had said. Nobody wanted to fight Vernell, who was tough, and there was me, ninety pounds dripping wet behind her, saying, "Yeah, leave her alone." It worked. When Vernell left school to have her baby, Vanessa and I stuck together.

Shaft had just opened, so it was a huge deal for us all. People showed out in high boots and miniskirts, and many had joined me now in sporting big afros. Vanessa and I were standing on the edge of the group, because I had a curfew and I was waiting for Skip to come pick us up in his car.

A cop car rolled up with one officer driving. "Come here," he said.

I looked behind me and realized he was talking to us. Now, I had just seen *Shaft*, so the spirit of Richard Roundtree's Black Power private detective was within me. Ever since Skip got beat up by the cops, my family had been harassed, but usually it was my father or one of my brothers stopped while driving. I walked up to the car but didn't say anything.

"What is your name?" he asked. Not a question. An order.

"Why?" I asked.

"I said, give me your name." He turned to Vanessa, who answered right away. He wrote it down on some kind of clipboard and turned back to me. "You need to give me your name."

"I'm not giving you my name," I said. Inside, I had my dukes up, because I was really sick of them. "I'm just waiting for my ride and you're harassing me."

"If you don't—" He looked behind me at all the kids, who were now starting to yell out, "Why are you messing with her?" and "Go do something." He continued, angry. "If you don't give me your name, I'm going to take you down to the station."

"Well, take me then."

He hopped right out of that car, grabbing me by the wrist to throw me in the back. Then he grabbed Vanessa. "She gave you her name," I yelled. "Just let her be." But honestly, I was afraid to be alone with him. Vanessa started crying when he put her in the backseat with me, which made me madder. Maybe he thought if he made a show of putting me in the car, I'd say my name. I didn't. "Fine," he said, swearing under his breath as he put the car in drive.

He took us to the police station, and when we got there, they didn't book us. They sat us down and said we couldn't leave. I watched that cop try to explain something to his sergeant, and I noticed they were getting heated. The sergeant seemed annoyed with him.

The sergeant came to us. "You know, y'all look like nice girls," he said, a mix of honey and malice. "You shouldn't be on the streets like this." He paused. "On the *corner*."

He was implying that we were prostitutes. We were kids. "What are you talking about?" I asked. "Sir, we were at the movies. We are *students* at Ball High. Issa bunch of kids that can verify that we were at the movies and then this cop came up and started asking me my name. And why should I give him my name? When I'm outside the movie?"

"Well," the sergeant said, done with the nice act. "He's gonna take you girls home. And not to the corner where he found you."

Vanessa and I were going down the steps to leave, and the original cop followed us. "We don't want you to take us home," I said quick. "We're good."

He was after something bigger. "Your name Beyoncé?"

I kept walking. Vanessa looked back.

He sneered. "I'm the one that kicked your brother's ass."

I turned on my heel. Now I recognized his small frame. His anger. That snivelly rat face. "Oh well, it looked to me like he kicked your ass."

"If you Black bitches don't get home, I'm gonna arrest you for curfew."

I borrowed a line from *Shaft*. In the movie he said it slow and dismissive. I did too: "You ain't gonna do *shit*."

With that, Vanessa and I started running. Not only to get away from him, but because I was so sheltered that I'd never walked at night without Johnny or one of my brothers—

Skip! I had forgotten that Skip was going to pick me up. If someone at the movie told him I'd been taken by a cop, he might be heading to the station. And then what would happen to him? This same guy would be there from that awful night, angry.

Thank God, Skip's car was at my house when I got home. He'd waited at the theater, then drove to our mom and dad's, thinking I must have gotten a ride home. They were all about to go out driving to look for me.

I told them all about the police. My parents were mad, but they couldn't do anything. It felt like none of us could. I went to bed, still channeling Shaft. One of the many times us kids broke out in applause during the movie was when Shaft calls his girlfriend to say he can't make it tonight. "You got problems, baby?" she asks Shaft. He answers with a sly smile: "Yeah, I got a couple of 'em: I was born Black. And I was born poor."

We *all* laughed in recognition. Because so were we. And we knew what Shaft knew. People could try us. Accuse us of being something we're not. Harass us. Hurt us. But we could look them in the eye and say, "You ain't gonna do shit."

SENIOR YEAR WAS A BLUR, A MIX OF EXCITEMENT, NERVES, AND admiration of the kids who knew exactly what they wanted to do as soon as they got out of school. A mechanic. A doctor. A parent. A nurse. College. But instead of a profession, I had a place in my mind: Los Angeles. I told everyone I was leaving on the next thing smokin' right after my Class of '72 graduation. I think my parents expected me to go up and get my diploma with a suitcase behind me and a car running in the parking lot. But I stayed to work all summer, saving money for an airplane ticket to L.A. I'd started earlier senior year, moving from just weekends at Sea-Arama to picking up shifts after school, stretching every dime to make it a quarter. My plan was to have enough to afford the flight in September. When people asked what I was going to do for work out there, I said, "Do hair, or something."

That summer was also meant to prepare my parents—ease them into it. But the anticipation only made them hold me tighter. They were in their sixties now after hard lives and needed more and more from their children. My mother didn't want me to leave her—I felt her binding me there in Galveston, using guilt to hold me. Whatever she said, I only heard what she had asked my father about me after the hospital exam. "Do you think she was pregnant?" It would only strengthen the wall between us.

By the end of August, I was close to my goal to purchase the flight. Late one afternoon I was at Selena's. Johnny was at work at the hotel, and I was watching my sister doing her seamstress work, as our mother did. I'd told my mama I wasn't sure what I'd do now that I'd graduated, but I wanted to do something that made women feel good about themselves. Something with beauty, maybe. Her answer was, "If you start really working as a seamstress, you'll never go broke."

There was a commotion, someone with a loud mouth announcing their presence. It was my nephew Ronnie, who I used to have all those fights with back in the day, even though we loved each other very much. He and his best friend Nap had driven out to San Diego and moved in with my niece Linda. Linda was Selena's oldest daughter, about thirty, and she'd moved out west after working for the Urban League in Houston. Something had happened in her marriage, and she was all of a sudden living alone in California. I just knew Linda was beauty-contest beautiful. And super smart, but nobody ever focused on how smart she was because she was so pretty. In her '64 Central High yearbook, every senior had to choose a meaningful quote. Linda's read: "Being a woman is a difficult task since it consists principally in dealing with men." She was on to them early. At one point, Linda had come home for Easter or some holiday, and I told her, "I'm gonna come visit you when I'm in California."

She chuckled good-naturedly at me with the big plans. "Okay then," she said. "Come join the party." That motivation was enough to power me for months and months.

Ronnie and Nap had driven out there and showed up on Linda's doorstep one day. She let them stay. "We're not in Galveston long," Ronnie said, swaggering, all California in a way that made me stand up straight so I could at least show I was still taller than him. They were going right back to San Diego in Ronnie's dark powder blue Dodge Charger.

"What's San Diego like?" I asked. "Is it far from L.A.?" Los Angeles and Oakland were all I knew of California—the land of stars and Panthers.

"Three hours up the coast," he said.

The way Ronnie said "the coast" sounded so glamorous. "I'm flying out there soon," I said. "I'm getting my money right and I should be good to go in a few weeks."

"Tenie, you should come with us," he said. "You could save all that money, just give us some for gas."

"Well, I want to be in Los Angeles," I said.

"Yeah, but San Diego is nice," said Ronnie. "And close. Linda won't mind you staying."

"She just took you in?" When he nodded fast, I lowered my voice. "When are you going back?"

"Day after tomorrow. Like I said, we're here real quick and gone."

Gone, I thought. Just the sound of that word and I knew I was going to be in that car headed to San Diego. I barely gave anyone notice, following my heart quick before my brain could catch up. It let me say my goodbyes in a rush, even to Johnny and my parents, swearing I'd be back soon. I broke my mama's heart.

Honestly, I don't remember what was said. My mind saw the opportunity to escape, and the next thing I remember is riding the whole way to San Diego with my butt on the floor. The Dodge Charger's front was long, but the backseat was about six inches off the floor. I sat on a couple of pillows my mama made me bring, and of course I'd even fought her on that. "I don't want these pillows," I'd said.

"Tenie, that backseat is so low," she'd said. "Spread these and you'll make a mattress. And take this blanket."

She was right, though at eighteen I refused to ever acknowledge it. The guys would let me switch to the front for an hour to stretch my legs here and there, but Nap was so long-legged it was cruel to make him sit back there. They took turns driving, one sleeping while the other floored it, and we would stop at rest areas because we didn't have money for a hotel.

Driving nonstop is why Ronnie's car started smoking from the hood, a problem that I guess now was the radiator. We just saw the steam of the car running hot, the water bubbling over. We pulled into a service station. "Tenie, you go on and talk to the guy 'cause we need it fixed *today,*" said Ronnie.

"Yeah, flirt with him," said Nap.

"I'm not doing that."

"Just give them a sob story," said Ronnie. If the car had to stay overnight, we didn't have money for a hotel, and I was already going to use what money I had to fix the car.

"You didn't even have enough gas money," I told them. "That's why you wanted me. Now I wind up spending what I would have spent on a plane."

"Yeah, but we're almost there, Tenie," Ronnie said.

"I could be looking down on you right now," I joked, hugging the pillow I hadn't wanted to bring. "Matter of fact, I am."

The man agreed to start working on it right away, but it was night-fall by the time we got back on the road. We drove the last four hundred miles with the windows open, racing under the starlit sky.

Finally, we got to Linda's house. She opened the door to see Nap, and Ronnie, then me with my one suitcase. I hadn't called, I hadn't asked—I simply showed up. Eighteen years old with such nerve.

"Tenie," Linda said, opening the door wider. And then, "Make yourself at home."

CHAPTER 11

GOLDEN HOUR

August 1972

I T WAS THE blue of the water that got me. I'd always been a junkie for the beach, but San Diego was different. In Galveston, the sediment and oil spills from the Gulf meant the stronger the waves, the murkier the water. The ocean water in California was the blue of crayons. Even the sand sparkled like gold dust, which every new San Diegan learns is just ground-up mica, but to me it would always be gold.

I'd made Linda dinner that first night, familiarizing myself with her kitchen and playing one of her Marvin Gaye records to bridge our nine-year age difference. Everyone loved Marvin Gaye. I made a pasta with what she had, cleaning as I went the way my mother taught me. This is what grown folks did—made dinner and a plan for the night with no one waiting up. Ronnie and Nap went out to let San Diego get another look at them, while Linda and I drove west to watch the sunset.

I was taking pictures in my mind, sending mental postcards back to Johnny and everybody. "I'd be out here every day," I said to Linda. I wanted to say, "I *will* be out here every day," but I didn't want to push it. I had already decided I was going to stay in California, no matter what it took.

That meant I would need a job, and soon, even if Linda put me up. I couldn't imagine not having one. I was my mother's daughter, even if I didn't feel like calling her to at least tell her I'd arrived. Maybe tomorrow. Or the day after that.

Linda was real busy at her job as an executive administrative assistant at the National Urban League's San Diego office. Anyone who's worked at a nonprofit knows you do ten jobs and there's still more to do. The Urban League focused on economic empowerment as the key to social equality. Linda might help host a jobs training seminar in the morning, then a small-business clinic, then take some high school student's scholarship application to look over at home. The Urban League was known for recruiting white corporate America into investing in Black communities, and often those checks came after a company had gotten bad press for job discrimination and needed to show it was "learning." Very much like it is today.

"I'm gonna hang around your office," I said, "and see what's going on in San Diego."

"And get a job," she said.

"Right?" I said. "I will."

"It doesn't look good if I work for the Urban League and I have got unemployment in my own home. Some roommate I'd be."

"*Roommate,*" I repeated. I hugged her and she laughed. She knew the opportunity she was giving me.

My mom reminded me there were plenty of jobs in Galveston when she called Linda's that first week looking for me. Nobody knew how to lay a guilt trip like my mother—we called it the "Full Agnes"—but I saw each call as a lasso she threw to pull me back in. When we lived at home, she was terrified of something happening to us. Then, she could at least wake in the night and pray over the sureness of our sleeping bodies, present and accounted for. Now, none of her children were home, and I, her wildest child, had gone and put a thousand miles between us.

Linda didn't want to hear any talk of Texas when I hung up. We were similar in that we left, and for her, that was enough of a statement. But I had bolted to California *to* a life, and she had bolted from one. She never spoke ill of the husband she left, but it was clear I shouldn't ask a lot of questions. I didn't know if they were divorced or separated, just that she had been there, working in the Houston office of the Urban League, and now she was here.

We would go out on the town, getting real cute. Linda had an incredible body, and like me, she sewed her own clothes. We would get all glammed out and put on the little midriff tops we made, pairing them with miniskirts and boots because we were women of the seventies. My color palette was whites and creams, or my favorite color, orange. Never boring black.

Her friends were bemused by me, this kid speaking so Texas that I brought the accent back out of Linda. The girlfriends were mostly from work and seemed so grown. Astrology was big in new-age California, and when Linda got a little closed off, she had a friend who used to tell her, "You're being such a Sagittarius."

"What does that mean?" I asked.

"She doesn't want you to know what makes her tick," said her friend. "She'll let you in just enough."

"Just enough to let you know I don't buy that stuff," said Linda.

"See?" said the friend. "And what are you?"

"Capricorn," I replied.

"Oooh, my sister is one," she said. "You know how to fight, right?"

"Yeah."

"So does she. I go to her when I want to fix problems, not talk about them. She doesn't like the boohoo stuff."

I thought about that. "Does my sign say anything about a job?"

That was my main concern. I finally lucked out with a job at a little Black-owned fashion boutique. I befriended the woman who worked with me. She was close to my age and beautiful, and we would make a day of acting like we were the most elegant, welcoming salesclerks in all of San Diego. She'd grown up in town and I would always ask her questions about California. She's the one who taught me about earthquakes, telling me that native Californians never walk into a room without looking to see what's sturdy. She hadn't been in a bad one, she said, but her mother had and that was enough. "It could all go." That phrase reminded me of my mother. Her fear that at any moment she could lose everything.

Then I met her mother, and she was nothing like mine.

"Your hair looks awful," she told her daughter as a greeting, then she complimented me on some random thing. I don't even remember any nicety she said because it was so weird. This became a routine, and my friend would be left deflated when her mom finally skittered out.

She opened up to me, talking about how her mom was so prone to jealousy that she'd even slept with her boyfriend. It shocked me.

I couldn't wait to get home to call my mother. "Mama, you are so good to me," I said right away, surprising myself. I hadn't known what I wanted to say, only that I needed to talk to her. The wall between us—built over something I'd overheard her say and never questioned—began to crumble.

I started crying. "You have always been so good to me. And I'm out here making you suffer, not calling you to tell you that."

"What are you—"

"Let me just talk, nothing's wrong except how I've treated you. You've been the best mom in the world to me. Me? I'm just an idiot, you know. I'm looking at these other people's moms and I'm like, *God,* I didn't even know moms like that existed. And here I have you and I'm sorry."

"Oh, Tenie," she said. And I heard her say to my dad, "She's fine. We're fine." She paused, and I realized she was crying. Now I'd gone and done this.

"I'm sorry," I said. "I, uh, I want you to kn—"

"No, no," she said. "I'm sorry for a lot of things too. I know that I was strict on you."

This was what I needed. This was what had driven us apart.

"Why didn't you trust me?" I asked. Why did she think I needed constant monitoring, or I would swing toward my true nature?

"It's not that I didn't trust you," she said. "I didn't trust *the world.* I know what people can do to *you.*"

I finally asked the question that had been unspoken for years. "Mama, did something happen to you? Because you were so scared of what boys might do to me. What happened to you?"

"Oh, Tenie," she said. I felt a door closing again between us. She didn't answer me, and she would never answer me. I had pushed enough. I told her again that I loved her, and that I was grateful for her. I didn't need to know what happened to her to understand her fear of it happening to me too. I gave my mother grace, first accepting the woman she was before I asked her to accept the woman I was becoming. That was the start of us reestablishing ourselves as best friends. What we had when I was little.

I had to leave her to realize how much I loved her.

. . .

I'D BEEN IN CALIFORNIA ABOUT FIVE MONTHS WHEN RONNIE AND
Nap moved back to Texas in early 1973. The morning they left they
lingered to see if I'd jump in again and go back. But I didn't. "It's
home, Tenie," Ronnie said.

Yes and no. I hadn't gone back for Thanksgiving or Christmas and
my birthday in January was with Linda and my new friends. I missed
Johnny. When I felt the California sun on my arm riding in a car, I
would think, *Johnny would like that,* and I wanted to send it to him.
But I couldn't mail California.

I was ready to move again anyway, but not back to Texas. Linda
had started dating a DJ who lived in Los Angeles. I would tag along
for her weekends there, which then became every weekend. Her DJ
guy was invited to everything, so he would get us into the best spots.
And I don't mean clubs. L.A. had a house party culture that reminded
me of Galveston. Linda and I would arrive in our cinched-waist
jumpsuits, convinced that the door to every party would have a
celebrity waiting behind it. "I know I know him," I would whisper to
Linda about some fine man sipping a cocktail. "I saw him on TV, I
know it."

I wanted to be in L.A., but I didn't pressure Linda. So the second
she said, "Maybe we just move here," I said "Yes" before she even got
to the "since we're here so much." Linda was smart: She lined up a job
doing administrative work at an L.A. law firm. It was good money,
certainly more than the Urban League could pay her. She figured she
could be a voice at the office suggesting pro bono work.

I had liked working in the boutique, so I went over to the Broadway, the department store on Crenshaw and Santa Barbara Avenue
before it became Martin Luther King Jr. Boulevard. It was upscale, and
at the foot of Baldwin Hills and View Park, serving the Black stars
and doctors who'd spent the last decade moving into those neighborhoods after the Supreme Court ruled you could no longer keep us
out. Integration led to white families fleeing, traded for the likes of
Ray Charles, Nancy Wilson, Roxie Roker from *The Jeffersons,* and
her little son, Lenny Kravitz. It reminded me of Galveston, with kids
having a specific place to run and ride bikes without being shot with

BB guns or cops coming to break it up. Only they were also rich, living on the palm-lined streets of what people were calling the Black Beverly Hills.

I went to the Broadway to get a job, any kind of job. The lady in the hiring department and I hit it off. "Your makeup is so professional," she said, then paused and leaned forward. "I'm not supposed to tell you this, but there's a Japanese company named Shiseido running a counter here and they're looking. They need makeup artists to just be in the Black stores."

I'd never heard of Shiseido, a Tokyo-based cosmetics brand that had recently expanded into the American market. But I knew makeup, and I had wished for a job that helped women feel beautiful. I had wished for a job, period. They liked me and told me they had Black women coming in and needed someone who customers would trust to work on them. "That's me," I said. I got the job on the spot.

I used the products myself and made Linda my model, road-testing everything at home. Linda loved L.A., but spending so much time with her, I could see the rhythms of her personality. She could be the warmest person in the world, and then a little switch would go off and she'd withdraw. Some people do that when the cup runs dry, and she would sometimes do it when the cup was full.

I could make room for it, though, because L.A. was too full of possibility to focus on anything negative. There was magic everywhere, and a sense that we had all come from somewhere to be right there. Los Angeles in 1973 was setting the culture for the whole country and you felt it. You would see the next makeup trend, the new hairdo, the must-have jeans on the streets before you saw it in a magazine or on TV. It was one big film set.

And then a star walked right onto my set at work. Tina Turner strutting down from her View Park house like Venus in blue jeans come down from Mount Olympus. I spotted her far away, because who could miss her with the long auburn hair falling down on the shoulders of a fitted leather jacket? I walked briskly over to my friend Paula, who did the makeup for Fashion Fair, which was just starting and was already the most influential Black-owned cosmetics company out there.

I whispered because this was a matter of grave importance that re-quired utmost discretion. "I think that's Tina Turner."

Paula, always sophisticated and beautiful with a brown lip framed by dark black lip liner, looked over. "Yeah, that's her," she said, so non-chalant. Paula was seven or eight years older than me, and sometimes she talked like that made all the difference. "She comes in here all the time. Lives up the hill." The woman who ran the Fashion Fair counter added: "There's all kinds of people in here."

"There's all kinds of people," I said, "and then there's Tina Turner."

"Just don't be, like, lame," Paula said. "Tina, I have to tell you, you are so country."

I went back to my spot and waited. And suddenly Tina turned, and really looked at me, right at me. I think she came over because I was looking at her like a sick puppy, willing her over there.

My hands were shaking. "Hello," I said. Meaning: *I wanted to be a singer and I never thought I was gonna get out of my little town and now I'm here and I'm meeting you, Tina Turner.*

"Hi," she said. "I'm looking for some lip gloss."

"Oh," I said, like nobody had ever asked for lip gloss and I hap-pened to have some here waiting in case. "Try this one." She had no makeup on but didn't even need any to be glamorous. She just exuded it. There's all kinds of people, and then there's Tina Turner.

I THOUGHT MY L.A. DREAM WAS OVER THE NIGHT LINDA TOLD ME she was moving back to Houston to reunite with her husband, George. The switch in her mind had gone off, and there was no arguing. I couldn't afford a place on my own, and she assumed I was going back with her.

I told Paula at work the next morning. She said, "Come live with me."

"You mean that?" I said, and instantly regretted even giving her a second to rethink handing me a lifeline.

"Yes," she said. Paula had a one-room efficiency apartment on Melrose. She said we could make it work, and we did. I moved in, saving up until I could afford an efficiency of my own in the same building. Paula and I still ate dinner together, taking turns in each other's apartment. When I needed her most, there she was in her Fashion Fair Cinnamon Crush lipstick and Perfect Finish foundation. (Paula, if you're out there, DM me.)

I always wanted Linda to know how much she meant to me, too. My gratitude for her was always on the tip of my tongue, so right there that out of nowhere whenever I would see her, I would randomly say, "You know, you really changed my life."

CHAPTER 12

RETURN OF THE PRODIGAL DAUGHTER

June 1974

I HAD A TOP that I loved forever, with a funky little repeating pattern. My mother had made it for me, and I wore it all the time as a teenager. When I started to outgrow it, Johnny cropped it for me. It became one of those "Why is your stomach out?" shirts my mom hated.

I wore that top all over L.A.; its origin was a remnant my mother spotted at a good price, then cut and measured for me, then made with her hands. No matter what alterations I made to it over the years, the pattern she chose for me remained.

Similarly, my pattern was ingrained. I went where I was needed, and now my mother needed me. I had gone home for the holidays, my first trip back to Galveston since I left, and saw that in those fourteen months, my mother had aged so much. This hadn't occurred to me in our calls. The able woman I pictured on the other end of the line was gone. Her arthritis now made everything more difficult, and her hesitance to do anything that might tax her heart seemed to take an even stronger hold on her.

"We don't have anybody to take care of us," my mother said, which was not entirely true but also not entirely false. All my siblings had their own families to take care of, and it was the age-old story that a dutiful unmarried daughter is supposed to care for her parents.

That winter, both my mother and father got really sick, and then the need was too great. They had to have someone there and I was their daughter. *"Lucy,"* Johnny said when he hugged me back to life, because I was very sad to be back in Galveston. "Lucy Ball, here you are."

There I was.

I could see what arthritis took from my mother, and I became her hands in the kitchen. I'd always watched her cook, especially her legendary gumbo, but now she would stand beside me, guiding me on cutting the celery down to the millimeter with an "Okay, that's right." Showing me how to core the bell pepper to not lose even the tiniest bit. Cut the three bunches of green onions with a quick sureness to not leave any of their juices to waste on the cutting boards. Slicing up the sausage to the exact width needed to make every person we fed feel taken care of and also stretch the meal so even a surprise guest felt like we had been waiting for them.

Then the lifting of the giant pot to the stove—itself a job—adding three or so gallons of water. I'd already washed the chicken because gumbo starts off with a base of boiled chicken. Season the water so every bite that you take has that seasoning in there, and also add in the vegetables. Once the chicken starts boiling, you put the crab in so that the seafood flavor can cook through the whole thing.

My mama would coach me through making the roux, first pouring even the vegetable oil herself with her unsteady hand, until she eventually trusted me. The small noises she made to measure out how I slowly added in the cups of flour to stir, telling me to quick add more oil if needed. A steady rhythm of stirring and talking, forty-five minutes until the roux and conversation deepened. To make it our Creole way, you wanted the roux to slowly bloom into the consistency and color of dark fudge, but if you or the heat got carried away, and the roux had already darkened to a peanut butter before the crucial thirty-minute mark . . . Well, you might still have a chance of cooling it, keeping a frantic stirring to salvage the work, but a *burnt* roux was ruin to your gumbo. If that happened, take the lesson, curse it while you washed the skillet and spoon, but start over.

Okra is essential to the gumbo, the vegetable carried to Louisiana with the recipe from West Africa—where in many cultures our ancestors called okra *gombo*. Now, in my mother's kitchen, we took another skillet to fry the okra for later. More heat and oil, but the enemy here was the slime. It's what makes people think they don't like okra when they just haven't had good okra. For that, my mother would have me splash vinegar— "a little more" she'd say, until she didn't need to. I saw how she listened to the okra frying, the sound of the sizzle going from dull to sharp as the vinegar deglazed the pan, the pitch telling her if the temperature was correct. All her senses in play, teaching me how to use mine.

It all cooked as you added the sausage that people looked for in the bowl to feel they got their share. More chicken—the dark meat of drumsticks and probably three chicken breasts shredded—and the essentials of the canned tomatoes and prepared okra.

Only then would we add in the roux, stirring it in gently, gently, gently. And I could feel my mother wanting to grab that spoon to gauge for herself how the roux separated into the water. She would taste it first, her face revealing nothing until I tasted it. "It needs more seasoning," I would say, and she would nod. If I'd overdone it, we'd add more water. Then it would be covered, three to four hours, time not hurrying or slowing down for man nor gumbo. The gumbo rooted us in place, taking turns or not, babysitting this pot like a child rich with promise that could go nowhere without you. Worried over, laughed over, but always that long-handled wooden spoon reaching down to the depths to circulate the heat and ingredients. When it was set—when a taste of this gumbo told you what it was (because no two gumbos were ever alike)—only then would my mother let me add the shrimp, their gradual pinkness the signal that the work was done.

There was some sort of peace that came over my mother then, her hand on my back, her head dipped to touch my shoulder in this mix of elation and pride. This everlasting meal, this tradition carried and passed down from mother to daughter—across time and tide and odds working against us—was served.

Gumbo became part of my game as I started dating in Galveston, making this intricate pot for a handsome guy and his friends, who thought I was this incredible cook. They were like, "Man, she's pretty but she can throw *down*." Not knowing I'd started at the top but ended there—gumbo was the only thing I knew how to cook.

I TRIED TO FIND FUN IN GALVESTON, BUT I KEPT THINKING OF MY other life in L.A. Johnny understood, and one night when we went out dancing, he took me to a drag show. I started helping Johnny with looks again, and the queens welcomed me back like someone with news from the front. I prefaced anything with, "You know what they're doing out there is . . ." or "The big trend now is . . ." and I had their attention. Johnny and I gave them the confidence to win trophies at the ball. As far as we were concerned, there was L.A., Milan, and then Galveston. I was *Vogue*.

I told myself I was only coming back for a short period of time, but I was still here. I was at the pharmacy getting a prescription for my parents when someone spoke behind me. "Is it just my imagination," a man's voice said, and then sang, "Running away with me?" I turned to see my friend Carlos from high school.

"Oh my God," I yelled. "I know that voice! How are you?" Carlos had been in a singing group like the Veltones, only his was modeled— I mean, as an outright imitation—on the Temptations.

"I heard you were in California," he said.

This is what I heard everywhere in Galveston, usually with a head tilt that translated to, "I heard you thought you were something." But Carlos was real about it.

"Oh, I was," and then I went into the whole story about my parents.

"Were you out there singing?" he asked.

"Pardon? Um, no. No." An older lady whose name I used to know was staring at us. *What was her name?*

"You should come sing at my club," he said. "Well, it's not my club, but I have a band." The old woman pursed her lips. She thought Carlos was trying to impress me.

"Oh wow," I said. "That's really cool." *Mrs. Williams*—that's who that was.

"You should come sing with the band," he said. "We do jazz but new songs too."

"Carlos, like, that was a long time ago," I said.

"You were *good*, Tina," he said. "Next Friday, just do a few songs. See how it feels. I'm not hearing no."

"Okay," I said, surprising myself and Mrs. Williams, who didn't bother to suppress a busybody shrug. "I'll have to get somebody to stay with my parents." Carlos gave me the address; it was by the Session. When he left, Mrs. Williams looked at me like we had been interrupted.

"Tina Beyoncé," she said. "I heard you went off to California." I could hear her tallying the gossip to share: "That Tenie girl is back and singing in a bar while her parents are doing poorly." If Johnny were here, he would have patted my stomach as a joke to really give her some news to spread.

"Yes, Mrs. Williams," I said politely. "I was out there. But I'm here now. You have a nice day."

CARLOS'S BAND LIKED ME, AND THE VENUE WAS THIS CUTE PLACE in Galveston. That first Friday night, right before performing again, I was surprised by how nervous I was. I'd never had these nerves in the Veltones because I had those two girls with me, and we were so close. I was too busy booting them up and building their confidence to worry about mine.

There was a little mirror at the club, and I looked at myself again. Someone had left a bouquet of flowers too long in a vase, but one pink lily was holding on. I rescued it, cleaning it off a bit and placing the flower in my afro, like Billie Holiday's signature gardenia.

I did slow songs the band knew, like Smokey Robinson's "Baby Come Close" and the Stylistics' "Betcha By Golly, Wow." I continued with the band at the club all that summer, finding a flower for my hair each time. And I loved it. I loved every second of performing, even if I stayed terrified.

It was bittersweet, though, in that I realized my singing career was never going to be some big thing. My crowd was always going to be a couple dozen tourists who would never remember my name once they went home.

BUTCH CAME TO VISIT ON A SUNDAY, CARTING FOUR DIRT BIKES IN case he was worried for a second about not looking tough to the guys who stayed in Galveston. They used to beat him up all the time because he was so good-looking, and all the girls talked endlessly about his beautiful green eyes. When he went to the military, he lifted weights and did karate to bulk up. He'd also been doing a lot of mechanical stuff in the Air Force and was starting a side gig fixing motorcycles. He wanted to get his own shop, which he eventually would.

There were a dozen of us, probably more, looking at the bikes. If anyone in the family got on one within ten blocks of Mama, she would be in the hospital again or worse, so Butch had us all go down to West Beach, far down from the seawall.

By now it was late afternoon, and we went west toward the setting sun. We were all barefoot—me in a cropped T-shirt and the lowest hip-hugging jeans, the wind in my afro. We looked like some beautiful hippie motorcycle gang caravaning past the city limits.

My nephew Ronnie wanted to race me, and I was game for that. We got out on a long strip and let go. Butch had gotten out, but why couldn't I? Twenty years old and I was still racing Ronnie to see who was first. I passed by a bunch of people who were staring at me, which is when I realized I must be going really fast. *At least I'm beatin' him,* I thought. *Wait, where was he anyway?*

I squinted to look in the little mirror to see about Ronnie, and what do I see but a police car chasing me? Flashing lights and the angry wail of a siren I did not hear until I slowed down.

And who was it but that cop? The one who beat Skip and tried to arrest me after *Shaft*.

"Not him again," I said aloud.

"YOU DON'T HAVE ON SHOES. YOU'RE SPEEDING. NO HELMET," he screamed, spittle flying out of his mouth. "I AM ARRESTING YOU!"

The police had been keeping track of my family for years, though harassment was more the word. Now the cop threw me in the car. He had a score to settle, so on the way to the police station, he deliberately made a left so he could drive me down the seawall to Menard Park. That had been a Black park, and he and I both knew that on Sundays every young person I knew in Galveston would be there.

The cop drove real slow through Menard Park so that everybody could see me. There were people all walking on the sidewalk, looking to see who was in the backseat. The cop laughed at the people peering in. "Oh, look at the monkeys," he said. "We're riding through the zoo."

I cursed him out, but I could hear the people outside say, "Is that Tina Beyoncé?"

When we were at the station, I saw him talk to this mean lady who came into the intake room. She said they had to do a cavity search on me.

"For a traffic violation?" I asked. "Really?"

She didn't answer, and instead grabbed a fistful of my afro and yanked hard.

"Ow," I yelled, trying to dodge her hand as she went to grab with the other hand.

"You gotta take it off," she muttered.

"I can't take it off, it's my hair."

"Well, strip down."

"For what?" I asked, looking for her humanity. "For what?"

But I did. It was the most humiliating, horrible thing. When it was over, I put my clothes back on, trying to put an armor of dignity over me too. She led me to a cell with a bunch of girls in there. These were the bad girls who were in for fighting and worse. I admit it: I was really scared of them.

"Where are your *fine* brothers?" one with really dark eyeliner asked. There was a little naughtiness to her voice, but it was wrapped in complete kindness. I looked up and she smiled. Then they all started in. "Wait, you're Larry's sister, right?" "Oh wait, Butch! Oh my God." One mentioned Skip and another girl piped up: "How many brothers you got?"

That got me laughing, and then I was in with these sweet bad girls. They were my brothers' ages, showing off for the scared new kid. There was a deck of cards in the cell, and they were playing Spades and trying to teach me the rules. We got to talking about makeup and went back and forth like this, having the time of our lives.

"You should spend the night in here," dark eyeliner said.

"Why?"

"'Cause if you spend the night in here, your fine is gonna go way, way down." They all nodded, pros at this.

"Really?" I said, not in a disbelief way, but a "that's a good tip" way. "Okay, well, I'm spending the night then."

Then another mean lady guard—where were they finding these mean ladies?—came to the cell door. "There are about thirty kids in the lobby," she said. My brother Butch brought everybody from the beach and then some into cars and they all drove in. They didn't want my mom to find out because she was so sick.

"Tell them it's cool," I said. "I'm gonna spend the night. Come by tomorrow." The lady snorted, then walked away. She was gone three minutes. Maybe two.

"Your brother said you better get your behind out of here, and 'Where is your money?'" Everyone knew I'd hidden all the money I came home with from L.A.

"Which brother is it?" one girl asked. "Send him in!"

I said goodbye to my new friends, and then to all my money. The cop had put a lot of charges on me, so I would end up using all my L.A. cash to make bail. I had to tell my mom then since now I was broke. She didn't care about the money.

"They're gonna kill my kids," she said, a hand to her chest like she'd been doing. Like she was trying to hold her heart still. "We gotta do something."

She called my sister Flo. Her husband's father was the chauffeur for a very prominent white attorney, Ballinger Mills Jr., which is a name that meant everything in Galveston. "I wouldn't ask you for this if I didn't think they were gonna kill them," my mom said to Flo. "I only need five minutes of Mr. Mills's time."

Mills ran the oldest law firm in Texas and was the great-grandson of the first Texan to be issued a law license. He lived, ironically, not far from where we did, I think because his mansion had withstood the storm of 1900 and the world went on around it. Flo's father-in-law brought us over, and we went through the service entrance into the kitchen. The floor was black and white tile, everything orderly. Mr. Mills came in, carrying himself like a judge entering a courtroom.

My mom tried to be poised and formal, but as she talked, she began to cry. She was telling him all the stuff the police had done to our family, starting with Skip, and the unfathomable number of times my father had been stopped while driving. She mentioned things I didn't know about my brothers, the humiliations of them being detained for no reason, and my strip search at the jail. I didn't realize how appalled she was that they did that to me. Mills was getting more and more worked up, taking off his glasses and making these shocked noises.

"This is really ridiculous," he said. "This is going to stop."

He made one phone call. And all of it stopped, just like he said. Probably five minutes of his time in addition to the five or ten he gave us. It's typical of what went on in every little town, a law you could see, and the law that was. Mills made a call that none of us had the power to make, and the years of harassment simply ended. But what if my brother-in-law's father wasn't a rich man's chauffeur? What then?

My mom then called my cousin Naomi. I knew Naomi as the woman who used to give me her old *Vogue* magazines, but my mom knew her for getting a job in Police Records. That mugshot went missing. My mama always saw to everything.

CHAPTER 13

INTO THE
UNDERCURRENT

August 1975

WE STARTED TALKING the way you do on the beach in Galveston. He was one of the finest guys I'd ever seen. Six-foot-three and twenty-one like me, but somehow distinguished even in a bathing suit.

This was at the 29th Street beach, which he knew was our beach since he'd vacationed in Galveston as a kid. His father was a professor at Fisk University up in Nashville, where Rusty was also a student. A philosophy major, which he managed to somehow talk a lot about in those minutes we were walking on the sand.

We waded in together when a strong wind came off the water, flapping a little flag by the lifeguard station. It drew our attention to the two young white lifeguards passing a joint between them. "Oh, they're out here smoking weed," Rusty said. "And they're supposed to be the lifeguards." We laughed and walked farther out.

Waves started coming in, one after another. The slow creep of the water up to my waist, and then all of a sudden it was at my chest. *Wait.*

"It's an undercurrent," I said, trying not to panic. This was what we called rip currents, when surging waves create strong channels of water that charge back away from shore. They'll take whoever is there and pull them out to sea.

"We need to start walking back," I said. Rusty was taller and had a better chance of staying up. "You go back and start pulling me." I knew the two of us together would have more of a chance of getting out. In Galveston you grow up respecting what water can do. You study it from infancy, learn how to angle yourself so that the water won't take you.

Rusty did not grow up in Galveston. He started walking back without me but didn't know what he was doing so he got pulled even farther out than me. I tried to go back, but all of a sudden, we were *in* the undercurrent. A swirling, taunting whirlpool, but we were still on the surface, both fighting not to get swept out.

"I'm gonna swim for the rocks," he yelled.

"No!" I said. I saw him looking at the long line of rocks into the water near the 29th Street fishing pier. Swimmers knew to steer clear. Undercurrents were worse there.

"I'm gonna," he said quieter.

Before I could turn to watch him, the water slapped me hard in the face and pulled me down deep. The undercurrent took me, and I reminded myself what I knew: Stay calm. It would pop me out if I didn't fight. But it sucker-punched me, tumbling me around till I lost any sense of where I was. Finally, with a force, it spit me out to the surface.

My first breath was a heave, my body desperate to keep me afloat, alive. *Move,* I told myself.

I looked to find the shore, blinking again and again because I didn't believe that I was looking at the end of the pier.

Oh my God, I am so far out here. The water had been calmer for that second, but it came back like a killer, rough and choppy. To escape the savage hold, I had to move even farther out. I could see some people on the pier. I got the breath to yell, but they didn't hear me.

I'm a good swimmer, I reminded myself. Adrenaline booting me up. Fear doing its job, giving me clarity. I worried about poor Rusty. I started trying to swim back, fighting the current now. It smacked me again, the same tumble and flow, until I was so far out that those people got smaller and smaller.

This, I knew, was how people died with undercurrents. You don't drown close to shore, you drowned way out here with the surge popping you out far, the water so rough that you can't move.

This was how that boy died. That boy from my fifth-grade class, *What was his name?* There were a bunch of us who died out here. That's why they gave us that spot, probably the most dangerous part of the beach, the pier right where the island started curving. So many of us gone, with a tiny little thing in the paper because they made their

money off tourism, so they never wanted anyone to know how dangerous the water was. *Oh God, what was his name?* I thought. *I should
know it.*

I looked up at the summer sky, darkening. There was a storm coming. I was twenty-one years old and I was sure that was the last time I
would see that disappearing blue sky. I saw my future disappearing
with that blue sky. I was so sure I would be a mother. I was impulsive
and always rushing, but I was sure I'd be a mother.

My poor mother. This is what she said would happen one day if I
kept going in the water. Her soft voice angry: "*Tenie,* they're gonna
find you in that durn water."

I hoped they'd find the body. I was that far gone. *My* body, I corrected myself. This was happening to me. *Keep moving,* I thought. But
instead, I closed my eyes, and tried to float again. Just to rest a little. I'd
swim more later.

I heard something above me and opened my eyes to see a helicopter
along the shore. In my mind, it was wanting to find me. Getting closer
to the water, and then swooping up, then down again. I raised my
arms. I splashed. I screamed.

The helicopter hovered above me. And then it went higher. "*Wait!*"
I yelled, but it kept going.

I watched my lifeline go, so I didn't see them coming behind me.
The high lifeguards, Cheech and Chong. They had three boogie boards
and brought one over to me. The helicopter was finding me for them!

"Lady, if you grab on us or fight us, we're gonna let you go and
you're gonna die," Cheech warned. They were used to people panicking, grabbing and tearing at them with their will to live making them
crazy. "You're gonna die."

"Don't panic," Chong kept repeating, attaching me to the boogie
board. "Don't panic." But as he said that, he accidentally moved us to
the edge of the undercurrent. It seized us, but way out here, its grip was
loose enough that we could swim farther out to escape.

Now it waited between us and the shore.

"This is rough, man," Cheech said to Chong.

Chong didn't answer. And I realized they were panicking.

We swam a ways over, parallel to the faraway shore, clearing the
area claimed by the undercurrent. I was kicking now. We tested the
force of the tide, seeing if we could risk swimming inland. As we did,

I could see an ambulance on land, sirens going and lights flashing. Together, first carefully and then frantically, we swam toward shore.

We were going to make it.

My legs gave out as I clawed to the sand. People lifted me by my arms, pulling me. Someone wrapped me in a blanket. I tried to keep my composure, but I was spent. EMS carried me to the ambulance.

And there was Rusty. Alive, by the grace of God. He was covered in blood, his chest sliced with gashes. He had swum for the rocks, collapsing when he thought he'd made it. Just as the water was pulling him back in, some crabbers raced over and pulled him up, but dragged him across the razor-sharp barnacles that lined the rocks. He was cut real bad, but alive.

"He'll be okay," someone told me. And I tried to nod but was too tired. *Ohh, God,* I thought, *I hope nobody goes and tells my mama.*

But they already had. With that huge crowd, people raced to the phone to tell her they saw her daughter pulled out of the water after nearly drowning. When I finally got to her, she was hysterically fussing at me: "I told you, I told you," over and over again.

Rusty and I were bonded by that experience. We tried dating for a minute, maybe two weeks that summer, but settled into friendship.

Not long after, my parents' health stabilized enough that I was able to move to Houston. I got a job in the Visa department at Bank of America. I dated a guy for a couple years, this young smart attorney named Jerry, who I thought was the love of my life, but it didn't work out. We were both alpha personalities. Meanwhile, Rusty, who also moved to Houston, would keep telling his friends about this girl from Galveston.

His friend from Fisk University, Mathew Knowles, was living in Houston, too, and he and some ex-roommates were hosting a house party. Rusty called me and asked if I'd go with him. "As friends," I reminded him.

"As friends," he said.

So I went to a simple party at some guy's apartment in Houston.

CHAPTER 14

THE PERSISTENCE
OF FATE

January 1978

WHEN RUSTY INVITED me to the party at his friends' apartment, I didn't know he had told them we were dating. Being Rusty's "girlfriend," real or not, strangely made me off-limits for conversation at the party, which was mostly guys. Since nobody was really talking to me, I busied myself looking at the host's record collection next to the stereo. Whoever this was had a serious vinyl collection, and I idly breezed through the jazz to pull out what they had for R&B.

I heard a man's voice behind me, right at my ear. "Don't put your fingerprints on my records."

I threw up my hands, offended by his tone. "Don't nobody care about your records," I said. "I don't wanna touch *nothing* you have."

And that was how I met Mathew Knowles.

"You're Rusty's girlfriend, right?" he asked.

I wasn't even going to talk to him, but I had to set the record straight. "Uh, no," I said.

"He says he's dating a girl from Galveston?"

"I am a girl from Galveston," I said. "That I can verify." It wasn't worth getting into anything else with him. But he persisted. He started telling me about himself, how he was from Gadsden, Alabama, and got a basketball scholarship to the University of Tennessee, then transferred to Fisk to study economics and business administration. He called economics "econ" and I nodded like, *sure*. When he said he was in sales, I thought that made perfect sense. I had just gotten his elevator pitch.

"How old are you?"

"I just turned twenty-four."

"I'm twenty-six," he volunteered when I did not ask. "Can I get your number?"

I smiled politely but didn't answer because I pretended to be distracted by something out the window.

"What's your name?" he asked.

"Beyoncé," I told him, not giving him my first name.

"B. Ounce?" he asked. "Like an ounce of weed?" I could not believe this conversation. I looked out the window again, maybe contemplating jumping. He grabbed his weed box—*this guy's got props!* I thought—and he started writing on it. "B. Ounce. And what's the number?" Real quick to close the deal. That was the sales training right there, but I still didn't answer.

"Well, where do you work?"

"Visa," I said.

"Oh, that's one of my accounts," he said, adding that he sold copiers for Xerox. "I know exactly where that is. I'm going to come and see you one day."

I smiled and figured I better make a clean getaway. I thanked him for the party, then told Rusty I had to get going. I'd probably never see that Mathew again.

WHEN MY PARENTS WERE BOTH HOSPITALIZED AT THE SAME TIME, my mother begged me to move back to Galveston. At least until they got stable again, she said. My mom would be sixty-nine that July, and my dad sixty-eight when he shook out his birthday cards in May. I did what I had to do: I gave my job at Visa six weeks' notice so I could train my replacement and started to pack up my apartment. For the last two weeks of my time in Houston, I would stay in my friend Pat's apartment, sleeping on her couch while I sold off everything in my place.

It was a few days before I moved back that I almost literally bumped into Mathew in the Visa lobby. He was doing a sales call.

"Oh, you're that girl I met, who lied and said you worked at MasterCard," he said. "I went over, and nobody knows you."

"No, I didn't lie to you," I said. "I told y'all I work at Visa, which is where you are. Right here. Where I *work*."

That was it, I thought. But only a few hours later, work brought me downtown and there Mathew was crossing the street. He said, "You know this is just meant to be. We've got to go to lunch."

"Well, I'm leaving town," I said, thinking it *was* strange to run into him twice in one day. I explained about my parents and how I was selling off furniture to move back to Galveston. That Saturday afternoon my friend Vernell was coming over to my old apartment to help me sell what was left dirt cheap.

"I should come by," he said.

He did, buying some stuff from me, including the wicker sofa on my sun porch. I'd found it somewhere, the arm broken. My daddy fixed it, and I'd spray-painted it bright yellow and bought these royal blue pillows. It was so cute, but I was ready to give it away. I noticed Mathew eyeing it.

"It's forty dollars," I said.

He handed me twenty. "I'ma pay you back." He paused. "Let me take you on a date." I took the twenty but didn't answer.

As Mathew's friend helped him get the sofa out, Vernell said, "You ain't never gonna see that other twenty dollars." But I had another way for him to pay me back. I was supposed to drive to Galveston that night for a Mardi Gras ball. Holy Rosary ran it at a nice convention center on the beach, and it was always a big deal for my family. I dreaded the ride there and back in one night, but my dad was in the hospital again, and with him not being able to attend, it was especially important to my mother that I be there.

I told him about the party later that night, saying, "I'm too tired to drive. If you want to take me, that's how we're gon' have a date."

It was the one chance I was going to give him, and he took it.

Mathew picked me up later in his Mercedes, all shiny. "This is really a pretty car," I said on the drive to make small talk.

"Yeah, but it's a piece of shit," he said idly. "It breaks all the time. Takes all my money."

"Then why do you have it?" I asked. "Just for appearances?"

He nodded. "I like this car," he said.

"I have my little orange Honda Civic," I said, "good on gas and practical." He started chuckling.

We were starting to learn about each other, but the night was a crash course in my family. First, I asked if we could stop at the hospital so I could see my dad. Mathew surprised me by not waiting outside but coming in to introduce himself. He was kind to my dad, respectful to him in his weakened state. I was impressed, but he still wasn't my type. Though admittedly I didn't have much to show for my type: these pretty-faced guys with a hint of danger.

At the Mardi Gras ball, Mathew followed me to our family's table. Slack was there with his current wife, plus my mom and my sister Selena.

"Oh, you *must* be Mr. Beyoncé's brother," Mathew said to Slack. "Y'all look so much alike. I'm here with your niece."

People started chuckling and I told him, "It's complicated. I'll tell you later."

But Mathew was undeterred, and started acting to everybody like he was my boyfriend. He was charming, handsome, and successful, and my family was all in. It was not lost on our neighbors that he'd parked a Mercedes outside. "Tenie's got a *good* boyfriend" was the talk of the party.

"He's a real hit," Selena told me as Mathew made the rounds, meeting Johnny and Ronnie and Skip too.

"You all can date him then," I said. "He's just not my type."

Selena took a puff on her cigarette, rolling the smoke along with her eyes. "We'll see."

That night we rode back to Houston together and Mathew dropped me where I was staying at my friend Pat's apartment. My bed was her couch, and she had a room upstairs. I was closest to the front door when someone started banging it after midnight.

"Who is it?"

It was Pat's boyfriend—he didn't like me much and it was mutual. He was a drug dealer, though she was always sugarcoating it as "He has a business." I opened the door to see him dripping in sweat, wearing a hoodie and sweatpants. It was so cold outside.

"What's going on?"

"I was jogging," he said. "Let me in." He didn't wait, then ran past me up the stairs to Pat's room. I went back to sleep, until I was awakened when they came down an hour or so later, making all kinds of noise as they kissed goodbye at the door. He left, but now I couldn't sleep, so I turned on the radio. Pat, who was all nerves, joined me on the couch.

There was a news bulletin that somebody got shot near the Astrodome right down the street from us. I looked right at Pat.

"That's where he was," she said, saying her boyfriend's name like it was the wildest coincidence.

"I know he did it."

"What?" She gasped. "Oh, they're not talking about him." Now she was sputtering, holding on to her belief in him. "He loves me but he said he's going away and he didn't tell me anything. He told me he has to go away."

"Girl! He's gon' come back and kill us! We gotta get outta here."

"He wouldn't kill *me*." Just like that. I thought, *Well, gee, she didn't mention* me, *did she?* This guy was on the run, and I wanted no part of this.

"I'm getting out of here," I said, already packing but suddenly trying to be polite. "Thank you for letting me stay here, Pat. I really do appreciate it."

I dragged my two suitcases to my car and drove to a payphone, going through my mental Rolodex for which girlfriend I knew who would have their own space to put me up for the night. For some reason, a little voice told me to call Mathew. I went over, explained everything to his widening eyes. I needed a couch for a few hours, and no funny business.

"This crazy stuff happens to me," I said. "I'm sorry."

"I understand," he said. He was so calm that I thought, *He actually does.* Mathew gave me his room, and he slept out on the couch.

The next morning, I realized two things: One, with no place to stay, I was moving back to Galveston earlier than planned. I called the bank where I worked, and they were very understanding. I had to go where I was needed, and my family needed me now.

And two: I really liked this guy.

For a year, Mathew and I dated across the distance of Houston and Galveston, more than an hour's drive. I found myself falling in love, our conversations never losing urgency or humor. We'd go out to clubs, and we shared an endless energy, dancing all night and becoming the couple that other people built their nights around seeing. There was tremendous passion between us, and I felt protected by him.

But I didn't see him as much as I wanted. The plan to stay with my parents only a few months went out the window early. I cared for them full time in Galveston as they got sicker and sicker, to a point that I was finally able to get them to agree to have a home health aide visit during the day so I could work. I got a job at Pennzoil, where Skip worked, and my parents were pretty stable for a while. My solace was riding the ferry, stepping on to let the water and the rocking movement soothe me. "This is our own boat," I remembered my mother telling us as children.

Just before New Year's, I went for a night walk with Johnny like we used to, meandering through Galveston and ending up on the beach. We looked out on the waves that we grew up playing in, and the waves that showed me how much I wanted to live when they almost took me.

We sat there in the sand, on the edge of the water, and also the edge of 1979. At twenty-eight, Johnny finally had a serious boyfriend: Peanut, as everyone called him. He was younger than Johnny and didn't have the family support Johnny had. Peanut's mom died when he was twelve or so, and he had lived with a mean aunt. His family had put him out all the time and now they didn't have much to do with him. Johnny had given Peanut a place to stay when he got thrown out again, and their friendship turned into love. People didn't perceive Peanut as gay when they met him—Johnny joked that he was "trade"—and I think his family put pressure on him to be straight, as if he could.

Johnny had found a partner in Peanut and was able to have his own life in Galveston while staying in the family. Meanwhile, I was resisting the undertow of my parents' needs and my siblings' expectations that I would always be the one to help our mom and dad.

"You know, I gotta live my own life," I confided to Johnny. "I'm gonna get married."

He sneered at my hand, "Okay well, that diamond must be small 'cause, uh . . ." He leaned in closer to look at my invisible ring and I lightly mushed my hand to his face. "Now where *is* that rock?"

"No, I mean he will propose soon enough."

"Lucy, you sure you want to?" Johnny asked.

"Yes," I said, realizing it was true. "Yes."

"And y'all gonna have a bunch of little brats?" Johnny laughed. "A bunch of crumb-snatchers runnin' around?" He joked, but Johnny was the only person who knew how important having kids was to me. I was never that girl who played with dolls. My mom got me a huge doll and I beheaded it to use as a baseball for me and my brothers. But Johnny had watched me watching his mother and mine. He knew.

"Yes," I said. "We'd be in Houston."

"He can't sell copiers in Galveston?" Johnny joked. *"Well."*

"I don't think so," I said. "He's getting into medical imaging."

We looked at each other and started laughing. "No, really," I said, and I explained X-rays and ultrasounds because I felt like I was already a partner in everything Mathew did.

"So, yeah, I'll be in Houston," I said. "And maybe you might think about it, too. You and Peanut. Because when I went to L.A. the one thing missing was you."

"Oh please, you were out there selling makeup with those Japanese girls," he said. "You had Tina Turner, okay? You missed your mama— that's what brought you home."

"And you!" I said, meaning it. "Houston needs you. You should see some of these looks on the street. They don't know what they're doing. They need you. *I* need you."

He rolled his eyes. "You need some sense," he said.

I pictured it anyway, a life with Mathew, Johnny, and those crumb-snatchers he joked about. I couldn't quite see their faces, but they were there with Johnny. I wanted to rush to them.

SHORTLY AFTER, I SAID YES TO MATHEW'S PROPOSAL. PENNZOIL was transferring me to Houston and when I told him I would look for a place, he said I should move in with him. "I don't do live-ins," I said.

"Then let's get married," he said.

"Is this a proposal?"

"Yes," he said. "I love you and I want to spend my life with you."

"Then, yes," I said. We went to the diamond district and got a ring for seven hundred fifty dollars, a diamond cluster that was the coolest thing. He bought a band that he never wore.

We planned a yearlong engagement with a wedding set for the next January. One afternoon that summer I was at his house, this beautiful duplex apartment with antiques. He'd gone out to play basketball with friends when the phone rang. I thought it might be him, but it was a bill collector. The guy asked me to take down a number, and I found a pen by the phone. I reached into a basket of paper to grab an envelope. I turned it over to see PAST DUE stamped on it. It seemed unlucky to write on that, so I grabbed another one—it read CANCELLATION NO-TICE. The *whole* basket was past-due bills.

He came back from basketball. "I wasn't being nosy," I started, "but you owe *everybody*! You're so in debt." This got a shrug and a smile, which surprised me. "Now, how do you have an oxblood leather brief-case with alligator trim *and* a past-due notice from Sears Roebuck? Who owes Sears?"

"Well, I bought the refrigerator from them."

"And JCPenney? I know that's not where you got those suits."

"The dining room set."

"You're just charging everything, aren't you?" I said. "I can't marry you."

"Look, when I was an intern, I was selling copiers like crazy," he said. "Now I'm promoted. Trust me, in six months I'm going to be out of debt. We'll get married and then six months after that, I'm going to buy us a house."

That became Mathew's mantra, and I rightly believed him. He always had a vision for the next thing, and he motivated me to think of practical ways to help make those dreams—our dreams—real.

I knew it was important to my parents that we have a church wedding and that we do it at Holy Rosary. Mathew and I would start Pre-Cana, Catholic marriage prep courses, at Holy Rosary, and I really liked the priest we met with, Father Saparito. He was a tall, good-looking, Italian priest—maybe a little flirtatious, but only enough that he seemed human and never holier than thou. I still had my reservations about the Church, but a church wedding was everything my parents wanted, so I would give it to them. Selena had been married at the courthouse and Flo had a garden wedding—my father was so excited to walk me down the aisle at Holy Rosary.

It was tradition that the bride's family pay for the wedding, but my parents could not, and I did not expect them to. "I want to buy you the most beautiful wedding dress instead," my mother said. She was too weak now to sew, but it was so important to her to be part of what I wore. I wanted it to be sexy, and our compromise was that it was low cut with plenty of lace at the top. I chose a little pillbox hat to pair with the veil because that's what was happening then. My mother talked me into growing my hair out, which I hadn't done for a long time, so for that year I simply wore braids.

Other brides were renting out big halls and blowing all this money on catering, but Mathew and I were saving up for that house he envisioned. So it would be a smaller wedding, and I wanted a party in Galveston, so everyone could come. My mother had a great idea a couple months out, which she called to tell me. "Tenie, this is what you can do," she said. "Every time you get a paycheck, why don't you buy a turkey to freeze and buy some of the stuff here and there on sale to start planning?"

It was exactly the soul food that I wanted to celebrate my family, a heavy, good meal with cornbread and baked mac 'n' cheese. When I asked my niece Linda, who hosted me in California, if she would make her potato salad, she offered to help cook everything. She and my sister Flo worked with the lady who ran the kitchen at Holy Rosary to prepare. We would host the reception at the ILA Hall, the longshoremen's gathering place where Johnny, Selena, and I had spent some of the best nights together at the Session.

And then it happened. The day before the wedding, my twenty-sixth birthday, my father had been running around driving people and doing too much. He leaned on a table, clutching his heart. He was rushed to John Sealy Hospital, where they told us he had suffered a minor heart attack.

We spent the night with him in the hospital, people periodically telling me to go home to get ready for my wedding. I had plans of getting my nails done, rolling my hair and getting it done perfect— I didn't care. I wanted to be with my daddy. Even more than my mother, my father had been looking forward to my wedding. Walking me down the aisle was going to be his big moment.

The next morning, I wanted to postpone the wedding, but my father was well enough to tell me not to. He wanted everything to go as planned, even without him. My mother asked me who would walk me down the aisle, and it simply hadn't occurred to me. Eyeing the tux we rented for my father, Mama said, "Let your brother walk you down the aisle. He's the same size."

"Skip?" I asked. "Skip is bigger—"

"No, Slack Jr."

"Mama, I don't know him that well," I said. And it was true. My mother's first son was fifty at that point, and I never formed the bond with Slack Jr. that I did with Selena. He didn't come around that much, and never went to church with us at Holy Rosary.

"Tenie, just do it," she said. I didn't realize how important that moment would be to her, the completed circle of her oldest son walking her youngest girl down the aisle. We wanted my dad there, but we could not have that. She took the remnant of that hope and made something lovely with it.

We had a beautiful reception at the ILA Hall, even while I thought about my dad the whole time. Flo and Linda offered to serve all that good food in chafing dishes, and my friend Carlos brought his band to perform. We danced the day away, this bride with her simple braids, two plaits my friend Sheila put into a French braid right before the ceremony, and a fast-dry manicure from Linda, who could not believe the state of my nails.

The day would not be complete without my dad, and Mathew and I were having such a nice time and I wanted him to be part of the day so badly, I got the idea that the whole wedding party should go visit him. He was all we were thinking about anyway, so we all left the ILA Hall and marched in our finery to the hospital.

It was night by then, and I got to see my dad on my wedding day. I hugged on him. Finally, he said, "Okay, you need to go."

Mathew and I planned to stay in Galveston that night, but he decided that we needed to drive to Houston that night, so we would be ready for our honeymoon flight to Las Vegas in the morning.

We lingered, saying our goodbyes to my family, and by the time we got back to our place in Houston, Mathew's whole family had beaten us there—parents, his sister, and endless cousins were all sleeping. We didn't have but two bedrooms, so they were sprawled out on the couch and the easy chair too.

Mathew and I slept on the hard tile of the kitchen floor. We chose the kitchen because it was so cold out—down to the forties—and I could open the stove to get us some heat. I found us a blanket to share. Our wedding night.

This is what marriage is, I thought. *You make do.*

Somehow, on the hard floor of our crowded house, we overslept. We rushed to the airport but still missed our flight to Vegas. "That's okay," I said. The next flight was in three hours.

There was no answer when I called my mom to check in on my dad. Then I tried Flo and got the same. Finally, Selena answered. "He had another heart attack," she said slowly. "It was when y'all were leaving. He's in intensive care, and Tenie, they don't think he's gonna make it."

Mathew raced me from the airport to the hospital. "Look," I said.

"Your parents are here and, you know, with intensive care I can only peek in every few hours. You go back and spend time with your parents." I wasn't married twenty-four hours and my impulse was still to go it alone. "I'll call you," I said.

My dad was hanging in. A bunch of us went to their house after to cook and keep our spirits up. The phone rang at eight o'clock and everybody jumped. But it was Mathew. Now *he* was crying because his godfather Reverend Walker had died. He had been Mathew's role model and mentor. His parents were flying to Alabama in the morning, and Mathew wanted to go with them.

I didn't see how I could leave considering my dad's state. Then on Wednesday, my father's doctors were hopeful he would live, but the heart attack had been so massive they were concerned about what life would look like for him. I wanted to stay with him, until my mother finally said, "Go be with your husband. You need to be there for him." I flew to Alabama the next morning to be with Mathew at Reverend Walker's funeral.

Right after the funeral, we came home to find out my *mom* also had a heart attack.

She was in intensive care, along with my dad, but they were hopeful she would make it. I stood there, watching them both with tubes and monitors showing their struggling hearts. Again, my impulse was to do this without my husband: I'd sent Mathew home so he could catch up on work and his accounts. It was what my parents, who worked all their lives, would have prioritized.

I went back to the waiting room. Johnny had gotten off work and joined me and Selena. Skip came in with Flo, who spoke the secret language of nurses and translated for us. We kids—who Mama nurtured into who we were, and who Daddy quietly provided for against every odd—now held hands to sit vigil over them.

We said the prayers our mother taught us.

WHEN MY PARENTS CAME HOME FROM THE HOSPITAL, THEY MOVED in with Selena, so for a time, I did too. Things had changed for good. It fell on me to pack up our childhood home, and I went out to the pecan tree one last time to think about all those stories my mother told me of love and sacrifice over generations.

Mathew's love for me extended to my family, and he never once made me feel guilty about not being there for him. One day at home, he saw how I was struggling trying to balance caring for my parents and working at Pennzoil. He sat me down. "Your parents need you," he said. "You don't have to work. Do it if you want, but don't do it for me. I'll take care of us. You don't worry about money."

It was that simple. I had girlfriends who kept separate bank accounts, not even knowing how much their husbands made. I always knew every penny that Mathew made because he put it in the bank and never set any restrictions on me to spend it. "What's mine is yours and what's yours is yours," he would joke, but we joked as equals. Mathew was brilliant and successful, but this feeling he gave me wasn't about the money. He could have made a fraction of what he did, and I would still feel protected.

All the times that I was coming and going, staying home with parents, he was so patient and never complained. Still, it was a hard way to start a marriage because my husband really didn't have a wife. When I talked to him about having to be "home," I meant Galveston and my life as a daughter. Living separately, I tried to bring him up in conversation with others to make things more real—referring to "my husband"—but it was like I was playing make-believe.

My parents wore out the revolving doors going in and out of that hospital, and once during visiting hours, I signed in as a nurse finished a call. She held up a finger because she wanted to tell me something about my mom or dad. While I waited, I idly looked at the name I had written again in the log: *Mrs. Tina Knowles.*

As my mother became sicker, what was essential to her in life became even more clear: her family and her faith. So it bothered me that she was not able to receive communion. In my mother's faith, being denied that sacrament meant that she would not meet God in heaven or spend an eternity with all the generations of her family in the afterlife. It was cruel.

I brought it up to Mathew and he did that little nod that always started a negotiation. He called Father Saparito, who had done our Pre-Cana courses, and arranged for me to get in a room with him to plead my case. Mathew booted me up beforehand, telling me nothing was impossible. If he wasn't a priest, Father Saparito would have been a fantastic actor in a Mafia movie. He had that kind of *Goodfellas* energy.

"Father, my mom is sick," I said. "I don't know how much time she has. It could be tomorrow, it could be months, but it's soon. God knows, not us, right?"

"Right," said Father Saparito.

"Her biggest wish in life is to receive communion. Is there any way?"

He paused a long time, considering. I started to talk to fill the air, but then he shared his thoughts on Jesus as the loving servant in the Bible. How Christ showed humanity in His divinity, but also showed something divine about being human, humbling Himself in His life here with us. Father Saparito arranged a meeting with the bishop to plead my mother's case. I liked being a team with Mathew in something so important, and the bishop was moved to give dispensation. My mother was finally free to receive the sacrament of communion.

When we went to the house to tell her the news, I made sure Mathew was there because he made it happen. She cried, tears of relief that she let fall. She took the hand of Mathew, who she and I would always love for giving her this moment. "You know," she said so clearly and with joy, "now I can die in peace."

I started to tell her no, but she talked over me. "Tenie," she said. "I need you to take care of Larry." My brilliant brother's eccentricities had grown, and he would disappear now for three or four days at a clip. "He's always going to need someone and that's you now. And Mathew, take care of her. Take care of my daughter."

Father Saparito came to give my mother communion at home. She tried to dress herself up for it, but I had to help her because she was so sick. But it was gratifying for us to see her do something for the sake of joy rather than only continued existence.

Some months later, on the last Monday of June 1980, I was in Houston, just back from Galveston. Mathew had made good on his promise, now out of debt and so successful he'd bought us a house. The move-in day was set for July 4th weekend. I was so proud of him and his ability to manifest.

Selena called. "You've got to come back," she said. "I think we've got to take Mama to the hospital."

Johnny and I took her to John Sealy Hospital, and she was so light and fragile over our arms as we helped her walk, practically carrying her. When she lost her balance and fell, we caught her, but not before my heart broke.

They admitted her, and a nurse told me that she was in her final hours. It is shocking that I was shocked, I know, but you have to understand that my mother had been counted out so many times and bounced back. Illness had lurked behind her my whole life, and together we'd kept it from taking her. I wasn't ready to give in.

And neither was she. When my mother did talk, it was not to us, but to someone we could not see. "God, just give me a little more time," she repeated over and over, all day and all night. "Lord, have mercy. Give me a little more *time*."

That was Tuesday, and she stayed relatively stable with the assistance of machines. We thought she was waiting for my brother Butch, because at the time he was stationed overseas in London. Flo kept telling me, trying to prepare me with the wisdom of a nurse, "Mama is hanging on for Butch to get here." But Butch got there Wednesday and while they had a meaningful reunion, my mom then whispered, "Larry." My unpredictable brother had disappeared again. Skip finally found Larry and brought him to the hospital that Thursday. He did not stay long, but when he left, I watched her exhale through the oxygen tubes. My brother was the missing piece, I told myself. *She just loves her some Larry.*

And then her litany started again: "Lord, give me a little more time. Please, God."

Later that Thursday afternoon, a doctor asked me to step outside her room. "I want you to understand something," he said. "Every breath your mother's taking is like her running up ten flights of stairs. She's really suffering—you've got to let go."

I didn't know how. Not when she was begging God for more time. I hadn't left her side, reclining one of the hospital chairs to turn it into a bed the size of a loveseat. If somebody came to visit, I would lie down on "my bed" to sleep briefly, then run to grab a coffee from the machine before they left. I was afraid that my mother would die without me there. I would fail her.

That Thursday night, as midnight turned to July 4th, Flo's mother-in-law, Miss Camilla, came in. "I'm gonna stay up here with you," she said, and I was so polite I didn't know how to tell her that I didn't want her up here. I only wanted to be with my mom. She sat on my "bed," and I was so annoyed with her taking up space. *I can't even lie down*, I thought. *She's getting on my nerves. Why she don't leave?*

Reluctantly, I made room for Miss Camilla on my chair, so much that I had to lean on my mother's bed. Then I put my head down, touching the crown of my head to her side so we could feel the sureness of each other.

Sleep took me. The deep, soul sleep of a baby in her mother's bed. The next thing I knew, Miss Camilla was waking me just before five a.m.

"She's gone," she said. I looked up, and my mother looked so peaceful. It was painful, but that same peace filled me.

"I came because your mama wouldn't have died with you looking at her," Miss Camilla told me. "It was time. I wanted to be here with her holding her hand through that transition. You had to let her go."

Flo came, and she agreed with her mother-in-law. "We kept saying she was waiting on Butch, then Larry. But Tenie, she was waiting on you. And you wouldn't go home."

My sister thought I wouldn't understand, and I *was* surprised that I was not as devastated as I thought I would be. Since I was a little kid, I remember my mom being sick, and never being truly at rest unless her kids were in arm's reach or when she lost herself in making something beautiful. I felt her now, free of all that. With us no matter where we went and arranging beautiful things for all of her beloved.

Now we were all living on our mother's prayers. Mama had joined her mother, and her mother's mother. She was now with all the mothers. The ones she could name under the pecan tree, and the ones who came before them. All of them watching over us.

I started the new year feeling nauseous. Not only in the morning, but all day. I missed my period and just knew.

The doctor confirmed what was already sure in my heart:

I was pregnant.

ACT TWO

A Mother

CHAPTER 15

BLOODLINE

August 1981

THERE WAS A magic to being pregnant. I know the joke is that every mother-to-be thinks she is the first person to ever bring life into the world, but this enchantment was more about connection. We—because me and my child were immediately "we"—were now part of this maternal line who defied all earthly things, whether they be time, space, or circumstance, to be together. I had even been on birth control when I got pregnant, and my plan with Mathew had been for us not to have a kid for a few years. Knowing my mom, she was probably praying so hard that I get pregnant, because I do believe she knew she was dying. I felt God had sent this baby to me after I lost her. This wasn't my mom coming back, but somebody to be that close to and love without any limitations.

The nausea of my first trimester left me in my second, and I was gaining weight in all the right places. I thought I was *so* fine. I resisted maternity wear, so I bought the designer dresses I loved in increasingly larger sizes. I liked Norma Kamali, ahead of the curve with her shoulder-padded jumpsuits, and Diane von Furstenberg's new shirt-dresses, a looser version of the wrap dresses she seemed to make just for me. To flatter my legs, I had the bottoms tapered until they were so pencil-skirt skinny that I had to take tiny steps to get anywhere.

Mathew and I held tight to the fun of being young. We kept up with our Friday happy hours at our favorite club in Houston, and I *dressed* for these nights. Even at eight months pregnant in August, I wore what I thought was beautiful and didn't care for the practical.

One Friday that became legendary in my family, I put on a long-sleeved black dress—crepe with a white Peter Pan collar, high-necked with a bow. I was big into hats that season and chose a black one with a wide brim and white band. The look said: pregnant fashion model.

I took my tiny steps into the club, "Fantastic Voyage" playing loud. The band Lakeside seemed to cheer me on, everyone dancing and singing, asking me to come along and ride. I spotted our friend George, a handsome doctor, sitting on a couch and made it my stutter-step mission to get there. Mathew got me situated there like he was parking a boat, then went off to work the room and run his mouth. George's good looks and career meant a beautiful girl quickly came to sit next to him. "It's kinda hot in here," I said to everyone and no one.

As I listened to them flirt, the air of the club seemed to become thinner and yet more oppressive. I fanned myself with my hand, and kept pulling at the white cuffs of my long sleeves to let some air in. I leaned back, then forward not to mess up my hat. I let out an exhale, then found I couldn't draw enough air back in.

"George," I said, "I think I'm about gettin' ready to pass out."

He absently put his fingers on the pulse of my wrist while he was talking to the woman. "You all right," he said, distracted and a little irritated. This girl was fine. "Your pulse is good."

"I'm . . . I'm so hot. I gotta get out of here," I said. I needed air. I got up, which was enough of a job, and looked for Mathew. I didn't see him, so I started my slow walk to the door, undoing the bow at my collar to open the clasp . . .

The next thing I knew I was outside, flat on the ground with my dress open all the way down to my stomach, my bra showing. Mathew and George were kneeling over me, fanning me with the hat they took off my head, revealing my hair all matted down in a bun. I started crying, not because I passed out, but because everyone was looking at me.

"Nobody's paying attention," Mathew said.

"Yeah, it's just us," said George, not as convincing a salesman as Mathew.

They got me to the car, and if I'd dared to look back, I'd see every face inside the club jammed into the big picture window to see my foolish self doing my little tiny step thing to the car, looking a mess. I know because my niece Linda—Selena's daughter, who I stayed with when I ran away to California years before—drove up to the house when we got home. She said exactly what I was thinking: "That's what you get," she said, laughing. "That's what you get for coming out, looking all fashionable, eleventy months pregnant, having on that stupid hat and hot dress."

That was it for Friday night happy hour. Even if I wanted to go back, I started to have heartburn bad in the last weeks leading up to my September due date. I couldn't even lie down. I had to sleep propped up, reading the books on parenting and babies I'd started collecting.

I was halfway through one of them late one night in the new house Mathew and I bought in Houston. Well, it was new to us, this beautiful old brick house on Rosedale in the Third Ward. It had the A-frame style of a church, and all those old houses had a carport with a pretty archway connecting it. The Third Ward is one of the oldest historical neighborhoods in Houston, originally white, but it has become a symbol of Black self-determination. After that first Juneteenth of 1865 in Galveston—when Texas became the last state to enforce the Emancipation Proclamation, at least on paper—formerly enslaved people traveled from the surrounding plantations of Texas and Louisiana to the Freedmen's Town of the Fourth Ward. As Black people moved nearby, white landowners started selling the devaluing property on the edge of Third Ward, and so Black families built their *own* homes there. The post–World War II "white flight" out of Third Ward and into the suburbs also left whole neighborhoods and big, beautiful homes for us to buy as prices went down. But by the 1980s, Black middle- and upper-class families were also beginning to leave the Third Ward for the suburbs. With Mathew's six-figure salary as one of Xerox's number-one sales reps in the country, that could be an option. But it was important to us that we plant our roots in the Third Ward.

Mathew walked in the bedroom, home from a dinner with clients. I tried to sit up, but it was impossible for me to get comfortable with my heartburn. "I'm never doing this again," I told Mathew. "After this baby, that's it."

I asked how the night had gone. He was so good at what he did, and I loved hearing his reports. I missed working, so I put that natural career interest into whatever deals or work dramas Mathew had going on. Our minds were both good at seeing the whole landscape and figuring out his best course of action. We were a good team, but our favorite subject was the baby on the way.

Mathew climbed onto the bed where I was propped, and he began serenading our baby in the womb, as he'd done so many times. We always sang a Smokey Robinson song together, "Here I Go Again." It's an anthem of blind love, going forward despite every sign of trouble. "Disregarding this just for you." It's Smokey with the Miracles, the lyrics drawn out in the harmonies that Mathew and I both heard as high schoolers in the singing group talent shows.

Maybe that's why we chose the song—nostalgia—or perhaps we were both acknowledging the field of red flags our child would be born into. There were already problems in our marriage that first year. Mathew had an ongoing struggle with fidelity, but the suspicions I had would get washed away by the fact that our love was stronger than a misstep. I could get past any kind of screwup because Mathew and I were so protective of each other on a soul-deep level. It was us against the world, taking on what life brought us.

Those responsibilities were very real, as my father needed me more than ever. After my mom died, my dad was diagnosed with lung cancer. He would come stay with us just about every weekend, showing up at the door unannounced, just like he used to with his family at Weeks Island. If he sensed a fragile time coming, he'd come right to me. On Fridays, my daddy would manage to show up just before I went to meet Mathew for happy hour, as I was doing the finishing touches of putting my earrings on. My whole body would tense from the weight of this caregiving expectation, but I couldn't show him. A couple of times, I was even supposed to go on a trip and couldn't go because he showed up to the house sick. He might stay a week, maybe two. Mathew never once complained.

On one of those visits, I told my dad my plan for the baby's name. If we had a boy, I wanted to name him Mathew. And for a daughter? "I was thinking about how I'm the last Beyoncé," I said. "I don't like the name getting lost. So I'm thinking about Beyoncé for a girl."

It was to honor him and the bloodline, I said, and I know it was also because I really missed being Tina Beyoncé as I got used to a quieter life as Tina Knowles. My daddy looked at me so long I thought he was touched by emotion. Then he scoffed. "This baby is gonna be real mad at you for naming them with a last name."

"Well, nobody'll know it's a last name but you," I said, falling right back into Tenie B's attitude. "Ain't nobody ever heard of Beyoncé, so this child will be original."

I didn't even tell him my idea for a middle name for a girl because I didn't want to hear his opinion at that point. When Mathew and I first got together, his roommate had a French ballerina girlfriend named Giselle. We went to see her perform in the ballet *Giselle,* which I learned was a coveted role for dancers because the title role only goes to those who have reached the pinnacle of technique *and* acting ability. I filed this beautiful, melodic name away in my mind, because if something is reinforced to me twice, I take it as a sign.

BY THE MORNING OF SEPTEMBER 4, I WAS REALLY READY TO HAVE this baby, though I had only finished decorating the nursery the day before. Not wanting to do pink or blue, I'd painted the room a pretty seafoam green by myself. That morning, I sat in the room, admiring the all-white furniture I'd picked, the white-eyelet bedding and curtains. I shifted to try to get comfortable in the chair—I still thought it was possible if I moved just right—and focused my eyes on the alphabet I put on the wall.

"I need to pack a bag," I said aloud, something I had been repeating for a week but never got to. There was always something else to do.

Mathew and I were set to host a party that night, our own Friday happy hour to kick off the Labor Day weekend for Xerox's Minorities United in the Southern Region. I didn't want to cancel it, because MUSR's mission mattered to us. Mathew was heavily involved in the program, which started in 1974 as a response to the discrimination Black executives faced after Xerox's affirmative action program drew them in. Now they sought out and promoted Black executives, doing what MUSR called a "Road Show" of career fairs at top colleges to invite Black talent to the company. MUSR brought in a number of Black women from around the country, and I was proud of these young professionals who were so sharp. Mathew would introduce these women to me, and I would mentor them as they got settled in Houston. It was a joy to see them succeed, and it reminded me of the brotherhood my father relied upon in the longshoremen's union, everyone sticking up for each other.

MUSR's goal was to show that diversity wasn't just necessary for appearances, but for a company's bottom line and future. I liked also that the group sent a message to Xerox corporate: These Black men and women were united, and you couldn't make them compete against each other for one management position like other companies did.

I was thinking about what I should wear for our MUSR happy hour when I felt a sharp pain. It passed and then, in a little while, I felt the same pain. At eleven o'clock that morning, I called my sister Flo.

"Yeah, that's labor," she said, her nurse voice matter-of-fact. "How far apart are the contractions?"

"Uh . . ." I could feel my big sister's eyeroll across the telephone wire. Of course, I didn't have it together to keep time. "Fifteen minutes?" That seemed right.

"Okay, Tenie, you got time, but start getting your stuff together. I know you didn't pack a bag."

By four o'clock I knew it was really happening. Mathew drove me to Park Plaza Hospital, his nerves starting up. He was so protective of me, but he was also very used to me not needing him. I was the strong one, and he could not stand me being in pain. At Park Plaza, he started doing too much, telling the nurses I needed painkillers. When they explained that contractions and pain were a normal part of childbirth, that answer wasn't good enough for Mathew. "Give her something *now*," he yelled. He was really getting on my nerves.

"People are gonna be showing up for the happy hour," I told Mathew. It was too late to cancel. "They're not gonna know what's going on." And then, as we got closer to five o'clock, I finally said, "Mathew, you should go. You can't let people down. I'll have them call you when it's time."

When Mathew left, I was surprised by the relief I felt. I was so distracted managing his feelings, and besides, in this vulnerable time, Mathew was no substitute for my mother. There was a moment when a nurse left the room to check on something, and I was alone. *My mom should be here to hold my hand,* I thought. *To greet this child and welcome them.*

I lay my left hand beside me and tried to imagine my mama's hand soft in mine, strong as it was when I was a child. When I felt nothing, the sadness was so huge I quickly backed away from it, shaking my head and placing my hand on my stomach. I labored alone. As I got closer to delivery, the nurses called Mathew so he could make it back in time.

Beyoncé Giselle Knowles was born at 9:04 in the evening, eight pounds, seven ounces. A new child in the Third Ward.

My siblings visited us in the hospital, and it was Larry who noticed it first: the way Beyoncé held each of the three middle fingers of her hands together, apart from her thumb and pinky.

"Oh my God," Larry said immediately. "That's *Mama.*" Our mother held her arthritic hands in that way, close like a pyramid with the middle finger on top. Beyoncé has always favored her, looking more like my mother than I do. Johnny came and held her, smiling at me. "Look at you, Lucy, you got yourself a little crumb-snatcher."

From the first night at home, Beyoncé was not an easy baby. She would wake up every two hours crying, and she wore me out. I bottle-fed her, because I didn't know about the benefits of breastfeeding, and that allowed Mathew to take turns in the night to feed her and soothe her. He brought me food, meals friends had cooked for me, but I know he wished he could do more. It would have been easier if I had a woman there.

Not simply a woman, my *mother*. My breasts got engorged, and the pain of the swelling was so excruciating that I didn't know what to do. I thought a warm shower would be soothing, but the water worked the opposite, and the swelling and pain intensified. I cried out; my first thought was to call my mother and ask what I was supposed to do.

The grief hit me so fast, caught me so unaware that I couldn't run away from it. There in the bathroom, I doubled over as the realization finally gripped my heart, this thing I had known rationally but not fully accepted: *My mom is not ever gonna be here for me to call.*

How was this a shock after thirteen months without her? I thought I had grieved, but my soul had not. Only days into motherhood, I fell into the depths of the loss, and all the future losses for me and my daughter—questions unanswered, prayers unheard, stories untold. Through my tears, I called Flo and asked her what to do about the engorgement. She told me I should be using cold compresses to get the swelling down. "The heat of the shower is too stimulating," she said, straight to the point. "You made it worse."

"Okay, Flo," I said, truly appreciative of her. I didn't know how to reach across the ten-year age difference, all the history of me frustrating my big sister, to ask how *she* felt the absence of our mother. I didn't realize at the time how young twenty-six had been for me to lose her.

I thanked Flo for the advice, but she wasn't my mama. Nobody is like your mom. She can see you at your most vulnerable moments, and she's not going to judge. There is no fear that she will stop loving you, and she has all the answers she spent years gathering for that very moment of passing them on to you. It's "mother's wit," a special knowing that helps you just figure it out. It would be so much easier if my mother was just here.

I didn't know anything about postpartum depression or the delayed grief of trauma, and I can't say which it was. My cousin Wanda had to come for a couple of days to help care for Beyoncé because I just could not function. Wanda was one of the first Black flight attendants for Delta, and she had cultivated such a certain grace to go with her natural kindness. There were two days of deep sorrow, and then I gave myself the job of getting better. "Listen," I said aloud to myself as I lay under the covers in my bed. "You got a baby to take care of." This was how I handled things then. All the way back from when I was a little kid, I would let myself have a good cry and then say to myself, "Okay, suck it up and keep it moving." That approach worked for me for a long time. I couldn't know how this only meant I stored the trauma in my body—stashed it in my mind and heart to lie in wait. *Keep it moving,* I said. So I moved.

Still, when it was three a.m. and Beyoncé would not stop crying, I kept thinking, *Oh my God, if my mama was here, she'd know what to do.* One night, I sat with my new baby as she wailed in her seafoam room, and I started to sing "Here I Go Again," the song Mathew and I sang all those times to my stomach. "Here I go again, walking into love," I sang, quiet, but strong.

Suddenly, she stopped crying. Beyoncé and I looked at each other as I sang. Right there, this song that had become all of ours was no longer only about the blindness love brings, but the courage love gives you. You could be scared, you could be overwhelmed, but you will keep going. Love is stronger than fear.

Holding my baby, singing to her, I vowed just that: I would not let fear dictate her destiny the way I felt my mother, despite her best intentions, had done to me. I could love my mother, call upon her strength in memory, and also learn from her what not to do.

Beyoncé fell asleep in my arms. It was the start of my own mother's wit, this new clarity that comes when the child that was crying in your arms turns quiet. The silence is astonishing. What seemed impossible minutes ago becomes real before you—because of you—and then there's this heavenly sense of peace. A feeling of accomplishment filled me as I held my newborn, an overwhelming mix of gratitude and exhaustion. I did the impossible. Didn't know how I would do it again, but I would. *You will keep doing the impossible every day, Tenie, because that is what mothers do.*

I would be the mother Beyoncé deserved. I'd been a young rebellious woman. I had a mouth on me and got into trouble a lot—my heart racing so far forward that my head was left to catch up. Never again. I'd found my purpose.

"I'm gonna do this right," I told myself. "If I screw everything else up in my life, I'm gonna do this right."

CHAPTER 16

JAZZ BABY

November 1981

AT TWO MONTHS old, Beyoncé was still waking up every two hours through the night. But we had found the remedy that soothed her: music. Nursery rhymes did not cut it; believe me I tried. When I was a little girl, my mother got me a little 45 record with nursery rhymes that I had memorized front to back. I tried my favorite, "Mary Had a Little Lamb," because I thought that's what babies were supposed to love. She cried louder to drown that out.

It was jazz that soothed her. We discovered that by accident, living our lives and playing the music we loved. We noticed that the baby always relaxed when her father or I would play Mathew's vinyl collection of contemporary jazz. I learned that when she was fussing or fighting sleep, it worked to fill the room with the complex melodies of Herbie Hancock's jazz fusion, hitting unpredictable but exactly right notes. Again and again, we played her "Street Life" off the Crusaders album with Randy Crawford, and then I bought the single of the version Ms. Crawford did on her own, the same song with a harder explosion of sound. She *loved* it.

But Beyoncé's favorite, maybe because Mathew and I were his biggest fans, was the spoken-word jazz of Gil Scott-Heron. Picture this infant swaddled in her princess crib, napping to "The Revolution Will Not Be Televised."

The jazz helped me get her to sleep, but she continued to wake up through the night. It was so draining, and eventually Mathew realized I needed a break. Later that fall, when Beyoncé was two and a half months old and he had to go to Padre Island on the Gulf of Mexico for a Xerox conference, he asked me to come along for the two days. "I think you would love the water," he said. "You're *so* tired. Just come with me so we can go to the beach and rest."

"I would have to take the baby," I said.

"No, that's the whole point," he said. "You need a break."

I called my sister Flo, and after some pleasantries, I announced, "I'm gonna let you keep my baby for a couple of days." I really thought I was giving her such an honor that I trusted her with the golden child.

Flo, always so dry, said, "What? You want to *let* me keep her?"

"Yeah, that's what I mean," not liking her tone. "I'm gonna let you keep her."

"Let me just give you a dose of reality, Tenie," Flo said, sure and certain. "Everybody in this family has a million kids. Your kid is not special. She is just another one."

I cut Flo off. "Ugh, that's okay. I don't *want* you to keep her."

I practically hung up on her, but I picked up that receiver right away to call Selena. My oldest sister would get it. "You know, I just called Flo," I said by way of greeting, "and did she get on my last nerve. I told her I was gonna let her keep Beyoncé and she said, 'Your baby ain't nothing special.'"

Selena chuckled. "Tenie," she said. "Understand that Flo has four kids and that you don't tell nobody that you're gonna let them keep your baby like it's such a big privilege."

"But it is."

"Tenie, this is your first baby," Selena said, practiced in breaking things down for people. "Everyone who has their first baby thinks their baby is the *first* baby, period. Girl, that baby is just a baby."

I called my cousin Wanda, who moved in for the two days while Mathew and I got away for some rest.

We had fun at Padre Island, and once again, the connection with Mathew was powerful. I found that we needed things like this to keep our relationship strong and remind ourselves that our desire to keep seeing the world together was greater than our individual faults.

On the beach, I took a piece of driftwood, drawing our names in the sand and including our new baby, *Mathew + Tina + Beyoncé*. I asked Mathew to take a picture of me with it, wanting to save the memory before it was washed away.

. . .

ONE AFTERNOON THE FOLLOWING SUMMER, JOHNNY SAT ACROSS from me on the couch. Beyoncé sat between us. She was nine or ten months, holding tight to the pretty blanket he'd made her—a shimmery silver that caught the light. I loved when my nephew visited, but I felt almost awkward around people who knew me before I was a mother. One of the strangest things about putting on new mother skin is how quickly parts of your old self shed away. At least in the beginning. Your vocabulary shrinks and suddenly all you know about is My Little Pony.

I'd run out of people to ask Johnny about in Galveston—all the queens he dressed and made up. But Beyoncé was putting on a show anyway. She put the blanket over her face, then pulled it off to look surprised to see us. "This baby playing," Johnny said.

I sang the line Stevie Wonder raps at the end of "Do I Do," which had become Beyoncé's favorite song, the one new song off the greatest hits compilation that she wanted on nonstop. "We just gon' play, and play, until it goes away." Every time Beyoncé heard that line, she would reach her arms up to be held up so she could "dance," headbanging like a rocker until you were afraid she was going to pop her neck.

"Chile, you're gonna knock yourself out dancing," Johnny told her. "You are just like your mama—no sense." He looked at me. "When's the last time you went out dancing?"

"Oh, gosh," I said, stalling, holding my baby up to let her deflect. "I'm here playing peekaboo." All these things I had loved—going to art shows, museums, dancing—I had stopped cold.

"Lucy . . ." he said, trailing off. "She sleepin' better?"

"Some."

"How about you?"

"I'm usually awake when she starts crying, or maybe I'm asleep and it just feels that way. Sometimes I think I'm sleepwalking."

"Just don't sleepwalk through your life, Tenie." Johnny had an expressway from his mind to his mouth. He'd always said what other people were thinking.

. . .

My father was enough of a responsibility for me to lose myself in. As we approached the summer of 1982 his health had already worsened to a point that he had to have a leg amputated. When he went for chemotherapy for his lung cancer, he only wanted me to take him. I got to know the other patients, and I would be devastated each time I realized another person had not come for treatment.

I now spent even more time back in Galveston. I had the baby with me, watching my daddy beat the odds going in and out of the hospital the same way my mother had done. The skinnier he got, the thicker his Creole accent became—the French and English melded into one. There was a white French resident at John Sealy Hospital who he loved, a doctor who could somewhat make him out. They had a special connection. "You know, your dad says everything backwards," the French doctor told me one day.

"What do you mean?" I asked.

"Like, instead of 'come here,' when he calls me over, he says to me, 'brought yourself *yeahr.*' It's already past tense—backwards." That was the Creole, and I was surprised this Frenchman could even understand him.

I spent the entire first week of August with Daddy at John Sealy, but my friend was getting married in Houston that Saturday. I had been gone from Mathew so long. *This will be good for us,* I thought.

I told my father I would be back Sunday morning. He never wanted to be a burden, so he usually said, "You go on, I'm go'n be fine." This time he didn't.

"Tenie, I heard the doctor say I'm dyin'."

"Who told you that?"

"I heard her. There were a bunch of them talkin' 'bout it."

"Daddy, they wouldn't have said that in front of you," I said, leaning in to smooth his hair.

"Yes, they did." He looked down. "They were talkin' 'bout it and they thought I wouldn't understand dem. But I did."

I found the resident and confronted her. "Did you guys say in front of my dad that he is . . . that he's dying?" She had a sweet face, and I watched fear first make it go white, and then shame flush the cheeks to scarlet.

"Well, he doesn't understand English?" she said as a question. This was a patient *she* could not understand, so she assumed that he wasn't capable of understanding *her*.

"He definitely understands you," I said.

"Well, I didn't say it," she said, looking away. I sensed she was lying, but I also wanted to believe my dad would be okay.

I went back to him to say goodbye for the weekend and try to convince him that he hadn't heard what he heard. "I'll be back Sunday morning and for sure you're coming home. You always come home."

"Okay, Tenie," he said.

"I love you," I said, kissing his cheek. "You ain't going nowhere."

He nodded but seemed so sad. It was only later that I realized my daddy, who had spent my life bobbing and weaving from affection, had let me smooth his hair and kiss his cheek.

The whole time in Houston, I kept thinking this wasn't worth leaving my daddy for. Sunday afternoon, Flo's husband tracked me down. My father had just died. Alone. He had told me, in so many words, that he needed me, and I had left him. I felt that wound until it became a scar.

It was Mathew, reading my daddy's obituary, who pointed out how extraordinary it was that Selena and Slack Jr. were listed as his daughter and son, with no indication about them being from my mother's previous marriage. It was so normal to me that I forgot how unexpected that might seem to other people. That a man could find simplicity in that complexity—they were his, just as they were Slack's. It would be a lesson I would return to again and again in my own life, mothering children born to other mothers. It's not taking someone's place, it's sharing that love, and all the burdens and joys that come with it.

Family isn't just about blood. It's who you show up for. I always tell people now that when their parents ask for them, *go to them*. "Brought yourself here," my father would tell me. And I still wish I had.

CHAPTER 17

IT GOES BY FAST

August 1984

M Y BABY GIRL was a month from three years old, and days with her stretched out like the days of my own childhood. There was so much to be done before noon. I'm not talking about the work of motherhood, but the discovery of it, which is harder to put into words. I would take Beyoncé on walks through gardens and explain nature to her as my mother did for me. Seeing roses like my mother grew, I'd stop to teach her what they needed to grow and feel like I understood the knowledge for the first time because I passed it on. We would go to the zoo to feed her favorite ducks, and everything felt new to me. At home, I'd watch her breathe in the smell of clean linen until I appreciated its beauty too. My baby girl would ask me to sing to her, and I leaned on the Isley Brothers, cooing the way my mama had sung to me. I'd thought my mother was the best singer in the world until I got a little older.

Motherhood was both the best and most important job of my life, and I was determined to do it well. Our home reflected that. I'd designed two stained-glass windows for the front of the house, both matching the pink and green of the rug I'd bought as an investment. Being my mother's daughter, I saw to every renovation myself.

I also glassed in the carport to turn the den into a little unofficial hair salon where I could do my friends' hair. I loved hairstyling, and my friends wanted me to open a salon. Even Johnny had been on me about getting my license and making it official. I couldn't imagine being away from Beyoncé, so going to beauty school just didn't seem to be an option.

An incident at the house on Rosedale made me see how fragile this existence could be. They used to have heaters in the walls of old houses like ours, and one night the one by Beyoncé's room caught fire. When the smoke detector blared, Mathew and I ran to her, and he called the fire department while I rushed her out of the house.

Standing out on our street, looking back at our home, I held my child and watched the flames reach a small spot on the roof. I could already hear the fire engines coming. I kept my daughter's face turned into me. "It's okay. We're okay," I told Beyoncé, but I was also saying it for myself.

The firefighters got there and put out the fire so quickly, and Mathew was already talking out the insurance process. We would stay in a hotel that night. We would renovate—another project for me.

That night in the hotel with my toddler, I kept thinking of my mother, holding her kids the night of the firebombing at Weeks Island. She watched her world burn, with no one coming to her rescue.

I knew what protected us: money. Pure and simple. But none of it was mine. What kept me and my daughter safe depended on a marriage I did not have faith in lasting. A man I was not sure of. We were so good half the time, a cosmic kind of love that made everything worth it, but then Mathew's erratic behavior would take hold. I was caught in this dance with him, each doing the same steps over and over: He would cheat or act up, and I would say I'd had enough. He would beg for forgiveness, crying and promising to get better. For a time, things would be wonderful, so consistent and steady that I would think everything was behind us, and then, boom, the same thing would happen again. But this is what married people did, I told myself. My parents stayed together through everything.

If I left him, what then? I'd been out of the workforce since I had the baby. *You cannot just run away this time,* I told myself. *You are not some little Badass Tenie B who can just do whatever she wants. You are a mother.*

So I had to make it work. I focused on the sureness of my child, as I accepted problems in my marriage. I allowed them to pass by me like time, one year upon the next, until suddenly Beyoncé was four and I was thirty-one.

It goes by fast, they'd warned me.

. . .

THEY LOVED SMOKE BREAKS AT THE BEAUTY SCHOOL. THE STUDENTS would file out like a fire drill no matter how cold it was in Houston, some not even to smoke, but just to keep chatting about whatever they were talking about the last smoke break. At thirty-one, I was much older than everybody at Franklin Beauty School, which was itself the oldest cosmetology school in the South. Made official in 1915, the school's founder Madame N. A. Franklin had also been one of the first purveyors of Black beauty products in Texas, following the incredible success of Madam C. J. Walker. Now, I found myself giving life advice to these young women at Franklin during their smoke breaks.

That day, though, I wanted to slip away quick to check on Beyoncé. This was her first week at the little school for toddlers at the Wheeler Avenue Baptist Church, right down the street from the beauty school. *I'll just go peek,* I told myself.

I smiled as I heard the sounds of kids in the playground, and as loud as they were, I still softened the sound of my heels against the pavement. As I got closer, I tried to pick her out of all the boys and girls running around, playing tag and huddling up. Where was she?

Then I saw her. It was the saddest sight: Beyoncé was alone at the swing set, pushing an empty swing.

A little girl stopped by me, pausing to catch her breath from running with her friends. I said, "You know, I think that girl over there is looking for someone to play with. She'd push you on the swing."

She looked over quick, then right at me with the clarity that pre-schoolers have. "I don't like her."

"Well, her name's Beyoncé and she's really nice," I said.

"No one likes her," said the girl. Just like that.

My sweet four-year-old kept pushing the empty swing, and I hurried my steps to get to her. "Beyoncé," I said. She blinked at me, coming out of some spell, then stopped pushing the swing. She put her hands behind her back in embarrassment.

"Mama" was all she said.

"I know," I said, reaching for her hand. I withdrew from beauty school that same day. We were not ready for this.

Later that day, I asked if it had been an imaginary friend in the swing. No, Beyoncé explained. It was just something to do while she sang to herself in her head. Nobody liked her, she stated, just as matter-of-fact as that girl. I thought it was because she was too shy, and I didn't understand that it was discernment that kept her quiet in new spaces. I wrestled with this: How could I help this child, who at home was this huge personality always singing and joking, stop hiding her light from the world?

MONTHS LATER, MY FRIEND CHERYL CREUZOT WAS OVER WITH her two-week-old baby, Coline. I'd offered to do Cheryl's hair, remembering those first weeks of new motherhood when you just want to feel like yourself again. She was a financial planner on maternity leave, and she brought her CEO-in-training efficiency to making every minute of that time count.

We were with our girls in my bootleg hair salon I'd built in the den. Beyoncé couldn't wait to hold Coline. My daughter had been asking me and asking me for a baby brother or sister, but my first pregnancy had been so hard on me at the end that I was keeping my vow not to do it again. As I worked on Cheryl's hair, though, I looked over at Beyoncé holding the baby and the sweet way she worried over her neck. Here I was constantly telling my daughter she could be anything she wanted, and what she wanted most of all was to be a big sister.

"I wish you'd open a salon," Cheryl said when I was almost done, curling each curl and stacking her asymmetrical bob really high to give it a lot of volume. "You really could, Tina."

Cheryl liked her regular hair salon, but she would be in there five or six hours for one appointment, double booked while the people working there gossiped or ran over time. Professionals like Cheryl couldn't set aside all those unpredictable hours in a day.

Beyoncé interrupted us. She wanted to show Coline one of her dolls in her room. "You go get it," I said, "I'll hold her till you get back." I took Coline in my arms so Cheryl could keep relaxing. I breathed in the baby's scent; she smelled so good. Something shifted in me.

Beyoncé came back and looked at me holding the baby. She smiled at us, hopeful.

Oh shoot, I thought. *I think I'm gonna do this.*

That October, Mathew and I headed on a three-week trip starting in Turkey, then Egypt, followed by a trip down the Nile River, and then back up to Greece and Italy. Another vacation package that my husband earned as a bonus at work. Wanda would look after Beyoncé, along with Johnny checking in. I'd let him in on my secret: Mathew and I had a plan, and I'd been off the pill for three months. "I'm getting pregnant on this trip," I told Johnny. "You watch, I'm going to have a boy. Another Mathew."

"We'll see," said Johnny.

"*You'll* see," I said.

And sailing down the Nile Mathew and I fell back into our rhythm as we shut out all the distractions. The cruise director asked me if I would dress as Cleopatra for their gala night, with Mathew playing my Mark Antony. He said they pick one couple on every trip.

"Oh, no," I said. "I don't think so."

"But you *are* Cleopatra," the man said, excited. "You have to do it." He showed me the wig, which was beautiful, and the gown, which was not.

"Okay," I said, "but I'm gonna get my own outfit." I wanted to be a sexy Cleopatra. At the next port, I bought a gold rhinestone dress, and the crew had someone do my makeup. Mathew had a costume that showed off his body, his tall frame in the barely-there red tunic of Rome.

We laughed so much on that trip—sneaking off the boat to do our own excursion to a Nubian village. This was the new home of Black people who were forced by the Egyptian government in the early 1960s to leave the southern border of Egypt and Sudan—their ancestral home for thousands of years of culture and progress. We had a lovely meaningful day in the village, and I ended up giving all my bracelets away to little kids I met. Then our tour left for Greece, where we accidentally visited a nude beach on Mykonos, and the people thought we were crazy voyeurs for staying clothed, facedown on our blanket to avoid looking at anyone. Even in Italy, where we finally got the dysentery that had plagued the ship, we were at least bonded in our suffering.

But when we got home, Mathew had a black Jaguar with a white interior waiting for us in our driveway. He'd bought it without asking me. "What is that?" I asked him.

"I wanted to surprise you," he said.

He couldn't have picked a more impractical car for a person with a four-year-old who was trying for another. He told me it was perfect for us, but it was a perfect choice for *him*. Someone without impulse control. Who was he trying to impress, anyway? I came crashing down from my vacation high. So much for those nights over Egypt.

But then I, the Queen of the Nile, was pregnant, just like I said I would be. I'd had a couple of weeks of nausea, then confirmed it at the doctor's. My due date for this second blessing was June 14, and I realized the baby was conceived on the Nile. Mathew agreed this was a boy. I wanted to name him Mathew Niles to honor the trip of a lifetime and the latest time we were truly happy.

The marriage was deteriorating faster than I could possibly find ways or even reasons to make it work—even with the pregnancy. Mathew's infidelity became so out there for all to see that I could not possibly stay in the marriage. I had gotten used to these extremes—incredibly joyous half the time as we shared life's adventure, then being disgusted and heartsick over how brazen his cheating could get. He was a wonderful father, but he had issues that did not make for a good husband then.

There was a night, early in the pregnancy, when I'd had enough. I can't even remember the specifics of what Mathew did, but I remember the miserable, suffocating feeling that seized me.

Standing behind Beyoncé as she brushed preparing for bed, I caught my reflection. My chin was raised, my hand up by my throat. And I remembered where I'd felt this claustrophobic before: anytime I was about to run out of Galveston. Every time I needed to escape to save myself. I had to leave Mathew.

In Beyoncé's room, I played the jazz she loved to sleep to. As my baby climbed into her bed, I sat beside it. I stroked her back, grounding myself in something real and present. I was afraid if I spoke, this panic attack might consume me, so each pass across her pajamaed back was a silent "I love you. I love you. I love you." The music was Miles Davis, side two of *Kind of Blue,* and in the glow of her night-light, my eyes fell on the passage on the back of the record, all about improvisation. It said Miles went into the studio with basically a sketch of a song—he trusted the spontaneity, his and the group's. Overthinking would kill it.

I needed to improvise. I had been asking myself, "What have I done?" I needed to be asking, "What do I do *now*?" I'd been out of the job market for four years, and who was going to hire me pregnant? I

had put myself in a position where I was totally dependent on someone, and I never wanted to be in this position again. Not a husband,
and surely not a boss.

You'll have to be your own boss. This thought sprang up so clear in
my mind that I tried to remember how it got there. Was it Johnny? Or
Cheryl? Each had told me what I knew: I should open a hair salon.

Beyoncé had closed her eyes, her face softening as she teetered on
the edge of sleep. My codependency with my daughter was holding us
back. I used her too long as an excuse to stay in a marriage and on a
track that was not healthy. Maybe I thought a second baby would fix
things, but now this new life growing inside me inspired me to move.

In the low light of my child's seafoam green room, as Miles's trum-
pet climbed higher and higher, I started to plan an escape.

CHAPTER 18

ORDER MY STEPS

March 1986

I NEEDED TEN THOUSAND dollars to start with.

I had gone over my business plan again and again, my proposal to create a hair salon that would cater to professional women. I was inspired by all the time my friend Cheryl and I had wasted in salons, and I wanted to treat my clientele and their time as valuable. Get them in and out and have an establishment that banned gossip and uplifted women. People forget that women could not open our own credit cards until 1974. A little over ten years in, and we were lawyers, doctors, and financial planners like Cheryl. As women rose in society, Black women were constantly scrutinized and held to higher standards—I wanted them to have a place where they could relax and have all the extra pampering they deserved. I envisioned a salon that would be a place for networking, so if someone on the come-up had to save up a little to be there, the price would be an investment in themselves and their ambitious goals.

My baby was due in June, and I saw that as a deadline to really start my new life without Mathew. I'd already knuckled down and taken the cosmetology boards, and at thirty-two was probably the oldest person in that room. But I passed. Now I had to find a space to make mine and be ready to open in the fall, just after Beyoncé started kindergarten.

Mathew was supportive of the idea when I presented my plan and asked him for the initial investment. I could have paid that ten thousand myself, because even though I hadn't worked for five years, my mom always taught me to put a little something away for when a hurricane hit. As I'd balanced the checkbook and paid our bills, I stashed some money for myself. But I knew I was going to need that money in my new life, so I was going to get his money to fund the escape route.

When Mathew urged me to take out a small-business loan, I knew the paperwork would just entangle us further. "No," I said. "I don't want to be in debt. I want to make money right away."

Now I had to find a place. I took Beyoncé around with me to look at the address the realtor gave me on Montrose Boulevard in Houston. The place was in the Museum District, a cool artsy area that was heavily populated by gay men in the eighties. A neighborhood my clients could visit to feed their spirits going to antique shops, quaint restaurants, and art galleries.

We pulled up to the building, a cute tan-brick two-story with black trim built in 1925. The building had a little restaurant to one side, and a florist on the other, just as I envisioned. There was decking out front, almost like a stage framed by a black filigreed gate and surrounding trees. I took Beyoncé by the hand and walked up to our future. The realtor was there, and as we walked in Beyoncé started to hide a little behind me.

It was a shell of a space upstairs to the left; maybe it had been an apartment because there was a kitchen area. It would be tight with my plans for three stations, but the place had great light with a big window in the front. It just needed some love. I looked at the space with Agnes's eyes, examining everything for its potential. I said my thoughts as they came, and if a building could nod as I talked, this one did: "I want a black and white tile floor, the reception here. . . . Lots of art . . ." I didn't realize I was talking out loud, and Beyoncé was staring at me. I smiled, and she smiled back.

"What are you gonna call the shop?" the realtor asked, trying to get me to commit. He didn't need to.

"Headliners," I said.

THE MONTHS LEADING UP TO MY BABY'S JUNE DUE DATE WERE A whirlwind of finding used beauty shop equipment to get Headliners ready. I went to a flooring place and asked them to teach me how to lay tile if I bought it from them. They probably thought I was crazy, but there I was, pregnant and sitting on the floor with Mathew to put the black and white tile in just so.

I'd bought a bedroom set for my home that had a huge black lacquer headboard with shelving. When it arrived, I thought, *You know what, I'm gonna turn this into my station at the salon.* I had it moved to the shop on Montrose and set it up with slick countertops. As I worked, I listened to Sade's *Diamond Life* and my Angie Bofill and Phyllis Hyman tapes on the stereo. I about wore them out.

It was all coming together. I would have the baby, and then prep for a grand opening in October. And then what? Leave Mathew? Be left? I wasn't sure. There was a woman, a sort of recurring character in his misadventures, and I had my suspicions that they were having an affair. I needed to be prepared to provide for Beyoncé and the baby.

The baby's Friday due date came and went. *Now I'll have it on a weekend,* I thought, worrying I'd end up with some random doctor. Then the weekend passed, and each day was an eternity—all the way to the *next* Friday. Beyoncé could not wait to be a sister and kept staring at my huge stomach.

"C'mon baby!" she said. "Come on out!"

Mathew told Beyoncé the doctor had said that if I walked a lot, it might get the baby moving.

"Okay, then," she said, going to the door to put on her shoes.

Do you know we marched for an hour? All over the neighborhood in the Texas sun, Mathew and me with Beyoncé leading us. She made up songs to keep us in rhythm, then switched it up with the Jackson 5 and then New Edition's "Cool It Now."

"Anything?" she asked me at a corner.

"No, Snoogums," I said. "This baby has its own mind."

As I fanned my face, Beyoncé whispered to my belly, "I just want to meet you."

When we got back inside, Mathew and I called the doctor before he left for the day. "If I don't have this baby by Monday," I said, "I'm coming up there, and y'all gonna take this baby."

"We don't have room for you on Monday," he said.

"Well, you can do it in the bathroom, I don't even care."

Maybe he thought I was kidding. When the baby didn't come

Saturday or Sunday, I just showed up Monday morning. The baby was ten pounds, so they agreed to induce.

"We're gonna have to find a slot for you," the receptionist said.

"I'll wait," I said, patting my stomach as I tried to take a breath. "Where'm I going?"

We sat in the lobby and a nice lady asked when I was due. "As soon as possible," I said.

"Are you thinking boy or girl?" she asked.

"Boy," I said. "I felt okay during this pregnancy. And I just kinda know."

"You never know," she said.

Hmm, I thought. I didn't have a backup name if we had another girl. I looked at my bag, which had a book of French baby names on top. I bought it for Cheryl when I was in Paris for one of Mathew's trips. She gave it back to me after I told her I was pregnant. "I don't need it," I'd said. "I just know it's gonna be Mathew Niles."

"Take it anyway," she'd said. Cheryl was always sensible. I leafed through it and saw the name I'd seen so long ago when I first checked out the book in Paris.

Solange. I said it aloud, liking how musical it sounded. *Even if,* I thought, *it's not gonna be a girl.*

But what about a middle name? I put the book down. On the slim chance it *was* a girl, I wasn't sure I wanted a double-Frenchy name. I scanned the room and saw a collection of medical books on a shelf. One was *The Psychology of the Child* by Jean Piaget, a Swiss psychologist.

"Piaget," I said aloud. Maybe. I picked up the June *Vogue* I'd brought with Shari Belafonte on the cover and turned through the pages and pages of ads up front. On page seventeen, a hand with nails like mine held a beautiful gold watch. "Piaget," it read. "Created like no other watch in the world."

I like to think I listen when God tells me something once, but twice? That's Him trying to tell me something important. *Solange Piaget,* I thought to myself. *Too bad it's not gonna be a girl, 'cause that's really nice.*

Finally, they told me they had a spot for me and would induce me. I was ready for another all-day labor like the first one, going through all that suffering. But this second time? I had a baby in an hour and a half.

To our everlasting joy, it was a girl. And I could use that beautiful name: Solange Piaget Knowles.

THIS WAS A TIME WHEN THEY DIDN'T RUSH NEW MOTHERS OUT OF the hospital with their babies, and Solange and I were there at Texas Women's Hospital three days. The night before we were set to be discharged, Mathew told me he would be going to an MUSR conference in Atlanta.

"You're gonna leave the day that I'm coming home," I said flatly, hoping he would realize how crazy this was. "With a new baby."

"I can't miss this conference" was all he said.

Then he casually told me he would take me to my niece Linda's house.

I suspected that a woman was involved, and that Mathew had a plan to meet her in Atlanta. We had a huge blowout at the hospital, but he wouldn't budge. He was going to Atlanta. Sure enough, the next day he dropped me, Beyoncé, and our newborn off at Linda's, his suitcase in the trunk so he could head right to the airport and catch his flight. When he practically ran out of the house to his getaway car, I said to myself, *Okay, I'm done.* It was time to move up the plan to leave him.

We stayed at Linda's a few days while Mathew was away. It was kind of her to take us in, but I didn't want to be there. I didn't want to go home either. Before Mathew arrived home, I called my friend Marlene. "I can't stay there," I told her. Meaning my home, this place I loved. Now home was "there." I was already mentally leaving it. Let Mathew have it. Marlene was a nurse, married to a doctor, and they had three bedrooms and a dog. "Stay with us," she said. "At least until you figure out what you want to do."

Mathew returned home to an empty house. He called around looking for me, and when he finally found me at Marlene's, I held Solange tighter and refused to speak to him. Beyoncé had no idea, ricocheting through all the feelings of becoming a big sister at five.

There was just one flaw in the plan: the dog. Marlene and James were concerned about security, so they'd gotten this Rottweiler they named Killer. One hundred pounds or more of mean, midnight black muscle and a dark khaki muzzle. While I was pregnant, Marlene had been on me to come over so I could meet the dog with the trainer. "He has to know your smell so he doesn't attack you when you stop by."

"Uh yeah, no," I had said. "I'm pregnant, I'm not coming over to meet a killer dog." So we never had the meeting with the trainer before we moved in. But once we got there, I eased into an okay relationship with Killer. For about two weeks, as I avoided Mathew's calls, we all got to know each other. Marlene and James kept Killer in a glassed-in den next to the kitchen during the day and then at night, Killer stayed upstairs in their bedroom, behind a heavy door that would protect us.

But one night, while the girls slept upstairs, James took the dog for a walk. Marlene and I played cards, sitting on the floor in their bedroom. When Killer came home, he charged up the stairs to go to their room and when he saw me there with Marlene, he snapped, foaming at the mouth and growling as loud as a freight train.

Killer circled Marlene and me, baring his teeth until we both started crying, begging James to get the dog. Finally, in a strong, deep voice, he commanded the dog to sit. It snapped the Rottweiler out of whatever spell he was in. We later realized that Marlene and I had shared her perfume, the way girlfriends do, and it had confused him on whether to lick me or attack me.

I called Linda. "We might have to come back over there 'cause this dog could have killed me," I said. We made a plan to return, but we would have to spend one more night there first. Killer would spend the rest of our stay in James and Marlene's bedroom.

Of all the times, Mathew called again, begging me to come home. I was so angry for what he put us through and annoyed with myself for having escaped a lousy marriage to almost get killed. I felt I had no choice but to go back and reclaim our home—but only under one condition.

I gave Mathew an ultimatum that if we did not get intensive counseling, our marriage would be over. It was the only way I would go back to the house—and to him.

ONCE MATHEW AND I GOT COUNSELING, OUR FAMILY HAD THE feeling of a fresh start. Beyoncé was our Snoogums, and now Solange was our Punkin', all three of us doting on her. Mathew and I sang to the girls at home, the two of us harmonizing on Peaches & Herb's "Reunited" and Marvin Gaye and Tammi Terrell's "You're All I Need to Get By."

Even as a baby, Solange responded to words the way Beyoncé loved music. Beyoncé had never cared about me reading to her, but Solange was captivated early by books. Mathew and I read to her constantly, and even early on she would pick favorites. The book that made her happiest was one that Mathew bought special for her, a fable about a tree on an island that didn't stand as strong as the other trees, so it initially didn't know how special it was. But there was a storm coming, and the villagers needed to leave the island. And the wood of the tree, the kind that didn't seem so strong, turned out to be the kind of wood needed to build a boat. The tree, small but still mighty, saved everyone.

I found the old 45 record of nursery rhymes that my mother gave me as a child. Solange responded to the repetition and storytelling of Mother Goose in songs about Jack and Jill going up that hill, Mary's little lamb, and "Row, Row, Row Your Boat." Beyoncé would hold her baby sister as I sang, joining in when she wanted.

I was always so in love with these moments with my daughters that it was only later that I realized Beyoncé was starting to harmonize.

As I prepped in these last months leading up to the October opening of Headliners, Selena's youngest, Denise, came to live with me. She brought along her daughter Ebony, who was a little under six months older than Beyoncé. My niece Denise was one of my favorite people—level-headed and funny. But she'd had Ebony at seventeen and she was still young herself, needing a place to stay while she got her bearings on adulthood. I was happy to give her one.

Before she moved in, I asked her if she would like to be the receptionist at Headliners. I wanted to start staffing up, so I had already asked another young woman, Ada, if she would work for me, encouraging her to go to beauty school on the side. That was part of my aim with Headliners: to not just serve the client but set the staff up for success too.

Beyoncé was getting ready for kindergarten at St. Mary of the Purification Catholic School, so we offered to pay for Ebony to go there too. The two got along great, and my shy girl would have a built-in

1 Odilia Broussard Derouen

Eugene Gustave Derouen *2*

My maternal grandparents

& great-grandmother

3 Célestine Joséphine Lacy

My paternal grandparents

Amelie Oliver Boyancé, Alexandre Boyancé *4*

Agnes Buyince   5

Agnes Buyince   6

Mama and Daddy — the early days

4   Lumis Buyince

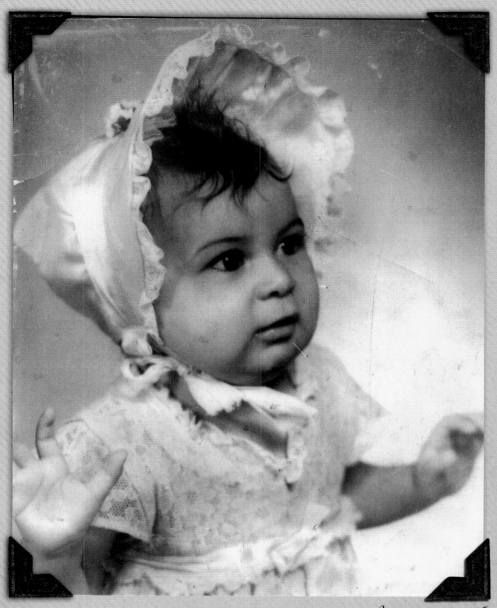

Baby Celestine in the bonnet Mama made

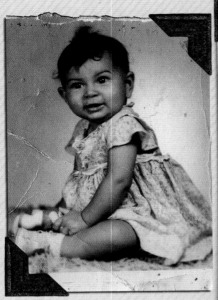

Larry, Skip, Tommie, and Ronnie, c. 1960

Larry, Butch, Skip, and Florence, c. 1960

Celestine Beyince

Johnny and "Lucy": best friends for life

13

14

Butch, c. 1971   15

Flo, c. 1960   16

Looking up to my big
sisters and brothers . . .

Mervin,
c. 1949

17

18   Skip, c. 1967

Selena, c. 1954   19

Larry, c. 1966   20

Tina, Gail, Polly, c. 1969

The Vettones rehearsal:
We just knew we could sing!

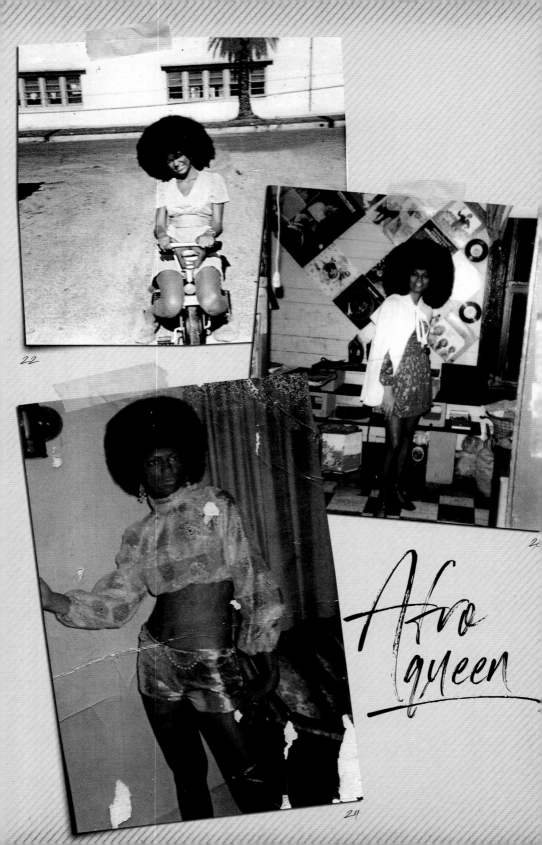

22

2c

Afro
queen

24

25

The day I got locked up by that Galveston cop

Tina and Denise, c. 1970

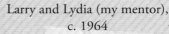

26

27

Elouise and Tina, c. 1967   28

*We were rich in smiles
back then. . . .*

29   Tina, c. 1972

30

31

32

Forever a
beach goddess

33

Mama always said,
"Pretty is as pretty does."

34

35

Always been about style

Mama Lou Helen and Mama Agnes

35

Mr. & Mrs. Knowles

and

our beloved Matriarchs

39

Wedding day,
1/5/80

40

41

7 mont preg bfyt

42

43

Pregnant with our future . . .

friend for the first day. St. Mary's was one of the best schools around and had a large Black population, but I was very anxious about it being a Catholic school because the Holy Rosary witches still haunted me.

When I went over there, I got a Louisiana kind of vibe—warm and family-oriented—and they didn't have any nuns. I met with the principal, Miss Rose Ellis, who had just started as the first lay principal of the school, which would eventually be recognized as the first African American Montessori school in all of Texas. Best of all, it was a two-minute drive from our house on Rosedale. I was already thinking like a mom with a work commute.

And Ebony had me rethinking how I had been mothering, or at least showing me there was more than one way to have a great kid. Denise had worked all the time, so she made an effort to train Ebony to do things herself. Neither of us judged each other's parenting, we just took advantage of the great opportunity to observe each other and see what worked.

When Denise moved in, she had this little step stool that she put in the kitchen. I didn't think anything of it, until I made lunch for the girls that first day. When Ebony was done, she picked up her plate, got up on that step stool, and put her plate in the sink to rinse it out.

Beyoncé gave me a look of *What is she doing?* and I looked right back at her thinking, *This girl has never picked up a plate in her life.* Ebony's independence revealed the kind of habits we had fallen into, just doing what was easy. Beyoncé was close to five, and when she got ready in the morning, she literally just stood with her hands out like a princess, waiting for me to take off her pajamas and put on the day's outfit. Meanwhile, we watched Ebony lay out her school uniform by her shoes. I'm looking at her and I'm looking at Beyoncé like, *This girl don't do nothing!*

Suddenly Beyoncé started trying to keep up with Ebony—doing things for herself and being proud of it too. The six-month age difference would show up, and I taught Ebony to be patient with Beyoncé, and Beyoncé to be patient with herself. When kindergarten started, my daughter was just turning five and had no interest in Ebony's diligence about schoolwork. If you asked Beyoncé what happened at school, she'd look at you like, "It was boring the first time, let's not redo it," while Ebony would tell you every shape and letter they learned. From the beginning, Beyoncé was always leaving her homework at home, and there would be Ebony with her little pencil at the ready. The teacher noted this and would go out of her way to praise Ebony, but only in the context of pointing out Beyoncé's shortcomings.

The teacher's constant comparisons made me anxious. If the girls were pitted against each other and made to compete, they would miss out on the gifts each had to offer. Ebony modeled responsibility, and Beyoncé showed her that she could also be fearless and have fun. That age—five years old, what I was in those early days at Holy Rosary—is such a formative time. I didn't want their personalities to be shaped or stifled by external pressures.

I leaned in to what I needed to hear as a kid. "This is just the start of great things for you," I told each girl. "Whatever you set your mind to, you will achieve."

IT WAS HARDER TO TAKE MY OWN ADVICE AS WE GOT CLOSER TO A month out from the start date of Headliners. I began to panic as I faced what many mothers do: How do you divide yourself to be in two places at once? You can't.

The phone sat across the room and I looked at it, knowing I just had to pick it up and make the call. I dialed the number to Mathew's mother, Miss Lou Helen Knowles, in Alabama. "I need your help," I said, "because I have to open a business." I asked her to keep Solange for a month, just while I got Headliners started. Two weeks before opening, and the two weeks after. I could work around Beyoncé's school schedule, but not a baby's. It was so hard, bringing Solange to her grandmother and leaving her there. I had breastfed Solange those months, and now had to switch to bottles for Miss Lou Helen.

Mathew's mother was a stern, strong woman who would really soften on her grandchildren. Beyoncé would go around there and she would melt, and the same was now true for baby Solange. Miss Knowles had a life of service, going to school with Coretta Scott King, then marching for civil rights. When I met her, she was taking in foster children in need. I was there once when she got a call from a new social worker making a placement. "Hi, Helen," the young white woman said when she answered.

"Now, honey, what did you say your name was?" And to Miss So and So, she said softly, "My name is Miss Knowles and I'm gonna hang up on you now and you're gonna call back and address me right." As she returned the receiver to the cradle, she said to me, "I don't take that off them. She thinks she's gonna call me Helen and she's a young woman?"

"You're my hero," I said as the phone began to ring again. I meant it.

Now Solange was in loving, capable hands. Still, as I left Mathew's mother's house, I promised myself that my girls and I would never be in this position again. Back home, my house felt empty without my baby. I looked at her waiting crib and thought of my mother having to leave Selena behind when Slack threw her out. That was so much worse for her, I knew, but her story . . . well, if it didn't repeat, it echoed. We were both moms of two when we knew it was time to leave our husbands.

I did what she would do. I closed the door to the baby's room, and I went to the salon to do more prep work.

CHAPTER 19

HEADLINERS

October 1986

I PLACED THE LAST flyer under the windshield wiper so the $9.95 showed just right above the name of my salon, Headliners Hair Salon for the Professional Woman. I'd hit every car parked at the light company, saying a little prayer with each one. The street marketing team Mathew hired was doing a blitz of advertising in the last week before Headliners opened, but I wanted to be hands-on about it. I'd given them a list of places to target where I knew a lot of women worked. The ladies at the light, gas, and water companies—and post offices too—needed to be cordially invited to the grand opening of Headliners so I could get buzz going. We also focused on other professional women, doctors, lawyers, and Cheryl's network of Black women in finance. The flyer offered a $9.95 shampoo-and-blow-dry and reconstructive treatment for a first-time visit only—Mathew's idea for a can't-resist deal that would get people in the door. The stylists I hired didn't like me for that—this was a thirty-dollar value, plus I told them we would throw in a trim if the client needed it. The women we drew in would love how they looked, and their happiness was a great marketing tool: We would have a customer for life. "We'll lose a little money up front," I said, "but sometimes you have to give a little to get a lot."

I could do that because I was confident in the service we would provide—and the power of deep conditioning. We catered to professional women, and I didn't feel bad about it. Anybody could come if you could afford it, but it wasn't cheap—and that's because I respected that their time wasn't cheap. Every woman I'd talked to hated that they'd sit in a salon for five hours—eating lunch under a dryer, listening to gossip—when they had a job or kids to get back to. I had found my niche, the consumer need that is vital to a new business: time and respect.

At the grand opening, all the worry paid off. There was a march of heels on that tile floor I put in, women who begged to be squeezed in, but I had to schedule for the next day. And when that was full, the next day, and then the one after that. As Denise took each woman's information, the clients marveled at the computer system I'd put in. It was Mathew's idea to put everyone on file in the database, which was unheard of in salons at the time. This would ensure that each client would feel important and remembered when she returned, because the secret of good branding is belonging; the person greeting her would know when she was last in for a perm, and if she preferred red or white when we offered her our complimentary glass of wine on arrival. We would even know how she took her coffee, and we were famous for the gourmet brew we offered, which was just regular with a little scoop of Texas vanilla Blue Bell ice cream.

Someone would always be at the ready to lead her to the dressing room to put on her smock, a gorgeous pink that leveled the playing field for all our clients. A doctor would be next to an opera singer performing that night at the Wortham Theater Center on Texas Avenue. And next to them would be an up-and-comer spending a bit of her first or second paycheck to look and feel good. There was no class system at the salon, no private green room that a VIP was whisked to. Everyone was special under the dryer.

I used only high-end products, but I married the science of hair care innovation with the ritual of what my mother had passed down to me. Looking at a client, I could hear the voice of Agnes, and how many times she'd told me, "You need some grease in your hair 'cause it looks dry." Most often, she used olive oil, heating it up to do a hot oil treatment, then wrapping it in a towel. She would also use butter and mayonnaise to nourish the hair, egg whites to make it stronger. "You've got to get the root," she would tell me. "You can make the hair as strong as you want, Tenie, but it will pull right out if it's not strong at the root." At Headliners, I became a mixologist, honoring what had worked in the past but modernizing the methods. There was no one product that mixed high-tech hair care with the moisture and oils that are so important to textured or color-treated hair. In fact, they said a Black woman could choose a perm for her hair or color—but not both. I proved them wrong.

I created my own protein treatments—making the hair stronger for curling, heating, and braiding—especially for clients choosing perms or color. Then I would work to balance all that protein with the moisture each client required, providing hydration and shine without weighing her hair down. Some stylists I'd met would never reveal their secrets, but I wanted to share as my mother had done. It would sometimes unlock stories in the clients about grandmothers and great-grandmothers doing their hair as little girls, the feel of their fingers on their scalp, caring for them. Hairstyling is more than the act of doing hair—it's how a mother's love is transferred through that care.

We got our stylists right out of beauty school, so none had developed bad habits. I did not care how it was done at another salon—this was Headliners. As we expanded our hours, we let new staffers know the culture of the salon before they were even considered for a station: This was not a place of judgment or gossip. If you were caught gossiping, you were fired. I would end up letting go of some people I really liked, but we just couldn't have that kind of atmosphere. Because the next thing you knew, everybody would be fighting and backstabbing.

The staff started calling themselves Tina's Girls, and they became an extension of my family. I had so much mother love to give that I wanted them to reach their full potential. The ones who worked at Headliners were taking home fifteen hundred to two thousand a week, unheard of in the late eighties. They were often making more than the women who could afford their services, and it allowed for a feeling of mutual respect.

Being my own boss, I could think of exciting ways to help them. We had a psychologist come in to do talks that would motivate them to pursue goals. If it took them away from Headliners, that was okay. Some went back to school. One of our best, Toni Smith, started as a shampoo girl, and when I quickly realized she could do anything she set her mind to, I encouraged her to get her license to cut hair. Succeeding at that, she then got her bachelor's, then her master's, and then ran for political office. I was also proud that so many Headliners "graduates" would later go on to become salon owners themselves.

I could already see a glimmer of that success those first two weeks, making every minute count before I went to Alabama to get Solange.

My goal had been to become independent, make my own income to prepare for a life without my husband. But now we had been in a good place since Mathew and I did counseling. I did not want to live without this Mathew, who was devoted and encouraging. He was an idea machine then, inspired by my budding entrepreneurship and simultaneously feeling bored with his own job at Xerox.

So bored that Mathew told me he wanted to quit and leave for another job. He said he had a 401(k) plan he wanted to cash out, which would give him about sixty thousand dollars. "We could sell this place," Mathew said, "and get a house on MacGregor."

The dream was always to be on MacGregor in the Third Ward. Not just our dream, but the dream for families who'd made it but wanted to stay in a Black neighborhood. MacGregor was the main street on Brays Bayou, thirty miles of green space and culture set beside the slow-moving river. To live on the bayou, for the kids to walk by the water like I did as a kid, and be so close to good schools, the zoo, and great theater, that was irresistible. It was also hard to resist that status symbol of a house there. Our neighbors would be much older than us, having saved and saved to establish the kinds of lives and bank accounts that granted you access. And here we would be, in our early thirties, self-made and ready for moving day.

I said yes, feeling like Mathew's commitment to us and his new life was something to celebrate. It would be my job to find the next house, one with space for Ebony and Denise too. I was already stretched thin, knowing it was only going to get harder since I was about to go bring Solange home. *This is what mothers do,* I told myself. *You said you were going to do this right. So do it.*

On the way to Alabama to get Solange, the adrenaline was still in my veins. I felt it in my arms most, this tension that I hoped would ease once I held my baby. I was scared that she had forgotten me, and that Miss Lou Helen would watch as Solange rejected me. Selena was going to come up to help for a few weeks, and then I would line up a nanny for the girls. My friend Cheryl had a housekeeper, Myrna, whose daughter Chunga was interested in working for me.

Solange was just rousing from sleep when I got there, and I picked her up. She looked at me with her big, beautiful eyes, and we breathed each other in. She worked her mouth and made a noise, as if she were talking, and I joked back, "Tell me everything." I recited all that I knew she had done that month in Alabama, everything that Mathew's mother told me in our frequent phone calls. "I know you were playing with some leaves with all these trees here. It was still hot when you got here but now it's a little colder, right? This is autumn. . . . I know, it's your first one. I don't like the cold, but we'll let you decide how you feel about it."

We went on like this, me hanging on every turn of her head and wide-eyed look. A conversation with my four-month-old that didn't seem so one-sided.

As SOLANGE AND I CONTINUED TO BOND, I RENEWED A CONNECTION with my niece Angie, the ten-year-old daughter of my brother Larry. Larry's divorce had been bitter. And after Angie's mother was done with him—and his erratic nature had given her plenty of reason to be—she decided she was done with all of us. For the first four years of her life, every Christmas, Flo and I would buy Angie and her brother Larry presents and leave them at her mother's doorstep. Finally, I said, "I'm sick of this," and just knocked on the door like Aunt Santa Claus.

Angie, a funny, smart little girl, had recently decided to move in with her grandmother. At ten, she was five years older than Beyoncé and as no-nonsense as summer is hot. She was an early example for me of what a child is capable of if you believe in them. "I want to know what grades you're making," I told her. "You need to send me your report card." This girl would go to Kinko's and make a front-and-back copy of her report card, put it in an envelope, and send it to me in Houston.

When I got the letter, I would make a big deal of it, calling her to talk it through. "What girl would do this?" I would ask my niece, my bonus daughter. "You are one of one."

She wanted to be at our house as much as possible and began to spend entire summers with us. Always a planner, she would call me before the last day of school, telling me, "You better have somebody picking me up." And we did. One way or another, we would not be separated again.

CHAPTER 20

PARKWOOD

December 1986

EVEN IN WINTER, on nights when it wasn't too cold, I drove home from work with the top down on the convertible, playing Luther or Sade loud. The drive was my reentry period from closing up Headliners to the kids' bedtime at home. This was my time, leaving behind the high-stakes pressure of hairstyling, creating sculptures to crown women who could make you or break you with word of mouth. In three months, we were so busy and so crowded I was able to take over the right side of the building's upstairs, too. We would gross half a million dollars that first year.

Tonight, I had Tina Turner on the tape deck, "I Might Have Been Queen." I did a mini-concert with Tina and I only quieted down as I got to the residential twists and turns of our neighborhood.

We had ended up buying a house the next block over from MacGregor, on Parkwood Drive. We were in a rush and none of the prized houses on actual MacGregor were for sale. But this was perfect: a five-thousand-square-foot white-brick dream home, with a little apartment in the back for my niece Denise. Her daughter Ebony lived with us in the main house, and by then I had taken most of the responsibilities for Ebby. Denise was a great mom but needed time. Let her party and be young—I had time and love to give.

There was a yard to play in, and it reminded me of my home in Galveston—a place for all the kids to hang out. "You can have parties for all your friends," I'd told the girls. Ebony liked that idea, but Beyoncé got quiet. I never understood why Ebony would be so full of stories to tell me about other kids from St. Mary's as soon as I came home. I'd turn to ask Beyoncé about her day, and she would shrug, find somewhere else to be as Ebony filled in the blanks of their day for her.

Easing the car into the driveway, I admired the house as I always did. It had a small U-shaped driveway, like something out of *Dynasty*. "I'm home," I announced, and Ebony and Beyoncé came at me in their pajamas, each grabbing a side of me.

Ebony didn't start telling me about her day, which should have been the first sign of trouble. She was standing by the door like she was just waiting on something. Beyoncé walked away, toward the kitchen where Chunga was drying the last dish before leaving.

Once Beyoncé was out of earshot, Ebony about exploded. "Aunt Tina," she said.

"Yes, Ebby," I said.

"Miss Jones took us out of the lunch line and gave us a peanut butter and jelly sandwich. And you know I don't even *like* peanut butter and jelly."

"Why, didn't they have school lunch today?"

"They did!" she said, like it was the big reveal. "She said just Beyoncé and me couldn't." I paid for them to have school lunch. Had I sent it in? I couldn't remember. "Beyoncé told me not to tell you because she said, 'You know my mama will get mad. You don't need her coming up here. Just eat your sandwich.' And well, I don't like peanut butter and I—"

"You don't like jelly, yeah, I know." I glanced to where Beyoncé was dancing around in the kitchen, up on the ball of her foot and doing a twirl. "Ebony, you did the right thing telling me." I looked at the clock. Nine o'clock. I would bring the money to school in the morning.

As Chunga left, the girls hugged her, and I went back upstairs to check on Solange.

"Hmmph," I said, climbing the stairs, repeating what Beyoncé told Ebony. " 'Don't need her coming up here.' "

The next morning, before I brought the lunch money to the principal, I met with the teacher. She said, as if this were an offhand remark: "You know, I know you needed to start Beyoncé young. But she is struggling."

I heard the "needed to" and felt the hair on my neck stand up. I did nothing with my child for my convenience, but what mattered more was that this was the first I heard she was struggling. I started to talk, genuinely concerned, and she cut me off. "I think she needs to be held back," she said. "And I think she might be a little slow."

I got heated. "What? It is *December*," I said. "They've only been in school a few months and you have determined that? What do *you* plan to do to help *her* the rest of the year? If she needs a tutor, I will get her a tutor. I will work with her, whatever, but you don't tell me that you've already given up on my kid."

She said I was overreacting, but I could tell this teacher had given up on Beyoncé, and it wasn't enough to hope that changed. When I gave the principal the check, I asked if she could recommend a tutor. She suggested a teacher who had recently retired, Miss Little. I called her right away. I could not let anyone write off my child.

It must be said: Miss Little was strict. There was a firm directness to her after decades of managing kids in classrooms. Even I was a little scared of her when she showed up at our door. But what a difference. Miss Little *saw* Beyoncé and booted her up. She understood the challenges introspective kids can face in learning environments. After the first couple of visits, Miss Little met me at her door to speak to me privately. "There's nothing wrong with this girl," she said. "The girl is *bright*."

Miss Little was one of Beyoncé's biggest supporters, booting her up until she excelled at math. Teachers hold so much power over how kids feel about themselves. Parents have to pay close attention to how they wield that power, because that one person can make or break a child's self-esteem.

Already, my girls—and all little Black girls—were being bombarded with messages from so-called mainstream culture that they were less than. When I was growing up, if ever I had access to a TV, everything that was "good" was depicted as white. Now my kids had access to TV and how many channels, but this was still the case. The most Black people they saw onscreen were on the news, being hurt or doing the hurting. Sure, there were a few more Black characters on TV shows, and there was *The Cosby Show*, which we all loved. But most everything on the air was to be palatable and enjoyable to white people. And certainly, the commercials were all about white America. When my daughters and their cousin Ebony saw a shampoo commercial, they saw long flowing hair, always with a white woman spinning it around to catch the light.

I thought it was important for my little girls, who wore braids most of their young lives, to also be bombarded by powerful images of Black women. As I selected art to purchase and hang in the Parkwood house, I looked at pieces through my daughters' eyes too. Did a work of art convey power and strength? Did it allow for vulnerability and being delicate? I used the same principle at Headliners, because wherever they went that I could control, it was going to be a place that let a little Black girl know that she was beautiful. Not beautiful "too"—there was no need to factor in a certain criterion of beauty that centered whiteness. The pride should be based solely on her own self. Black is beautiful.

I also wanted them to know the beautiful people in their own life, the ones who were discounted by that same "mainstream." It was important to me that the girls understood the value of their uncle Johnny's life with Peanut. Peanut didn't have family that saw and loved him the way Johnny's did. But Johnny had chosen Peanut as family, so he was our family too. The girls understood this. Johnny and Peanut were married in every way but the paper.

BEYONCÉ'S SHYNESS PERSISTED INTO FIRST GRADE AND TOOK EVEN more of a hold of her in second grade. She walked into every classroom trying to be invisible. Complicating things, after three years of her living with us, Denise decided to get her own place with Ebony. We were all devastated because it was almost like saying goodbye to a child and sister. But my niece wanted her own place and her own life, and I of all people understood that need.

Without Ebony, Beyoncé was on her own at school. There were popular sisters at St. Mary's, who I'll call Heckle and Jeckle, beautiful little girls who had my shy daughter jumping through hoops, she idolized them so much. Whether or not they were friends that day went with their whims, and I would tell her not to let them bully her. When I asked her to do a dance again that she had loved, she would say, "Well, Heckle and Jeckle said I looked stupid dancing." At Neiman's once, I bought Beyoncé a white rabbit coat with a little hood and she adored it. But then she came from school holding the coat under her arm, not even wearing it.

"I don't want this coat," said Beyoncé, throwing it on the ground. "I'm never gonna wear it again."

Of course, it was because Heckle and Jeckle told her it was ugly and silly. That was the last word for fashion at St. Mary's.

In a situation like this, my mother would not have told me the answer, she would have *shown* me. She would have figured out a way to give me the lesson I needed without fussing and flat out yelling, "They're jealous of you!" I could tell Beyoncé that fifty times and she wouldn't have gotten it.

"Okay, I'll tell you what," I said, mother's wit kicking in. "I'm gonna put the coat in a bag and you take it to school. You tell Heckle and Jeckle that they can have it."

"They don't want it," she said. "They think it's ugly."

"No, no, just give it to them, because I bet they secretly like it."

The next day after school I asked, "Did they take the coat?"

"Yeah!" she answered, still surprised. "They really *liked* it. They were *fighting* over it!"

"Well, you know the lesson in that, Beyoncé," I said, "is that sometimes people will put something down that you have or do because deep down they're actually sad they can't have what you have or do what you do. It's called being jealous. You gotta understand that because you can't let other people's jealousy change your mind on how you really feel about something."

It was an important early lesson for her. But as the years went on, there would be more times that I just didn't have answers when she dreaded going to school. So, some mornings, when I had time away from Headliners, I would surprise the girls with what I called a Beach Day. "You're not going to school today," I would announce on a blue-sky Wednesday morning, and Beyoncé would act like she'd won the sweepstakes. Solange would not be happy, feeling it was irresponsible for anyone to skip school. But I knew once she got there, she would have a ball.

I'd drive Beyoncé and Solange down to Galveston Beach with the top down to have a girls' day playing in the sand and going to ride the same ferry to Louisiana that I grew up loving. One day at the beach, I laid out a pretty blanket where the good sand was, and we looked out at the water. Some teenagers were already there skipping school like us, and they started blasting Michael Jackson on their boombox. Beyoncé and Solange leapt up to put on a dance show for me. There weren't many people out, but the few people there stopped walking to watch. Solange noticed them first, and kept going, even playing to the crowd. Her glances at their growing audience made me look, and meanwhile Beyoncé was dancing with such joy that I was afraid she would see too, and the attention would make her freeze. But she kept going, laughing with Solange as the two fell in and out of step with each other.

My girls were happy and free.

Later, when I saw St. Mary's posted a sign-up sheet for a dance class, I thought of that smile dancing brought her. They were bringing in a teacher named Miss Darlette to do a group session one day a week. I figured Beyoncé might enjoy it.

Maybe this will help her shyness, I thought, writing her name on the sheet. *Help her fit in.*

CHAPTER 21

"THOSE LITTLE KNOWLES GIRLS"

January 1989

I WAS LATE AGAIN. I tried really hard not to be, especially picking up Beyoncé. She hated to be the last one waiting anywhere. On Saturday nights, I would get off work and race over to Miss Darlette Johnson's dance studio to get her. Beyoncé had liked the class at St. Mary's so much that I decided to enroll her in the real dance classes twice a week: Wednesday nights and all day Saturdays. Mathew would drive her over on Saturday mornings at ten with me covering the six o'clock evening pickup.

I arrived that Saturday night to see Beyoncé alone in the studio with Miss Darlette. I was all apologies because I really liked Miss Darlette and was respectful of her time. She was young, with the energy and gentle persuasion to keep a roomful of girls in line. The parents all took the class seriously, most coming from the surrounding working-class neighborhoods. They made sacrifices to scrape up the money to send their kids to dance class.

"Miss Tina," she said, and it was the "I have something important to talk with you about" tone. I braced myself. I wasn't *that* late. She turned to my second grader. "Beyoncé, can you put away those tapes for me? Thank you." Bey moved to the cassettes quickly. I saw her eyeing herself in the mirrored wall, admiring her own precision as she walked in the style of whatever dance they'd practiced. It was pride on her face. I was scared my being late was going to blow this for her.

"Miss Tina, I noticed something today," she said. I nodded in exaggerated active listening. "So I was singing along to the music to-night, just sweeping up . . ."

"Waiting for me, I know," I said. "I'm sorry, it won't—"

"No, no, that's not . . . *So,* I was singing a song and I was out of tune. I stopped singing but Beyoncé kept singing it for me." I nodded again, with absolutely no idea where this was going. I glanced over her shoulder at Beyoncé for a clue, but she was acting like some kind of music librarian, making those tapes look perfect.

"I asked her to sing it again, but she wouldn't because, you know, she's so shy."

I shrank a little. "Yes, yes, she is. We're working on that."

"So I told her I'd give her a dollar if she sang it again."

"Oh," I said. "Uh, well . . ." She was Tenie B's child for sure. "You didn't have to do that."

"She's *really* talented."

Now, I never wanted to be that braggy parent who was like, "Oh, my child is so amazing." I told my daughters that, but that was for them to know. Other people knowing just how special my girls were didn't matter as much to me. I just smiled and agreed, "Yes, I think she's talented."

"So you know she can sing?"

"Yeah," I said, quickly. "She sings with me and her dad all the time."

"Well, Beyoncé can *really* sing," she said. "You know, they're having a talent competition. It's all the parochial schools . . ."

"You mean that it's gonna be, like, high school singers?"

"Yeah, high schools. Junior high."

"Aww, no," I said, picturing my little seven-year-old competing with all these teenagers. I liked her in the safety of Miss Darlette's stu-dio, dancing in a room of little Black girls around her age. "I don't want to ruin her confidence before she even gets started."

Miss Darlette held back a chuckle. "Miss Tina, she can do this. Beyoncé can really sing and y'all should work with her."

I called Beyoncé over and asked Miss Darlette to explain the com-petition. I figured Beyoncé would look at me to get her out of it.

"I'll do it," Beyoncé said quickly, looking right at Miss Darlette.

"We'll check with Daddy," I said, hiding my surprise. "But I want to make sure this is something you want to do." Beyoncé was nodding yes before I even finished the statement.

Miss Darlette entered her in the contest, and Mathew and I worked with Beyoncé to practice John Lennon's "Imagine." On the day of the show, as he and I sat in the audience, I was ready to go get my baby if she froze or even sent out any kind of distress signal. I felt that energy around me too as she walked out. Sometimes an audience thinks they have to carry the performer, especially a child. Smile to encourage and nod to get them through it. Every kind-hearted person leaned forward in their seat, as if to catch her.

With that four-bar piano introduction, I tensed up. *Let go,* I told myself. I wanted her out of her shell. Maybe this would make raising her hand in class easier.

Beyoncé started singing, and I had the same reaction as everyone else in the place: *"Oh."* Mathew, too. We did not recognize our shy daughter. As an audience, we were in the hands of a gifted performer. She didn't need us to anticipate the notes and hope she could make them, or clap midway to give her confidence—she was doing this with or without us.

I grabbed Mathew's hand. He squeezed mine back. It was shock. It's funny that people sometimes assume that I was some sort of stage mom. I was busy enough trying to be a *mom* mom, just like so many women I've met. Watching Beyoncé perform in front of an audience for the first time, that was *my* first time seeing her onstage too. I was catching up just as much as the rest of the audience, but anyone could see she was *home.* On that stage and on whatever stage she took from then on—home.

As she finished that last note of "Imagine," I got up with everyone in that audience to give her a standing ovation.

A few minutes later, Beyoncé came from backstage to where we were sitting. "I'm hungry," she announced, my seven-year-old coming back to earth and what mattered.

"Okay," I whispered, pulling her to sit on my lap. "We can get something after, but we gotta stay 'til it's over."

"I just wanna get my trophy and go home and eat," she said.

I answered, "You don't know if you won."

Beyoncé turned to face me, and raised one eyebrow in that way she still does. I shook my head like "watch yourself."

But she was right. She won.

. . .

WE WERE RUNNING LATE OF COURSE. I DROVE STEADY OVER THE limit as Selena rode shotgun hemming the dress Johnny and I had spent all night making for the day. Beyoncé was in the backseat, humming the song she'd prepared. We were heading to her first pageant, and I thought probably her last.

This had also been Miss Darlette's idea. She had another girl who was active on the circuit in Houston, and she came to me after the talent show, wanting to enter Beyoncé into pageants.

"Oh, absolutely not," I said. I preferred people telling Beyoncé and Solange they were smart, and not just that they were pretty. The last thing I wanted was for them to get stuck on their own beauty.

"Well, Miss Tina, she only has to do the Beauty portion of a pageant one time, the first time, and then she's qualified to just do the Talent portions at all the pageants after." There was one coming up, and Miss Darlette could get us in last-minute.

All Beyoncé wanted was an outlet to perform in this home she had found on the stage, so I reluctantly agreed. Johnny and I had put off making the dress until the night before, when I was already so tired from working twelve hours at Headliners. We chose Beyoncé's favorite color of pale pink, putting a beautiful beaded lace at the top with a bubble peplum, and then a little straight skirt. It was going to be cute if my sister hemmed it in time. Selena blew smoke out the window, expertly sewing as I passed the car in front of me.

We had no idea what we were walking into. Backstage were all these little girls standing around racks of dresses—full-length *Dynasty* formal gowns made pint-size with towering heels to match. And here we had this one little girl's dress homemade the night before. Moms were leading their kids through march-like walks, peppering them with questions they might be asked in the Interview portion as they pestered their hair nearer my God to thee. Girls grinned in hand mirrors, switching smiles on and off like robots, practicing them to razor-sharp perfection.

"There is no way she can compete with these girls," I whispered to Selena, who did not argue.

Miss Darlette gave us the run-through fast because we only had a few minutes before Beyoncé had to go on. There was the Beauty portion, the Walk—which showed your poise—the Interview, and then the Talent. Honestly there might have been more categories, but Selena and I zoned out, all wide-eyed and "What have we gotten ourselves into?" Beyoncé was one of only two Black girls there, and I saw her turn her eyes this way and that, watching the intimidating girls practice their walk. Five minutes before the show started, she learned the "pivot turn" of the Walk, a move these second- and third-generation pageant girls had done since they were in baby shoes.

"Okay," Beyoncé said to herself.

"Okay." Selena laughed. I could tell this was fast becoming a story to tell people later, something silly we endured and never did again. The pageant had already started, so while Miss Darlette stayed backstage, Selena and I went and found two open seats left to the side of the audience. "I wonder what Mama would say about this?" I whispered.

"She would say 'Pretty is as pretty does,' but she would have loved all this," said Selena. "They're like dolls. That's what she wanted you to be, you know."

Selena hit at the contradictory messages my mom had given me. She told me I was more than my looks, but once I grew into them, she changed that to "God, if you're pretty you can get by a lot on your looks."

"I think that's why I was a mischievous little kid," I said.

"No, you were bad, period," Selena joked. Then a little girl got up to sing, her mouth somehow staying in a straight flat line as she sang Shirley Temple's "On the Good Ship Lollipop." Her mom stood up in the audience, hissing "Smile, smile!" as the child's face remained blank through the dirge. I bit my lip as the mom started doing the choreography to get her child to do the moves, flapping her arms in the animated way she probably did as a pageant girl herself.

Selena began to giggle. I bit my lip harder and closed my eyes, holding in a laugh. I gripped the arm of the seat.

The mom started *singing*.

Selena burst, which made me start laughing, and the more we tried to stop, we couldn't. That wheeze-laughing that takes you over. The mom was too in her Shirley Temple zone to hear, but the people around us shot daggers.

"Ma'am, can you please step outside?" It was a schoolmarm type holding a clipboard, and Selena looked at me like *I* alone had been caught, which only made me laugh more. We left the show area, taking deep breaths doubled over. "They put us *out*!" Selena yelled.

Well, Miss Darlette came through the doors like we'd disrupted mass at Holy Rosary. "This is very unfair to Beyoncé," she said. "She is three people down, and she will be judged by you, too. So you have to pull yourselves together."

"Yes," I said. "Right." Miss Darlette turned and went back in while we collected ourselves. Selena muttered, "These people are crazy."

We got back in our seats just in time for Beyoncé. Selena and I were now bone-sober nervous while she did the Interview onstage. But we saw the same transformation in her that Mathew and I had witnessed seeing her onstage the last time. She was poised, yet wholly herself. Then she had to do her Walk, which all those other girls had spent those years practicing. She did it so naturally, then hit that required little pivot-turn and looked back.

She threw the judges a kiss.

I saw the effect, a wave going over the crowd and the judges melting. No one had ever told her to do that. It was just the instinct of a born showperson.

For her Talent, she sang "Home" from *The Wiz.* "Oh," Selena said, her turn to be at a loss for words. Beyoncé had sung in the backseat the whole way here, but now it was different. This girl we barely recognized up there was interpreting the song so that the lyrics had new meaning, a song about being between two places. Dorothy knowing that she was stepping into something magical, but still hoping for time to slow down so she could enjoy a normal life: "Giving me enough time in my life to grow up."

That would be the challenge for us now. With the stunned look on Selena's face, I couldn't deny that this was Beyoncé's calling, and she was already on her way. By the end of the pageant, she'd won for Talent. And Beauty. And the Walk. And the Dress—the one that Johnny and I had made, and Selena hemmed in a rush on the way over. *Everything.* I think it was refreshing to the judges that here was this little girl who dressed and acted like a little girl.

More important, now she could compete solely in the pageants' Talent portion. Beyoncé never competed against another girl in Beauty ever again. She never had to dress up in anything more than the costume she requested I make to serve the song she'd chosen.

And she won up every one of those trophies.

Beyoncé spent two years on the pageant circuit. When we were approached by agents after shows, the line was "Not only is she beautiful, she's really talented and we would love for her to do commercials." Mathew and I would give a direct "Nope." There isn't anything wrong with modeling, but Beyoncé wanted to be a singer, and we didn't see how commercials had anything to do with that.

Instead, we focused on talent. Mathew and I got Beyoncé additional dance classes. Luke tells us in the Bible that to whom much is given, much will be required. Our daughter had a gift and a passion—some artists only get one of those—and that required Mathew and me to make sure we helped her nurture both. The same with Solange. I have no problem saying that my children are geniuses born with gifts, but all that just remains unrealized potential if they don't work on their craft.

When a child is that talented that young, it can scare you that they feel so at home in a place that is solely theirs. You worry you'll lose them to their gift. Parents do. I promised myself I would not. I wouldn't hold her too tight like my mama did me, telling herself she was keeping me safe. Beyoncé could have this home she found, but her family would always be a home for her too. It didn't matter that her passion was for entertainment: Mathew joked that if our girls were interested in medicine, we would figure out a way to buy a hospital and I'd be finishing up a nursing degree so I could assist in the OR.

Because it *was* both girls. At four years old, Solange was already showing her own artistic promise in performing. She began dance lessons with Miss Darlette, and emerged as such a bold little star that Darlette created a way for her to nurture her talent by dancing with the big girls. The shows would start with all the little girls—including Solange—dancing in a line, doing pretty simple routines, with the older kids waiting behind them. Then the line of little girls would recede to the back, leaving Solange and this other little girl up front. The two of them would have their little solo part, doing slightly more complex work. When the bigger kids came on to really get down, Solange and the girl were supposed to leave.

And Solange decided she would stay. The first time it happened, I leaned over to whisper to Mathew, *"She don't want to go back."* But she kept up with them! She knew every single dance step from watching them and practicing herself. From then on, Miss Darlette let Solange stay out there with the bigger kids because she proved she could do the work.

"Those little Knowles girls, they just take all the attention," parents would say. They didn't try to—they just wanted to dance, and I had to start finding additional outlets for them. We lived near the Shrine of the Black Madonna community center, and I'd mostly visited because of its amazing bookstore and art for sale by Black and African artists. It was here that I could find children's books with kids who looked like mine and paintings they could see themselves in. They also had programs that served children in the Third Ward. One day while I was there, I checked out a kids' dance program. My mouth dropped open— these children were *good*.

I had Solange and Beyoncé in the car for the very next class. "You might think you're bad at your dance school," I said as we pulled up. "Lemme take you here and these little girls are gonna teach you something."

I remember that first class, the surprised flash of a smile on Beyoncé's face as she was challenged by the elevated skills of the other girls. Solange was right there too, holding her own, with none of the baggage of being the little sister. They brought this electric energy back to Miss Darlette's class, where the two worked even harder. If people said they took all the attention, they could not deny that these girls who lived and breathed dance worked really hard.

I would come to get them, see my girls dancing to Miss Darlette's favorite, Janet Jackson's "Rhythm Nation." I watched the precision of the choreography with growing awe. They were only kids, but it felt real that there was something magical happening. And as I took in Janet's bold lyrics, it clicked for me that Solange and Beyoncé were also each taking in the message of stepping into power—and belonging there.

CHAPTER 22

LESSONS IN SURVIVAL

Spring 1990

THE TWO LADIES had come to see Beyoncé perform at the Evelyn Rubenstein Jewish Community Center. They approached us after, telling Mathew and me that they wanted to form a girl group with her as the lead singer.

"Okay," I said, very nonchalant because my thoughts were not about "the business." In my house, the business was the shop. I'd sped home from Headliners to take Beyoncé to this. I figured this might be something nice for her to try—maybe she'd meet some kids who liked the stage as much as she did.

They called the group Girls Tyme, and in the beginning, there were about a dozen girls total, mostly eight or nine years old. After a few months, the two ladies who organized the group brought in another partner, a sweetheart who we loved, Andretta Tillman. Miss Ann would manage the group. Beyoncé had just turned nine and was in the fourth grade, but she had gained confidence from performing as a singer for two years. So as the girls worked out routines in near-daily rehearsals, Beyoncé assigned them their parts to get the most interesting harmonies, and she would make up choreography for each girl in the group right there on the spot. She also knew who needed more support, and who could be pushed if they were singing flat or dancing low-energy. My wallflower, who would sooner disappear rather than raise her hand in class, was telling other girls what to do, directly and with care.

The adults in charge were wearing Beyoncé *out* with all that extra work teaching all these girls. On the ride home, she would melt into the seat, resting her head on the passenger side door. When I asked if it was too much for her, she said, "It's fun."

Beyoncé's role in the group was lead singer, but she was also their teacher. Gradually Beyoncé's voice became hoarse from all the strain of teaching and reteaching everyone their parts and arranging the harmonies as she did her own lead vocals. This little fourth grader sounded like one of my daddy's longshoreman friends.

The managers decided to bring in another lead singer because Beyoncé was hoarse, and asked her if she knew anyone with a good voice. Not knowing the plan, my daughter had recruited the girl for them, a strong singer with a beautiful voice in the People's Workshop, a community arts program. Ashley was a year older and had such a pleasing personality that Beyoncé knew she would be a great team member. So this cute girl who looked older than them came in with a fresh, strong voice. Mathew and I hired a vocal coach to meet with Beyoncé once a week and teach her how to use her voice without damaging it, but she *hated* the voice lessons. The sessions seemed tedious to her and she wouldn't keep up with them.

Beyoncé came home one day, crying, and at first, I thought she was just upset, but then I realized she was mad. "Mom, they have taken all of my parts from me, and she is singing all the leads," she said. "It's not her fault that she is taking my place—I like her and she can really sing—but I've worked so hard and they still have me doing all the harmonies and teaching everybody. It's not fair!"

"Well, Beyoncé," I said, maybe a little too calm, maybe a little too preacher-like. "Life is not fair, and I've been trying to get you to have these vocal lessons."

"They use me to do all the teaching," she repeated, completely ignoring my point.

I remembered how much I needed my mother to stand up for me, to at least know that she understood how I felt. "You know, you do deserve a thank-you from these women. They brought you in to be a lead singer." I paused. She looked hopeful. "But . . ." Her head dropped—there went the hope. ". . . I'm not going to argue with these people, Bey, because you got an opportunity to take your voice lessons, and you don't want to take them. So, if I were you, I would get busy with those sessions."

"Yeah, but you should—"

"*You* get past your hoarseness, and *you* get your voice stronger, and *you* take your spot back, but I'm not goin' up there fightin' with these people about that. This girl is older than you, so her vocal cords are more developed and she's not doing all the stuff you do—overusing your voice, teaching everyone their parts—so she's singing fresh when it's time for her to sing. That's why she sounds better than you."

And, oh, what did I say *that* for?

"I. Hate. You," Beyoncé said slowly.

I knew it was a reflexive response—I had hurt her ego deeply. Kids can say things like that, thinking it gives them power. But I stayed calm. "That girl is not your competition. *You* are your only competition and that's how it always will be. Focus on you and what you're doing, and not on her. You gotta work harder."

She started to walk away. "Well, you think about it," I called after her. "And you decide what you want to do."

Beyoncé emerged from her room a little later after calming down. "You're not my friend," she said, "and I'm mad at you." I nodded. She gave a half-smile of determination. "But I'm gonna take the voice lessons."

She started twice a week, then three as she found that it was making her voice strong. The teacher's lessons were about how *not* to use her voice; what would destroy her vocal cords. Within about three months, she got her spot back.

On the way home, she didn't seem tired at all now. "Mama, I'm happy that you didn't go up there and fight with them," she admitted. "You made me work for it."

Instead, I'd said the tougher thing for a mom, but the true thing: "You need to work harder." I couldn't just be her mom for that moment; I needed to be her mom for her whole life.

The lesson was: Work hard and then even harder in order to get what you want. Nobody is going to give you something 'cause it's "fair." She says now that that's what made her go work her butt off, and it's the life lesson that inspired the song "Survivor," which amounts to, "It's nothing personal: I'm not gonna talk about you. I'm just gonna work harder, because I'm my only competition." She doesn't have to—or even want to—wish ill will on someone, especially a nice girl like Ashley, who was just doing *her* best too. Because, as Beyoncé sings, "my mama taught me better than that."

.   .   .

IT WAS AROUND THIS TIME THAT JOHNNY'S PARTNER PEANUT GOT sick with breast cancer. It is rare, but studies show that Black men in America have a higher incidence of breast cancer than white men. By the time Peanut got diagnosed, he was very sick but still managing. I had them over for coffee on one of their visits from Galveston, and I invited a neighbor who was also friendly with Johnny. She lived a few doors down, and Johnny had actually done her wedding dress. That was just Johnny, one conversation and people were hooked.

We were all sitting, chatting, and I noticed my neighbor was staring at Peanut. He looked frail at that point but was holding on to his vigor. I hadn't noticed that she was no longer drinking her coffee. But Johnny did.

Peanut cleared his throat, which turned into a cough he tried to stifle with a fist.

"What is *wrong* with you?" this woman asked. The last words she would say in my house.

"He has breast cancer," Johnny answered for Peanut.

She got up and left. Not a word; left her coffee to get as cold as her heart.

I called her to let her know how strange I thought that was. When she called me back that night, she practically hissed, "Tina, that guy has AIDS."

"No, he has breast cancer," I said. "Peanut is not 'that guy' either. You are talking about family, so—"

"Men don't get breast cancer," she said, furious with me. "He has AIDS, and you need to be careful because you're all up against him, hugging him."

Badass Tenie B came out: "You don't know what the hell you are talking about." I hung up.

I wasn't mad that she accused Peanut of having AIDS. I was mad that she was so ignorant about it. But that was an excuse people used, not wanting to know about HIV and how it was transmitted in an era of misinformation. People hid behind "fear." It compounded the hate that the gay community already had to deal with. Peanut did not have AIDS, or even HIV, but what if he did? He would be just as deserving of love and care.

But that neighbor made me second-guess things because I still had more to learn myself. When Peanut had to be hospitalized, I admit to wondering if they *were* covering for AIDS. My sister Flo, a nurse, set me straight. "Tina, I've just been up there to see him and there's nothing about any extra precautions," she said. "Peanut's getting cancer care. Men *do* get breast cancer."

I stayed with Peanut in the hospital in Galveston to give Johnny a break.

"You know, Tenie, they just got all these rumors about me," he said.

I pulled that chair right to him to sit close and wipe his tears. "You can't worry about them, Peanut," I said. "You just got to fight for your life. That's all you have to focus on, okay?"

But he didn't make it. The cancer took Peanut so fast, within a year of his diagnosis. Johnny was devastated. Worse, he couldn't even focus on his grief. The day after Peanut died, he called me at Headliners. Peanut's old evil aunt had showed up, probably waiting for just this moment. She took the car Peanut and Johnny bought together, which was only in Peanut's name because he had better credit. As a gay man married only in spirit, Johnny had no rights to shared property. But that wasn't all she took.

"Tenie," Johnny said, trying to sound cavalier but I could hear his voice about to break, "she said I can't come to the service."

It was just so cruel. "You can't let them do that."

"Tenie, I just . . ." he said. "I'm not going to fight with them."

Funerals are supposed to be sacred, and Johnny couldn't even say goodbye. I wouldn't go, and I wouldn't let my children be in the room with people who would close the door to Uncle Johnny.

The weekend of the service, I went to Galveston to be with Johnny so we could get through this together. We would remember Peanut our way and celebrate him the best way we knew how: We went dancing.

All that first night and the next, Johnny and I danced to house music. Losing ourselves and our sorrows in pounding beats, tailoring the dance routines we worked to precision in childhood to newer songs like "Buffalo Stance" and "The Power." We danced until the night stretched into the early hours when deep house music took over, the relentless hypnotic beats for the true devotees.

Peanut's aunt barred Johnny from the service to keep it holy, but that kind of hate is blasphemy to God. Peanut's spirit had flown away anyway. He was somewhere in heaven, just above our heads, admiring his Johnny dancing in swirls of sweat and loss and revelry and remembrance.

AFTERWARD, THERE WAS JUST NO LIFTING JOHNNY UP. WITHOUT Peanut, Galveston—even with all our history there—now seemed to hold no future for him.

I prayed on it, and then Chunga came to me with the answer. She told me, near tears, that she would no longer be able to work for us full time. She had been studying me and my success with Headliners and so both she and her mother, Myrna, my friend Cheryl's housekeeper, had secretly been going to beauty school at night to get their cosmetology licenses. Now they were going to open their own shop. She worried I might be upset. But I was thrilled for her. "We love you," I said. "You have to live your life, Chunga."

This was the solution. I called Johnny and begged him to come live with us in Houston and I would pay him to run the house. If I had told him I was worried about him, he would have rejected it. This way, it was him being there for me.

"I'll give you a year," he said. "Help you with these crumb-snatchers you went and made. They need some good meals. Never too late."

And so, Johnny, the center of my childhood, became the nucleus of our family. He moved into the apartment behind the house where Denise had lived and kept everything running for much longer than one year. Picking up the girls from school, cooking them delicious meals, making them the most beautiful dresses, and being there when I came home to them.

My daughters already adored Uncle Johnny, but they each began to form a bond with him that was theirs alone. Solange formed a special connection, my dreamy four-year-old who loved order. Who tested people and the limits of their love from a young age. *Do you love me now? Do you love me if I say this truth about how I feel? And if I say* this? He did—he just got her. They each accepted the other wholly.

Johnny was getting his bearings living with grief while the poetry of Solange's life was just starting. She was developing her innate *cool,* and there was no better mentor in that than Johnny. They would drive around in my convertible, each with a knee up, Solange wearing a bandana made to match his. He was her heart, the way he'd been mine.

There are moments I treasure, ordinary bits of time that I didn't see coming. Me walking in the door and seeing Beyoncé and Solange, already in their pajamas, wildly dancing with Uncle Johnny. The radio was so loud they didn't hear me come in. I was going to make a joke about me and Johnny, how my house was now the Down Beat or the Session. But this moment was theirs, just Johnny's and the girls'. I took a picture with my mind and tucked it in my heart to keep safe forever.

CHAPTER 23

THREE GIRLS

November 1990

BEYONCÉ TOLD ME there was a new girl at rehearsals. "Kelly," she said. "Oh my gosh, she's got the most beautiful voice." That was high praise from Beyoncé.

Kelendria Trene Rowland auditioned with Whitney Houston's new single "I'm Your Baby Tonight," which really impressed Beyoncé. "She knew all the words." It actually *is* a complicated song, and not just for nine-year-olds like Kelly was. Whitney could fill all that space with tons and tons of lyrics, making herself a staccato instrument. Beyoncé picked up on how Kelly made that song look easy. Here was this girl who was her same age, was always on key, and stayed loose enough to take direction? *And* she was sweet?

The first time I met Kelly was at our house on Parkwood, because all the children in the group would hang out at our house when they weren't rehearsing in our backyard. By then, the original two women who had recruited Beyoncé to the group were no longer involved and Miss Ann had become the manager, with Mathew as the unofficial co-manager. The group was shaking out to be six girls—Beyoncé, Kelly, and Ashley; LaTavia, who would do raps; and two sisters named Nikki and Nina, who were dancers and cousins of LaTavia. Kelly went to elementary school with LaTavia, and they were playing Barbies when LaTavia heard Kelly sing. She asked Kelly if she'd be interested in trying out for this little group she was in.

All the girls had three settings: rehearsing, eating, and lying about on and around the couches of my home. They were doing the last one when I walked in from work. Kelly remembers now that my hair was in a fresh set, and I was wearing a casual flowy dress and the bright red Revlon lipstick Beyoncé and Solange teased me about always putting on, the same shade I'd idolized on my sister Selena. I recall Kelly first as this sweet kid sitting close to Bey, looking like friends from stroller days.

As I got to know Kelly in the group, her mom, Doris, became part of our lives too. She was straight-up *funny:* In a few seconds she could squint to better size up a situation and find something to say. If people didn't immediately laugh, *she* would, and her infectious little-girl laugh would take over everybody. Doris was a single mom—Kelly only had vague recollections of her father, Christopher, because he had not been in the picture for so long—and she worked job to job as a live-in nanny for white families. This meant a lot of moving, as Kelly would live in these houses with her. Doris didn't have a great support system, so Kelly was aware of adult problems at a young age.

Kelly got to know us too, spending so much time at the house on Parkwood. Her family might not have looked like the ones she saw on TV, but ours didn't either. We were never going to be that "sit down every night for a meal" family—not with our schedules and me coming home at nine. That meant our main family meal was Sunday lunches at Luby's Cafeteria after Mathew and I took the girls to church. That meal was a special time when we would talk about the whole week with the girls.

We both worked very hard, and if that meant some nights Mathew had to go pick up some dinner for the kids on the way home from work, he would. When I cooked, I cooked a lot. Soul food and my mother's gumbo, things the girls could microwave and have all week. Kelly would join us for my spaghetti, which was all about this Italian sauce I'd mastered. What makes it good is wine—lots of wine—cooked long and slow with bell peppers and onions, then I put beef sausage in. My house was the hangout house for friends and family, something I got from those years of watching everyone call my mother Tenie Mama as she made them feel secure. I never knew what girls from the group would be there for lunch or dinner or both, and always wanted people to feel welcome. Parent meetings for Girls Tyme were most often at our house, and I sewed the costumes with the material I bought for the girls.

As the girls came and went, it was sometimes easier for Doris if

Kelly spent the night. When Doris needed Kelly to stay with us for the weekend, we were happy to help because Kelly was a pleasure to have around. Even then I worried that Kelly's demeanor, a kind outgoingness, might have been developed to fit in as she moved into strangers' homes. But it was more complex and real than just being a people pleaser. She was special. I watched her ground every room she entered, and if a situation lacked stability, she brought it. She and Beyoncé shared a discernment beyond their years, two old souls with new ideas, so relieved to find each other.

If Doris had to miss a performance, we drove Kelly home. We'd be heading out of a community center, and the girls would start talking about their concert, not just to rate what went wrong or right, but what was *fun* about it. Maybe they'd been promised three mics and there was one when they got there. They would be laughing, reliving the mental rhythms of "five, six, seven, eight, okay, pass the mic so she can do her part. Okay, now pass to LaTavia. . . ."

Then we'd take them home and music education would continue, watching Mathew's VHS collection of Motown concerts and videos. Mathew was becoming more and more invested in the girls' performances, even as he excelled at his new job at a competitor for Xerox. He had a laser focus on the group and could be tough, but never cruel. It was assumed even then by people outside the group that Mathew showed favoritism to Beyoncé, but he was far harder on her than anybody. The kids had a running joke about Mathew's criticism—whether it was that they were low-energy, or the choreography wasn't precise—and how it always ended with one particular phrase. They would all beat him to it, saying in unison: "Especially you, Beyoncé." He saw a leader in her and wanted her to take on that responsibility for the group.

We put a deck in the backyard, built by my brother Larry, to be a stage for the girls. He got a book, used or out of the library, and put his engineer mind to work designing one, just like he did building the little bench he put in the pecan tree when I was little. Larry laid the foundation, then had someone come over to help him put the boards on and nail them. It was my mom all over again—she built our kitchen cabinets after she bought a woodworking book at a garage sale.

My deck, their stage, was beautiful, and they were on that stage all the time. The girls wanted to get better, the same way up-and-coming athletes their age discover that the hours alone in the gym—developing a work ethic that is just as vital as building muscle—pay off when it's time to perform. Their court, their field, was the stage. For them, Mathew developed summer "boot camp," part of which involved taking them jogging along Brays Bayou. He had them sing the entire run, to increase their lung power while they did their choreography. Solange would join in, wanting to be wherever the action was.

One night, Beyoncé and Kelly looked like they were going to collapse on the lawn when they got back from an extra run along the bayou. Mathew had gone inside.

"Is it too much?" I asked the girls. I had asked this before, but it felt important.

Beyoncé looked at me like *I* was the crazy one. "No," she said.

THE *HOUSTON CHRONICLE* CALLED THE SALON IN NOVEMBER, wanting to send a reporter and photographer to our home for an upcoming feature on how different families celebrated Christmas 1990. We were the Black family, and I was the news hook as an entrepreneur in town. It was still fall, so Johnny got the Christmas ornaments down from the attic to hang in the window with garland and made the girls Christmas dresses overnight.

Of course, I was late getting to my own house because I was held up at the salon. Mathew was working late too, so the girls were there with Johnny, who was doing his best to steer clear of the reporter and the *Chronicle* staff photographer. Making small talk, the reporter complimented the girls' matching dresses, red-and-green plaid skirts with holly-green tops. "Johnny made them," Beyoncé and Solange answered in unison.

"Your house is so Christmasy."

"Johnny decorated."

"Oh, something smells so good," she said.

"Johnny cooked," they answered.

"Your hair looks so beautiful, girls."

"Johnny combed it."

"You have such a pretty home."

"Johnny cleans it."

When I finally got there, beating Mathew home, the reporter turned to me. "I have been hearing all about your husband Johnny," she said.

I laughed. "No, actually, Johnny is my *wife*."

She looked startled. She thought this meant we were a lesbian couple. This was not in her notes.

"No, no, no," I said. "That would be cool, but I am kidding. Johnny is my nephew."

"Oh," she said.

"He's really my best friend and he does all the things that a wife does, so that I can work long hours. I can only do that because I know my kids are taken care of."

Not long after the article ran, Beyoncé, Solange, and Kelly gathered in front of the TV to watch Whitney Houston sing the national anthem at the 1991 Super Bowl XXV. I was as entranced as the kids—from the land of the free to the home of the brave; from the buzz I felt in my head to the chills on my arms. "The Star-Spangled Banner" was not supposed to be for us, but Whitney made it so.

When it was over, Beyoncé said in a quiet voice, not bragging, not even dreaming, simply stating a fact: "I'm gonna do that someday."

I nodded. I thought of the times I'd dreamed out loud to my parents and how their fear had replied for them. "Yes, you will," I said. "If you want it, you will have it."

As Beyoncé began working toward those goals, Solange was starting to discover her own gifts. I was very conscious that she not feel overshadowed. I remembered how people used to make a big deal of my older brothers. Butch's good looks, Larry's brilliance, Skip's athleticism—people sometimes acted like I was just *there*. Any younger sibling could feel diminished by an older sibling, but in Solange's case there was the added element of her big sister being a performer. I understood this, so I always celebrated my daughters' differences while never comparing them.

I started taking Wednesday afternoons off to set aside alone time with Solange. As a mother, I know it is important to see when a child needs that extra bit of attention. "Solange's Day," as we called it, was a time she could just *talk*. Because this girl loved storytelling and had the most vivid imagination of any child I'd known.

One of those Wednesdays, we headed to the bookstore after school—the top down and the radio up. Solange loved reading, and I was always on the lookout for books where she might see herself in the stories.

"Why do we have to have this kind of car?" Solange asked. It was always zero-to-sixty with her at that time. She would be thinking hard about something all on her own, come to all these conclusions, and then—bam—she was going to let you know a thing.

"You don't like our car?" I looked out at the hood of the Jaguar gleaming black in the Texas sun.

"Well, the Browns have a Toyota Camry," she said, matter-of-fact.

Oh, Lord, the Browns. This was an imaginary family Solange had created. They were any kid's ideal family: The Brown parents worked at Chuck E. Cheese, she would explain, came home at the same time every night, and Mr. and Mrs. Brown cooked dinner together for their four kids. And now, apparently, they had a sensible car, too.

"A Toyota Camry?" I said. "That is so nice. We have a Jaguar. And that's what works for our family." Even with my eyes on the road, I could feel the piercing judgment from the passenger side.

At first, I'd laughed at these stories, but she was dead serious about them. It came to a head once because she was supposed to go to a pool party and was sick. "Solange, you've got a cold," I'd said. "You can't go." The Browns, she informed me, let her go swimming when she was sick.

"I don't care about them," I said, too harshly. "They're made up anyway." Her whole body recoiled. She looked so crushed. I knew she had based the Browns on our friends the Creuzots. My best friend Cheryl Creuzot had four kids—one of whom had been the inspiration for me even having Solange. Whenever we had to go out of town over-night for Beyoncé and couldn't take Solange because of school, the Creuzots were the people I trusted for her to stay with. She would come home from the stay, going on about how they were the most perfect family. Cheryl was hard on her four kids about schoolwork in a way I never was, and her husband, Percy, would go to the grocery store with her. When Cheryl came into Headliners to get her hair done, Solange watched as Percy would sit and wait on her to be done. It was so different from the way our family operated with all of our individual schedules. The Creuzots did not need an Uncle Johnny to take care of them because Cheryl was working late. Running her own financial planning service, she had managed her life to be home at the same time every day to check the kids' homework, with hands held open to say grace across the dinner table at exactly 6:01. Like the Browns—and not like us.

Beyoncé loved the freedom our family dynamic gave her, but I didn't yet understand how much Solange longed for practical structure. Life had given her a Jaguar, and she wanted a Toyota Camry.

Close to the bookstore, we stopped at a light, and I looked over at my singular, unique daughter. I'd always looked for books that might show her some character that she might identify with. I was starting to realize that she and I both were still finding out just who she was. Now, I had a better idea of what to do.

When we got to the store, I led Solange to a table of journals. I opened a few for her, showing the blank lined pages—all that structure for her unwieldy, already wise thoughts, each crisp page a new start.

I told her to pick one out to buy to keep as a diary. "This way," I said, "you can write your own story. In your words."

GIRLS TYME WAS GETTING MORE AND MORE KNOWN IN HOUSTON, playing huge events like the Sammy Davis Jr. awards benefit for the People's Workshop, and also the Black Expo. Kelly remembers that one as the first time she was onstage and thought, "We are going to be big."

There were a lot of little moments that seemed like the big break for Girls Tyme. In October 1991, a record producer, Arne Frager, flew the girls out to Sausalito in northern California to record demos at his famous studio, The Plant, to begin to shop the act around. Mathew just had to tell the girls that Frager had produced Michael Jackson's song with Rockwell, "Somebody's Watching Me," to get them excited. Arne was kind, with hair that had already gone white and a daughter who was Beyoncé's age. We met Arne through Lonnie Jackson—a young songwriter and producer who was as funny as he was talented. Lonnie kept us all cracking up in those days, working tirelessly with the group to define their early sound.

We took Solange along because we didn't like to leave her. As Girls Tyme worked on songs, we had to keep an eye on our five-year-old, a confident wanderer who was liable to walk off at any time. One afternoon we realized Solange had slipped out of an open door.

We all took over the place in a panic, enlisting everyone to look for her in the halls and the bathroom. *"Solange! Solange!"* we yelled. There was one last closed door to one of the studios. We walked in and found her sitting in a chair, smiling ear-to-ear and holding court as two young guys smoking Marin County's entire supply of weed hung on her every word.

"Hi," said Solange, looking dreamier than usual.

"This little girl is a trip, man," one of the men said, smiling just as much as her. He looked to be around nineteen or twenty. "She's been in here talking and dancing!"

It was Tupac Shakur. He was there with Shock G, recording with Digital Underground, who the girls were more excited to see because of "The Humpty Dance."

"She's really special," Tupac told us as I hustled her out the door before she really got a contact high. "Come on, Punkin'," I said to Solange, grabbing her hand as she turned to say in her Texas sweetness, "It was nice meeting you!"

When Tupac got big, it was Beyoncé who recognized Solange's buddy. I didn't see anyone *that* cute in the studio, but she remembered him. "Solange was in there probably telling Pac all these stories about us."

Arne worked his connections, but he just couldn't get them a record deal. We did a showcase, and Suzanne de Passe wrote us a note after. She not only helped develop Michael Jackson and the Jackson 5 as an act, but she was also the legendary president of Motown Records and the genius behind *Motown 25,* a TV special on tape our girls grew up watching. She was all business in her letter. Suzanne said "the little girl"—meaning Beyoncé—should be solo or we had to cut the group down to two singers and a rapper, because nobody was going to sign a group with that many people. Especially one with two dancers when no label ever signed dancers—they just hired them. But the girls were friends, and they had worked hard, so we couldn't do that to them. I tore up the note, knowing it would be hurtful to the other parents, who might pass the message on to the girls that Beyoncé had been singled out.

I did take Suzanne's critique about the costumes as a lesson. I had dressed them in these sequined tuxedos, which she said were way too old for them when they needed to have a funky vibe. It was a reminder that they were still just kids. The girls were so talented, but really, the problem boiled down to the fact that they were only ten years old. Beyoncé was the peacemaker, the mother holding meetings to settle every dispute among the girls fairly. LaTavia, the sassy one who would speak up for the girls, was also my road dog—if I was running errands, she would be right there. Ashley was already wise at just a year older than the girls, and they looked up to her. And sweet Kelly the cheerleader, keeping up morale no matter what.

Because Doris worked such long hours and a lot of times could not be there, I found myself becoming more and more protective of Kelly. Not getting her special treatment in that group, but just looking out for her.

"You are a princess," I would say, just to her. "Don't you forget that."

CHAPTER 24

BREAD OF LIFE

Summer 1992

RAISING OUR GIRLS in our middle-class neighborhood, I wanted them to truly know people who had less than them so they would learn to have empathy for others and be reminded of their blessings. I wanted them to know all sorts of people so they would care about them. If you teach your kids to care about other people—that they are important too, no matter where they come from—that's a value that will stick with them. Even in our middle-class neighborhood, the city had put a halfway house in, something they wouldn't dream of doing in a white part of town. Early one evening, Solange and I were watering the flowers when I heard Beyoncé around the corner of the house talking with the kids in the neighborhood. These were the children and grandkids of judges and doctors, and they parroted some of what their parents said.

"Well, homeless people are drug addicts and alcoholics," one said. "They're either crooked or lazy."

I waited for Beyoncé to say something to push back. To say, "No, that's not true." She was silent.

Down went the hose. "Solange, come, 'cause you need to hear this too," I said. I popped right around that corner like a wise witch in a fairy tale. "Guys, everybody that's homeless is not a bum," I said. "Some people are educated or just smarter than you know, and we are lucky, but many people don't have housing they can afford even if they have a job. The system is working against them, so we're not going to kick them while they're down. Remember, there but for the grace of God go I. Go *us*."

They all looked at me like I was crazy.

Then God provided the lesson my children needed. On a Sunday soon after in 1992, we were at a lovely church service at Windsor Village Methodist, the megachurch we had been attending for years. We loved it there—they had the best choir in town, and the best preacher.

It was during his sermon that we were called. "We've been given a church downtown," the preacher said. "And we need you guys to occupy it. And so, the people who live on that side of town must leave us for this blessed opportunity to be part of the community downtown." He began calling out several families, starting with the Knowles family. "We'd like for you, these ten families, to go and occupy the church."

I was heartbroken. I loved Windsor Village, and being cast out to this new place, St. John's, felt like we were being exiled. The Methodist Church gave them this derelict church that had nine white members downtown. The church had kind of died, and we were supposed to give it new life with a mission of ministering to the homeless people in the community near the church. Now it was our mission too.

The church itself was in terrible disarray, but we all got together and painted. We were inspired by the incredible work ethic and faith of co-pastors Rudy and Juanita Rasmus, who founded St. John's mission and started the Bread of Life program to feed people in need. The sanctuary of the church was the dining room, a place for the family meal.

Every other Sunday, I volunteered the girls to serve food at these meals. Usually, we would have gone straight to Luby's Cafeteria after church. They had the best mac and cheese, jalapeño cornbread—good hot food as if your mother made it knowing you were coming. Solange and Beyoncé always got Salisbury steak.

"We have to wait like two, three hours now," said Beyoncé. "It's not fair." But it's what we were called to do, I told them. As the weeks passed, they got into being of service and they learned the lesson, getting to see and *know* families that were homeless. Kids who looked like them. They had the opportunity to treat them with dignity.

The things that the girls learned at St. John's are in their toolbox now: Beyoncé using her sense of order to portion out the meals so nobody felt cheated. Solange standing up on the stool to pass out the bread because she wanted to look everyone in the eye. When Angie spent summers with us, she was right there with us at church. Going around after the meal, the girls were hungry themselves, but they shook hands and visited with people as *they* ate. I wanted to teach them that being rich had absolutely nothing to do with what was in our bank account. True wealth was measured in their ability to share blessings, feeling the honor of someone letting you care for them, and staying grateful that you even have anything to give.

There was still more I could do. I went to Pastors Rudy and Juanita Rasmus with the idea to offer the women we served free services at Headliners. I knew the power of self-esteem. I decided to invite about nine or ten each Wednesday and made a point to not isolate them or have them come in after hours. Our new trainees would care for them, not because I thought their time was less valuable, but to let them know the culture of Headliners. If they didn't treat these women with dignity, I knew they didn't deserve to be at my salon.

Every Wednesday these women I met through St. John's would come to Headliners and be among the attorneys and utility executives, people who would inspire them and sometimes even be able to help them get back on their feet. The professionals who came to Headliners had access—they could help navigate a form to get services and they knew about jobs that might be available. "Listen, if y'all got clothes that you're not wearing," I would say, "then share with them because they've got to go to job interviews." And I loved connecting women to those opportunities. I would say, "Oh, you know who's looking for work?" I would know this woman by now, describe her strengths and things that I thought she could work on. "You know anybody who has any positions open, or how you can help her?"

This was networking in the classic way, which you understand if you're like me and grew up poor with dreams. When somebody wanted to get a job, you talked to people about it and prepared them for the interview because it's different when you don't have the resources of the outside world. Not everybody's daddy has a friend he can call and say, "Can you get my child an internship for the summer?" or "Well, can you help my child get into UCLA?" That's what people think networking is now, but we networked in a different way, and it was to survive. I knew exactly what it was to have to be creative. How to answer the age-old question of "How can I get this done with no money?"

I was that girl in Galveston; I was that woman standing there putting two people together in Headliners; and I am that woman writing to you now. I am so grateful for every hurdle in my life that turned into a gift.

That is how God works. Sometimes you don't understand it, but He is giving you things that you can take out of the toolbox and use.

AS A SIDE PROJECT FROM HEADLINERS, MATHEW AND I STARTED A magazine called *Hair International*. This was pre-internet, so the way salon owners and hairstylists found each other was through print media. I wanted to publish my own large, glossy magazine devoted to Black women and hair trends.

We went around getting people to invest, usually about a thousand dollars each, and Mathew and I put in about twenty-five thousand dollars of our own money. I would track down some great stylist in another city—especially Atlanta, D.C., and New York—cold call them from Headliners, and talk them into having a hair photo shoot, which most of them had never done before. I would give them guidelines about getting the right light and being close enough to show texture and details. But a lot of my time was spent talking women into understanding that their work was worthy of documenting. Back then, so much of a beauty professional's work was supposed to stay behind the scenes. It was life-changing for some of them to hear, "*You* are an artist. Let's let people know about you."

I didn't know what I was doing, but I did it. I wanted nice thick paper with big full-color photos, and the publication was very successful. We charged twenty-five dollars a copy when we presented it at beauty trade shows like Bronner Bros., which was the premier Black hair show, bringing thousands of attendees to Atlanta.

After the first issue of *Hair International* was a certified sell-out hit, stylists and salons from all over the world were sending in submissions to be featured. It helped them to be in the magazine, which I was proud of, but producing it was so expensive that we could only afford to do two issues a year. The problem was that Mathew and I realized we were in the shipping business. We sent the magazines to the shows—places like New York and Tennessee, anywhere the big shows were—and we had to ship these huge metal frames to display them.

They were as big as room dividers, and of course we would wait until the last minute to send them, so the shipping would eat up all our money. Soon, we realized we were *losing* money. It was a drain. I kept wanting to stop publication, but Mathew was so gung ho about it. It was another of his obsessions that I didn't fully understand.

So I would focus on Headliners, bringing our girls with me to help out when they weren't rehearsing. Even at the salon, they performed, and they had a captive audience. The women would applaud, and sometimes not. You have to get used to all kinds of audiences. Sometimes when they were still in earshot, a client might ask a shady question, one designed to give us a reality check. They might be talking about the young singer Brandy and say, "When we gonna see *your* daughter do that?" and then, "Is your daughter still in that little singing group?"

Then, once they had local success, the question evolved to "When am I gonna see that little singing group do something big in Houston?"

"They're already going places," I would say, more for the girls to overhear than for the client.

Finally, someone asked, "Are they still only doing stuff in Houston? When is your daughter gonna be on TV?"

Imagine how I felt when I had an answer.

"Well, you're going to see them on *Star Search*."

CHAPTER 25

THE LOSS IS
THE FUEL

November 1992

THE LOSS ON *Star Search* is now part of the auspicious origin story of Destiny's Child, but that November day it was just six excited girls in Florida, getting ready to go on a show they were obsessed with. They watched the competition program together every week, judging with the judges, deciding how many stars—from one to four—each act deserved. Arne Frager had secured the spot, thinking it would be an easy win and launchpad for Girls Tyme to go national and get a deal. We would tape in early November, then keep quiet about the results until the episode aired in February.

Lonnie and the other adults really pushed for a hip-hop song that would open with a rap. Mathew felt strongly that they should do a ballad, "Sunshine," that would showcase the vocals. He was overruled.

So our girls—"the hip-hop rappin' Girls Tyme" as host Ed McMahon introduced them—were up against the returning champions, a group of white thirtysomething guys named Skeleton Crew. The ones who would become famous for getting a perfect four stars to Girls Tyme's three.

Afterward, Mathew went up to Ed McMahon. "Do you know why the girls didn't win?" he asked. "Can you give them any advice?" Ed said they were just too young, which was true, and that they had more work to do. But he also reeled off a list of people who'd lost on *Star Search* but went on to do great things. "The ones who make it, win or lose, don't quit."

This was exactly the inspiration that Mathew needed to boot up the girls and himself. He cast the loss as a step in the right direction: "Don't worry about it. We're gonna go back and rehearse and we're gonna get better. We're gonna use this as fuel."

Mathew saw the *Star Search* loss as a sign that he needed to step up—he was not going to be outvoted on something as important as the choice of song. He needed to take more of an official role as a co-manager, not just a parent who did the work of a co-manager.

It wasn't long after that Mathew came to me with another decision. He had decided to leave his corporate job and devote his life to managing the group. He hadn't quit yet, but it was like every other decision he made: done.

I was just as clear. "It's your life and I'm not going to argue with you," I said, "but I'm scared. You make a lot of money, and how are we gonna keep up?"

"Oh, the salon is booming," he said. "And I'm gonna help you manage Headliners because we can make so much more money there."

Oh boy. Mathew came in and worked there for a while, but it didn't work out. First off, it was my space, and I didn't like the changes he wanted, even if he was right. He correctly pointed out that I used very expensive products but that wasn't reflected in the price of the service. I would either have to use cheaper products—which neither of us wanted to do—or I had to go up on my prices. Now "our" prices.

"It's not just products, Tina," he said. "You are charging the same prices as other places that do not serve wine. That do not offer the service you do and do not get to people in fifteen minutes."

Without asking me, Mathew came up with the idea of charging every client a two-dollar service charge to spread out the increase. He wrote a whole letter, printing one for each client, folded neat in an envelope to be handed to them as they arrived. I watched them read it as they came in, getting pissed. But it was needed, and the charge kept the salon profitable without raising prices across the board. His ideas for growing the business weren't wrong, but our communication styles clashed, and I cared about people as much as I did the bottom line. Finally, I told him, "You gotta go. Focus on the girls."

I got what I wished for, but then it was all on me to keep us afloat. Not just the family, but the group and the hopes of these little girls. It did not help that Mathew still spent money like he had a six-figure paycheck. When the cellphone came out, this man ran up two-thousand-dollar bills letting the kids get on the phone to call all their friends. I'd find him with them sitting in the driveway, calling just to tell their friends they were using a cellphone.

Along with this huge shift in our lives, there were changes in the group. Ashley's mother made the decision she would be better off solo, so everyone was sad to see her go. The dancing sisters Nikki and Nina also left.

That left Beyoncé, Kelly, LaTavia, and a new addition, Beyoncé's classmate LeToya. In addition to having a beautiful high note, LeToya was the funniest kid I'd ever been around and would do great impressions.

And then, of course, Solange, always on the edge of things at seven. Her mind worked nonstop watching the girls practice at our house every day. She would offer opinions about choreography, and yes, tell someone when they were singing off-key. I would be in the kitchen, and I'd hear a girl harshly say, "Be *quiet,* Solange." Beyoncé's answer was to remove Solange to keep the peace. "Get out of here, Solange."

Where could Solange go? This was her home, and her childhood too.

CHAPTER 26

THREE SISTERS

Summer 1993

T HERE'S A HOME video we lost in a move, and it hurts my heart just to think about it. It's of Solange at seven, the night she won the same People's Workshop entertainer award that her sister had won around her age. She sang Shanice's "I Love Your Smile" in a dress I'd made for her with these cute leggings and my rhinestone belt. She completed the look with rhinestone cat-eye glasses, so unexpected and so *her,* even then. I worried she was too young to compete, but she wanted to go up against the big kids. At the end, whereas Shanice sings "Go, Branford, go," in response to Branford Marsalis's saxophone solo, Solange changed the lyric to "Go, judges, go." She charmed them, not just winning the night but getting a standing ovation.

Solange was invited to repeat the performance at AstroWorld, which had a huge amphitheater frequented by established acts coming through. The People's Workshop show had been for about four hundred people, but now Solange would be performing outdoors for probably a couple thousand kids. They would have to set up a little platform for her to sing and dance on, because she was up on a high stage, and they wanted everyone to be able to see her.

I'd been at shows there before, and I was scared for her. I said, "It goes *way* back." Meaning not just the audience, but the force of the star power this tiny girl would have to send out.

"She's gonna be fine," Mathew said. "She's gonna go out there and love it."

That day I watched as this little girl magnified herself and gave the crowd no choice but to go crazy. She moved to another level, right there before our eyes. She killed it, and more important, she *loved it.*

After all the celebrating was over, all the play-by-play moments of her moves and the crowd reactions, I went to bed uneasy that night *because* she had moved to another level. The truth was that I didn't *want* Solange to be an entertainer. I saw the downsides of the business, mainly that I felt Beyoncé and Kelly missed out on a lot of the things that should be natural to a kid. Not having to worry about things so much or watch what you say. To just be kids.

I wanted that for Solange. She and I had spent all this time back-stage at places for the girls, adrenaline finally ebbing because we made it somewhere on time. People would be pushing past us, and I would hold Solange close to me as she watched the girls onstage. "You could go be anything you want to," I would tell her right there backstage. "You got the grades, you got the smarts, you got the per-sonality, you got everything it takes to have a really happy life. And not do *this.*"

I was that clear: This was not *my* first choice for Solange at all. Her dad always encouraged her interest, but I tried my hardest to steer her away from entertainment. As Solange grew, her pursuits and hobbies were so varied that I felt she could choose any path and suc-ceed. "You have so many friends and other things that you can do," I would tell her. "You can go to college and be free. Don't have all these pressures."

But, like I said, this was not my choice. It was hers.

I FELT A DIVISION GROWING BETWEEN SOLANGE AND BEYONCÉ. IT was the way of sisters: The girls were seven and almost twelve, and any parent of girls with a five-year age difference like mine can tell you about that time when the older one starts to want to be more indepen-dent. This comes as a shock to the younger one, who has literally spent her life in the presence of her sister. When the door gets slammed, it can really hurt the younger sibling. Now, Solange was not some little angel—she was a mess. She would stir things up all the time, like any other kid sister.

Solange was nurturing her gifts and I worried she would feel eclipsed before she even started to do what made her happy. I also wanted Beyoncé to be more aware of how her actions affected her sister. Yes, she was driven, and that was commendable, but that drive couldn't block out all her responsibilities. I wanted my daughters to grow up close, so that when they were older, they would remain sisters not just in blood relation, but as best friends.

I looked into getting a therapist who specialized in child psychology. I had read enough to know that there was nothing wrong with focusing on mental health, but when I mentioned it to certain family members, they outright told me it was a mistake.

"You're going to *make* them crazy because they're too young for you to take them," one sibling scolded me. Meanwhile, I had brought it up to them to try to have a conversation about our relationship and our history together.

It was important to me that the therapist be Black, and I found a gentle gay man with a special ability for communicating with children. No gift would have worked for Beyoncé, who hated therapy because she didn't like to talk. But Solange *loved* therapy because she got to talk nonstop. She clicked with the child psychologist right away and looked forward to therapy every week. The man had a small office on Kirby in Houston, and I would sit in the little waiting area as the girls talked. Then the therapist would discuss their conversations with me without being invasive of their privacy.

As much as she didn't like therapy, I saw the biggest changes in Beyoncé. She was way more sensitive and protective of Solange. A noticeable change was during rehearsals. Solange offered advice on a step, and one of the girls snapped at her.

"Don't talk to my sister like that," Beyoncé said. "Solange, come on and show us the step." Solange did just that, and it was a good note. But even if it hadn't been, Beyoncé showed her sister respect and kindness. Now eight years old, Solange began coming up with steps for the group, offering a "Y'all should do it like this 'cause that's not working." Not all of the steps, of course, but enough to earn the respect of everyone there. Enough that they followed Solange's eye as she examined each performer, waiting to hear her verdict.

Once we had the tools to help them anticipate and work through issues with sibling rivalry, Beyoncé stopped going to therapy, but Solange continued. Sometimes, she and the therapist would talk over ice cream he brought her, and Solange would bring her diary to go over some of her feelings. Writing had already become a place where she could express her frustrations and then figure out a way to voice them with him.

In one of her sessions, I learned that Solange had written, "What kind of mom lets you miss school to play hooky?" This was about the Beach Days. The therapist asked how I felt about Solange saying that about me, and I was honest: It didn't feel great, but it was her right to ask that question. As we delved further into it, it was clear that part of Solange feeling some type of way about me letting them play hooky was that she thought I didn't value her education. That couldn't be further from the truth, however I also was never that serious parent who demanded, "You gotta bring home straight A's." I was the one who said, "Do your best."

Solange was still so young, and I trusted her to find her passion and thought I was doing the right thing telling her, "You can do anything you put your mind to." With the therapy sessions, I realized Solange didn't understand I really meant *anything*. She wanted what other kids got: concrete ideas and nudging guidance toward college. "If you want to go to college, I will definitely be right here to support you," I said. "But I'll be honest with you, Solange, college is just not that important to me. You are."

I took the lesson. When Solange visited the salon, I made a point of asking women of different professions questions about their career path, and what types of education opened doors for them. Solange absorbed all the journeys of these women—she later called them her tribe—and they mentored her by investing their stories in her future.

Months went by, and then there was a Sunday morning when I heard Solange and Beyoncé singing together, and I realized it had been a while. I crept toward Solange's room, afraid that my presence would break the spell. I could just see them sitting on the edge of the bed. Beyoncé held Solange's hand in her lap, their eyes closed as they sang in harmony.

·   ·   ·

AT THE START OF THE SUMMER OF 1993, KELLY'S MOM DORIS CAME
to us with a problem. She had begun working with a new white family, and not only did they not want Kelly to live in their house, they
were not comfortable with Doris taking their kids along as they
drove Kelly to our home in the Third Ward. We felt they didn't
want their kids coming to our Black neighborhood. There was some
discussion about how we as a group could look after Kelly, letting
her stay and shuttling her back and forth. To me the answer was
clear.

"Doris, why don't you let Kelly stay here for the summer?" I asked.
We didn't know it would be six years and then forever in our hearts as
family. Doris was grateful, but so was I—Beyoncé was *so* happy to have
Kelly there. When Kelly moved in, Beyoncé shared her room with her,
and their bond only got deeper.

There were growing pains that summer. I overcompensated to help
Kelly get adjusted. At dinner I would say, "Oh, Kelly, you can have the
last piece of chicken." Solange, six years old with the watchful eye of a
writer, might seize the moment to express her feelings. "You know, you
just give Kelly everything," she'd say. "You don't fuss at her. Kelly gets
away with murder."

Solange and Kelly did butt heads sometimes, but I never once saw
Bey and Kelly get in a disagreement. Even with the other girls in the
group, Beyoncé would naturally have arguments, but not those two.
That August, however, something came up: It was time to go school
shopping for new clothes, and I was not sure yet how Doris would feel
about me buying Kelly outfits for school. It was no secret I was paying
for a lot of her things, but I was aware of her position as a mother and
never wanted to overstep.

"You need to share clothes with Kelly," I told Beyoncé privately.

"Well," she said, like it was a negotiation. "I don't really want to
share my clothes."

"Well," I said, matching her tone. "You're going to have to share
some of your stuff."

"I'll give them to her," she said. She's still like that: Will give you
the shirt off her back, but once she does you can keep it.

Kelly stayed with us beyond that summer, our home becoming hers.
Solange and Beyoncé were her sisters, and she became our daughter.

As "Aunt Tina" I never tried to replace Doris, just stand by her side supporting our Kelly. At some point, as years passed, Kelly would start calling Mathew "Dad" like her sisters did. She was always such a sensitive sweet kid, and it says so much about their relationship that Beyoncé did not tell Kelly that it was hard for her to hear that in the beginning.

"She is calling my dad 'Dad,'" Beyoncé told me when we were alone in the car. "And I don't like that." We talked, and I was proud that my quiet, accommodating girl could explore her honest feelings about it. I explained to her that Kelly seeing Mathew as a father figure didn't take him away from Beyoncé, just as Kelly hadn't made Solange and Beyoncé any less sisters. It was an adjustment, and she accepted it, even growing to like sharing her dad. There is a long tradition of Black families expanding to include people as need and love have called for it, and that is just who we were.

Eventually, years later, Kelly and I would have a conversation when she was eighteen. We talked about how we both had always held space for Doris—who she called Mama—to be her mother, but I could be her mother too. Kelly began to call me Ma, and I am continually astonished and grateful to God for giving us this gift of Kelly.

SOLANGE HAD KEPT UP WITH THERAPY, AND I WAS RELIEVED SHE had a safe place to talk about all her feelings. When she was eight, here and there her therapist had to cancel appointments because he was ill. He began looking skinnier, drawn around the face, the weakness of his body slowing him in the session, though his spirit compensated.

And then we got word that Solange's therapist had been hospitalized and quickly died from AIDS. There was no way for it not to be traumatic for a third grader, losing this sweet man who listened to every word she said without judgment. She went into a depression that felt like winter falling on all of us. Her reawakening was slow, leaden with stops and starts.

Even before this difficult time, Johnny and I were coming apart. It was over his new boyfriend, who he had moved into the back apartment with him behind our house on Parkwood. I did not trust that man for a half-second with Johnny's heart—he would talk crazy to

Johnny and he said enough things around me that led me to believe he was a cheater. I thought Johnny was settling because he was so lonely after Peanut.

With the death of Solange's therapist still fresh in my mind, I worried for Johnny being with someone I felt could put him at risk for HIV. "This guy is not the guy," I told Johnny. "I think he's promiscuous." That was a loaded word then, wrapped up in morality. He had always been a one-man guy, and if this boyfriend was sleeping around, I didn't think Johnny was someone who could have conversations with him about safety. He would just accept it, and I could not.

It hurt Johnny that I couldn't stand this man, and we had a falling-out. It wasn't long before he told me he was going to move out. He started working for my old friend Marlene, who I stayed with when Solange was a newborn. They became inseparable, and I admit I felt some sort of way. Johnny still came over to visit all the time, he loved the kids, but we were not as tight as we were.

I was dealing with that loss of my soulmate, hoping it was temporary, when the bottom dropped out on me. Mathew and I were hit with a huge tax bill that would change everything. We were taking care of too many people to let them down; we didn't want to let on that it was hard. Because of the tax lien, we had to file for bankruptcy and would have to sell our dream home on Parkwood.

I had always had it in my head, and a lot of Black people do in Houston, that I was going to stay in the Third Ward. As I watched all these people make it and move to the suburbs, getting brand-new houses for less money with less upkeep, I would say to myself: *I'm gonna stay and make my neighborhood better.* Now I couldn't afford to. We needed enough space for the three girls, plus our home had become a girl group headquarters, and we needed room for them. I'd also assured the kids, "We're gonna move into a smaller house, but it's gonna have a pool."

We got $60,000 from the sale of the house. One place I looked at fell through after we'd already sold Parkwood, so I was desperate when I walked into the ranch-style house on Braes Meadow Drive with a pool for the girls. But the house was such a 1970s time capsule. The entry hall had a disco-ball light fixture and was covered in a rice-paper wallpaper in an avocado green shade. This was only outdone by the dining room, which had a wall of mirror tiles with blond veins running through them. There was more wallpaper in the living room, a style the designer might have called Crazy Floral.

"But what can you work with?" I heard my mother saying. So I took it. The house was very clean, and they built a modern annex of a den. The bedrooms were okay, with skylights because that had been a big thing in the seventies. And it had a beautiful pool in a great neighborhood.

The next day I got some paint and covered the rice paper in the entryway with a soft cream. And it actually looked nice. I took out the disco ball, bought a smaller fixture to open up the space. The mirror wall taunted me, so one night after putting the girls to bed, I could not stop thinking about it. I went to the supply closet to grab a hammer and an old blanket to use as a muffler. 'Cause I meant business. I took that muffled hammer to every one of those tiles, shattering each one. Like some crazy person, I was at it all night, but I needed to make this house our home.

Then I tackled the living room. And took that wallpaper *down*. The kids loved the *new* new house. I loved the opportunity to bring order into my life.

At Headliners, I had a young assistant named Abel Gomez who had come from Mexico, his accent remaining thick as my parents' Louisiana while he learned English. His work ethic also reminded me of my parents', even before I learned what sacrifices he and his family had made for him to go to beauty school. I felt a kinship with Abel as he worked his way up through Headliners.

There had been so many stylists "graduating" from Headliners to form their own places, but it was Abel I related to the most. This young gay man was a Capricorn like me, and, also like me, was only comfortable in forward motion. If a client was having a hard time, he wouldn't charge them for the service. I did that as needed at Headliners, not doing it for any motive other than that I wanted to. When I saw Abel do that, I told him I was proud of him.

"Everything is not about the money," I told him as we were cleaning up. "That's not the measure of success."

One morning, over coffee, I told Mathew my plan: "What I really want to do, Mathew, is I really want to pay the rent up for like a year in advance." I know paying all that rent up front didn't make much business sense. But the money was safer there. Mathew was so intent on getting the girls' careers going with a new record deal, or making our *Hair International* magazine go big time, that I knew he would put every penny of our money in either pursuit. Mathew was that person who, if for some reason we would ever be down to like a thousand dollars, he'd go and spend seven hundred on some FedEx packages to send out tapes to record labels or magazines to potential beauty advertisers.

After paying the rent, we had $25,000. To Badass Tenie B, that was a fortune. For a breadwinner like I was, at least for the time being, it was watching the pressure going up to the roof.

CHAPTER 27

THE DOLLS

Summer 1994

M ATHEW KEPT PUSHING for Girls Tyme to make it, and sent a
VHS tape to Daryl Simmons, who had been a partner with
L.A. Reid and Babyface, two record-producer executives
who'd been in the R&B group The Deele in the early eighties. The
partners had recently gone their separate ways, and Daryl started his
own thing, Silent Partner Productions, in midtown Atlanta. Daryl
signed the girls to a production deal, and decided they should be called
The Dolls. The way a production deal works is that Girls Tyme weren't
signed directly to the label, they were signed to a deal with Daryl, who
was the one who had the deal with Elektra Records. The danger is that
when you're not signed to the label, you will always have that go-
between.

In 1994, Daryl wanted them to move to Atlanta for the summer
months off from school to record an album. Kelly had just turned
thirteen and Beyoncé was still twelve. Daryl was young but rich and
had a huge mansion in a gated community. We only agreed once it was
understood the four girls would have a parent-chaperone present at *all*
times. LaTavia's mother, Cheryl, went to live with them, and she had
already been a constant chaperone, taking good care of the girls. I had
Headliners, so I couldn't go full time, but Mathew and I would fly in
when we could, staying for four days at a time to allow Cheryl to go
home to her husband.

I would never have sent my kids if I thought it was risky. Daryl
understood that we were super-protective of our kids, but he thought

we had too many rules. For one, nobody could curse around the girls, and people couldn't smoke around them. These were rules that were very different for the music business, but Daryl told us he got it.

The girls were in heaven, mainly because they got to meet TLC and other stars in the Atlanta music universe, like Usher and Monica. Monica was produced by Dallas Austin, who had a studio next door to Daryl, so they got to hang out with her all the time. It was inspiring for them to see a girl their age who already had a hit record.

Cheryl was beyond reproach as a chaperone, but there were small things that seemed harmless to the adults around the girls that still troubled me. One time, TLC was having a birthday party for one of the members. Cheryl and I had discussed whether the girls could go if she chaperoned. I advised her, "You should take them to the party, let them stay an hour until she blows out the candles, but then bring their behinds home." But when Cheryl's hair appointment ran late that day, the group all left for the party without her. Cheryl called me immediately and I said, "You call around until you find out where that party is, and you get in a cab and you go." She did, and the girls had a great time, because they got to stay an hour or so longer than their moms would have let them. It was all innocent, but our agreement was that they would always have a chaperone, and I worried Cheryl felt disrespected by the other adults.

Right after, Cheryl's husband happened to be driving to Atlanta to spend time with her for an extended weekend. I was already scheduled to fly there to bring the girls back to Houston so Cheryl could have a break, so while I was in Atlanta, I asked to speak to Daryl. I wanted to check in to make sure our rules were respected. I told him, "I heard some guy was smoking weed in one of the studios." I reminded him I didn't want the kids exposed to these things and added that when Mathew and I came out to Atlanta, "we don't feel welcome with you because I feel like you wanna be in total control." We had noticed them having an attitude whenever we started asking questions about the work.

Daryl got defensive. "Y'all are just not gonna work in the industry," he said, and I'm sure my neck was rolling a little bit at him getting heated. I listened to him say the girls would never make it with me and Mathew—with all the parents—because we were too "square." I'd never been called square in my life. "This is the music business," he said, "and you need to get with it."

Before I could say anything, he rolled on. "This is a huge opportunity for them. Look at me. This totally changed my life. I remember me and Babyface and L.A. going to the mall and we couldn't buy anything and then all of a sudden, we could just go buy *whatever we wanted,* and the money just flowed. . . ."

I was getting more pissed off as I realized he thought money was our goal.

"*Listen,* that is not our story," I said. "Every one of these kids' parents will see that they have a good future. This is not that life-changing to *them.* They're gonna be happy and healthy no matter if they're singers or not. That's not the only way out."

And that's what pissed *him* off. He seemed to take it personally, but he shouldn't have implied that this was all about money.

"Well, you need to take the girls home because I'm dropping them," he said.

"Oh no, please don't do that." *How had it gotten to this?* I wondered.

"Yes. Y'all, this is never gonna work because y'all are too protective," he said.

"That's gonna devastate them," I said. "It's gonna *really* hurt them. Let's talk about it."

Daryl dismissed me with a wave. "You have yourself to thank that you messed it up for them, they're not gonna make it."

"You are not God, and you are not in control," I said. "You can't tell me what's gonna happen. They will get another deal." That was a bluff.

He shooed me out. It was over. I was shocked. I left and went and got the kids. At first, I didn't tell the girls what had happened. I let them think we were sticking to the original plan of going to Houston for an extended weekend, then bringing them back Tuesday.

I couldn't tell them. I felt physically sick that I had ruined all of this for them. Back home in Houston, all they talked about was how they were going to go back and hang out with TLC. They thought they were going to have this kid-sister relationship with them, and as they talked, I felt less and less able to tell them. "They're gonna hate me" were the words I heard over and over in my head. "They're gonna hate me."

Mathew was not upset with me at all. "You did the right thing," he said. That said, he added, we had to tell the girls. My plan was to tell them after work on Saturday, but when I got home, I couldn't bring myself to. Finally, after church on Sunday, I told them at lunch at Luby's. There were lots of tears, and I kept saying, "I'm so sorry."

I was such an obvious wreck that the girls started to reassure me, telling me they understood. Comforting *me*.

As usual, Mathew launched into why this was going to work out for the best when they got a real record deal. "It was just a production deal," he said. "It would be better if you were signed to the label—this wouldn't have given you any power."

They nodded, kids who only wanted to sing. "Still," I said, "I messed things up for y'all."

For decades, I thought that was the full story. Then Mathew had a conversation with Daryl. Mathew told me that Daryl graciously shared that his production deal with Elektra was discontinued before our conversation. Daryl said he didn't have the heart to tell the girls, so he kept trying to get another deal. When I showed up talking about rules, Daryl told Mathew he saw his opportunity to get out and not let the girls down.

I had never understood how the discussion had escalated to me packing up my kids and going. Now I did.

I wish I'd known the full story then. Instead, I carried that weight all those years. Someone might have assumed success made my lonely burden lighter, that having to tell my daughters "I messed things up for you" would become an increasingly vague memory that blurred with each blessing.

It did not.

JUST AS WE WERE ADJUSTING TO THE GROUP HAVING THIS SETBACK, Solange was having trouble with her teacher, an older white woman from the South. When I went to our first meeting, the teacher walked by me several times until I asked if she was Solange's teacher.

"I just wasn't expecting someone that looked like you," she said to me.

"What do you mean?"

"Well, your daughter is very . . ." She searched for the word. *"Ethnic."*

When the meeting started, she immediately pointed out that Solange wasn't going to fit in, not even with the other Black kids. The teacher mentioned the five kids in the class and explained that they had been grouped together since kindergarten. They were meek and mild, never using slang—what we would have called "whitewashed" in Galveston. And then there was my daughter in her braids, wearing Cross Colours and combat boots. Already conversant in the language of hip-hop. *Ethnic.*

"They won't accept her," said the teacher.

"Well, they will if *you* accept her," I said. "And it's your job to make sure they do."

She urged me to take Solange out of her class, an A group for advanced kids.

"I'm not gonna put her in the B group because *kids* won't accept her," I said. "She is staying."

There were ways, small and large, that the teacher showed Solange she wasn't welcome. I remember my daughter being so proud of a school project on heroes, for which she chose to spotlight Oprah Winfrey. The teacher had students go in alphabetical order, but when she got to *K* for Knowles and Solange was prepared to go up, she suddenly announced they would be starting backwards from *Z*. I said something to the teacher, trying to explain how strange I thought it was, but she acted like I was seeing things. This is an effective technique of undermining you early on for when the aggression becomes more blatant.

Which it did. A boy sitting next to Solange in class developed a fixation on her, pulling her hair and touching her skin. Solange's complaints weren't taken seriously. When the child began copying off her quizzes, I sent in a note, trying to be civil, asking that Solange be moved away from him. The teacher put Solange in "the corral," an area of the classroom reserved for kids who misbehaved. I once again had a conference, and the teacher acted as if she had simply honored my request. She feigned confusion, asking me to repeat myself, and wondered why I was "overreacting."

It was not long before the final straw fell on my baby. One night I got home from work late, around ten. Solange's bedtime was 8:30, but she was up waiting for me. She had called the salon and told Vernell what happened, but hearing Vernell's reaction, Solange made her promise to wait because she knew I would be right up at the school.

Now Solange took a breath and told me that that day the teacher explained what the n-word meant. Solange said the full word because the teacher did.

I said, *"What?"*

The teacher had presented an improbable story to the class that a child had privately asked her to define what an n-word is. To illustrate the slur—and allow her to repeatedly say the word in class—she made up the story that once upon a time a little Black boy was swinging in a tree when he called a little white girl the n-word. The teacher clearly created this narrative so she could have the little Black boy say the bad word. Solange's teacher continued this bizarre tale, saying the little white girl went home and asked her mother what an n-word was. And then she defined it in front of my daughter and all these kids: "It's someone who's low class, trashy, lazy."

"I'll handle this," I told Solange. "You did the absolute right thing telling me."

I could not sleep that night. Mathew and I had a meeting the very next day. The principal was there, and the teacher said she was trying to give an example because one of the kids had asked what an n-word is. Again, she said it fully to our faces the same way she did to our child.

Mathew got so upset. "Don't ever use that derogatory term," he said. "My child has never even heard that word." I was sure she had, but context matters.

"This kid who asked you," I asked, "was he white?"

"Yes," she said, "but he told me a Black child had called him that . . ." She said it *again*.

"That is some bullshit," I said.

The principal cut in, telling us that the teacher was their finest, and reminded me how parents begged for their kids to be put in her class. She had a lot of power with the school board, he added, but perhaps Solange wasn't a good fit and would be happier in another class, naming the teacher of the B group. This had been the plan all along.

"No, that's not fair to her," I said, "because she is doing well with accelerated learning. She will stay in this class if you're keeping this teacher, and she is gonna teach my kid because we pay our taxes and pay her salary. And she is gonna treat her right."

My husband suddenly asked the teacher, "Where are you from?"

"I'm from Alabama."

"Oh, that figures."

"Well, what's that supposed to mean?"

"Because I'm from Alabama too," he said. "Maybe we're cousins."

Her face scrunched in confused disgust. "Oh, I'm sure your people are Southern Baptists. My family is Catholic."

"You know, I don't want to have to come back up here again," I said. "I don't care who on the school board likes you. All the parents who like you, too. If you pick on my kid one more time, it's going to be me and you."

She looked at the principal, who took a stern voice. "Miss Knowles," he said, "we're not going to have any violence."

"I'm not talking to you," I said. "I'm talking to her." I looked right into the teacher's eyes, saw this little person who had amassed all this little power in her life and used it to hurt a kid. "And I'm just telling you I mean it."

We left. This was our baby. The teacher was okay with her for the rest of the year, but I decided it would be Solange's last one at that school.

ALL OF THIS WAS ON MY MIND WHILE I PREPARED THE FINISHING touches on the next issue of *Hair International*. I had that feeling mothers can have looking at our lives, where we look at what's essential to our children. The first thing to go is what we *want,* buying time before we cut what we need. That August, I felt like my children's futures were in the balance—Solange's education needed my full attention, and by losing the deal with Daryl, the girls had seen their third big break in a row crash and burn. First, they couldn't get a deal even with Arne Frager and the Plant behind them, and then the tragedy of *Star Search*. Now this.

I looked at our finances and declared that I was over the magazine. I told Mathew I didn't want to print the issue that we had ready. This wasn't really true—I loved writing and the community the magazine gathered—but *Hair International* took sixty thousand dollars to produce and ship. Too much money up front to hope to break even. I had to think of my kids.

Not long after, Mathew came to me. "Tina, you're gonna be so mad."

"What?" I said.

"I was going to surprise you," he said.

I could tell he was trying to sound happy. My heart was up in my throat immediately. I was just home from work. The three girls were watching TV in their pajamas. "Surprise me how, Mathew?"

He'd taken the money to print up the magazine, he said. He had rented a booth at Bronner Bros. without telling me, had the magazines printed and shipped to the show. "I said to myself, 'I'm gonna do it one last time, and I'm gonna surprise her and make this money.'" He kept talking. I blinked, swallowed, nodded out of reflex.

"We don't even have sixty thousand."

No, he assured me, he'd just taken the twenty-five thousand we had. Threw in maybe five thousand more on credit and did it for half the price. He went to get the copy of the magazine he had and handed it to me. I saw how he'd cut the cost in half. The paper so thin the images bled through. On top of that, they were dark and had a blur to them. All the detail of the hairstylists' work was lost.

It was the last straw for me. There were so many things wrong, but I could withstand them. This was going to affect my daughters. I started crying, and I had done everything not to cry about my marriage, no matter what. I could yell, I could state my case, but not cry. The tears came this time before I could stop them, swallow them with my pride.

"I can't believe you *did* this," I said.

"It's gonna be fine," he said. "Tina, I'll go to Bronner Bros. this weekend and I'm gonna sell all of them and we're gonna get the money back and everything's gonna be okay."

He left for the show on Thursday.

Friday, I would go and find me and the girls an apartment. I had to leave Mathew.

CHAPTER 28

MOTHER OF
INVENTION

August 1995

I COULD NOT AFFORD to cancel any clients. I had about two hours that Friday to find an apartment on my own, and the time limit gave a clarity to my thinking. The first day of school would be here before I knew it, and the biggest priority was getting a place with access to good public schools.

My focus was on schools for Solange and Kelly. Beyoncé was already set for ninth grade. She and Kelly, along with LeToya from the group, had tried out for the High School for the Performing Arts. Beyoncé and LeToya both got in, but the school had not accepted Kelly. She had been devastated, and Mathew and I had gone up there to tell them exactly what a big mistake they were making missing out on this incredibly talented student. "You are going to regret this one day," I said. This was what Mathew and I were good at: agreeing on how great our kids were.

Had been good at, I reminded myself at a stoplight. This marriage needed to end. I shook it off. *Worry about that later,* I thought. The best public schools were in the most expensive zip codes. Kelly needed a really good school to make up for the hurt of not getting into the one she wanted.

I looked over at the *Houston Chronicle,* folded on the passenger seat to show the apartments I'd circled. This was the same newspaper I'd been in years ago as a perfect family in a perfect house. I turned left to make the drive to River Oaks. Houstonians will laugh at "I was looking for a cheap place in River Oaks." It's the most expensive area with big, beautiful houses. But in that same area, which was not far from my salon, you could cross Kirby and find apartments in high-rises. They called it "an annex of River Oaks," but it was still in that zip code. I would pay more for less, but that would open doors for Kelly and Solange.

The woman renting out the apartment had agreed to meet me there. I practiced what I was going to say on the way up, putting on the armor of grace to deflect any questions about my credit. She opened the door with a smile, glasses on her pleasant face, and as she showed me the two-bedroom apartment, my script fell away. I told her what I had worked so hard to hide from everybody.

"I'm married, but this is just going to be me and my three girls," I said, aware that because we had filed for bankruptcy, my credit had not yet been reestablished. "I really need to get them in good schools. I might not look like much on paper, but I don't have any debt and I make good money myself so I can pay the first, the last, the whatever months you need in advance. Anything to get in the apartment because I really need this. For them."

I could feel us making a connection. Woman to woman, she understood. "I'm guessing you need to move in right away," she said.

"Yes," I said. "I can be ready tomorrow."

"Okay," she said. "It's yours." So easily and with such kindness that I wondered if someone had done her a favor some time back and I was reaping the benefits.

I raced over to River Oaks High School to start the process of getting Kelly enrolled. Then I went over to a magnet school down the road on San Felipe, T. H. Rogers School, for Solange. I had our new address memorized for forms like we'd been there months.

Now I had to tell the girls. I waited until all three were together, just us in the living room. Maybe it was *this* exact moment, telling them I was leaving their father—that had made me stay for so long. To just make it to the next good patch. I also had to break the news we were moving again. Ironically, I presented this as Mathew always spun bad news, getting the facts out of the way, then talking up the opportunity that change presented.

"But the good news is you will still see him all the time, and you guys are gonna get into really great schools," I said. "It's gonna be good and we are just all gonna be together and you know . . ." They stared at me. Beyoncé and Kelly then looked at each other. Kelly was fourteen, Beyoncé almost that age—they both kept their emotions close. Solange took it worse than her sisters, angry with me that I was upending her life at nine years old. She felt righteous about us abandoning her father. "But we love him," she said. *You love him.*

I did. Of course, I did. But I packed up the house and we moved Saturday. I left Mathew a lot of furniture, but I brought some of the things that I thought would make the girls feel at home. I stuck all this big, dramatic, beautiful furniture into that apartment, which I know now was silly. I think the minute the movers left, my cousin Wanda came over to look after the girls because I had to go work to pay for all of this. Wanda took one look at this big black lacquer wall unit and the giant sectional sofa that took up so much space in the apartment. "Why would you bring that in here?"

"I don't know," I answered, sounding lost. "I just want my kids to have all their stuff."

I told my daughters I was going to write about this time, and I asked Solange what she recalls. "Oh, I just remember that place being a one-bedroom tiny little apartment. . . ."

"What?" I said. "Girl, that apartment cost more than our house. It was a nice size. And it was a *two*-bedroom. Beyoncé and Kelly had a bedroom, and you slept with *me*."

"Are you sure, Mom?" she said. "I remember that being a one-bedroom."

"I'm going to call Beyoncé." And I did. "What's your memory of that apartment?" I asked her. "That two-bedroom one."

"Mama," Beyoncé said, "I don't remember much about that apartment because I did *not* like being there."

"It wasn't that bad," I said.

"I was so sad," she said. Just as I was taking that in, she added, "And it was a *one*-bedroom—"

"No, it was not," I said, laughing. "It was a two-bedroom. You and Kelly had a bedroom and me and Solange had a bedroom."

"I just remember it being *so small*."

Beyoncé *was* sad that first weekend in the apartment, when Mathew wasn't home yet to even know we had left him. But I had blinders on. I was unable or unwilling to see how much this was affecting my girls.

Wanda had to take me aside when I came home from work. "Beyoncé's been crying," Wanda whispered.

"Really?" I said. Because as mad as Beyoncé could get like any kid on the edge of fourteen, she was not a crier. She could withdraw, kind of go someplace else even when you were right there talking to her, but there wouldn't be tears.

"She's saying their lives have changed so much," said Wanda.

I could see the uncertainty wear on Kelly too, though she tried to hide it. She had had so many disruptions, moving from house to house with Doris's jobs. I had hoped to give her a sense of permanence, and I worried she had lost that again.

I knew how my mother would have made this a home: starting at its heart in the kitchen, committing time and energy to cooking a meal, putting hours into creating a gumbo. The ritual of cooking and cleaning up can give a parent and child structure. The cause and effect of gathering ingredients and making a meal, then the sink full of hot soapy water and the sense of completion children get from drying dishes and the belonging that comes with knowing where to put them away.

I knew that was the answer, but I did not have time. I needed to work. That weekend, it was easier for me to think that the girls' feeling out of place was about losing a big house. But kids sense things and my girls were all smart. This was about their mother and father.

Mathew got back on Tuesday to find that we had left him. "I can't do this," I told him. "It's too much." Mathew, who could sell a heater in the desert, did not fight me. We still wanted to do what was best for the kids: Mathew as a father and manager, me as a mother and provider.

We separated, and I didn't know how to tell people. I was too busy anyway. Every morning, there was the race to get three girls to three different schools. Then I would go to work, squeezing the seconds out of every minute with the timer set to blow at three o'clock when Solange's school let out. I would time it to put people under the dryer, so I could race over to her, then get Kelly at her 3:30 pickup, and Bey at 3:45.

I did what moms do—I made it work. I would take them through the fast-food line to get them an early dinner of Burger King to eat at the salon or drop them off at the apartment. When we first moved in, I thought the one thing that would save money was that the girls from the group were not going to want to come over to the house every day like before. I loved them, but it was expensive to feed all these girls and their friends too. "We won't have that pool anymore," I said, not realizing the pool was never the draw.

IN THOSE FIRST MONTHS LEADING UP TO THE HOLIDAYS, THE three girls visited Mathew at what had been their house. He didn't say anything bad about me, but Solange would come home mad at me. "My daddy doesn't have *any* food at his house," she would say. "All he has in his refrigerator is beer." When I bit my tongue, refusing to say what I thought of that, she got to what she saw as the heart of the matter. "He's lonely and he's sad. You *left* him." I had abandoned her hero.

I protected that image of him, just as my mama let me think my daddy was a hero. Like Solange, I thought my mother didn't appreciate my father. When he came home drunk on weekends, so loud he woke us, what I focused on was my mama fussing at him and nagging him for doing it again, spending the money we needed to live. "You don't even work," I would tell her in the morning, discounting the importance of her seamstress work because it was so everyday to me. Woman's work. She didn't say, "Girl, if you only knew." My mom probably made more than my dad, but she was not the type to ever say that. She would simply work on another beaded jacket, sewing and hustling to keep us afloat. She let him be "the man," always saying, "Well, your daddy's supporting us."

I realized I had married this version of my father—a good man who could make bad decisions—passing that burden down generation to generation. When Solange came home and got on my case to make me the mean monster, I dutifully played my mother's role. I didn't say to her, "Oh, well, your daddy just spent up all of our money," or "Your daddy is running around with women." How are you going to tell a little kid that? You can't tell them that if you care how it's going to affect them.

One time Solange returned from visiting her father and decided to run away. What she did was hide in our apartment building while we were in a panic for an hour or so. I thought someone had taken her, getting more and more terrified until she finally came from her hiding place. "This is why you should let Daddy come back," she said.

Our daughters' time with Mathew was greatly focused on singing and rehearsing, and now I can see the pressure they were under. Each thought if they were just good enough, that would make things right: Mathew was so intent on getting a record deal for them, maybe to prove his worth as a manager and father, and both Kelly and Beyoncé saw the missed opportunities that led up to our family falling apart.

The girls had lost tangible things kids can understand: their parents' marriage, the house, a car. All kids blame themselves for adult problems, no matter how many times you explain it has nothing to do with them. I added to the issue, though. In trying to never say anything bad about their father, I barely spoke of him. I left blanks for the kids to fill in.

PREPARING FOR CHRISTMAS, I WENT AROUND EVERYWHERE UNTIL I found a skinny tall tree for the apartment. Maybe I should have cut back, but I overdid it on presents to compensate for them being in this place they didn't like. If I planned my money right, I could keep things as nice as possible for the girls.

Of everything, the big gift was an electric guitar for Kelly. She'd wanted one for a while, and when I finally found one at a good price at a pawnshop that fall, I knew she was meant to have it for Christmas. I bought it on layaway, stretching out the installments until Christmas Eve, and had everything set before midnight mass, just like my mother would.

Christmas morning, Doris came to spend the day with Kelly and us. And I let Mathew come over too. He seemed intent on working on his issues, and the girls seemed happier with us all together as we opened presents. I felt that myself. *This* was the Mathew I loved—the inside jokes we'd spent years storing, and the passion when I looked at him. When we got sick of Christmas music and played soul records, Al Green sang "I'm Still in Love with You" like he was dictating my thoughts. The hurt of admitting that you are wrapped up in love with somebody after all these years, and that the good times are so good they outweigh the worst of bad times. I stood up, trying to break the spell by scanning the room for something to do, stray wrapping paper to pick up, a child to hug, but my eyes fell on Mathew, looking right at me. The man I was still in love with.

We kept our Christmas traditions, which only added to the feeling that Mathew and I were fully husband and wife again. Brunch was at the Westin Galleria hotel, where Doris kept asking the waiter how they made the Bananas Foster dessert, just because Kelly liked it so much. When the first guy just smiled and didn't answer, she asked another waiter, then another. Finally, Doris told one, "I *need* to make this for my daughter."

"The chef doesn't like to give away his secrets" was the response.

"Well, I can just go back and talk to him," Doris answered back.

"He's very busy," said the waiter, zipping away.

I noticed Doris eyeing the swinging door to the kitchen. "Doris, don't," I said. And she just smiled as she got up. Next thing I knew Doris was in the kitchen chatting with the chef, the two of them laughing. Having borrowed a pen and a piece of paper, Doris emerged holding the recipe. She won the day, and I was so proud.

After, we continued our Christmas tradition of going to the movies. We already had our tickets to see *Waiting to Exhale,* the girls knowing the drill of covering their eyes whenever there was a risqué scene. Every Christmas, when we went to brunch at the hotel, I'd bring a Ziploc or two and fill them with the restaurant's chocolate-covered strawberries to save for the movie. Mathew always rolled his eyes at this, telling me "Y'all are so country," and we teased him back for being so bougie.

At the start of the movie, he said, as he always did, "Give me one." And we, us country girls enjoying our treat, gave the same response we always did: "No, can't have one." Then we relented and passed him the bag. We had fallen back into this pattern so easily.

The next Sunday we arranged to have all the ingredients for Bananas Foster in the apartment so Doris could make it for us, but mostly for our Kelly.

And Mathew came back too. We started 1996 letting go of the house he had been living in and I allowed him to move into our apartment. After six months in that place, we moved into another house back on Braes Meadow.

AS TEENAGERS, THERE WAS A HUMILITY TO KELLY AND BEYONCÉ that I mistook for shyness. Neither wanted to pop off about the group.

Kelly, for one, had a biology teacher who saw her in the paper and then teased her constantly—a man who singled her out as needing to be brought down a peg. Though she never discussed music at school, he was aware of her performing in the group. Handing her back a quiz, he would say in front of everyone, "Maybe if you weren't trying to be a singer, you'd do better."

Even going to her performing arts high school, Beyoncé would command a stage on the weekend and then on Monday act like it never happened. Still, Beyoncé blossomed at that school, a creative space where all the kids were talented, and everybody was always doing something that made them stand out. Down came the everyday bun of hair, and gone were the oversized T-shirts of middle school. She started wearing her little Chanel knockoff suits and St. John Knits jackets with pearl necklaces.

She and Kelly mostly kept to themselves at their schools, no matter how much I pushed them to be more carefree. I wanted those two to have friends outside the group, to have crushes, and to go to a school game where they didn't just sit talking to each other.

I overheard them discussing a party a classmate had invited them to in the neighborhood. "Everyone is gonna be there," said Kelly. Then a noncommittal "yeah" from Beyoncé.

"You're *going* to that party," I said.

"We are not," said Beyoncé.

"You guys never go anywhere," I said. "But you are going to this party." Oh, it was pulling teeth. I made them dress up and drove them over as they acted somber, like I was pulling up to the guillotine. I parked and they didn't move. "Get in there," I said. "Go."

They called me an hour later. "Come get us," said Kelly. I knew Beyoncé had Kelly make the call because I never could say no to Kelly. "Nobody's talking to us," she said, "and we are just uncomfortable." But I took my time to come get them.

In the car, Beyoncé explained it with a sigh. "We just don't know anybody like that."

"Like, we're not popular," said Kelly.

"Well, nobody's talking about being *popular*," I said. "I just want you to have fun. Do more than singing."

"But singing *is* fun," said Beyoncé.

.   .   .

As we settled into being a family again, Mathew's new thing was "We're going to get this record deal at Columbia." Columbia was a division of Sony, and we'd met the Texas talent scout for them before, Teresa LaBarbera Whites. Teresa first met Beyoncé and Kelly years before, back when they were in Girls Tyme. She was an A&R scout in Texas for Columbia, a beautiful Italian lady with an earth mother vibe. She had tried before to get Columbia interested and had no luck, but was now working with Kim Burse at the label to make things happen.

When Teresa called with the news that Columbia wanted to sign the girls, Mathew could not wait to tell them. "Let them finish their day in school," I said.

But he was already in the car. "Oh, hell no," he said. "I can't *wait* to walk in there." He started at Kelly's school, where the teacher had singled her out as needing to be brought down a peg.

Mathew marched right into the classroom and made a huge production of Kelly being signed to a label. "Maybe *you* need to go back to school. . . ." Mathew told the teacher, becoming Kelly's hero. And for the kids in the class, too, because when he said, "She doesn't have to come here anymore," her classmates started clapping.

Then he went over to the High School for the Performing Arts with Kelly to tell Beyoncé and LeToya, then they called LaTavia on the phone.

They didn't look back.

CHAPTER 29

NAMING THEIR DESTINY

Spring 1997

WHEN I GOT to the house, Kelly, Beyoncé, LeToya, and LaTavia were still sitting at the dining room table where they did home school. The teacher was packing her bag like she was mad at it, and I could tell it had been another raucous class. This uptight little white lady had trouble with the girls from the moment she introduced herself at our new house back on Braes Meadow.

"Good morning, girls, I'm Mrs. Dick."

That name was too much for four fifteen-year-old kids. Yes, they'd signed a record deal, but they were still just kids. They started cracking up and were never quite able to stop. Worse, Mrs. Dick had a thing about being addressed as an elder, even if she was around my age. If the girls said, "You want us to . . ." She would stop them with, "It's Mrs. Dick. 'Mrs. Dick, would you like me to . . .'" That would start the avalanche all over again. Mrs. Dick would lecture me about the girls, and I would promise to talk to them, but even I thought it was funny. She really should have used a different name: If you're a teacher, you can't be so strict *and* be Mrs. Dick.

It got ridiculous when Mrs. Dick mentioned her husband. Harry.

"Harry Dick?" said LeToya, disbelieving.

"*Mister* Harry Dick," corrected Mrs. Dick.

LaTavia lost it. Kelly jumped up, waving her hand. "I can't. I can't." Beyoncé followed her running out of the room as they burst, so unable to hold their laughter they fell onto the floor.

We would soon get a new teacher, one they would love and who would tutor the girls up to the time they finished high school. But of all the tutors, it was Mathew who gave the kids the best education. I give him so much credit for teaching them to look after their money in a business that would happily exploit their talents. At rehearsals, he would sit them down for pop quizzes on the entertainment industry. "What's the two ways you make money in this industry?" he said.

Before they could answer—because by now he'd drilled it into them—he wanted to make sure they *understood* it. "Do you make money off of selling records?"

"Noooo," they would say, in singsong voices to show they would never be that naïve.

"How d'you make money?" he'd ask, raising his hands like a conductor.

"Writing songs and touring," they'd recite.

"Yes," he said, grinning. "Those are the two ways, so you don't miss it."

Mathew would continue, his years of coaching corporate sales teams brought to bear on his most important project. "The other thing I want y'all to understand is that the label is gonna be willing to buy you a bunch of stuff and spend all this money," he said. "And y'all want all the best hairstylists and the biggest directors and the fanciest hotel rooms and ice cream room service in a silver dish. That's fine, but just know that you're gonna have to pay back every penny."

So many artists missed this. They thought record labels advanced you a pile of cash to keep, but that cash today is your debt tomorrow. You used it to pay for recording studios, talent on the album, your videos, your hair and makeup, and ice cream from room service. You had to pay the label back once you sold music. For generations, Black artists had been targeted with bad royalty rates, losing the control of and profit from the music they made. They'd create number-one hits and still owe work or money to the companies they made rich. We were not so far from sharecropping and Weeks Island.

Mathew would not let that happen. Knowing kids are visual, he would make little charts to show them how their money was going to come in. "Don't fight to spend all this money *for* them," he said. "You can go stay in the Four Seasons hotel and fly first-class and do all that. I want what you deserve. But just remember until you negotiate that into your budget, at the end of that trip you're not gonna make any money."

Understanding this history as they began to make their own, Kelly, Beyoncé, LaTavia, and LeToya buckled down and didn't waste money on the crazy stuff. They were frugal—when we had to stay in New York to record, they doubled up on rooms at the hotel. Sometimes four in one room with two double beds if the place was nice. They watched as other artists made mistakes. One young man always had his own room at that nice place, also booking a room for his mom and his assistant— just a friend he'd hired. He didn't realize what the girls knew: That's not free money. And that money will be your freedom.

As the girls worked on their first album, the label had suggested the group change their name but hadn't given any guidance. We'd been through so many iterations at that point, and none had stuck. There's so many stories about the name of the group, but here is the truth: I prayed on it. I kept a picture of the group, a promotional photo I loved, in the NIV Study Bible I carried with me. When I want to manifest something or keep people safe, I keep them there so they stay in my prayers. When I opened my Bible, I saw I'd left the photo in Ecclesiastes 9:1–12, with the heading "A Common Destiny for All."

Destiny. I knew that was it, and I was relieved the girls liked it. They each said it aloud, trying it on like something meant to be theirs. Prayer works, but so do lawyers, and the label came back and said that name was already taken by a gospel group that had done some stuff in the eighties. Mathew had the vision to add one additional, important word, and the group now had a name, one they loved: Destiny's Child.

THE PHONE RANG EARLY, LIKE SOMEONE WHO'D WAITED UNTIL THE first light of morning to call. Marlene, who was now my best friend's best friend, got right to it. "Tina, I don't want to talk about Johnny's business," Marlene said, panic in her voice. "But he's been having night sweats."

"What's that mean?" I asked. I knew she was a nurse, but I didn't know what this was supposed to signify.

"Tenie, I think Johnny's sick," she said. She paused. "*Sick* sick." She wouldn't say more.

Now I realized she meant AIDS. I called him immediately.

"Let's get together," I said. "It's been too long since it was just the two of us." Johnny and I had grown apart since he left Parkwood and

I moved, but we had the girls keeping us together. There was always some concert or birthday party to invite him to. Beyoncé was so busy, but he and Solange would still spend a day together. Sometimes I'd be at Headliners when he brought her back to the salon, and I would think, *Let's all go to the beach.* Even if I wanted to go be kids again with Johnny, I couldn't.

When we met up now one on one, just for coffee, I looked for signs of this illness Marlene was on about. He was thin, but not too thin. I could tell myself he was okay. "Are you healthy?" was all I had to ask to set him off. He got angry, accusing me of talking to Marlene. She'd probably been on him to get an HIV test. Johnny was pragmatic. He had lost almost all his friends to AIDS at that point—the people he began to gather as a second family from our first night at the Kon Tiki had been taken one by one. He had said they would get sick and then be gone like that. Now he didn't want to talk about it.

"Okay," I said. "Okay. You're here." I changed the subject to the girls and clothes—the common ground of what we cared about.

Beyoncé had been invited to prom, I said. I could see Johnny's mind whirring with a vision before he even found the material. A high collar that would please my mother, with cutout holes we would have loved when we were sixteen. Johnny designed a white dress of endless sequins, adorned with swirls of lavender and pale green—the colors of our childhood Easter Sundays in Galveston. The promise of spring I hoped Johnny would see.

Beyoncé loved that dress. Through the years, she and I would fall in love with dresses, but never again like that.

I put a picture of Johnny in my Bible, joining one of Solange and the one I kept of the girls, now Destiny's Child. All of them pressed in the pages of my heart. That summer I carried him in that Bible onto planes and into studios. So much was happening for the girls: July 4th weekend of 1997, their song "Killing Time" was released on the *Men in Black* soundtrack. Mathew had fought to get them on there, making their Columbia debut on *Billboard*'s number-one album as fifteen-year-olds alongside Will Smith, Nas, and Snoop Dogg.

There was so much beginning, but in the back of my mind, I felt something ending.

CHAPTER 30

A WAY OUT OF
NO WAY

Summer 1997

WYCLEF WAS LATE.
As the girls weighed where to put money into their album, they agreed it was a smart investment to add Wyclef Jean to one of their best in-progress songs. We'd first heard "No, No, No" when it was played for us by a popular producer, Vincent Herbert, with the understanding that it was not meant for the girls but was written with another young popular artist in mind.

"No, this is their song," Mathew said.

"You have to at least let them record it," I said, and Teresa LaBarbera Whites at Columbia secured the song for the girls. "No, No, No" was written as a ballad, and it was always Mathew's concept to have the slow version but also have a hip-hop remix with a rap. Not necessarily fast, but something for radio.

We recorded the original version in New York City at Chung King Studios on the edge of Chinatown, a music landmark for Run-DMC, the Fugees, and the Notorious B.I.G. The girls were doing a small tour supporting Wyclef while they worked on the album, and Mathew asked if he would record an addition to the single while he was at their Houston stop.

Now Wyclef was behind on making it to the studio, and Beyoncé was especially concerned. Studio time is money, her father had drilled into her. I think we also knew Wyclef had a plane to catch, and it all made everything seem like each moment had to count double-time.

Triple-time even. When he did show up, he sat at the control table while Beyoncé was in the recording booth, and he made some joke about needing to rush.

"You mean like . . ." And she began to rap-sing the ballad in triple time. "You'll be sayin' no, no, no, no, no," she rhythmed super-fast. "When it's really yeah, yeah, yeah, yeah, yeah . . ."

People went crazy, and Wyclef said what we all felt: "Yo, that was amazing. That's how I want you to sing it."

With that, "No, No, No (Part 2)," the girls' first single, was born in a couple hours. On budget, and with Beyoncé's new improvised rap-singing innovation.

BEYONCÉ TURNED LEFT AND GUNNED THE ENGINE JUST A LITTLE on the Ford Explorer. She'd only turned sixteen the month before in September, but she'd already been driving a year. I'd gotten her a hardship driver's license as soon as she was fifteen so she could take Solange to and from school.

All of Destiny's Child was in the car, racing over to Solange's school to be on time for pickup. They had the radio on, of course, and were pulling up just as the DJ introduced a new song "from H-town's own Destiny's Child!" Columbia had released the song to urban radio to get buzz going for a November release. The girls started screaming—their first time on the radio.

Kelly turned the radio up so everyone outside could hear the song, especially Solange, who came out of her school like she'd arranged the whole scene, picking her sisters' single as her walkout song. They parked right there to get out and join Solange in dancing around the car. Doing the routine they'd practiced countless times, right there on a school day in Houston.

They all called me at Headliners, each screaming, "Our song was on the radio!" all at once. I told Vernell, who told the whole salon. Before they hung up, Beyoncé said quietly into the phone, "Mama, it was on the *radio*."

I HAD GATHERED ALL THE SUPPLIES TO BRING TO LOS ANGELES to shoot "No, No, No (Part 2)," their first video as Destiny's Child.

The group chose a young Black director named Darren Grant, who Beyoncé found after scouring through a trove of music videos Camille Yorrick at Columbia compiled for her to find the perfect person. Even on the edge of sixteen years old, she was so clear about her ideas and already becoming conversant in a visual language. This was when she began learning from the choreographer and creative mind Frank Gatson Jr., who had worked with En Vogue, one of her favorite groups. Beyoncé and Frank would mutually teach each other so much.

I was working as the group's hairstylist, an alternative to the more expensive stylists needed for four girls. Each girl wanted something special, and Beyoncé's request was that I would let her have highlights for the first time. I had light blond ones in my own hair, but she would have fake platinum blond hair I would glue in as little streaks.

The soundstage had a big room set for hair and makeup, and I lugged all my stuff to the door. I could hear people laughing inside. *The makeup crew must be already here,* I thought.

I opened the door and the laughter stopped. Two men looked at me—*scowled* is the word. Sharp-eyed and pursed-lipped, they stood at two giant tables *covered* with their stuff. This big old room and they'd left this one little spot at the end for me.

Kill them with kindness, Tenie, I thought. And I did. I tried at least. Chris Maldonado and Eric Ferrell were best friends, both around thirty and so handsome, both incredibly talented and both determined to not be nice to me. I set up all my curling irons and equipment, and just found myself another little table to drag into the room to put my stuff on. They warmed just slightly enough in that confined space to give that strained smirk that said, "Excuse me, I need to get by your tired ass."

Then Beyoncé came bursting into the room. "Okay, put them in," she said to me.

I started the platinum streaks, and as I placed them in, I could tell I didn't bring enough. Beyoncé saw it too. "It's not there yet," she said, frustration in her voice.

Chris's and Eric's heads popped up like little Siamese cats ready to see the show. They must have thought, *Now she is gonna get it.*

"Oh, Mama," Beyoncé said.

"Mama?" Chris and Eric both said at the same time. "You're her mother?" asked Eric. "Why didn't you say something?" The guys started laughing, not at me, but at themselves. They confessed they had been freezing me out. "Our friend was supposed to do the hair and they canceled them," said Chris. "They said that the director's girl-friend was gonna do the hair."

I laughed. "Darren is about fifteen years younger than me," I said. "You think I'm his sugar mama?"

"You could be," Eric said, looking me up and down.

"I never heard of a hairstylist sugar mama, but okay."

That started a deep friendship that day, and Eric and Chris would later re-create their conversation from before we all met. "We are not giving this bitch *any* space. We gonna be so mean to *her*." But our new friendship did not solve the problem at hand in that hair and makeup room. Beyoncé needed more blond streaks.

I did what I had to do: I looked at myself in the mirror, took a little scissors, and began to cut some highlights from my own hair, just enough here and there to glue into my daughter's hair without leaving me bald-headed.

"Now we know you're the mom," Eric said, watching me snip my hair.

"*That's* a mother's love," joked Chris.

They were both brilliant artists, and Eric had helped Aaliyah craft her look from her very first album. Kelly and Beyoncé already idolized Aaliyah, but that love only grew once they met in 1998 at a dance re-hearsal studio with Fatima Robinson, perhaps the most accomplished choreographer in the industry. Destiny's Child was practicing for the video for their single with Timbaland, "Get on the Bus," a track off the *Why Do Fools Fall in Love* soundtrack.

They had been at it awhile when I walked in to join them, and I saw there was a young woman sitting on the floor by the door quietly re-winding the cassette tape so the girls could start the song again. We smiled at each other, and she pressed Play on the tape.

When Beyoncé came over, she said, "Aaliyah, this is my mama." Aaliyah stood up and brushed her hair back as my mouth fell open. I just thought she was a friend of Fatima's helping out. She was, but here was this superstar who was so humble. We got to chatting and after

Mathew came in, Aaliyah asked permission to take the girls along to a video shoot that night. Mathew hadn't recognized her either, so Beyoncé and Kelly were just humiliated as he went into full dad mode. "Well, how old are you?" he asked Aaliyah. Even when he realized who she was, he still asked, "Do you have your driver's license? Okay, let me see."

Aaliyah laughed, showing her ID. "I'll get 'em back," she said. "I'll get 'em back to you." Aaliyah said it was very sweet that the girls were so protected. They all kept up their friendship, always excited just to be around this artist who proved you could be great—have hits and be in the movies—and stay so humble.

Later, we would be devastated when we lost Aaliyah and Chris together in August 2001. Destiny's Child was headlining MTV's summer *TRL* Tour, and we were on a tour bus from Indiana to Chicago when we heard the news: A Cessna carrying Aaliyah, Chris, and seven other people had crashed leaving the Bahamas. They were there to shoot Aaliyah's video for "Rock the Boat," and Eric had his best friend Chris fill in for him while he was on tour with Macy Gray.

A depression fell on the group, and for the two-day break they had between Chicago and the L.A. show, they could just barely speak. They were so close in age to Aaliyah, who was twenty-two to Beyoncé's nineteen. There were a lot of tears and late-night talks while we played her music.

I didn't hover but was there to hug and be hugged when they needed it. Sometimes being present is both the best thing and the only thing a parent can do.

When "No, No, No (Part 2)" came out, the single would become Destiny's Child's longest-running Hot 100 hit—thirty-five weeks on the chart—and one of the biggest-selling singles of 1998. One of the first uses of their power was when Beyoncé and Kelly found out a boy at Solange's school had singled her out for bullying. All four girls got in the car to go pick up Solange at school and asked her to point out the kid. They surrounded him, each one telling him in their own way to stop messing with Solange. Until Beyoncé finally hissed, the executioner in his ear: *"Destiny's Child has warned you."*

As the four girls traveled nonstop doing appearances and promotion, any little hiccup that came up, it was *"Destiny's Child has warned you."* And then laughter. On the road, LaTavia's mom, Cheryl, was the chaperone, and together we were everything: the hairstylist, the luggage carrier, the steamer, the packer, the travel agent, the whatever that was needed. We would show up at a Holiday Inn, usually getting there late, and they wouldn't have anybody to carry luggage in. "Oh no, girls, you can't carry the luggage," we'd say, "'cause y'all are stars." Yes, they were doubling up at a $73.25 room rate, but even as they paid their dues, we wanted them to feel special. It needed to be *fun*. As the hotels got better and the appearances bigger, and people started fawning over them as the Talent, Cheryl and I were cautious about them getting spoiled. If some staffer at an event acted like the girls couldn't carry a single bag, we would stop whoever was helping. "Oh, they can carry it."

"Well, you told us we didn't have to carry our luggage," one of the girls said after. "Now we got somebody to carry it and you want us to."

"You're good," we'd say. As moms we'd boot them up, but they needed to stay grounded and not become teenage divas.

Cheryl and I were willing to do the work it took to help the girls succeed. Columbia would assign Destiny's Child a stylist, but only pay this person to pull the clothes. Then they would send the outfits to me or have them waiting at the event for us to see last-minute. Sony would not pay to send a stylist to the location because they knew that I knew how to style and that Cheryl and I would get the girls dressed, iron the clothes, then pack everything up to send it back.

The stylists always sent clothes that were all one color: black—never prints or vibrant colors. It was cheaper and low effort, not requiring care or thought in coordinating the four looks. We would get to some event, look at the rack of clothes, and get depressed. "Who died?" Worse, the looks were pulled for how the stylist saw these girls—as interchangeable twentysomething women at a club dressing just to attract men, not sixteen-year-old girls performing for an audience they wanted to dazzle. The clothes were super sexy, too clingy and tight. So I would go buy some fabric, adding flair to the outfits the way Johnny and I did in Galveston.

A lot of times the clothes got lost in transit, and oftentimes there was a problem with the looks showing up on time or even being stolen. I would have to run to a mall and do a speed-sweep for four performance looks to customize with barely any budget and no time to spare. Sometimes there was literally no time, like when we were in Germany for an event and the showroom sent four pairs of shoes, one with two lefts. Beyoncé took the hit for everyone. "I can handle it," she said, putting on the two left shoes. On the red carpet, she turned her foot just so, enough that no one would notice. This was always her, the peacemaker who could pull off anything.

Like my mom, I carried a needle and thread with me at all times to alter clothes in the backseat and backstage. I became an expert in finding the nearest dry cleaner because they always had a sewing machine. It was all about making a way out of no way, just like my mom always did.

She would be proud that I was also mentoring her granddaughter and my bonus daughter Angie on the road as the girls' assistant. At twenty-one, my brother Larry's girl looked about sixteen, but she was capable and not to be messed with. Angie had spent every summer with us for years, which meant that wherever we went on vacation, Angie went. She got used to nice restaurants, nice cars, and nice things. When she was twelve or so, she told me she wanted a Dooney & Bourke bag like the one I had, and I bought her this little tiny one. That was big time back then, but she didn't try to hide that she was disappointed in the size of the bag.

"Let me just tell you something," I said. "You got a real high-minded way of thinking. You better get a hustle going because your grandmother Agnes would say you got champagne tastes on a beer budget." It wasn't ingratitude on Angie's part—it was an awareness that she deserved the best.

And after that, she worked for it. Never dependent on anyone ever again. At thirteen, Angie went on her own to get a job at a clothing store, and I still think she lied about her age on the application. Then she worked at Walmart and was managing adults at eighteen. I had recently talked her into moving in with our family, and then I hired her to go on the road with us as the girls' assistant. Angie was my eyes and ears on the girls whenever I had to even step away for a moment or be home with Solange. This girl could walk into a promoter's office at the end of the show with our road manager Craig, saying, "I'm here to collect the money." At first glance, this little girl with the baby face looked like you might be able to get something over on her, but Angie had a presence that was like six feet tall. If there was a dollar missing— a penny—she would count it again until the promoter suddenly realized where that missing cash got to.

HEADLINERS KEPT HAVING TO COME SECOND TO ALL THIS. By then I had moved the salon to Bissonnet Street in Houston, a smaller space with eight chairs, and a staff of five stylists. My former assistant Abel, with all his kind steadiness, had taken a lead role in my absence. There were clients I had to simply turn over to his capable hands, because to pretend that I would always be there for them felt unfair. I knew what I had to do.

Abel and I were the last ones in the salon one night, and I had to act before I overthought. I handed Abel the keys. He seemed confused. I always locked up.

"It's yours now," I said. "I decided."

"Are you serious?"

"I'm very serious," I said. "I know you'll take care of Headliners."

"I don't have to pay you anything?"

"No," I said. "Just take over the rent and take care of my clients." This was the only way I could say goodbye to this life I really loved— give it to someone whose dreams were as big as mine, who could love and nurture Headliners. "We can have a staff meeting tomorrow, Abel, and I'll call the clients and let them all know."

He started to cry, which I knew would put me over my own edge, so I turned on my heel to look around. Where I had invested in myself and women and provided for my family. Where I'd innovated hair treatments and service standards, graduating out countless stylists who brought what they learned to their own shops, providing for their own families. I saw where my girls had sung, where they'd all swept hair for tips to spend on roller coasters, where Solange had done her homework. This empire that was wholly mine. I closed my eyes.

"I can't believe it," he said.

But I wasn't at Headliners anymore. I was back at Holy Rosary, watching Linda Kendeson crown Mary in the white dress my mother gave her—my dress. Seeing her so happy, learning how good it felt to give up the things that were important to me. Headliners was important to me, too.

I'd made my choice. I turned, opening my eyes to look right at Abel.

"I've seen you give things to people who can't believe it," I said. "I know you know this, but it's easy to give away shit you don't want. Stuff that's not important to you. But if you can give it to someone who will love it as much as you, it's like the best joy."

CHAPTER 31

THE STYLE IT TAKES

March 1998

T HE MTV PEOPLE were freaking out about the showers in the forecast, but I'd only been in Negril, Jamaica, a few hours and a little rain was the least of my worries. The girls were at rehearsals, scheduled to sing "No, No, No" the next day on *The Grind,* which we knew was *the* prime time of the annual *MTV Spring Break.* Every year, MTV took over some tropical locale, filling it with audiences of college kids—and millions of people at home—to watch live music and bikini contests.

This was exactly the kind of audience Columbia said was out of Destiny's Child's reach. The label prized white consumers, and acted as if they would never accept the girls because they were Black. Not just Black, but *too* Black. The girls would not change who they were to "cross over," and the label lacked the imagination to see that audience coming to the group.

But this opportunity was about to be wasted because the clothes sent from the stylist that Columbia insisted on hiring had been held up or lost. We had nothing for them to wear.

Negril was a resort town, and there wasn't some mall I could run to and fix this. I couldn't just buy them souvenir T-shirts and have them looking like every girl in the audience. Cheryl and I didn't want to panic in front of them, so we stepped out of the room. I closed my eyes and took a breath.

It had been a two-hour drive along the coast from Sangster Airport.

I remembered the van had slowed down right outside Negril. Right by a little roadside market . . .

"Cheryl," I said. "We passed a place. They had camouflage shirts hanging." I remembered the military stuff because it had made me think of Master P, a Louisiana rapper who was huge in Houston. He'd popularized wearing camo for guys in rap—musicians calling themselves soldiers—but I'd never seen women doing the fatigues look. "We're gonna go back," I said.

We got someone to take us, paying cash for the camo shirts, shorts, and several pairs of extra-large pants to have the fabric. Then overnight I cut up and then sewed up everything to make the tops and a little dress for Bey. Wyclef was coming to do his guest part on the song, and Pras, his old Fugees bandmate, was already there. I eyed his green cargo sweatpants. If I cinched the waist, they would be perfect for Kelly. I borrowed them right off his body, saying, "Give me your pants" and figuring I'd explain later.

The girls were anxious about the look, which was so different for them yet more in keeping with their true style. I had these platform boots for them, which made Beyoncé so anxious that she would trip.

When Wyclef came over just before they went on, he stepped back in surprise.

"*Yo,* who *styled* y'all?" he asked.

Beyoncé nervously answered, "Oh, my mom." Wyclef knew me from the studio and looked right at me.

"Well, you need to style them all the time," he said. "Because this is unique—they don't look like everybody else."

The girls went out there and killed it. Beyoncé was right about those platform boots, but I watched her fall back, then twist around and pop back up like it was part of the act. This would become a signature move of hers, yet another moment of a star finding genius in necessity.

Stomping the stage in those boots, the clothes we made with minutes to spare, the girls dared those storm clouds on the horizon to even *try* it. After that, Destiny's Child wanted me to be their stylist. They let Columbia know I was doing the hair *and* doing the clothes.

· · ·

I HAD CONVERSATIONS WITH EACH MEMBER OF DESTINY'S CHILD about how *she* wanted to look, not who someone in a boardroom wanted her to be. Each girl was beautiful, but everybody deserves the chance to say how they want to be perceived in that beauty. What clothes made them feel strong? Beyoncé loved long dresses, Kelly and LaTavia wanted to show off their legs, and LeToya wanted looks that showcased her midriff.

Big picture, we wanted to embrace the classic, sophisticated look of Motown, when all the artists honored their fans by dressing the part of bigger-than-life stars—you not only wanted to hear them sing, you wanted to see what they were wearing. Destiny's Child didn't need to have much makeup on, so the girls could just be the fresh-faced young people they authentically were. In many ways, I was unconsciously re-creating my own girl-group days in Galveston, designing for Destiny's Child with the love and care my mother and I brought to every look for the Veltones.

The girls had more freedom to be themselves with me officially as the group's wardrobe stylist, but we still faced limits. Columbia gave me barely any budget, so I had to take what we had and then invest in beautiful fabrics to make something wonderful.

I was already a regular at High Fashion Fabrics, a large store on Louisiana Street in Houston. I used to say my kids grew up there, and while other children had memories of smelling cookies baking, mine would remember the smells of the dyes and the fabrics. They didn't like it there, but it's where I would get inspiration, the same way my mom did when I was a kid. She made those beaded jackets, most of them white or silver pearl beading, and I would follow her around, saying things like, "Why don't you do some red beads, or some green beads?"

She'd laugh. "Oh no, I would never be able to sell that." Now as I walked around High Fashion Fabrics, feeling the material so it could tell me what it could be, Solange would sit on one of the little pedestals they put mannequins on. First she colored in the coloring books I brought; now she was reading. The staffers would keep an eye on her as I pulled fabrics and imagined stage costumes for Destiny's Child.

I began designing clothes out of necessity, not because I had some dream of being a designer. But I'd found a calling, waking up in the night with visions of the four of them in blue metallic leather. Or see-ing a photo of Cher, the happiness on her face as she danced in a Bob

Mackie flame dress sparkling like fire, and wondering how could I create a tribute that gave the girls *that* joy? When I worried, "I'm going too far," or "People aren't going to understand this," those were the outfits that got the most love from fans.

I know that didn't always work. Sometimes, the clothes needed more time and money that I didn't have. The irony was that Columbia became more stingy about budgets as they felt "Mom" was making the clothes anyway. My niece Linda was a hell of a seamstress, so she helped with the first outfits, before it became too much even for her. Thanks to LaTavia's mom, Cheryl, I had found Jaime Zelaya, a tailor who was a wizard with leather, taking my sketches and ideas and making beautiful outfits. I also found another seamstress, Miss Enid, an older Jamaican woman who was an artist with the sewing machine. Miss Enid became like a surrogate mother to me, but time was always so short, so I would end up helping with the tailoring and sewing with her anyway.

When I tried working with designers, the reality was that many did not want to give their clothes to these curvy Black girls. And even if I did work out a deal with a designer to do the wardrobe for an appearance or shoot, I needed four equal, distinct looks. And that was always a problem, because I noticed early on that even the best designers often had what I called "star clothes"—one specific look or dress that was the one in the collection, and maybe two that were super strong.

Well, I had *four* girls. In the past, the girls' stylists would settle, coming with a rack with two great pieces or even one great piece. Then, the dreaded instruction: "The designer says this one is only for Beyoncé." But these were four beautiful girls, and Beyoncé was very sensitive to being singled out. If there weren't four amazing outfits, I wouldn't use them. Instead, I would pick the two best of one designer, then the two best of another. I did not know that was breaking a time-honored rule: Designers did not like to mix with other designers. When other stylists or people in the fashion industry saw me doing this, they didn't view this as a declaration of independence but a confirmation of my naïveté. Someone else might be able to get away with it—a *Devil Wears Prada* type or a man with his nose high in the air—but not this grown woman perceived as a country girl.

There were times the girls heard these cutting remarks. One time someone treated me so badly backstage that Beyoncé saw I needed a lift. She wasn't going to pull the "that's my mother" card—we were both too professional for that.

"Mom," Beyoncé said, "if you got some locs in your hair and you talked with an accent *they* would love you." We laughed. It was true—we'd seen these people fall for anything in a European accent. She looked me right in the eye. "But *I* love you."

BECAUSE OF THE NUMBER OF OUTFITS WE WERE MAKING, MISS Enid was often running behind on sewing the clothes. I would go to her place to pick them up, and she might have two outfits made and hadn't started on the third. I would wind up staying there, taking a seat at her second sewing machine to finish the work. So often that she grew to expect it, and I had one more person counting on me. There were many times we had a red-eye departing at eleven o'clock and I might leave her place at nine. I would still have to go home, telling the girls what to pack on the way over, and then not be able to sleep on the flight. When we got to the event, I'd still have to hem the pants or take something up to fit the girls.

It left no time for myself. I was so overworked, seven days a week, that I stopped doing my makeup. I couldn't even make time to comb my hair. I wanted to, but how could I when I was working until the last minute?

For all the work, what was really wearing me out was trying not to be an absentee parent to Solange. At eleven years old, she was steadfast in her refusal to travel with us. Other kids were always begging to tag along, to go to L.A. and New York to stay in hotels and use the pools. When we dragged Solange with us, she complained the whole time. People who didn't know my girls suggested that maybe she was jealous of the attention Beyoncé got in the group. They lack information on two fronts: One, Beyoncé got the least coddling of any of the girls, including Kelly, whose feelings I still went out of my way to protect. And two, they underestimated how much Solange, a homebody Cancer like my mother, needed the practical magic of feeling rooted in place.

"We would get you a tutor," I said. "Your education is really important to us, and we'd make—"

"No, I don't wanna travel with them," she said. "I don't wanna leave my friends."

I asked my friend Cheryl Creuzot to keep her for me, and I had a hard rule that I would never spend more than four days apart from my youngest, no matter what it took. I can't tell you how many times I would catch a red-eye to come home and spend a day with her. But Cheryl's regimented, orderly life was in stark contrast to mine with the traveling circus. Solange had school, then homework checked by Cheryl, dinner at 6:01. Solange kept up with St. John's church services and joined their Wednesday night youth group, the God Pound. She accepted the office of Secretary of the God Pound, a job that suited her so perfectly.

One Wednesday I had a clearing in my schedule, and I killed myself jumping on a plane, racing to be with her. I pictured the surprise on her face, could feel the grip on my neck, trying to get me to either lift her or bring me down to her. The two parts of us whole again.

Instead, she glowered at me. "You cannot just show up," she said.

"Well, I'm here," I said, trying to smooth it over. Anxious to get that hug.

"I have my own life, and you just pop up and want me to spend the whole time with you."

"Well, let's go get pizza," I said. I was not about to complicate this further by showing how hurt I was.

"I have plans."

"What plans?"

"I have my meeting."

"What meeting?" I thought it was something she was making up. Still my little girl playing pretend.

"The God Pound," she yelled. "It's Wednesday night!"

"Oh, of course," I said, covering that I forgot this thing that had become so essential to her. "It's Wednesday."

"You don't even know what day it is," she said, dismissive.

"No, I understand," I lied.

I went to Cheryl. "Solange don't wanna spend the evening with me," I said, sounding like Miss Pitiful after hiding all that hurt. "And I gotta leave on Friday."

"Well, Tina, you *can't* just be popping up," she said. "You should have told her that you were coming."

I told Solange I would drive her to the God Pound, and I was ready at the door when she came down to go. I wanted to offer her that sureness. Fit myself into her life while I was here. "Solange, I was thinking I would like to come to your school tomorrow," I said.

She paused. "Okay," she said, but the happiness showed in her voice. Thursday, I was at her school right as lunch began. All kids need different things. Solange required the dependability of a schedule and time with her peers. My vision—her being with me, her father, and her sisters—creating a home wherever we were, worked for us but not for her. What I saw as togetherness, she felt as loneliness. A world of adults where she was always told where to stand and what to do.

In summer, though, I couldn't simply leave her with Cheryl. I made her travel with us, sometimes bringing Cheryl's daughter Coline for a week in New York or L.A. Coline got to be in a couple music videos, which thrilled her, but Solange approached that the same way she felt about room service or getting to go to shows and meet famous people. There was no place like home.

"I'm missing my meetings," she would say, once she got going. "I'm missing God Pound. I'm missing my life."

NEAR THE END OF THAT FIRST YEAR, SUCCESS MEANT THE GIRLS got their first big checks, $85,000 apiece. It was so much money, kind of unheard of for new artists, but they had been so frugal and not incurred debt with Columbia. As soon as the money was in their hands, all four girls said, "We're buying cars." Kelly wanted a Cadillac Escalade; Beyoncé wanted a convertible Jaguar like the one I'd had when she was little.

I knew our minister at St. John's, Pastor Rudy Rasmus, was trying to get some money together to get a set of vans for the church to do more outreach to the homeless. I told the girls about tithing, watching my mother put the few dollars we had into the church basket, and her telling me that this was how we made it. "She was right," I said, and they only had to look around themselves to see the proof. "I promise you if you tithe, and y'all buy these vans for the church and get yourself a used car, next time, you'll be able to buy whatever you want. God will bring it back to you in ways you can't imagine."

They weren't that happy about it, but they bought those vans—two white ones at about $20,000 apiece. With the money left over, Kelly bought a used red BMW convertible—she looked so cool in it—and

Beyoncé got a used silver Jaguar with a convertible top. It's not like they went without, but the lesson still stuck. What you give comes back to you, which was proven when six months later Kelly had the money for a new Escalade.

The funny thing is Beyoncé found out she is just not a car person. That Jag is still in storage somewhere, the last car she bought that wasn't some vintage thing for a video.

EVEN WITH ALL THIS SUCCESS, THERE WAS CONSTANT PRESSURE from some at Sony and Columbia for Destiny's Child to change who they were.

The label just thought they knew better. Mathew had a great plan to break into European markets and conquer overseas, then bring that international success back to America. Back then, artists didn't spend a lot of time in Europe. There were so many people at Columbia who worked hard to support the group, but the suits higher up seemed to cling to the belief that Destiny's Child didn't have a prayer of being as successful as pop acts because they were Black. They were very happy with the girls staying in their lane. "Mathew is always talking about how he wants the girls to cross over," they would say, "but in order to cross over, they have to tone things down."

To remind us, they would make dismissive comments about me and the looks I created, and the go-to was "pageanty." Someone high up sneered out, "They look like the Supremes. With their big hair and their shiny sequins."

"Yeah," I said, "that's the idea, because the Supremes were amazing. And yes, they have looked at Motown tapes. And what we noticed is that when you're sitting in the sixtieth row and you see some sequins up there, you feel like you're in the front row because it's bigger than life."

"They're not gonna work with white audiences," I was told. "They don't want to see those kinds of clothes they can't relate to." When the label X'd out costumes before a shoot or video, I knew from experience it was exactly those outfits that would *hit*. Yes, it was a hit with the Black audience Destiny's Child respected and loved—and which the industry didn't value as much as white consumers. The girls and I would fight to keep the looks, sometimes winning, sometimes losing.

They said things like "These colors are hideous"—looking at vibrant purples and greens that were too bold, too bright, too Black for them. It was the same way they hated that Beyoncé braided her hair. "We want her to look pretty," someone said.

"She is beautiful," I said, ending the conversation that I knew would never end. "She is a beautiful Black girl."

In those early days, we proved them wrong over and over again. But what we saw as growing proof that the girls could draw wider audiences without changing who they were, the label saw as success found *despite* their being Black. And despite me.

CHAPTER 32

JOHNNY

Summer 1998

WE WERE SO busy traveling that it was easy for Johnny to hide that he was getting sicker. He began having episodes where he acted erratic, which made him withdraw more from family. Then he was hospitalized, and Selena found out. Johnny was her heart and best friend. She called me immediately and I caught the next flight to be with him.

The diagnosis was AIDS-related dementia, which was causing a sort of delirium and paranoia. Johnny had always been thin, but now he was *very* thin from wasting. "Tenie," he said. "The doctors are trying to do stuff to me. They said I have AIDS and I'm gonna die." At first, I tried to soothe him, but he would get frustrated. He preferred Badass Tenie B, his protector.

"Who said that?" I would say, curling my lip to show I was ready to do battle for him. "They don't know what the hell they're talking about."

"They're listening in, Tenie."

"Oh, are they?" And I would whisper a flood of curses at them that made Johnny smile, hitting a savage rhythm as I read these poor innocent doctors to filth. Cursing their every flaw—real and imagined—to start him laughing that beautiful laugh until he forgot what he was so mad about. We were safe together.

Johnny got medication which helped him get a little better, but not for very long. He started to lose motor control, so he couldn't live alone. We got him into a long-care facility, not quite a nursing home but close. The staff was lovely, but very clear with me that this would be Johnny's home until he went into hospice.

When the family wasn't in some city with Destiny's Child, I would bring Johnny home with me on the weekends to spend time with Solange and Beyoncé. Saturday mornings, my daughters would put on the house music he used to play as he helped raise them. Now they played it to him, dancing around as he bobbed his head to Robin S singing "Show Me Love" or Crystal Waters going "la da dee, la do daa."

Solange was eleven, and would clown for him, pulling out all the stops to make him laugh. She would get him his "funny cigarettes" as he called them. They would sit out on the little patio where I let Johnny smoke weed because it eased his nausea. I had always lectured the girls about Johnny's funny cigarettes and how I didn't want him smoking around them, but we were focused on more important things now. Solange had already lost her therapist to AIDS, and watching Johnny decline was very hard on her. She feels things so deeply, internalizing pain until it reappears later as art or words.

Because he was losing control of his body, Johnny wore diapers, which made caring for him hard. But he wanted to stay with us, so we would extend the visit as long as we could, from Sunday nights to first thing Monday morning. When it was time for me to take him back, he would cry. "I don't want to go."

I WAS AT AN AIRPORT WHEN I GOT THE CALL. JOHNNY NEEDED TO move to hospice over in League City, halfway between Houston and Galveston. It was getting to be his time, they said. I visited him at the facility there often, staying overnight sometimes. Selena and I took turns, and occasionally Flo and Johnny's sisters Linda and Denise would come. I made the decision that the girls were too young to come and see Johnny so vulnerable.

Johnny liked me to get him into a wheelchair so I could take him outside the hospice. We loved the sun, and it would relieve his chill, the one he felt down in the bones that his skin clung to. We would leave this place and could have been sitting high up on the plank Larry put in the pecan tree, a landmark of our shared childhood. I have a picture of him with me outside near the end. There's white around his mouth, and he would look already gone if he wasn't so insistent on showing his sense of humor: He made this funny face to make me laugh.

Those moments outside were an escape from a kind but lonely place, filled with so many men dying who had been abandoned by their families. Johnny was fortunate to have a private room, but across the way there was a room with two guys in there. There was a man in that room, and on a morning that I came for Johnny, this man started calling for me. Well, not me.

"Mama," he said. "Mama, come here. Please."

I put my head in. "Good morning," I said. Just to say it. Give him a chance to realize I wasn't his mother. But he still thought I was—"Mama," he sighed—and the rush of relief in his voice was enough to make me start crying. I was not his mother, but I am a mother. What could I do but go in?

He must have had dementia worse than Johnny, because even as I got closer, he didn't waver in thinking I was his mother. I took his hand and stroked his head. I made the soothing "shhh" noises mothers do for their children until he slept.

I told Johnny about it. "That damn queen," he said. "Taking up my time with you."

"Johnny, I was there ten minutes."

"Then he owes me ten minutes."

"Oh God, Johnny, I don't know how much time he has left to give you."

"Well," he said. "He can't have mine."

I talked to the nurses, and the man was one of many who never had a visitor. As a parent, I could not imagine abandoning my child to die alone. The next day I went early to give the man a few minutes without telling Johnny, but then when I was rolling Johnny outside to the sun, he called for me again.

"Come here," the man said from his bed, a voice so pitiful and alone. "Mama, please."

Johnny snapped up quick, "You ain't going over there."

"Oh, Johnny, come on now," I said, not waiting for his answer. "Just one minute."

Johnny must have counted those sixty seconds. "That's enough, Mary," he yelled to the man. "That ain't your mama, you know. She's an impostor."

"Johnny, you gotta be nice," I said, though Johnny might as well have been on the moon to this poor man.

"Okay, you had your visit with Mama," Johnny said, kinder but no less loud. "Lucy, this one is trying to hog you up."

The man went to sleep again, and I stepped out to grab the handles of Johnny's wheelchair. "You will find drama wherever you go," I whispered, chuckling like we were back in Holy Rosary, cutting up.

"You're mine, Lucy."

"I always will be," I said.

Maybe to protect him, or just because he was so proud of them, I'd hung a framed Destiny's Child poster in his room. It was the photo from the first album cover, the girls in black with Kelly and Beyoncé on each end. One night I was sleeping over in his room and at two a.m. he hissed me awake. "Hey, hey," he whispered, gesturing his chin toward the poster. "They're laughing at me."

"Oh, that's Beyoncé," I said. "She wouldn't laugh at you. She would never, ever—"

"No, they're making fun of me."

I took the poster down, turned it around on the floor to face the wall. The next day, he asked me what happened to his poster. "Oh, it must have fallen," I said, putting it back up.

I knew then it would not be long now until we lost him.

Johnny took his last breath on Sunday, July 29, 1998. He was forty-eight. He was my best friend. Selena was devastated. They had a bond like I have with my children, this give and take of ideas and love where the story is always going, and you think it will never end.

We had his memorial the following Saturday at Wynn Funeral Home in Galveston. Beyoncé and Kelly sang with the other girls from Destiny's Child. They had just been touring with Boyz II Men and now they were here crying. I don't know how they got through "Amazing Grace," but they did.

Johnny lived *life,* which is different from just living. Every day, he found something funny or made it so, and you just couldn't be around Johnny without laughing your head off. Years later, in the summer of 2022, I was in the Hamptons at Beyoncé's home. She and Jay were hosting those closest to them for a *Renaissance* album drop party, and Blue and Rumi—then ten and five—had decorated the place. This album was her tribute to the house music Johnny had schooled my daughters in. I hadn't heard the song "HEATED" yet and as we all danced, Jay suddenly said to me, "Listen to this."

Then I heard the next line, Beyoncé singing on the record: "Uncle Johnny made my dress." I started to cry and smile at the same time, knowing this was what Johnny wanted. To be loved and celebrated. I hugged my daughter, and we raised a toast and danced on it. "Here's to Johnny."

When we went on the Renaissance World Tour, fans all over the world would turn to sing the line to me, and every single time, my hand went to my heart in love. I wished Johnny were there to dance with me because we would have tore it up. But I would always see people in the crowd who reminded me of Johnny—just his spirit—and I would do everything I could to get to them. I drove security crazy: "Bring him! Yes, that one!" I would send the movie cameras their way. "Make sure you get them! Oh, they're fabulous." I collected pictures of so many Johnnys.

Beyoncé closed the show with a photo of me and Johnny huge across the stage. It shows me out one night, looking at him with adoring but skeptical eyes, readying for the next thing out of his mouth. Beyoncé had asked me to give her a picture of Johnny and me for *Renaissance*'s album art, last-minute of course. That photograph was right on top of a pile when I opened a box, Johnny picking just the right one for us to admire him. When the photo of us was up there on the stage in stadiums across the world, all the young people who felt kinship with our beloved Johnny erupted in cheers.

"Yessss, Lucy," I heard, Johnny's voice so close in my ear, loud over the house music he and my daughters loved. "They know what time it is!"

CHAPTER 33

NEW BEGINNINGS

October 1998

I FOUND BEYONCÉ SITTING at the control room in the studio in Houston, with the girls in the booth.

"Where is everybody?" I asked, meaning She'kspere and Kandi Burruss, the hottest producer-songwriter duo out there. They were already famous for creating TLC's "No Scrubs" and Mathew hired them to produce parts of Destiny's Child's second album.

"Mama, they are *so* nice," Beyoncé said. "They're letting me give all this input. It's amazing." Newly seventeen, she had been in plenty of studios, but people had mainly just let her produce her own vocals and the girls'. A producer might call her in for the harmonies to give the other girls their parts, but then they would conduct the performances for recording. Kandi and She'kspere had a very hands-off approach as they wrote these great songs, like "Bills, Bills, Bills" and "Bug a Boo." Now, when I showed up, there was Beyoncé by herself, saying things like, "They need more harmonies there."

I was a little concerned they were too hands-off, and that she was going to do all this work and not get any credit. Mathew wanted to say something to them, but I stopped him. "On second thought," I said, "she couldn't buy this kind of education." She was already a writer and arranger; now she would know what it takes to be a great producer. I am eternally grateful to Kandi and She'kspere for seeing that talent in her and not being gatekeepers.

Near the end of recording, in the spring of 1999, the album was set to come out that July, but we couldn't settle on a name for the record. We had a meeting about it in the studio, with them being there all day anyway. I said that the title should be something spiritual. "We should pray on it. It's gonna come to us." I had my NIV Bible, the one that had inspired the name Destiny's Child, and I had just read some scripture from the Book of Daniel, the writing on the wall that appears when God has measured your value. You know your fate by the effort you've put in, and I felt the group's success was ordained because of their hard work.

"What about *The Writing's on the Wall*?" I asked the group. They loved that, and Columbia was fine with it. That same day, the girls were doing mafioso accents with each other, imitating the *Godfather* film they'd just watched. They decided to create an intro track for the album, one reenacting the meeting Don Corleone called for the leaders of the five crime families, in their case four. The idea was wholly theirs, showcasing them as individuals forming an alliance. Somebody said to me, "What guy came up with that idea?" I answered quick, proud of them: "There was no man there! That was the girls." It was very empowering for Destiny's Child to have an idea, execute it, and then place it square at the front of the album.

Director Darren Grant was back to shoot the video for the first single, "Bills, Bills, Bills," and he had a whole treatment that the girls made their own. Destiny's Child wanted a futuristic, high-end salon with its roots in Headliners, the girls looking amazing and convincing as hairstylists after all their years in the salon. I had this idea to do black and white dresses composed mainly of string, buying yards and yards of it. It was a nightmare—making it and wearing it—but it was such a big hit with people that the next season I saw strings all over the runway. Yet the label fought us on every design, desperate to cut the pink and purple outfits and blue leather looks that people would love. The girls held strong, giving the label one "victory" of cutting my favorite design, a purple leather outfit with lime green accents. "Oh, we could never," the label rep said. "We could never do this."

The single's success grew over weeks, rising from number eighty-four on the Billboard Hot 100 to number one. They had a hit—the writing was on the wall.

By that winter, sadly, LeToya and LaTavia would no longer be with the group. Beyoncé saw it as the end of a marriage of ten years, and she began to grieve it as such. Rumors and negative stories took hold, casting Beyoncé as the daddy's girl who made demands, and people even ran with a lie that Kelly only stayed because she was Mathew's biological child from an affair. It was all incredibly hurtful. Just as things were starting to look better for the album, with sales inspiring Columbia to plan a bigger push for the third single starting in 2000, a depression fell on our house.

BEYONCÉ WOULD BARELY LEAVE HER ROOM, COCOONED IN HER bed. Mathew seemed paralyzed; his racing mind of ideas slowed to a stop. They were upset about the departure of the two girls from the group, but this was something deeper. Beyoncé and her father had always motivated each other, but in January 2000, the two people who kept each other so driven each retreated into themselves.

I gave them a few days—they would right themselves, they always did. Then a few more. Kelly seemed unsure, and the stress on her was part of what sent me into Beyoncé's room that winter morning.

"Get up," I said, throwing back the curtains to let in the light. "We're not gonna do this."

"Do what?" she asked, a kid again.

"Whatever this is," I said. "We're gonna figure this out." We needed to replace the members as soon as possible. We were scheduled to shoot the video for "Say My Name" in L.A. in a matter of weeks, and we wanted the lineup set. Beyoncé and I started going to performing arts schools, auditioning young women in Philadelphia and New Orleans, but nobody felt right.

I made calls the way we would have done in Galveston—to get things done. See who knows who. I started with my cousin Junella Seguro, a choreographer and dancer for MC Hammer, who had started doing work with Destiny's Child. I asked if she'd met any nice backup singers on the tours she'd done.

"Oh, there's this one girl that was *really* nice," Junella said. "She lives in Chicago, and she was a backup singer for Monica. And, um, I think that y'all will really like her."

Tenitra Michelle Williams had been told someone representing Destiny's Child might be in touch. Now here was the girls' mother calling her in Rockford, Illinois, and she was a little blown away that it was me.

"Is this an okay time?" I asked, to break the ice. "What are you doing?"

"I'm staying with my grandma," she said. "Taking care of her."

"Oh, that's so sweet." I had met a lot of young women around her age of twenty lately, and not many of them were the type to look after their elders. We talked about her life, how she had enrolled at Illinois State University to major in criminal justice, but singing had been a passion of hers since she was growing up in the church choir.

"Can you send me some pictures of you?" I asked. I wanted to make a case for this girl to come in for an audition.

Michelle sent "Glamour Shots" from a mall store, and they'd given her hard curls in her hair and harsh makeup that had done nothing but accentuate what looked to be a mustache. But she looked cute to me.

I took Michelle's Glamour Shots to Mathew and Angie Phea, who was helping run his company Music World Entertainment. They laughed me out of the office, saying variations of "Unh unh."

I showed Beyoncé the pictures, not giving up. "Mama, see if she has some pictures without some makeup on. Just some natural pictures, 'cause she looks so cute."

A little envelope came, and there she was, as cute as could be. Got that little mustache, but she was cute. I called her again. "Can you come out tomorrow?" I asked. I booked her a flight, using my own money. I didn't tell Mathew or Angie anything—I was in this girl's corner.

Solange and I drove to the airport to pick up Michelle, then brought her right to the house to meet Beyoncé and Kelly. I could see the girls breathe a sigh of relief at Michelle's kind presence.

I asked Michelle if she would be interested in a makeover to give her the advantage she deserved at the audition. "You just need a little polish." I took her to my esthetician Sherrice for a facial. Sherrice was blunt. "Baby," she said to Michelle, "this mustache gotta go."

Michelle giggled and said, "That's my boyfriend."

"Well, you gotta kiss your boyfriend goodbye," I said, and all three of us laughed. I think she was just scared of the wax, but it was over like that. I did her makeup, and then we took her to the salon to wash her hair, roll, and set it. She smiled seeing Beyoncé and Kelly's reaction, and they gave her a little midriff top to pair with her baggy sweats for the audition. They asked if she wanted to practice harmonies so she'd be ready.

"I would love that," she said. They shorthanded the song Michelle wanted to try—a gospel song called "Walk with Me"—already working out their own language as partners. When they began to sing, the three of them sounded so beautiful. "I want Jesus every day of my life," they sang together, "to walk with me." It's a variation of a song generations before them had sung in turbulent times.

Hearing them, I started to cry. Beyoncé and Kelly had so many years of singing harmonies together, and now Michelle was just naturally falling into this. Better than just fitting into their vocals, her talent inspired them. Michelle led the song, and Beyoncé added her spin to the arrangement, with Kelly getting just the right tone.

"That's the song we should audition you with," Beyoncé said. "It's 'Walk with Me' for sure."

We went to the office and just walked in on Angie and Mathew, and the three pretty much sang the song for them. It was so clear we had a new member and a fresh start. We took them all to lunch at Pappadeaux, introducing Michelle to Cajun seafood. As they bonded, I saw something shake loose in Beyoncé, and also a sureness in Kelly. We were moving in the right direction.

I still love that song, "Walk with Me," because it's not a plea for help, wailing and waiting for God to come save you from your troubles. You are on the journey *through* your trials, humbly asking God to be with you as you put one foot in front of the other on the path laid before you.

We rounded out the group with a young woman, Farrah Franklin, who answered a call for auditions in L.A. She unfortunately didn't work out, and I always wish her the very best on her journey.

. . .

YOU WOULD THINK AFTER HOURS AT DISNEY WORLD WOULD BE more fun. Destiny's Child was there the Friday of Mother's Day weekend, set to perform for the 2000 Grad Nite concerts. The park opened up just for high school seniors, and the girls were going to perform twice that night. Jessica Simpson was also performing, a Columbia labelmate who understood all the pressure on the girls, but she was also just a nice person. She was and remains a friend.

But immediately there was a difference in how the concert organizers treated Jessica's team and ours. They gave her the bigger dressing room, which she thought was strange too, because it was just her and we had four girls. It wasn't just that Jessica got preferential treatment, it was that there was an assumption that we were trouble. Jessica got the singsong Disney voice from them, but they were very rigid with the girls, repeating themselves as if they were dumb. It got tense, and Mathew saw a Goofy costume backstage and decided to put it on to make the girls laugh. Someone with a lanyard and clipboard scolded him like a child. *"Go take that off!"*

We did what we always did, laughing and keeping things light to prevent the stress from affecting the girls or the performance. Each artist did two shows that night for the different time slots. During the first one, Beyoncé threw a towel into the audience, and the crowd went crazy. It was the mark of a true superstar, creating that interaction with an audience when girls weren't even supposed to sweat. She had complete control of that crowd, born of mutual respect. "There's a barrier right there," she said, pointing to the front. "Y'all can't jump it and you have to not hurt each other."

The organizers had the *police* waiting for her as soon as she came offstage. These officers talked to her so crazy, practically spitting as one said, "If you throw *anything* out there, we're shutting the show down and we're arresting you."

I got right between them. "You are not *arresting* her."

"Yes, we are," the cop said to me. "If she does that again." Then, right in Beyoncé's face, he said, "You could have caused a riot out there."

It wasn't just that she was Black, it was that the fans were. The ones who were up front, singing every word to "Say My Name."

For the next performance, the police officers had the nerve to stand onstage while they performed. One kept his hand back to his cuffs, sending a message not just to the girls, but to the audience. Destiny's Child didn't let their anger show, but I was never so pissed off in my life.

Near the end, I saw Beyoncé flick her eyes this way and that, acknowledging the cops, but keeping her focus on the audience. "Thank you for supporting us," she said to the crowd. "We *love* you."

CHAPTER 34

"TINA IS THE PROBLEM"

May 2000

MATHEW CAME BACK to Houston needing to tell me something.

Sony had asked him for a meeting in New York—just him. It was right after the huge jump in sales for *The Writing's on the Wall,* and the people at the meeting shared some pleasantries about the album still hitting new highs so many weeks after the release of the "Say My Name" video. They said they were projecting it to be one of the top-selling records of the year. *But* they needed to talk to him about a problem.

Me. They told him I had to go.

"Mathew, you have always shared your dreams for the girls," one of the suits had said. "But your *wife* is going to be the reason Destiny's Child will never cross over like you say. Not the way she is styling them. Tina is the problem."

Mathew started to say something but was cut off. A scared assistant rushed over to the main person in the group, holding up a board with flattering photos of the one-name pop acts: Britney, Jessica, and Christina. "Your group is an R&B act, so they will never be as popular as these people," the suit continued. "And they definitely aren't going to be that big with your wife limiting them."

Mathew said they all piled on, saying things like, "People love their music, but they will never love them." Their hair was too big, *"too Texas,"* someone supplied. Their clothes were "not something an average girl can go to the mall and just get for a date." The look, a higher-up said, was "Motown." Just that word started a wave of gri-maced nods.

Mathew and I both knew what this was code for. They were too Black, and any kind of Black was too Black. But the girls *are* Black. Delighted to be and unapologetically so, because there was nothing to apologize for, and they were confident in the looks.

He said they pointed to Britney Spears as the proof of what the girls could never be. "They said, 'This is what stars are wearing—jeans and midriff tops. Nothing flashy. Not these homemade clothes. Tina is what's holding them back.'"

"They really said 'homemade'?" I asked Mathew.

"They did."

"So what did *you* say?"

He chuckled. I thanked God again that with all the things wrong with Mathew as a husband, he was a team player you wanted going to bat for you. "I said, 'You are not going to tell me that my wife is limit-ing this group. Not when everywhere they perform, people are coming up asking who does their clothes. And not when we are selling millions of records. You are not going to do *that,* so just get over that.'"

I hugged Mathew. "Thank you," I said. A week later, he went back for an all-hands executive meeting at Sony. He reached for the light switch and flicked it off. They sat in darkness for one beat, two beats. Three. He turned the switch on again. "Destiny's Child is keeping the fucking lights on in here," he said. "Just don't forget that." That mo-ment became legendary. "That man is crazy" was the word, but he was right. It was true.

With his corporate mind, Mathew thought that the group would increase its market share if they mixed in pop songs on the next album. The label said this was yet another industry rule he would be breaking: "You cannot mix R&B with pop on one album—people will not buy it." Which sounds ludicrous now, but it sounded dumb to us then too. We didn't think Destiny's Child needed to *move* to pop, because pop would move to them. "Change the world," I would tell them. "Don't let the world change you."

I knew this because as mean as the people in the industry and other stylists I met could be, they stole our looks all the time. I would see a white pop singer dancing in a Swarovski rhinestone–covered outfit or watch a model walk down the runway in camouflage couture and think, "That's Destiny's Child." We were inspired by our own Black culture, and people have always wanted our swag and copied our work.

Shortly after the move to fire me, we were in Cologne, Germany, for a Destiny's Child performance. We saw Britney Spears backstage, and she was so sweet—which was always the case. She and the girls were each living a singular experience that only they could understand, and yet the industry tried to pit them against each other. This was true with Jessica Simpson and her younger sister, Ashlee, too. Solange and Ashlee bonded as the little rebel sisters cursing together to be funny, each shocking the older sister they saw as a goody two-shoes. "Mama, Solange has a partner in *crime*," Beyoncé said.

Now, in Germany, Britney talked about loving the girls' outfits. "One day, Miss Tina, you've please got to do something for me."

SONY PRESENTED THE GIRLS WITH AN OFFER THE LABEL THOUGHT they couldn't refuse. The song Beyoncé wrote, "Independent Women, Part I," had been selected as the lead single for Sony's *Charlie's Angels* soundtrack. The single would also forecast Destiny's Child's direction for the album they were working on now, due out in early 2001. Sony said that Pat Field, the renowned stylist for *Sex and the City*, was willing to dress the girls for the video. This was an honor, and we loved Pat from shopping in her beautiful, eclectic store in New York's East Village. But I knew what Sony was up to. They didn't want the girls to be too Black for the soundtrack video.

The girls knew it too. Mathew had sat them down after Sony tried to get him to fire me. We never told them everything Sony said about making them change to fit an imagined demographic, because they were already under enough pressure. But this time, Mathew had told them exactly what they said about me and their look so they could make an informed decision themselves. "We've got to stick together, and y'all got to stand up for Miss Tina," he said. "Y'all can't let these people do this to her, because she's been riding and dying with y'all the whole time."

Sony had tried it this one last time, and I was actually the one willing to fold. I told the girls that they could go with someone else to style the video, but they refused. As I made plans getting ready for the late August 2000 shoot in Los Angeles, I talked up designers we could approach.

"Mama," Beyoncé said. "You don't have to change our—"

"No, we gotta step it up," I said. "So I'm going to do designer stuff."

"Well, you can do *some* designer stuff," said Kelly.

Beyoncé added, "But we still want your look. We want you to do one of your leather cutout outfits."

"Okay," I promised. I had to make outfits last-minute for a fight scene they added two days before. The scene would involve the girls doing flying kicks on harnesses, so I wanted the clothing to float in the air to add to the flying effect. I went and got a whole bolt of this purple and white fabric that just flowed. There was enough time to make the pants, but for the tops I literally draped this fabric over each girl on set and took another piece to make a sash to tie around them. It took five minutes, and the scene was beautiful.

The film's stars visited the set that day: Drew Barrymore, Lucy Liu, and Cameron Diaz. They were so lovely, and Lucy admired the sashed tops on the girls: "Where'd you get those from?"

"My mama made them about fifteen minutes ago," Beyoncé said.

"I just draped some fabric," I said. "It's not even made yet."

The line made everyone laugh, and it really was *fun* for all of us. Even under terrible circumstances, when Sony was trying so hard to have me not do it. We just always turned the lemons into lemonade.

Soon after, Destiny's Child was honored at the VH1/Vogue Fashion Awards in New York, and we sat in the audience with John Galliano, Betsey Johnson, and Oscar de la Renta as *Vogue* showed a tribute to the girls' style. When the group won the award, they told me *we* won, and they grabbed my hand to pull me up the stairs onstage with them. "We want to give thanks to this lovely lady right here," Kelly said. "Miss Tina Knowles, who definitely set the image for Destiny's Child."

The night marked a turning point, as there was something about the *Vogue* seal of approval that legitimized what the girls already knew to be true. And now Columbia was done messing with me for good.

BACK IN HOUSTON, PEOPLE HAD STARTED SHOWING UP AT OUR home for an impromptu meet-and-greet with Destiny's Child. You would be just halfway unpacked or happy to be in your own bed, and you'd hear a crowd in the yard. In the beginning, you think that situation is crazy, but now it was at a point I thought *I* was crazy not to be looking for something with a gate.

Vernell and I were driving out to Lake Olympia outside Houston, real estate listings in hand and reminiscing about Galveston. We pulled up to a five-bedroom house for sale on Swan Isle, and I walked in to see a huge picture window overlooking the lake. I was in love. The girls would no longer have to share bedrooms, and I could make a project of each of their rooms to create a refuge from all the pressure.

That new home was the start of a good time for Mathew and me. You cannot watch each other fight so many individual day-to-day battles on behalf of your daughters and not continually fall in love again.

And I had also fallen in love again with Galveston, this place I'd always been so eager to leave. We often couldn't plan family visits far ahead because of Destiny's Child's schedule being so unpredictable. It was like when my parents would return to Weeks Island unannounced, my daddy having us just show up in Louisiana. I get a better sense now of what they felt—a homecoming to yourself.

As they reached these new heights, I wanted my daughters to draw strength from the foundation of their relatives and history. In between stops, we popped in. Beyoncé loved the ease of Galveston and the beach, and I could see Solange just storing all these images in her mind. Kelly may not have been born into our family, but she was loved into it. They needed to hear our stories and suffer through their Uncle Skip's corny jokes. Inevitably, each person would share a memory of Johnny, and the girls, exhausted from touring, would completely relax.

I could not leave Galveston without having my daughters and Michelle ride the free ferry that had been my escape all those years. They'd been on jet planes and in limos, but this was special to me. "Riding the ferry was my saving grace growing up here in Galveston," I told them. "Especially when I was a teenager. Every new boyfriend I had, I would say, 'Do you wanna go on my yacht?'"

The girls laughed, and I kept going. "Then when we were out on the water, I would sing to them. It was part of my Tina game, that good old Tina game I can pass on to you now. Along with this boat my mother gave me. It's all yours now."

I paused, looking out on the water that held such possibility when I was a kid, this route back toward where my parents were from. "It's yours now, too," I said again. "All of it."

CHAPTER 35

TWENTY-FIRST-
CENTURY WOMEN

Summer 2000

M ATHEW AND I were standing in the kitchen at the house on Swan Isle in Houston. We were either just back from a trip or leaving for one—this was the constant state of change we were living in.

Solange walked in and opened up a cupboard to reach for a glass. "You know, I've been in the studio," she said, half-turning to us as she filled the glass with water.

"What?" we both said. By then, we owned a studio in Houston, because it was cheaper than renting one for all the stuff we were doing. We knew that she was always writing songs, and her journals were now full of lyrics. But we thought she was at the mall, not the studio.

She sipped the water. "I want a record deal," she said, just like that. This girl didn't wait for nothing.

"You know, Solange," I said. "You don't even want to get up in the morning if you think it's too early. You want to have fun, so just go have fun. You don't need this."

"No, I want a record deal," she said.

"Okay, if you want a record deal," I said to Solange, "then go with the girls on tour. You be a backup dancer for them. We want you to see how hard it is getting up at four o'clock in the morning."

I figured those early wake-up calls would do it. She'd had a big taste of that life because she had traveled with us, but we always gave her an out. She wouldn't get up before dawn for a flight, so we would often let Solange and her nanny-tutor stay behind to catch a later plane.

"If you're working, Solange," said Mathew, "you can't go take a later flight, you gotta go with everybody else."

I leaned on the island countertop. "You go be a dancer this summer, and if you prove to us that you're gonna work hard and *keep up*, then we'll talk."

Maybe I'd set myself up in giving her the challenge. Because of course she rose to the occasion. The girls were opening for Christina Aguilera on their biggest, longest tour yet. She hung in with these backup dancers who were twenty-five or thirty years old and had been at this for ten years. She kept up the whole time, and in fact choreographed a little ballet intro for herself.

Summer went into fall, and she kept up her commitment. That October of 2000, we were in Denver for a show, and as so many dancers were struggling maintaining their breath at such a high altitude, there was Solange, determined not to let it show.

It was at that concert that a small disaster happened. The girls had two or three quick changes during the show—which was crazy, I know. No opening act did all that, but this was Destiny's Child. It was decided that they could not use the room at the stage to change, so to pull off the quick changes, they had to run down a ramp in the dark. Racing in the pitch-black, Kelly broke two toes on her right foot.

Other bands would have canceled the remaining dates, but we were not going to let that stop us. I rhinestoned her cast *and* a stool for Kelly so she could sit and sing. I also made Solange a costume to match Kelly's, as she was doing Kelly's dance moves with Beyoncé and Michelle. Solange now had the pressure of doing Kelly's steps as an extension of her, which is a lot for someone at fourteen. But she killed it.

She knew it too, because as soon as we got home, she went into the studio and started producing her own vocals. *This is a nice project,* I thought. *We'll see where it goes.*

Some time went by, not long. "Mom," she said. "Um. I have a song that, uh, Pharrell did."

Once again, I yelled, "What? How did that happen?"

"Well, I just got his number from Bey."

"And what?"

She slowed her voice down to help me. "I called him and asked, would he do a track for me?"

"Well, how did you pay him?"

"I haven't paid him."

"Did you negotiate anything?" Because Mathew had a philosophy that you negotiated up front so that you wouldn't have to pay so much later. And Pharrell at the time was on fire.

"No," she said. "I just arranged him to . . ."

"You *arranged* Pharrell to do a song? Are you kidding me?"

But that was her, no time to waste. Mathew contacted Pharrell and he was lovely. He was one who immediately saw the writer in Solange, the young storyteller. She went to Miami to record the song "Crush" and there was no stopping her. Solange insisted that she would be able to write her own songs and get credit for her work. She picked out all her own producers and started work on the album she would release the next year, *Solo Star*. "Solange is so ahead of her time," her sisters and I would often say to each other. She knew the hottest producers before we did and wore a mismatched print that she would declare over once other people did the same. But she was also ahead of her time in that she was accomplishing these things so young, and I wanted her to stay in that childhood as long as she could.

As Solange made her plans, Destiny's Child continued their rise. In January 2001, we had two days to shoot the video for "Survivor," starting on a stretch of Malibu beach called Point Dume. It seemed too perfect a name, given that we were all freezing. For this opening scene I had the girls in torn chiffon dresses, three survivors washing up on a desolate island.

Ty Hunter was next to me watching the girls "wake up" on the beach, and I could tell he was worried they were cold. Ty was a young man we hired to assist me after years of seeing him at Bebe at the Galleria mall in Houston. I would race in there needing last-minute outfits for backup dancers, and he had always been so kind, with such great energy.

I had started calling ahead of time, asking for him and saying, "What y'all got?" He would put things aside for us. "Don't worry," I told him once, "I'ma get you outta here one day." I kept my promise, calling him and saying, "Look, I need some help on this video. Do you wanna leave?"

"I have been waiting for this call," he said, and immediately got on the whirlwind with us.

Now Ty held his arms around himself tight, this empath who was cold just watching the girls in the water. He murmured to me as the cameras rolled, "Only you would have them in chiffon in the middle of the ocean."

"Well, they were performers on the ship that went down," I said.

"Don't you think it would be more realistic if they had on, like, jeans?"

"They were onstage when it happened," I said, matter-of-fact.

"And how *did* the ship go down?" he asked. "How was it just them in that raft?"

"I don't want to talk about it," I joked. "It's too painful." And we both started laughing. I just wanted them to look beautiful. We were delirious from being up for two weeks straight—I designed the outfits and Jaime made them, then me and Ty would do the finishing touches of shredding dresses or gluing all the rhinestones. We were always bedazzling *something*. The looks these fur bikinis Beyoncé insisted we have, a tribute to Raquel Welch in *One Million Years B.C.* I also wanted to take the camouflage look they'd popularized, which started with Master P, and step the battledress up a notch. Make it camo-*flaunt*. We hand-rhinestoned the patterns of the bikini tops and shorts, and also dressed all the backup dancers in camo too.

I think I told Ty we'd be traveling a couple weeks, but it was four months or so before he got to come back home. He would pack and unpack the clothes and dress the girls. We worked sixteen-hour days unless we needed twenty-four, and Ty became a brother to the girls, someone we could trust. We threw Ty in the deep end doing the Grammys that February, when they performed "Say My Name" and took home their first two awards: Best R&B Song and Best R&B Performance by a Duo or Group with Vocals. We needed at least two wardrobe changes—one for the carpet and then a stage costume for the performance, but Beyoncé said that wasn't enough. "I want to do a wardrobe change at the awards show."

"Oh my God," I said. Then, "Okay."

I started designing where I always begin, with the fabrics. I went to High Fashion Fabrics in Houston to see what inspired. I started with the stage costumes, finding blue sequins that I loved. It was a medley starting with "Independent Women, Part I," so I sketched out something that went with the look of that. When the stage went dark,

Beyoncé would snatch some of the fabric off to toss it, then come out in the sequined top and little shorts. I'm not a great sketcher, but I could always work the designs out with Jaime, first in Houston on the mannequins designed to their measurements. On the mannequins, you could really see the possibilities. I'd walk around one, draping this way and that, talking to myself: "Okay, on one side, I want it to look like a bikini, and on the other side I want it to look like a dress." Once we had the designs for the blue costumes, I started negotiating for the arrivals looks, these beautiful Versace slip-dresses that had just come off the runway, all in different champagne shades. For the final look of the night, I picked this bright green bugle-beaded fabric with sequins at High Fashion Fabrics. We wanted things that would stand out and fulfill the progression of the night: starting off subtle and classy, then the blue, and then something really bright and popping.

Jaime and I were still creating up until the last minute, spray-painting boots and putting extra stones on. It was so much work, but my God was it fun. So many trends came from those looks, some we got credit for and a lot we didn't, but the sweetest tribute was when Hasbro made Barbie-like Destiny's Child dolls to match the blue per-formance outfits. I had to get involved to get the looks right, and the initial faces they sent looked nothing like the girls. But the finished product was so sweet. When my children were little, I had worked hard to find dolls that reflected my kids, and now here they were.

Representation mattered so much, and yet there were so many attempts to control how Destiny's Child was perceived by larger audi-ences. Beyoncé was invited to take part in *Vanity Fair*'s November 2001 Music issue, one of their huge tri-fold pull-out covers, and as usual, it was photographed by Annie Leibovitz. We were so excited because she was going to be on the cover with legends like David Bowie and some of the hottest acts of the time. We were in the trailer on set preparing when some assistant came in and announced, "Miss Leibovitz wants Beyoncé's hair back in a bun."

"Oh, her hair is not going back in a bun," I said. "It's part of her trademark."

We were told it was "too distracting" with Jewel's hair also down. "There's too much hair in this shoot, and we want it in a bun."

"No," I said. When I was young and fled Galveston to go to Denver that time with Butch and his wife, I worked as a model for a hot minute.

I noticed that they never hired Black hairstylists so the crew at the shoot or show didn't know what to do with Black hair. The solution was always "Put it in a bun." I have met enough Black supermodels to know that this happened at the absolute height of fashion modeling— including Condé Nast titles like *Vanity Fair* back in the day. The phrase I always heard in these directives was "It will look classy."

The assistant returned, stone-faced. "Miss Leibovitz would like to speak to you." This was said with such solemnity, but I did not know Leibovitz's history and portfolio. "Okay," I said.

She came in, saying, "Can you just slick her hair back in a bun? You know, a classy bun. It will show her in a different light."

"Tell Jewel to put her hair in a bun. Go tell another girl there's too much hair—she's not gonna be the one."

"Well, if there's no way I can talk you out of it . . ." she said as she left. I finished working on Beyoncé's waves, and when I got out to the set, I saw these famous musicians here and there. And sitting on the floor where they'd arranged him, looking so sad in a huge hat, was Maxwell. He was twenty-eight then, famous for his beautiful voice and the most gorgeous natural hair.

I went right to him. "Why do you look so sad?"

"I hate this *hat*," he said.

"Well, why do you have that hat on?"

"They want me to wear it."

I took the hat right off his head, then used my pick to begin fluffing out his hair. I didn't know him from Adam, and I was shy back then, but I was Mama Bear. "Do not let these people put something on your head," I said. "Tell them they can put a hat on somebody else."

I looked over and saw Beyoncé trying to hide her face like, *God, my mom is crazy*. Maxwell's manager came running. "What are you all doing?" he asked Maxwell.

"Your hair is your trademark," I told Maxwell, focusing solely on him. "Your crowning glory."

JAY-Z HAD BEEN FEATURED IN THAT 2001 *VANITY FAIR* SHOOT, and Beyoncé had developed a friendship with him, solely over the phone. They provided good counsel to each other as they discussed the industry, each sharing a singular confidence in their artistic vision.

The girls also happened to be home in Houston when he came in to do a concert, and whenever a group or solo artist was in town when we were, I would invite them and their entourage over for a Sunday soul food dinner. People on the road need a home-cooked meal, a chance for all these people working hard on a tour to break bread. As Beyoncé and Jay then kept up with each other in calls, the friendship deepened. She would tell me, "He's just so *nice*." There was another guy in the industry talking to her, a friend who maybe wanted to be more, and while we were in Los Angeles for her to film *Austin Powers in Gold-member,* she told me they were both coming to town at the same time. "I don't know what to do."

"Well, who do you like the most?" I asked. "Who do you enjoy talking to more?"

I watched her think. It was Jay. Isn't it humbling how love can begin with such a simple feeling? You like talking to someone over the phone. You're twenty-one years old and you can't know someday you will take that love to the stars, but it begins with such a small instinct.

Once they got more serious, there was a meeting of mothers— Gloria Carter, her mother Grandma Hattie White, and myself—on Mother's Day in New York. We decided to rent this suite with a kitchen, and I would cook. We invited Jay's two sisters, Annie and Mickey, not knowing that they have a tradition in their family that the girls take Gloria and Grandma Hattie to a play and dinner on Mother's Day. They are incredibly close, the funniest people who spend so much time together.

His sisters are so funny that they good-naturedly gave Beyoncé a hard time as a joke. During the meal Jay said, "Can I have some water?" And Kelly being Kelly, the most hospitable person there ever was, got up to get Jay some water. Even though Annie and Mickey are indepen-dent women and don't really feel this way, they saw a chance to poke fun at Beyoncé: "You're gonna let another woman get your man some water?" teased Mickey.

Beyoncé reacted with an "I'm sorry," like she should have known better. Now they pretended to haze her. "Do you know how to cook?" Annie asked.

"No, I don't really cook," Beyoncé admitted, "but I used to." Kelly and I chuckled, remembering those Hamburger Helper days of Beyoncé cooking for all the girls.

"Well, do you clean?" they asked. "Do you know how to wash dishes?"

I jumped in to turn the joke back on them. "Look at these hands," I joked, stealing a line I'd seen Diahann Carroll use on a talk show and filed away. "Look how beautiful they are. Do you think she could ever put these in . . . in *dishwater?* No, she makes way too much money to be wasting her time washing dishes."

Beyoncé pulled those hands back, because the very last thing she'll ever be is arrogant, but Jay's family *laughed* and let her know it was all in fun.

That was the start of the Carter and Knowles families joining as one family, and we are all very close to this day. Our gatherings would become parties, rich with laughter and storytelling, drinking and dancing. In the Bible it says to eat, drink, and be merry, and that's what our evenings are like with the Carters. Two of my favorite dance partners are Jay's sisters, Mickey and Annie, and for years, when Gloria knows I need a boost, I wake up to this beautiful scripture or an affirmation that lifts my spirits. And Miss Hattie White, always the quintessential matriarch, is the sharpest and kindest woman, one who would give words to so many of our feelings when she delivered a speech at her ninetieth birthday, words so wise Beyoncé would eventually feature them in her song "Freedom": "I had my ups and downs, but I always find the inner strength to pull myself up. I was served lemons, but I made lemonade."

DESIGNERS NOW APPROACHED US ALL OVER THE WORLD, ASKING me to go to their showroom in New York. "Tell them to give you whatever you want." I would walk into the same places that someone had almost literally thrown me out of before, saying they would never dress the girls. The gatekeepers' voices would shake as they hoped I'd forgotten what they'd said to me before. But I remained civil, asserting myself while making the most of these relationships.

I could do this sort of thing in the service of my children or other people's children like Maxwell, be that advocate they needed and call on Badass Tenie B. But I had a harder time showing up for myself. In 2002, people had started to try to interview me more and more, and I found my own voice shaking sometimes. Oprah Winfrey *made* me come out onto the stage of her show when we were there in Chicago, knowing my importance to these young women and refusing to allow me to hide. On top of my nerves, I did not want to be in front of the camera in the first place, not liking how tired I looked. There was no way for me to get more sleep with the constant checklist of what I had to do, so I just began to go invisible, a ghost dressed in dark clothes, flitting in and out of the room as she saw to things.

Even when the group had time off, I had difficulty slowing down. We were having one of those rare days when it was just me, Solange, and Beyoncé at home in Houston after Destiny's Child finished a world tour. Beyoncé was cocooned in her room, in her crash-landing uniform of sweats and a weathered tee. I was restless, aware that the cycle of rushing and last-minute sketch-to-stage looks would begin again. I'd spent weeks looking forward to just being still, and now that it was here, I couldn't.

The second Solange said, "Mom, come go to the mall," I jumped on it and grabbed my keys.

I called up to Beyoncé's room when we were at the door. She had been resting after all the work, just watching TV and probably having the same problem I was. "We're just running to the Galleria, baby," I yelled.

I heard a soft "I wanna go."

"Oh," I said. Solange and I exchanged a quick look. Of course, we wanted her there, but it was getting to be a production to go anywhere with her being recognized and stopped. "It's gonna be really hard for you to get through the mall."

"Yeah, but I'm bored," she said, already coming down. "And I wanna go."

Driving over, I found myself planning the best entrance to get in and out. The Galleria was one of the largest malls in the nation, and Solange wanted to go to the Versace store. As we arrived, I was thinking how great it was to be in Houston, where people just did not care about all that fame stuff. Beyoncé could still have a refuge here. I had been so silly to think she didn't.

All of a sudden, all these people started filling the Versace store. Word got out that Beyoncé was there. The staff was trying to keep people out because it just wasn't safe. People were screaming my daughter's name here in Houston. They were happy to see her, and I appreciated their love for Beyoncé, but this was just too many people at once.

The panicked staff hurried us into a storage room and led us out a back door. It had been so loud, and now there was silence—us and a couple of dumpsters. Glamorous.

"We didn't even get to shop," I joked, trying to keep things light. "We went through all that trouble parking, too."

As we walked all the way to the parking garage, I realized how Beyoncé's life had changed—all of ours. Even here in Houston, where we were still used to being able to do anything. We drove home quiet, empty-handed. I knew what she now knew too: Her life would never be the same, and the time of being able to go to the mall, or do any simple thing, was over.

CHAPTER 36

EYES LIFTED TO
THE MOUNTAINS

Spring 2003

T HE OFFICES AT the Sony building in Manhattan were intimidating. You might be on top of the world, you might even be a member of one of the bestselling girl groups of all time, but as you went solo, the place could make artists feel out of place. There were some amazing people at the record company, women like Yvette Noel-Schure and Stephanie Gayle, who truly cared about artists. But there were also people who got ahead by sticking to some of the worst aspects of the industry rulebook.

The Columbia executives were waiting for us in the boardroom, which we thought was a last-minute meeting about the upcoming rollout of Beyoncé's first solo album, *Dangerously in Love*. As a group, Destiny's Child had decided to take a hiatus, allowing the girls to pursue projects that were wholly theirs. Michelle was the first with *Heart to Yours,* which became the bestselling gospel album of 2002. Then Kelly took over the summer with her single with Nelly, "Dilemma," our princess creating a classic and number-one single in the United States and in places all over Europe, forever launching her as an international star in her own right. It was one of the reasons her album *Simply Deep* debuted as the number-one album in the United Kingdom.

Beyoncé had pushed back her own album so her sister Kelly could take full advantage of the momentum of her own success. People oftentimes say that the goal was always for Beyoncé to be solo, but if that were the case, she would have done that out of the gate. She loved being part of a group. But now it was time for *Dangerously in Love*. She had submitted the work to New York, and Mathew was flying to London, personally bringing the album to Sony's U.K. office to drum up excitement and get them thinking globally about promotion.

"Do you think you can handle the meeting with Donnie while I'm gone?" he had asked me, reeling off a list of about five other suits whose names I can't remember. Donnie was Don Ienner, the head of Columbia, and soon to be the head of all of Sony now that Tommy Mottola was gone. Ienner was legendary for his temper and what he called "war meetings," where he and the other guys at the company planned an artist's fate. But I liked Donnie and thought he was a good man. I understood his passion even if I knew his success came from mastering the mentality of the music business.

"We got this," I said. Mathew had been an executive and top sales rep for Xerox: He knew every intimidation trick a suit could pull on what they saw as this little country girl who didn't go to college. I never spoke in meetings like this, only giving my opinions to Mathew and the girls before and after. Beyoncé and I went into this alone, sitting across from these suits not knowing this was a war meeting on *us*. A principal's office setup timed for when they knew Mathew—who they mistook as our only fighter—would be thousands of miles away.

"We listened to your album," one of the suits said. "There is not one single on here."

"Not one," another echoed, fiddling with his pen like we'd disappointed all of them. This album already had "Crazy in Love," "Baby Boy," "Naughty Girl," "Me, Myself and I," a "The Closer I Get to You" cover with Mr. Luther Vandross. . . .

"We don't think the record is ready," Ienner told us. "We'll need to push back the release." He looked right at my daughter. "Back to the drawing board."

"No," said Beyoncé. "I mean, I think the record is really ready."

For twenty minutes, we went back and forth, with me letting Beyoncé speak for the quality of her work. "Tell you what," the pen fiddler said. "We're going to invite a few tastemakers here tomorrow and we can get their opinions."

"Oh, that's great," said Beyoncé. But when we walked into the boardroom again Friday afternoon, we were surprised to see the room packed with about twenty people, some from the label, a few radio DJs—a gathering of what would eventually be called "influencers."

They grimaced as a greeting, but we stayed gracious. Pressed Play and watched as these people did everything they could not to bob their heads to Beyoncé's music. "Yeah, well, you know, that one is all right," someone offered. At the end, the parrots chirped out their talking points: "Aww, it's got potential, but I think you need to go work on it." Only a couple people said something *mildly* positive, but even as they did, they looked around ducking for fear that they would be ostracized.

We left that meeting and as soon as we were in the back of the car, Beyoncé got out her phone. "I need to put Jay on 'Crazy in Love,'" she said, pressing his number in her little flip phone. "'Cause they wouldn't do this to *him*. They wouldn't talk to Jay like that."

He was in the city, and we picked him up to go to his apartment in New Jersey to play him the completed album in sequence to hear his thoughts. "This is a smash," Jay said. "Every one of these records is a smash." He spoke as a fellow artist with the drive the suits could never understand. We left there and immediately went to a studio they booked. It was my first time witnessing Jay work. He didn't write anything down, just listened to "Crazy in Love" two, three times in a row, and went to the mic and started rapping. Beyoncé and I were dancing, screaming, throwing fists in the air. It was a solution—not a compromise of her artistry, but a doubling down.

We took that record back. Marched right in there and played "Crazy in Love." With Jay on it now, they suddenly said, "You've got a hit on *this* song." Meaning they still wanted to hold the album. "The feedback from the room was not good."

Mathew was still in London, but now on a speakerphone courtesy of a box in the center of the boardroom table. The connection was not good, and Mathew's speaker box was one long line of static talking as he lost it. They turned the volume down.

"Well, I have to say," Beyoncé said slowly, her voice dropping to a lower register. "I don't agree with anyone in that room."

But now I was mad. I thought about all the times I had to fight. Fighting with TV directors and lighting people who didn't know how to light Black girls and turned them gray. Teaching them their jobs in the moment. Or fighting with someone I was so intimidated by on a set, saying, "No, you gotta let them do this over. The music didn't start on time." Advocating for my girls so that people would just stop being so careless with their feelings and their art.

"By the way," I started, revving up to getting really country, "they were all a bunch of haters. Every single person in there, with the exception of one or two. And in case you don't know what a hater is, it means *none of them* wanted this to be good." Now I was giving the full Galveston, the wind of the Gulf breezing up through the Manhattan skyline. "I resent the fact that you guys will go and gather together people that don't know they ass from a hole in the wall. . . ."

Beyoncé sat up, letting them have it too. Not country like me, but with the same fire I had worked to protect all those years.

"We are *not* pushing the record back," she said. "Listen, I am the artist. And I know that this is a hit record."

"Okay, well," one of these suits said. "We're going to put it out, but we just want to say our opinion."

"Thank you for your opinion," said Beyoncé. "But we are putting the record out. So let's get moving." End of discussion. In the hallway, Beyoncé quoted Erykah Badu, saying, "Now keep in mind, I'm an artist and I'm sensitive about my shit."

"Crazy in Love" was already a hit, but here again, adversity had made something even better. Jay was meant to be on it. Beyoncé only became fiercer in her protection of the album, adding more instruments to make every song even better. She worked on the record for another couple weeks and she put the record out on time.

Years later, opening the Wynn in Las Vegas for an ABC special and video album, she joked about the label telling her she didn't have one hit on the album. "I guess they were kinda right. . . . I had *five*."

IN THE FALL OF 2003, WE WERE IN ONE OF THOSE TIMES IN WHICH Solange created stillness around herself as she moved forward. It was like a disappearing act she'd perfected. Even at seventeen, no matter how extraordinary her life might seem to everyone else, it would no longer satisfy her creative impulses. She would have to leave whatever village she had built around her to go cultivate another one. When you have a child as creative as her, you get used to these comings and goings. At first you accept it, when it's a closed bedroom door and a journal, and then you respect it.

Solange was still recalibrating after the January release of her first album. Columbia had wanted a junior Beyoncé, and instead were met with this artist who'd been paying attention all those years traveling the world. She was Bohemian *and* Western, drawing from elements of Jamaican and Japanese cultures with true curiosity and not costume. The label would complain that she didn't want to dress like Beyoncé, but really, she just wanted to dress like herself. The other issue was that though she had the eye and taste of a veteran performer, she did not have the budget. She had an answer for that too: her college fund. The one Mathew and I had been putting money into for years. I still had the dream that she would surprise us all again, announce an interest in college. Get away from this business that could leave me feeling so hollowed out.

"Mom, I want to take my money," she told me. "And put it into my work. I want the styling, the sets—it all just has to be bigger."

We compromised. I wouldn't let her take it all out, but she could invest some of her own money in the project. My daughter's vision of what she wanted was so creative, so different from other first-time artists who just nod yes at whatever keeps them in the game. If Columbia wanted a little baby girl skirt, the next thing I knew I was designing her vision of a ten-foot-long dress, helping her climb the tallest stepladder we could drag to the beach to tower over these men with small-cage ideas.

I did anything to maximize the money she was putting in. While we were in New York she announced she wanted a horse in her album packaging. "Solange, we can't afford a horse," I said. "We're so over budget."

"I want a horse."

We talked to Stephanie Gayle at Columbia, a genius at getting things done, and we came up with a plan: I remembered I'd seen horses up by Central Park West, and she arranged the shoot simply, hair and makeup, a grip and photographer. Solange wore a lovely white dress, and we simply walked from the hotel over to meet the horse.

I stroked its face. "We're going to have to retouch you," I assured the horse. "But you'll be beautiful." The horse was, and the photo looked like we'd spent a fortune.

The album did well, but she was frustrated when she went out to promote the work. Imagine creating an album you care so much about and when it's finally out, the interviewer who hasn't even listened to the record asks one quick question—"Wow, the littlest Knowles! Are you excited?"—before steering the entire conversation to Beyoncé and Destiny's Child.

"I'm not here to talk about that," Solange would say. It got so she didn't want to do interviews and would naturally go quiet. After one really bad interview, when she shut down, I gave her a talking-to. She had the experience of a veteran, but people couldn't understand that. "Listen, you're trying to get out there. You don't have the luxury of doing that. This is your debut."

"I'm not doing it," she said. She felt the same way about acting, when she did the rounds of guests on teen shows. But the actors her age weren't always welcoming to her. She had done so well filming *Johnson Family Vacation* that the film's star, Cedric the Entertainer, was developing a TV series with her as the star.

But that would not be for another year or so. Solange had a boyfriend, Daniel Smith, a fellow Houston native who'd just graduated from Madison High School to become a college football player, first planning on Texas Southern before going to Los Angeles Pierce College. Home in Houston with Daniel away, Solange bonded with her friend Marsai Murry, who was just three months older than her and a senior at L. V. Hightower High School. Marsai was the ideal guide to normal life—exceptional herself, a veteran of the school debate team and dance team, a perfect friend for Solange. As I traveled the world with Beyoncé, the two of them would stay at the Swan Isle house with Mathew, and Vernell would check on them constantly. At tour stops, my youngest told me what they did that day, marveling at going to a high school party or, one of their favorite things, being under the lights at a high school football game. It seemed like the first friendship she had where they just did girlie stuff, sleepovers where they did their hair and then their nails. The novelty of a normal life.

Late on November 8, a Saturday, I was in England with Beyoncé. She had one more concert in Newcastle before she did two nights at Wembley, which would be taped for a concert special. Solange was in Houston. The night before, she and Marsai had stayed up long into the night, making up dances and naming the future kids they'd have, swearing they would be best friends too. Solange only named a girl, as certain as I had been that she would be a boy.

The two made plans to go to the Hightower High football game at Mercer Stadium over in Sugar Land. But the godfather of Solange's boyfriend Daniel asked her for a favor: Would she take Daniel's little godsister to the Houston Rockets home game that night? So Solange drove the girl to the new Toyota Center for the basketball game while Marsai went to the football game.

The call came for me in the night, so late in England. It was the little girl telling me Solange was on the ground screaming. All the girl knew was that Solange had received a phone call at the Rockets game. It was awful not knowing what was wrong and trying to help this girl through it. "Can you try," I said, "can you just get her to talk on the phone?" When Solange tried to talk to me, all she could manage was "They shot her, they shot her."

"Who?"

"Marsai!"

There had been an argument outside of Mercer Stadium after the game. Somebody got bumped by a car. A twenty-one-year-old jumped onto a car, fired a shot at a guy, and missed, killing Marsai as she simply walked by with a friend.

I called Cheryl Creuzot to get Solange and the little girl at Toyota Center, then I immediately booked a flight home. I couldn't get a nonstop and had to go through Atlanta. I just wanted to be with her. As a mother, I knew that my daughter had now lost a third person—her therapist, Johnny, and Marsai, these keepers of childhood confidences. You raise your children, filling them with love and strength, hoping they will never be tested. I spent a day with Marsai's mother, Nettie, who was in shock, feeling a desolation I could barely begin to imagine. The funeral was a week later at Windsor Village, our old church home, where Marsai had been an usher. Solange sang at the funeral, and I was again humbled by her strength.

In the aftermath, there was a quickening to Solange's life. When I was her age of seventeen, I remembered feeling that I would not have enough time to do all I wanted to do. I needed to run away to get it started. But Solange had proof of how short life could be. She didn't want to wait to get started.

I WAS TRYING TO STAY CLOSE TO SOLANGE, LOOKING FORWARD TO Thanksgiving at home in Texas with her and the family, when I received an early morning phone call. An Irish voice talking fast.

44

Baby Beyoncé in her bonnet . . . .
lookin' just like me

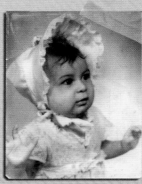

45

Matt + Beyoncé + Tina.

It was written . . . (in the sand)

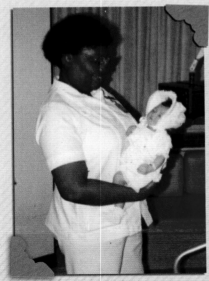

46

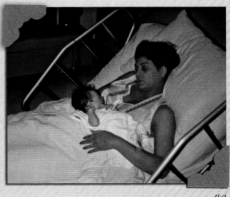

47

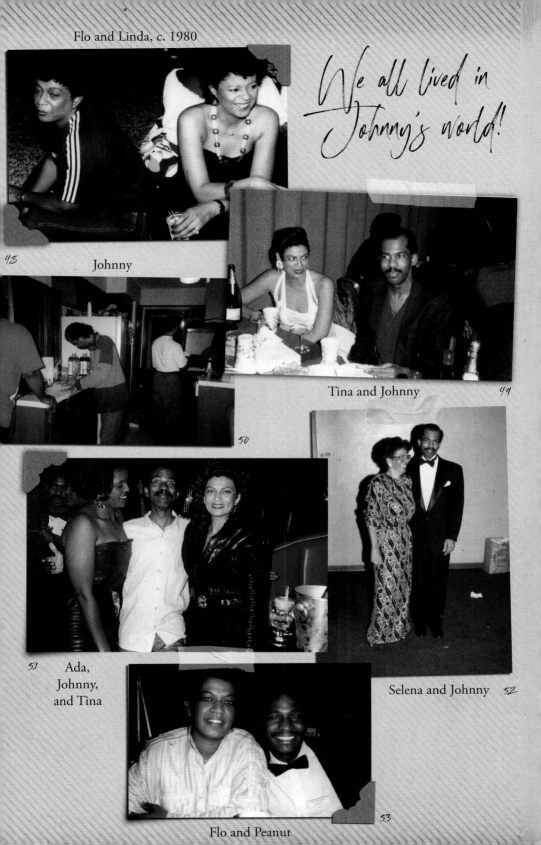

Flo and Linda, c. 1980

We all lived in Johnny's world!

48

Johnny

Tina and Johnny

49

50

51   Ada,
Johnny,
and Tina

Selena and Johnny   52

53

Flo and Peanut

54

The Knowleses

55

56

57

The many phases of me and Mathew

Mathew and Tina 59

60

EGYPT

58

Egypt: first trip to the motherland

61

62

43

On the Nile River
(little did I know I was pregnant with Solange)

Solange, 1988

64

65

Solange

67

66

Beyoncé, Solange, Ms. Tina,
Angie Beyincé, and Bono, 2003

68

69

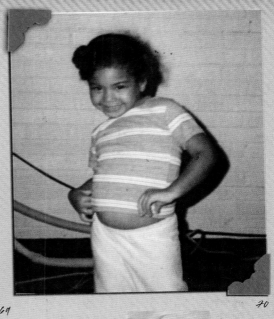

70

71

Beyonce
9 yrs

72

73

Big girl Beyoncé

← + her first car at 17

74

75

76

77

Sisters always

78

Headliners' head stylist

Headliners salon, 1986

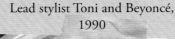
Lead stylist Toni and Beyoncé, 1990

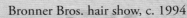
Bronner Bros. hair show, c. 1994

Ms. Tina

+ me always at work, sewing or doing hair

83

84   *85*

My sweet
Kelly

Doris Garrison and   *86*
Kelly Rowland

God's gift
to me

Christopher Lovett and Kelly Rowland   *87*

The evolution of 'Destiny's Child

88

89

90

91

92

93

Beyincé

Buyincé

Beyoncé

Beyoncé, Sir, Blue, and Rumi, 2020

My babies had babies

Solange and Julez, 2005

Kelly, Tim, Titan, and Noah, 2021

97

A new beginning—
Glamour Woman of the Year

98

99

100

"This is Bono," he said, "and I'm calling to appeal to you to have Beyoncé come perform at this concert we're doing in Cape Town to raise money for AIDS medication and education in Africa." He was so persuasive, talking about how the South Africa show would honor Nelson Mandela, and in fact this event would be named 46664 because President Mandela hoped to make something positive of the prison number he carried for twenty-seven years.

"The only thing," he said, bracing for my response, "is it's Thanksgiving."

"Oh, we can't go," I said immediately. "We have this big Thanksgiving with my family and my sister—"

"Tina, I am a white guy trying to raise money for AIDS in Africa. I had five or so people on the roster and everybody has canceled on me because it's Thanksgiving. This is important to your people, Tina. This is about lives."

I thought, *Now who is this white man to tell me about my people?* But that was the way to get me, and I guess that's how he's done so much good work. I now had to get everyone on board. Mathew was in, and when she heard what it was about Beyoncé said, "Mama, I'm down. See if you can get everybody else because I know we want to be together." I wouldn't do it without Solange, and she agreed, but Kelly had a commitment. Then I got Flo and Ty on board too.

In Cape Town, they tried to do a traditional Thanksgiving dinner to greet the Americans, and Oprah Winfrey and Archbishop Desmond Tutu were there. It was very sweet, but everyone agreed I should have flown out early so they could let me cook. What we *loved* was the jollof, a West African rice dish of tomato and herb, and we all filled up on that.

The concert would be incredible, with bands like U2 and Eurythmics, but at the last minute, Beyoncé was asked to perform twice. She would open the show and then return to sing a ballad and stand with Mr. Mandela. This moment would be important to her personally, and as a performer she wanted to honor the occasion and the audience by wearing a second outfit of a traditional African fabric.

With no time to spare, Ty and I jumped into a little car from production and headed to the local market to find fabric. My vision was kente cloth, and I prayed on the way over. "God, You gotta work with me. Whatever You want, I'll do." He put the most beautiful mud cloth in my line of sight at the fabric store—pigmented cloth of orange, tan, and brown woven together and then painted with patterns. "Oh, that's going to be better," I told Ty, "because it'll be stiffer than the kente cloth."

Ty and I raced back to the dressing area, a tent with a dirt floor, and I had maybe thirty minutes to hand-cut the dress with no pattern but memory to make a strapless column dress. We placed a sewing machine on a ten-inch stool to hand-press the push pedal. By the grace of God, it fit Beyoncé beautifully, and she then took the fabric I had left to wrap her hair, a move that was so perfect and befitting of the moment.

We said we wanted to do some good in the local area and visit with the people. They told us about a place in the Cape Flats, the Baphumelele orphanage for children with HIV whose parents had died of AIDS. Beyoncé was adamant that no photographers follow us, as she thought it would be invasive of the children we were visiting, but someone in the group took a personal photo. Beyoncé was holding a baby who was so sick, so near death that I was convinced this little one was already gone. But she carried the baby and the moment with such grace and authenticity, giving the child love for their journey.

As Beyoncé and Solange met the kids, I talked with the founder of the orphanage, Rosie Mashale, a primary school teacher who saw the need and answered the call. I noticed a girl, older than most of the kids at around ten years old, staying on the edge in clear sadness. "She has tried to kill herself," Ms. Mashale explained to me and Solange. "Her whole family died, and she is the only one left." As a mother my instinct was to go draw this girl in, but at seventeen, Solange understood her better as a peer who'd experienced loss. Solange took her to the side to talk alone, or just sit together quietly. I got caught up in conversation, and the next time I looked over, the girl was leaning into Solange, who was rocking her gently.

When we left, the ten-year-old was happier now, standing taller. Outside, Solange looked back, then whispered to me in the quiet voice of my little girl: "Mom, you see? She's *smiling*." My children can perform before millions of people, but it's always how they treat one person that fills me with pride.

.   .   .

On February 8, 2004, Solange and I were in the back of a car on our way to the Grammys. We were almost there, plenty of time to get to the Staples Center. Beyoncé was opening the show doing a medley of songs with Prince, then, two hours into the show, she would sing the title track off *Dangerously in Love*. She would take home five Grammys that night, and Jay would get two for his work on "Crazy in Love." Just the week before, she'd sung the national anthem at the Super Bowl in Houston, a wish come true after watching Whitney Houston sing it when she was nine.

Solange had seemed nervous on the car ride, and now that we were pulling up, she talked as if she was about to miss her chance at something. "Mama, I need to talk to you."

"Okay, definitely," I said.

She looked at the driver. We had just parked, and I asked him to please step out while we talked about something. Solange started with, "I just want you to know you've been the best mother."

I had no idea where this was going.

"And, you know, you didn't do anything wrong." She paused. "But I'm pregnant."

I started to say something and couldn't, but she kept going. "And I'm happy about it and I wanna get married. I wanna get on with my life because I'm not gonna live to be that old."

It was all too much at once, but that last part broke my heart. "Why do you think you're not gonna live to—"

She looked at me. It was Marsai, it was her therapist, it was Johnny. You didn't live because people wanted you to. There were no guarantees. "I just want to get on with life," she said. "I don't wanna do the television series, I don't wanna do music. I just want to get married and have my family."

I managed a stunned "okay" and a repeated "I love you." I hoped my hug could say what I could not. She knew I had to go, and maybe she had timed this for when my responsibilities would keep me from being able to talk too long to her about this. So she could go it alone.

Inside, getting Beyoncé ready, I was upset but not angry that Solange was pregnant. Of course, I was fearful that she was too young to be a mother and a wife, but I understood the urgency she had to live her life. I also worried she would regret giving up her career. She could be a mom and be an artist. We would help her do that. But she was talk-ing about walking away from all of it.

I knew small-minded people would judge her and talk shit about Mathew and me being failures as parents, but I never cared about that. My *least* worry was public opinion about my family, certainly not what people said about *me*. My first priority was what it always has been—to protect my family.

I told Mathew and he was devastated. He and I were going through another hard time, but we were together in knowing all the sacrifices both Solange and we had made so that she could have the career she wanted. "She doesn't have to get married," he repeated, again and again.

I tried to reason with her about waiting to get married, urging them to have the baby and hold off. When she insisted, I resorted to the plain-speaking jokes my big sister Selena and brother Skip would have used to get their point across. "We're not gonna help you," I teased, "and you're gonna have a baby and you're gonna run out of money and you're just gonna have to get a job at McDonald's."

It started as a playful threat, but it escalated because Solange will tell you what you can go do in a minute. My niece Angie and I came up with a scheme that would have had Johnny rolling his eyes and call-ing me Lucy. We knew there would be no convincing Solange to wait, so Angie and I would call Daniel to persuade him to. We hyped him up, convincing him that they were too young, and that they could love each other and still be together without getting married. Now, we said, he had to tell Solange.

He called us back, crying. "She said, 'Fuck you, and fuck my mama, and fuck Angie because I know they put you up to this.'" Solange hung up in his face, and then disappeared for two days. We were scared to death, and even if a disappearing act was always Solange's way, I was so mad. "Angie, you always think you know everything," I said.

"Yeah, but it seemed like it was gonna *work*," she said.

We called around until we found Solange at a friend's house. She had taken what I'd said to heart about her having to make her own money, so she'd gone and pawned her jewelry. It was what a kid would do, a reminder that she was just seventeen. It was all gone, including the *Solo Star* bracelet I'd had custom-made, a large piece covered in diamonds. I'd spent a fortune on it, and she pawned it for like a thousand dollars. All told, she said she'd gotten three grand for every-thing. She wouldn't tell us where she'd sold the stuff. "I don't need you to do anything," she said.

I went to the friend's house, if only just to hug her. "Okay, okay," I said, showing I wasn't going to fight her on this. "Well," I said, "if you're gonna get married at least let me give you a wedding. So you can have memories."

"I don't want a wedding; I just want to be *married*. I'll go to the courthouse. I don't want people in my business and they're gonna find out."

"They're gon' find out anyways," I said.

"I want to do it today."

I breathed out. It was a Wednesday. If this was happening, I wanted to bring the whole family together, show her we're here whether she wanted to reach her hand out to us or not. "Let me work it out," I said, quick, like it was easy. "Give me three days."

She nodded. She would get married Saturday, February 28. The race had begun. I called Stephanie Gayle at Columbia, then our friend Yvette Noel-Schure in the media department. Sony really stepped up, and somebody at the label reached out to John Travolta, who owned what amounted to a private resort on Grand Bahama island. He let us take over the place and we made plans to fly everybody down there. Stephanie even came down to look after us. I was so touched by how protective Don Ienner was of Solange and the family—any Sony employee who heard could have gone and sold a news tip and not one did.

I gave myself one single day to get bridesmaid dresses for Beyoncé, Kelly, and Angie, finding perfect rose-colored ones at a little boutique in Houston. Then Solange and I went to a David's Bridal to get her wedding dress. She tried on three dresses and picked the most simple one. A white lace strapless mermaid gown, perfect for the Bahamas. I ran over to Neiman's and found a suit for me in the same rose pink as her sisters' dresses. In one day, we had everything.

We flew to the Bahamas the next day. Beyoncé and Jay flew from New York, and Mathew also came separately from there. He was still very upset. "I'm not signing the papers for her to get married," he said.

"You can't fight this," I said, "and you can't control it. So you might as well go with it. You know your daughter. This is her life."

Mathew relented. He walked Solange down the aisle to Sade's "By

Your Side," a song that would be important to her for years to come. "I'll tell you you're right when you're wrong," Sade sings, a line that might confuse people who have never known love, romantic or maternal. No, I didn't want her to get married, but I trusted my daughter. During the ceremony, I meditated on that and on 1 Corinthians, which comes to mind at weddings. Not just the "Love is patient, love is kind" everyone knows, but the tougher lines: "Love always protects, always trusts, always hopes, always perseveres." It's God's way of saying that love, any kind, requires understanding.

WITH THE WEDDING DONE, I COULD FOCUS ON A MOVE. IT WAS TIME once more. People were sneaking into our Swan Isle development, walking up to the house and ringing the bell again. Then throwing rocks in the hopes of seeing one of my daughters at a window. Right before the Super Bowl, when Beyoncé was preparing to sing the national anthem, Angie and Solange were at the house alone when a mentally ill man showed up saying he was married to Beyoncé and had written all her songs. He threatened terrible things, foaming at the mouth, and Angie was left to think quick and get the cops involved. Another time, I walked out back to look at the lake and there was a huge white guy lying out on a lawn chair. "Can I help you?" I asked.

"I'm looking for Beyoncé," he said.

"Oh, hold on," I said. I went in the house, locked the door, and called Mathew. "We gotta get out of this house." I left that day and never went back.

I found a furnished apartment downtown and moved into it the next day. Mathew and I were happy there for a while, but then he fell back into old patterns. Once again, I began to think of a life without him. When I found out Mathew was selling Music World Entertainment, the family's management company, to Sanctuary Records, I made him give me half the company and used that money to buy my own house. At fifty years old, for all the times I ran away, I had never lived truly alone in my life.

The empty nest scared me, so I did some magical thinking. *If I buy a house big enough to fit everybody, they'll visit all the time.* Solange was living with Daniel in L.A., but she was due in October. She would need her mom, the way I wish I had, so I needed a place where I could make a whole area for her and Daniel, complete with a nursery for my first grandchild.

I bought this huge house in our home base of Houston, eleven thousand square feet with these gorgeous tall walls for all my art, and the whole back of it was glass with a view of the bayou. I planned a wing for Solange, Daniel, and the baby who was due soon. The nursery in my home came as a surprise to Solange. "Mom, I never told you to buy this house."

"Well, I told you that I was buying a house big enough for y'all to stay in," I said. "I would never have bought a house this big for just—" I didn't finish it: Just me.

I found ways to avoid moving into the house alone. There was the spring tour with Beyoncé, then I was constantly renovating. I have always had insomnia, and dreaded what it would be like to sleep alone in such a huge place. At night, Mathew would text me about something important for work, and then in the quick back-and-forth of that late hour there would be some plea for forgiveness, or a line that he thought might work on me. Even "I love you." I knew he meant it. *I* meant it, though I would not say it back to him.

I wouldn't reply. I would put the phone down and let love and pride have their old fight over who would win. Until finally I was so exhausted from the battle that I slept. And then I was so exhausted I just gave in and let Mathew back in my life. But before I did, I got him to sign something saying that all of our property was separate. Whatever he owned was his and whatever was mine was mine. I told him that was the only way I would continue the marriage. He happily signed it, and Mathew and I ended up moving into my getaway house together.

Our pattern continued: I didn't know how to live alone, and he didn't know how to live without me.

CHAPTER 37

JOY AND PAIN

July 2004

WHEN I WAS little, I wondered if my mother cooked so much on Sundays because people came over, or if people only kept coming over on Sundays because my mama was cooking. Either way, the tradition had continued, even in the New York apartment Mathew and I kept on the Upper West Side. This particular Sunday I was frying up fish in a skillet, one by one feeding the revolving door of people coming in to say hi and grab a plate. I was dressed down in a T-shirt and my Stella McCartney stretch jeans.

Solange was on the phone, surprising me by planning her own Sunday cooking nearly three thousand miles away in Los Angeles. "Mom," she said as a greeting, "tell me how to make your baked chicken."

I turned the fish in my own pan, a glorious golden brown. "You have the cooking bag, right?" It had been my mother who turned me on to the cooking bags you buy at the store, the grocery item she rightly predicted would be my best friend. I even do my Thanksgiving turkey in a bag.

"Yeah," she said.

"Okay, you're gonna take the chicken, wash it, season it real good with garlic powder, onion powder . . ." I said. "Then I want you to cut up some onions and throw them in the bag with the chicken. Then put a tablespoon of flour in the bag and shake it around to dust it so it's not sticky. Then I usually put three or four tablespoons of water in the bag."

I could hear the chop of the onions. I pictured her, seven months pregnant, these nesting instincts kicking in. I was knee-deep in plans for her baby shower I was hosting at the new house in Houston the following Sunday. "I'm really proud of you," I said.

She didn't hear, always on task. "But how long does it take to cook?"

"How much does the chicken weigh?"

"It says two pounds."

"Well, believe it if it's talking," I said. "That's about forty-five minutes."

"Okay."

I went back to my fish. Ty had arrived to eat, so I made him some. The grease stayed super-hot, the fish frying. "Can you cook us just one more piece of fish?" Mathew asked.

I added the last portion to the boiling oil when my phone rang with Solange again.

"Ma," she yelled. "You did not tell me to put it in a pan!"

"Oh, no, are you crazy?" I yelled. I started laughing, unable to help myself. "You just set the bag right on the oven rack—?"

"The juice started spilling out and then I picked up the bag and my chicken fell on the floor, and I'm so pissed at you. *This is your fault!*"

I laughed so hard. So hard she hung up on me. So hard I threw my hand down, and I hit the handle of the skillet.

The skillet jumped from the stove, falling right off toward my stomach and pelvis. I turned to run, knowing what was about to happen.

The cascade of boiling oil hit the side of my left leg, boiling lava spilling down my leg, *burning burning burning.*

The oil melted through the stretch of the jeans, then my skin, continuing down through my skin to the muscle. I fell to the floor, unable to scream. Making some sort of breathless, guttural sound. Mathew and Ty were in the dining room, unable to see me. I was on the floor, desperately trying to pull at the leg of my jeans, burning even my fingers. Desperate.

I did not leave my body. I stayed trapped in the excruciating pain, the heat of the oil penetrating farther and farther into me, down to bone. Finally, Mathew came in and said, "What?"

I managed a "take them off" and he tried, but it was too awful. The skin and jeans sticking to each other, pulling the muscle off the leg with the pants.

"Oh God, I'm pulling your leg off," he yelled.

He did not know what to do, screaming for Ty to get ice. In a panic, Ty filled a trash bag with ice and water to put my leg in. This was not the thing to do, but it was done. While Ty called 911, Mathew struggled with the jeans, recoiling from the sight of my bone as he yelled to me, "Don't look. Don't look." The pain was all encompassing, rooting me in place. Besides that, I'd burned the nerves of my fingers. I couldn't feel them and thought they were gone. I couldn't look at anything.

The police arrived before the ambulance. They saw this woman on the floor crying, screaming about her leg and afraid to look anywhere but to heaven. Mathew was holding my upper body. Cradling me and crying too. The cops stood there as he whispered in my ear, "Oh my God. I wish it was me." Again and again, *I wish it was me.*

"Sir, we need you to step into the other room," the white cop said.

"What?" I asked.

"If we're going to help her, you need to step into the other room." Mathew would have done anything in that moment to help me. I wanted him to stay with me.

"What is going on?" I asked.

"Sir," said the cop, grit in his voice. Mathew got up.

Once Mathew was in a bedroom, the cop looked at me, still writhing.

"Did he do this to you?"

"No," I managed to say, Ty joining in. "No, no."

My life was now anger and pain. I gasped out, "I was frying fish. Why are you doing this?"

"He was whispering to you. Was he threatening you?"

"No," I said, another wave of tears coming. Even at a time like this, we were suspect. Presumed guilty.

The EMTs were at the door to rush me to the hospital, and it was in the ambulance that I screamed again, the nerves of my hands so haywire. "Do I have fingers?" I yelled. "Do I have fingers?"

"Yes, you got your fingers," the EMT said. I could not look, afraid to find out he was lying. Afraid of everything. At the hospital, waiting for the burn doctor, I begged to be put to sleep, anything to stop the pain. "Please help me."

"We have to wait until the doctor gets here," someone in scrubs said.

Mathew finally broke. My crazy husband, the man I loved, turned over a tray in rage. "Give my wife some fucking pain medicine. Give her something right now."

They did. I saw the shot coming, hoping for oblivion. The pain edged slightly, and I finally peeked at my fingers. They were there, the skin mottled and blistered. I still could not look at my leg.

The doctor came, explaining directly that my leg would not simply grow back. My left leg would likely be much smaller than the other. "I want my leg," I said. "I don't care what you all gotta do. I want my leg."

AFTER THE SHOCK OF THAT SUNDAY, THE DAYS BLUR IN MY MIND. Sony lined up a great surgeon and corner room with a view. The doctor made a plan to perform a skin-graft surgery, but first I would have to receive a little over a week of daily debridement, a procedure that removes dead and infected skin to help the wound heal. Each morning, they shot me up with morphine and took me to the torture chamber. I called it that, because though they were kind, the procedure was showers of high-powered hoses held on the burnt skin to get the top layer off. When I heard them coming to bring me, I would start crying, begging not to be taken. When the door opened to the debridement area, you could hear the other patients screaming, and the worst part was knowing you would be too.

During the day, I tried to proceed as normal, planning Solange's shower for Sunday and a Destiny's Child shoot for a magazine cover Monday in New York, the day before my surgery. The girls had reteamed to do one more album, *Destiny Fulfilled*, so all the art had to be special. I turned my hospital room into a showroom, Ty pulling the clothes and hanging them on a rack we put together. Nurses would come in and laugh, then admire the work. I wanted any escape from the pain.

Mathew was my greatest advocate in the hospital, fighting to get me the best care and doctors. This was the side of Mathew that made all the pain of loving him seem worth it. The worst husband had it in him to be the best.

And what I wanted, in that moment, now seems absurd. But he went with it: I wanted to go to my baby's baby shower. I would not miss being there for Solange. My mother missed seeing me pregnant, missed all the rituals that come with this joy. I would be there to hold my daughter's hand.

The doctors understandably did not agree. "You cannot fly," one said. "You can't have your leg bent up three and a half hours."

Mathew saw my face. The desolation. "What if she had a private plane where she had a bed?" he asked, negotiator mode. "Where she could stretch out?"

We were told it wasn't worth the risk, but the doctor could not begin to weigh how I valued things. It was decided. Mathew called Donnie Ienner to get a plane, and I would fly Sunday morning, be there for the shower, and then fly Monday morning to be back the day before the surgery. I was there for my daughter, even if I had to be on crutches. Hugging Solange was medicine.

And then I pushed it. I wanted to go to the Destiny's Child photo shoot when I got back to New York. "I worked so hard on this shoot," I said. "I just want to be there and see it."

When I got there, the girls were putting on these leather pieces from Dolce & Gabbana. "What are you doing here?" yelled Kelly.

"Hopping around on one leg," said Beyoncé.

"I just wanna make sure," I said, already fussing with the neckline on Beyoncé, seeing to the perfection of things. My fingers were still healing, and I thought of my mother, willing away the pain of her arthritis to get the feel of the cloth. *To just make sure.*

I got back later than the hospital expected. I apologized, saying my plane was delayed. The next day, the doctor killed that surgery. He cut a whole sheet of good skin from the top of my hip to halfway down my thigh, then grafted it to my wound. I stayed in the hospital—no more baby showers or photo shoots—for another two weeks, and I remain so grateful for their work.

OCTOBER CAME AND WE ALL AWAITED SOLANGE'S DELIVERY DAY. Her sisters and Michelle really wanted her to be part of the video for "Soldier," the second single off *Destiny Fulfilled* after "Lose My Breath." It's a Southern song, and the girls planned to give their video the feel of a bunch of Texas–Atlanta transplants gathering in L.A. What would that be without their little sister?

The way things worked, the shoot happened to be on Solange's due date, but her doctors had told her she would likely be overdue—just as she was for me. The shoot would be near her, and I even figured out the best route to the hospital, trying to get her to be a part of it. She kept saying no. "I'm too big."

"Solange, don't you worry about it," I said. "You're glowing." Which was the truth. So we asked her husband to be in the video, and we knew he would convince her. "I don't want to come over there," she said. But she relented, smiling at all the love and blessings she received on the set.

It would be another seven days until Solange had the baby. She was in labor a long time, with Beyoncé, Kelly, Angie, and me at her side the whole time with her husband Daniel. It was so different from when I had my first child, when I felt so lonely without my mom. We could each hold her hands and surround her with love. As she delivered her boy, we were right there, the room filled with her song, now her family's, Sade's "By Your Side." When he came out, this beautiful boy they named Daniel Julez, she greeted him with all that love. "I'm going to treasure you," she said. "I'm going to give you the world." Over and over, she said it, this young woman who was now a mother down to her very essence.

As a grandmother, I could hold Julez and brag to him about his mother and how loved he was. It was something I said over and over to him. "Your mama treasures you," I would whisper. "And do you know what she's going to give you? *The world.*"

The new family came to live with me, just as I'd hoped. They were in Houston about a month when Daniel got the news. The University of Idaho had signed him; he would earn his degree while playing receiver for their football team, the Vandals.

Solange was clear: "I'm going with him, Mom. We're moving to Idaho."

CHAPTER 38

CONTEMPORARY
AMERICAN
LANDSCAPES

January 2005

A BRIEF HISTORY LESSON of Moscow, Idaho, because I had to learn where my baby and brand-new grandson were going: The town is six square miles, one tenth of Houston, in the upper skinny part of the state, right on the border of Washington. The Great Migration mostly missed Idaho, and certainly skipped Moscow. When Solange's husband Daniel became one of the Black student-athletes at the University of Idaho, the most recent census showed that only one percent of the *entire* population of Idaho was Black. But Solange, a Cancer like my mother, who also found herself as a teenager with a baby away from her family, wanted to be with him and do her best to make it a home as a wife and mother.

I wanted to be there all the time, but I couldn't. First, I was preparing for the Academy Awards in February, incredibly time-consuming and high-stakes because I was styling Beyoncé for three performances of nominated songs. (Adding to the stress of the night, as Beyoncé was descending the stage staircase during the second song—"Learn to Be Lonely" from *The Phantom of the Opera*—her stiletto got caught in the tulle of her floor-length dress. She had to keep going down the stairs in *one* five-inch stiletto, the other foot up on tippy-toe—and never missed a note.) Then I would be on the road with Destiny's Child for a sixty-eight-date farewell tour starting that spring which would take them into September. But I kept showing up in Idaho when I could, and I resisted giving advice when Solange would mention marital trouble in calls. They were young newlyweds and parents, a difficult position. She and Daniel fought over things that seemed small but were fundamental to this new life. She wanted a nanny; he thought they could do without one. An argument would escalate to the silent treatment, and then I would get a call saying, "Mom, come."

Oh Lord, I'm in the middle of the video, I would think. But I would leave if I could. The thing about getting to Moscow was you had to catch two planes to get there, either running through the airport in Seattle to make the connection or sitting around waiting for the next flight to the tiny airport. By the time I would get to Solange, they usually would have made up.

That winter was so cold in Moscow, land that was somehow flat and hilly at the same time. Solange's home was wedged against a hill of forest behind her, and when it snowed the cloud cover felt close and oppressive. But she saw its beauty and had begun painting. Solange created abstract landscapes, mostly scenes with small people made tiny by their surroundings.

Whenever I visited, Solange wanted to go to the biggest attraction in Moscow. "Mom, let's go to Walmart."

"Walmart?" But we would go, and as I visited, spring came. We started stopping for ice cream after Walmart, Solange deciding that the ice cream place was the second biggest attraction in Moscow. I noticed her art getting even better, away from those first forays on canvas and into more interesting things. She just quietly went about the work, learning and perfecting according to her own standard. Whenever people I didn't know well asked me about Solange being in Idaho, they kind of tilted their head in concern. They couldn't imagine an artist's creative life outside of the gratification of the charts. Solange was not just an artist, she *is* art.

She was eighteen years old, having worked in the industry for five years, and she'd really been part of it longer. Trauma had played such a role in her life, losing her therapist, Johnny, and Marsai. She'd grown up in tour buses and airports, getting mad if I took her out of school. Now, she was rooted here, at least for now.

Her circumstances would change, and she would later make the decision to file for divorce in 2007. Daniel remains my bonus son and I am close to him to this day. Solange would then briefly split her time between Houston and Los Angeles. But when I think about that time in Idaho, I think of her as an artist in residence, giving herself the space and time to explore her mind in a new environment.

It was time for me to do the same.

WHERE DID I FIRST SAY YES? IT WAS A RED CARPET, PROBABLY London. One of the reporters asked, as many had done in the past, "When are you and Beyoncé coming out with a clothing line?" My go-to answer was always, "I would love that," and then a quick pivot to Beyoncé's great sense of style.

This time was different. "Oh, very soon," I said, then doubled down. "Very soon, we're working on it."

But we weren't. It just slipped out. So when I got back to the States, I talked to my attorney to make this outright bluff more official. They sent me to an industry trade show in Vegas to get a sense of what people were doing, but I was much more interested in the outfits I saw on real women when I slipped out of photo shoots last-second to find some perfect accessory. The clothing I saw on beautiful women of all sizes in Brooklyn or Harlem, or the streets of Houston. What I loved was stopping a woman to tell her she looked beautiful, and then seeing her pride as she took me on a tour through what she had created. The best looks were a mix of dependable pieces and things she had splurged on. What if our line also mixed the two—a couture brand combined with streetwear?

Beyoncé and I partnered with Arthur and Jason Rabin, an influential father-and-son licensee team who headed up Kids Headquarters, and we really liked them. They knew the fashion business, and we would provide the creativity, marketing, and design. Beyoncé would be the face of her brand. We did a fifty-fifty deal with the Rabins, but the problem was that they really didn't have time to deal with the business aspect of the line, so I had to step in with no experience. For that reason, I hired a co–creative director, Heather Thomson, who had worked with celebrity brands.

We decided to call it the House of Deréon, after my mother's maiden name, because Beyoncé said it fit her vision of incorporating fashions from the three generations: hers, mine, and my mom's. I brought in as much of my mother as I could, little touches that she would appreciate: the mossy trees and alligators of Weeks Island, the fleur-de-lis motif of her Creole culture. When we did the ad campaign, each setup included a framed photo of my mother so she could be part of this.

New York was where fashion happened, so we set up an office in the heart of the Garment District. Mathew and I got an apartment high up on the forty-second floor of the Bloomberg Tower. The floor-to-ceiling windows looked out on the landscape of New York, all glass and steel and possibility. Beyoncé got a place two floors above, Apartment 44B, a double of her lucky number 4.

House of Deréon's mix of high and low meant a price differential that some customers did not like. We were in high-end stores like Neiman's, and fans didn't want to invest in one piece. We wanted the fans to have the clothes, so the Rabins suggested we add a junior brand, Deréon, keeping House of Deréon as a halo brand. That junior line, a guaranteed success, would help fund the higher-end work.

It took off like lightning. In 2006, Beyoncé wore a fleur-de-lis hoodie in the video for "Irreplaceable." The replica did crazy numbers in stores, along with the jeans that women swore were the most comfortable and flattering they'd ever found. The secret of the fit was simply the darts that I had always put into all the girls' jeans to make them smaller in the waist for more room in the hips and butt. Of everything we made, it was the jeans that people became best friends with, wanting to stop me to say, "I've never had jeans fit me so well."

That year we cleared something like $100 million. I should know this number off the top of my head, but what I really remember, what I can describe in detail down to their lashes, were those people—of all sizes and backgrounds—turning to twirl on the streets. Grabbing my hand to tell me they loved how my clothes made them feel.

So much good was happening that year. I met Tina Turner at the White House, where all the celebrities were squeezed in before Beyoncé paid her tribute, doing "Proud Mary" at the Kennedy Honors. "You know, every now and then, when I think of inspiration," Beyoncé said onstage, "I think of the two Tinas in my life: That's my mother, Tina; and of course, the amazing Tina Turner."

I would get to talk with her more when Beyoncé rehearsed with her for a duet at the Grammys. "I met you so many years ago and it made my life," I told her. "I had just moved to L.A. and I worked at the Broadway—"

"Oh, I used to be at the Broadway all the time." She laughed.

"I sold you some lip gloss."

"Aww, that's so cute," she said, and I was nineteen again. And Beyoncé was like a little kid too. Literally skipping to meet her and embrace her. While they were talking, two incredible artists working out the performance, Tina squatted on her heels to really think about a piece of choreography. Nearly seventy years old, on stilettos. Beyoncé then squatted too, afraid to miss anything this genius said. This is something only a mother might notice, but in the years after, I always loved seeing my daughter backstage suddenly squat down on her heels to really think about a performance.

"Oh, now you're just tryin' to be like Tina," I told her.

"I thought that was so gangsta!" said Beyoncé. "That she had on those heels and just squatted down as she was talking so casually."

This amazing life could also be overwhelming. During a break from her ninety-six-stop world tour The Beyoncé Experience, my daughter and I were in New York, up high in our tower. She had absorbed the energy of all these people for months and was overwhelmed. You can love what you do and still need a break. But she couldn't go anywhere. Now her fame kept us in that tower, because to even be on the street was to draw a crowd. She didn't complain, but I could see the toll it was taking. There was a sadness to her, knowing her life was never going to be the same.

"Let's sneak down to Galveston," I said. I had just bought a beach house for my family to use, way down past West Beach and right on the water. "Nobody's gonna know or care about you being out there."

She gave me the look a child gives her mother when she has just said the craziest thing in a lifetime of crazy things. *"Mama."*

"No, it's Monday," I said. "Most of the people that live around me, they just come on weekends. Let's just go and see how it goes. We can come back Friday."

"Okay," she said. We flew to Houston, then drove right to the beach house. Security would stay in town, but we wanted to be by ourselves. My first plan was a walk on the beach. Out of habit, I stood behind my daughter to do her hair, tucking the sandy blond up under a baseball cap, then did the same for myself. We put large sunglasses on in the mirror.

"Somebody told me Beyoncé's in town," I joked, "but I haven't seen her."

"Oh, Mama," she said.

"I hear she's really nice," I said, putting on my sandals to head out the door. "That mom of hers is so pretty, what is her name?"

"Cuckoo," she said. "That's what they call her."

I had missed this, the spontaneity of announcing a Beach Day for my girl. It was so nice walking along the water that we wanted to keep the day going. We got in the car and first drove to Menard Park, where that cop who arrested me for riding a motorcycle paraded me through so everyone would see Tina Beyoncé handcuffed in the back of a police car. Then we drove to my old neighborhood, which seemed so small. "I've got to show you this backyard," I said, so proud. I took her hand, quietly walking into the back. The pecan tree was still there.

"This yard was so freaking big," I said, and Beyoncé laughed because it wasn't. "Girl, this was big for Galveston," I told her.

She was having so much fun she made a request: "I want to go to Walgreens."

"That's what you want to do most?"

She nodded. This girl stayed about an hour in the Walgreens pharmacy because she was so happy being able to go down the aisles, picking up every single thing to examine the item. When we were in the toy section, she had to say "Oh!" about every single pail and shovel. She took so long that I looked for a beach chair to open up and sit in.

When we left, she was glowing, so empowered that she said, "Now I wanna go to Ross." Here I thought we were flying a little too close to the sun, but I took her. The Ross Dress for Less store wasn't crowded, but it wasn't empty either. She went through the racks, moving hanger after hanger aside, holding things up to herself and looking in the mirror. Not a single person approached her. Not one.

Now this really felt like a fairy tale, and Beyoncé had one more wish. "Let's go to Luby's." This was the chain of her youth, the place we always went to after church on Sundays for her and Solange's favorite,

Salisbury steak. We sat at one of the tan wood tables, and then I spotted three girls sitting at a table across the way. One was practically pointing while the other two squinted. I read the lips of one of them, "Naw, it's not them."

I looked away fast, pretending to be interested in something outside. But the insistent one had come over.

"Miss Tina?"

I held a finger to my lips, nodding.

"I promise, we're not gonna . . ." she whispered, glancing at Beyoncé. "I promise you, I'm not gonna make a scene. I'm gonna be really *quiet,* but it's . . ." She smiled broad. "I'm just so excited."

We gave smiles back, conspiratorial. I watched her return to her friends, the girls stifling squeals. This was the reality check coming at the end of our little meal. "These girls were quiet, and we were just lucky about that," I told Beyoncé. "This was heaven, but it's time to go back."

She nodded. "I had fun," she said.

"You needed it," I answered. She stayed that whole week, recharging. In the mornings we each read from copies of books of prayer by Stormie Omartian, sharing what we thought would give the other strength or guidance.

At night Beyoncé and I would sit out on the balcony, no questions to answer or decisions to be made. Just us and the breeze off the water, watching the waves caress the shore under the light of the moon.

CHAPTER 39

IN MY FASHION

February 2008

I HAD TWENTY YARDS of the most gorgeous white silk *ever* stashed in my house in Houston. What I was doing was so top secret that only me and Jaime knew. Beyoncé was getting married in a couple months, and since she could not just go try on wedding dresses, I decided to make her one as a surprise.

I pulled out the mannequin and began draping the silk, pinning and tucking and literally making the dress on the mannequin with Jaime tacking it. I knew Jay had told her he liked the shape of mermaid dresses, and strapless was the only other thing she'd told me she had in mind. I resisted my urge to do lace and kept everything very sophisticated and modern.

When the dress was done, I flew with it up to New York and hid it in my apartment. During a regular visit, I said to her, "You gotta try on your wedding dress."

"Oh my God, you did a wedding dress?"

"Yeah," I said, and she answered, "Okay, Mama." She was so sweet about it, but I noted that she wasn't excited like I thought she'd be. Then she tried on the dress, and I got teary. "I love this dress," she told me. "It's beautiful."

They had the wedding at their house on April 4 because it was the only place that we knew it wouldn't get out. We had a lady make white curtains to cover the walls and windows, right up to the twenty-five-foot ceilings. It was a gorgeous ceremony full of flowers, with our minister, Rudy Rasmus, coming in from Texas with his wife, Juanita, to officiate. The details are my daughter and son-in-law's, but what I will say is that I joined Jay's grandmother and mother in cooking all the food. We did soul food, of course, the best food for a night of dancing and family love.

WE HAD RECENTLY REVITALIZED THE HOUSE OF DERÉON. THE junior line of Deréon had been wildly successful, but Beyoncé and I wanted to focus on dresses that conveyed our brand's original goals of sophistication and glamour. Girls had literally stopped me on the street and asked me to make them their prom dresses—and I often did—and this way I could help more of them.

To expand my reach, I also signed a deal with HSN to sell a line I called Miss Tina. It was a great opportunity, but the problem was that HSN headquarters was in Tampa, Florida, and as the line sold well, their expectations of my time grew and the atmosphere became unpleasant. When I became what they called a "Fan Favorite," that meant they wanted me down in Tampa monthly. You appear on the hour, every hour, staying in hair and makeup, talking and talking. But I would constantly get notes that I stayed on the line too long with callers, since I was supposed to be moving them along. Connecting with customers was my favorite part of working with HSN, but I eventually found the company's obligations too confining. I was running House of Deréon and working on Beyoncé's projects, and the last straw was when they refused to let me switch my time slot so I could go to Egypt for a tour date.

I looked for a new place to bring the Miss Tina line, and I opened my brand in Walmart. They could assure me a price point everybody could afford, and inclusive sizing so every *body* could wear it. On HSN, I always showcased women wearing our clothes in different sizes, three models if possible, wearing the same item. I had always noticed that when clothing lines were "inclusive" of women who wore larger sizes, that meant they selected only one or two items to actually produce. Pieces that *they* imagined were appropriate for plus-size women. These pieces usually amounted to camouflage, heavy smocks of monotone-colored fabrics that conveyed to women that they needed to hide their bodies.

I always fought to have at least up to 18 in our sizing on all our items, constantly being told, "We're going to lose money doing that."

"I don't care, that's what we're doing." I would rather accept that loss, because I never ever wanted my fuller-figured customer to see something I offered, then go to the store and she couldn't get it.

The fights I had. Anything that showed skin, I heard, "They wouldn't wear that."

"Yes, they will, and they're gonna look and feel great." Isn't that the point of fashion?

THE SUMMER OF 2008, BEYONCÉ WENT TO LOS ANGELES TO WORK on the thriller *Obsessed*. I came to help her get settled, and we stayed at the Beverly Wilshire while she looked for a place in town. She was a producer on the film and was inundated with questions. We were also both dieting, her losing the weight she gained to play Etta James in *Cadillac Records* shortly before, and me losing the weight I gained stress eating over the House of Deréon and Miss Tina lines. She had loved doing *Cadillac Records,* researching the role of the troubled but brilliant singer by getting to know real women dealing with addiction at the Phoenix House rehab center in Brooklyn. (She donated her paycheck from the film to the program.)

But now she was stressed. She had been filming all day and came to my room. "You saved me," I said, opening the door. "I am in here looking for snacks."

She didn't laugh. She looked so *sad*. I went to hug her, but there was something she wanted to say. "Mom, I don't know how to do anything," she said.

"Oh, now that's not true," I said. "What's anything?"

"I don't even know how to book a hotel room."

"Trust me, that's overrated, baby," I said. "You've got people to do that." She looked down, and I pressed. "Why do you care?"

"I don't know how to do anything, and I don't even have an office!"

"You're a singer and an actress, why would you need an office?"

"Because I need to start my own company."

"Oh," I said. "Okay." It was a low-key response, but I recognized this urgency. I had felt it before Headliners. Being the fixer that I am, the next day I started looking at chandeliers on Melrose. I thought that if Beyoncé had an office, it would have a chandelier, and it just contin-ued like that. I did a shopping spree, shipping things to New York.

I found an office in the same building as House of Deréon, up on the thirty-fourth floor. A space that wasn't too big, but with room for whatever she wanted to start with. In two weeks, I had it decorated: I made four little offices, a conference room, and a workroom. It was beautiful, but I realize it wasn't functional at all. I had bought the black lacquer desks, the all-important chandeliers, but I didn't have a single file cabinet in there.

"Mama, it's so beautiful," she said the first day I showed her.

"Now you got an office, and a phone system . . ." I trailed off.

"Well, what do we do with it?" she joked.

We started laughing. She would make her plans soon enough, but I get emotional even now thinking about how she was standing at the threshold of leadership. God puts this vision on your heart sometimes, this feeling of needing to be more when you think you've already given all you have.

He had a vision for me too, but I would have to be broken first. One of my favorite pieces of poetry in the Psalms is 34:18: "The Lord is close to the broken-hearted and He saves those who are crushed in spirit."

God was about to hold me very close.

CHAPTER 40

BEFORE AND AFTER

March 2009

THE WEEKS LEADING up to the start of a world tour are always a crunch-time blur. We were prepping for the March 26 start of Beyoncé's I Am . . . Tour, her most theatrical concert performance yet. And in that period when the stakes were so high, when even dreams in three-hour snatches of sleep were continuations of discussions with the team planning the tour, Mathew told me he had recently ended an affair.

It was over, he said, and he wanted nothing to do with her. Telling me was part of the counseling he was once again undergoing to figure out why he kept doing this, and he told me that my forgiveness would be the key to his recovery. That key might set him free, I knew, but it would trap me again.

"Don't you show up on this tour," I told him. "If you do, I'm not going to talk to you, and I will embarrass you."

Mathew kept his distance until the fifth date of the tour, an April Fool's Night in Seattle. We got to town the night before, but so did Mathew. He showed up at my hotel room, and when I wouldn't let him in, he harassed me until morning. Knocking at the door, begging me to talk to him. I did not sleep, and the next day there was no time for rest. The show had to go on.

After the concert, I was so tired, but I needed to do an all-nighter in my suite with Tim White at the sewing machine and Ty Hunter helping me organize and perfect the looks for Beyoncé's *Obsessed* press tour, set to start the next morning. But as we worked, Mathew returned to badger me again, talking through the door, and calling. What made me blow up at him was that I could not focus on the work. I opened my door slightly, leaving the door latch on and whisper-screamed at him. "Leave me alone," I said. "Once and for all. You are a torturer with this stuff. And if you don't leave this hotel, I'm gonna create such a scene."

Mathew hung his head. I closed the door. I didn't know what to do with all my hurt. The work needed to be done, and I asked my mother to give me strength as Tim, Ty, and I returned to the tasks before us.

I went along with Beyoncé to her interviews the next day, delirious from lack of sleep. I watched her set up for an interview with Billy Bush from *Access Hollywood*. He asked her the questions we'd come to expect about balancing acting and singing. And then he switched it up on her.

He told Beyoncé he'd noticed that anytime someone spent time with her, the person came away saying, "You're a very gracious person, very happy, very nice. Do you credit your mom and dad for that in you?"

She paused. I leaned forward, nervous. I was off to the side and out of the camera's reach.

"I definitely credit the people around me for keeping me grounded," she answered, slower in her response than to the other questions. "And especially my mother. Because I trust her, and I would do anything for her, and I admire her so much. I mean . . ."

Mothers know when their child is about to cry, and I tried not to myself but gave up as she continued. ". . . whenever there is something going wrong, my mother's there and she stays up all night to make sure everything's perfect. And I always can depend on her. . . . See, I'm starting to get emotional. . . ."

"You *love* your mom," Billy pressed. "You think about all she's sacrificed for you?"

"Yeah," she said, "I feel crazy. But I am very lucky to have her."

They turned on a behind-the-scenes camera to show me crying. I let the tears fall.

I *had* sacrificed so much. All mothers do, so much we stop noticing, and we certainly don't expect our kids to.

But even after that sleepless revelation, when I was running on fumes and faith, Mathew got his way. I returned to him. I was never able to stay away from him more than a few months. I convinced my-self the counseling had helped this time, and he was so pitiful in his apologies that it felt wrong to abandon him. *Keep it moving,* I told myself, when all I did was stay in place.

As predictable as the clock on the wall, we fell into the honeymoon stage of our cycle, five or so months of real closeness.

On October 2, during the second break in the I Am . . . Tour, Beyoncé received the honor of Billboard Woman of the Year. The luncheon was at the Pierre Hotel near Central Park in New York, and Gayle King would do an onstage interview. Mathew was there, walk-ing around the place being seen at this heavy-industry event. I had some deadline to meet so I left early.

When I walked out, there were about ten reporters outside, not unusual at events my daughter was scheduled for. Celebrity weeklies would send people to stand outside, hoping to get a quote they could use next to a paparazzi photo. They usually just asked me, "How's Beyoncé?" but today, one young woman led the group in asking, "Miss Tina, how do you feel about today's developments?"

I said something like, "Oh, I think's it amazing. I'm so appreciative that my daughter is being recognized for her work." Their faces got a little funny, and the girl who asked me seemed thrown. As I walked to the waiting car, I wondered what I'd said wrong. I didn't know what they knew: They were tipped off that Mathew had been served with paternity papers inside. It was the woman he'd told me about.

I got back to the apartment and was there for forty-five minutes working before Mathew came in. "Tina, I gotta tell you something."

When he did, I screamed, "Get out! Get out!" like he was some demon. *"I hate you!"* He tried talking to me, but this gifted salesman, this master of apologies, came up empty and walked out. The apart-ment now seemed so quiet, yet my world had exploded. I'd woken up that morning not knowing I was living in the Before, oblivious for a few more hours, and now I was in the After.

A call from the front desk broke the silence—an alert that there were reporters outside the building asking for me. The Bloomberg Tower had no back exit, and if I didn't leave now, I would be trapped. I threw some things in bags, sailed past the reporters to a waiting car, and headed to the airport to get the first thing smoking out of town. I could hide in Houston.

I was paranoid, convinced everyone in the airport was looking at me. True or not, the feeling was enough to send me to the Delta lounge. They had a sort of theater room where you could watch news, and I took a seat behind a few people. And what comes on the news but my daughter's face and then mine with Mathew's. "Breaking News: Beyoncé's Dad in Baby Scandal." As a reporter talked, there was footage of me leaving the luncheon without sound, smiling like a fool in her Before life. I expected the people in the room to turn around. Nobody even paid attention. I was still humiliated, and tried to stay invisible until my flight took off.

In Houston, people really were looking at me because I was in and out of there so much. I'd always smiled, always taken a second to compliment someone. I loved that moment of contact between people. Now, I kept my head down and sunglasses on to hide my tears. One more thing he'd taken from me.

I filed for divorce. This was different from the other times I had chosen to leave him. Now I had no choice. In the aftermath of that explosion, I kept pace with my life, as I had now for years, sticking to my routine and allowing work to numb and carry me. But losing myself in doing for others, turning my brain off again, was no longer a plan. I got through October, then stumbled to 2010, hoping to magically feel better.

When I did not, someone improbably steady presented himself for me to hold on to in my disorientation. The last man I expected.

CHAPTER 41

FRENCHY'S AND VEUVE CLICQUOT

April 2010

M Y ASSISTANT AND I were in my office at House of Deréon in Manhattan, going over a goals list for the next week. One of my favorite photos from the Spring/Summer 2010 campaign was on my desk, Beyoncé leaping in a radiant green dress that flowed with the breeze of Santorini. I loved the freedom of it.

As we talked, the insistent blare of a siren rose from the Friday afternoon traffic on Broadway. I checked the time. My assistant noticed and went to her phone to look at my schedule.

"I have to go to Houston," I said, handing her the stack of approvals I'd gone through. She was still focused on my schedule, but my flight wouldn't be on there. It was a secret.

"Oh," she said, confused. "Did someone else book it for you?"

"I just booked it myself," I said. "I've got some things at the beach house I gotta take care of."

"Weren't you just there last weekend?" she asked.

"I was," I said, getting up to conclude the conversation. "It's a . . . it's a lot of stuff there."

Nobody knew the truth. I was giddy heading to my gate at the airport, nothing but my work bag. I was the last one on the plane and the handsome flight attendant handed me a champagne. "Glad you made it," he said.

When you're sneaking around, every smile you get seems conspiratorial. Like everyone and no one is in on the plan. I had never hidden a romance before, never felt that thrill of doing something your brain knew was off-limits. I was finally having *fun* again.

The rendezvous had been going a month or so, first meeting up in New York, then settling into these secret weekends in Houston. Landing now, I couldn't wait to see him. I'd promised to be there in time for us to watch the sunset together. And there he was, waiting for me at the house.

Mathew.

Having an affair with my estranged husband was the last thing I expected after I filed for divorce in November. For three months, we did not speak. But then in New York City, he came to my apartment and laid his heart bare. He'd changed after new counseling. I didn't believe him, but he was persistent, proved he'd gotten help, and as he courted me, I found myself falling in love again. The magnetic pull between us, this cosmic cord I had tried to cut so many times, was stronger than ever.

We were realists, believe it or not, and we knew our bond seemed stronger because we were sneakin'. We told no one, certainly not our kids, until every weekend we had the same blissful routine. Meet in Houston, then drive over to League City where we kept our two boats. If it was a quick trip, we would take the *Miss Tina,* a speedboat naturally, fast like me. But we preferred the *Daniel Julez,* a forty-two-foot cruiser yacht, right under the legal limit where we needed a captain. It could be just us. We knew we had a court date for the divorce later in the year, but to call it off would draw attention. This was ours, and we knew the kids would be so mad at us if they found out we were together again.

This evening started like all our stolen nights on the water: We picked up a bottle of Veuve Clicquot and then fried chicken from Frenchy's on the way. Mathew would drive the boat out, and once we were safe on the water, we'd just sail around and chill. Eating, drinking, and dancing to every slow song on the CDs I'd packed. I wanted only the greatest hits CDs, our favorites of our favorites: Marvin Gaye, the Isley Brothers, Sade, and Teddy Pendergrass. With Mathew loving the water like I did, a calm came over us. The only deadline we had was the sunset. That was always our cue to head home, and under the cover of darkness we would sail to Galveston.

For three months, these sunset-cruise nights had ended at the

beach house. I would tell my girls—"I'm down here just chilling"—
and I am sure they imagined lonely Mom going for walks with a mug
of tea, hugging some cardigan to her instead of a man. When they
called, Mathew would go to another room, a couple of teenagers hiding out.

On Mother's Day in May, Mathew and I were having a lazy late
morning in bed at the beach house. All my girls were busy: Kelly in
Europe promoting her dance single "Commander," a follow-up with
David Guetta to their huge hit "When Love Takes Over"; Beyoncé and
Solange had some vague things they had to do that weekend and they'd
each apologized for leaving me alone on Mother's Day. "Don't worry
about me," I'd said.

My phone rang. "Guess where we are?" Solange said.

I looked at Mathew, holding a finger to my lips. "Where?" I said.
"Who's we?"

"Mom, we're in Galveston!" Beyoncé shouted.

"Oh my God," I said slowly, hoping my shock would read as delight.

"We're in the car," chirped Solange, so pleased with the surprise. I
started waving my hands at Mathew to get moving. "Okay, see you
soon."

"What do we do?" he said, gathering his things.

I jumped up. "Lemme think," I said. "Okay, I gotta tell them. I
think it's better if I tell them." Mathew had to leave quick and not be
there when they arrived. This was going to shock them, and they deserved time to absorb it. As he jumped in the car to head back to
Houston, I removed any trace of their father's presence from the place,
even washing the two coffee mugs from the morning.

They just missed him. Solange and Beyoncé burst in, so excited and
each finishing each other's sentences in a blur of: "We just thought
about you being here by yourself and we just wanted to come down
here and cheer you up." I let them get settled but couldn't hold it once
I sat them down. The moment reminded me of when they were little,
and I had to tell them I'd left their daddy.

"Listen," I said, "I gotta tell y'all something and I know you're not
gonna be happy about it. Your daddy just left here. He got help and
we . . . we decided not to get a divorce and we've been together ever
since."

It was dead quiet. Then Beyoncé nodded solemnly. "Okay. Fine."

Solange exploded. "Mom, what? *What?* What are y'all doing? What are *you* doing?"

I breathed out. Let her have this emotion, but I was still her mother. "That's not your business," I said. "You live your life. I don't tell you who to be with; you can't tell *me* who to be with."

Beyoncé was more understanding than Solange, who I know was just being protective of me. They each loved their dad in different ways, and I sometimes felt my youngest was so much like her dad that she felt his moments of failing on a soul-deep level.

I was torn, protective of my daughters and protective of Mathew. Only later would I realize I didn't worry about me. On the day our divorce came up in court, we were no-shows. We spent the day on the water, out where reason could never find us.

I HAVE A FONDNESS FOR THAT TIME OF REUNION WITH MATHEW, a year of my life. This coincided with a time when Beyoncé reluctantly decided to part ways with Mathew as her manager. The waters were muddied and she wanted her dad to be just that, her father. Like any young woman, she needed to get out of the nest and fly on her own. Take all of the amazing things he had taught her about the business— the control and authority he encouraged her to have over the work— and apply these lessons on her own. In March 2011, Beyoncé announced her father was no longer her manager. Her next album, *4*, would be wholly hers.

In the beginnings of her office, she had filled that place with twenty-five people, and there is video of her first all-hands meeting, a moment I love for being so cute: "Does everybody know who everybody is?" she asks, putting down her bag. "All right, I'm Beyoncé. And I'm the president." On that day, she came into her power and understood what a remarkable leader she had always been. She had been the person in charge, but now she claimed it.

You can be brave and scared at the same time. Stepping out on her own was a risk, and when a woman does that, there are lots of people waiting to see her fail. But there is also a legion of women and girls, and people who care about them, who need a model for that courage. You can own your own business—whether it's a hair salon or a record label—and instead of changing yourself to become someone's idea of a "boss" you can remain who you are as success brings new challenges and goals. In the way that all of my daughters smartly refused to change who they were in order to be successful, Beyoncé could become more *herself* as the boss.

She named her company Parkwood, her first thought for something so important and personal being the street of her childhood. It was where everything started. Where she and Kelly practiced every day, Solange keeping time and watch until she was right there with them. Parkwood was the nucleus of Destiny's Child, where it all began.

I distinctly remember watching Beyoncé in her process of formatting the album and figuring out the sequence of songs. Before, her father would take the album and there would be a back-and-forth. "Do you think you need an intro there?" and she would say, "Well, I think we need it there." She would test her ideas against his, him sitting in the studio day and night to have everything mixed and mastered. All of a sudden, it was just her, and she was not going to trust anybody to do that. She had to trust herself. It was a whole 'nother level of working really hard and not getting any sleep. With that came an understanding for all of us of two things: how much Mathew did, and also what Beyoncé herself was capable of.

From the artwork of the *4* album cover to the early plans for the rollout, *4* began in that packed little office. When she outgrew those fifteen hundred square feet, we went down the street, securing the whole twenty-fourth floor for a girl who just a short while ago thought she couldn't book a hotel room.

She was setting an example, taking a leap. And I needed to as well. I clearly knew my relationship with Mathew was unhealthy, and it was the fear of going it alone that kept me stuck. I had been avoiding Mathew lately, afraid to cut the cord, and he had retaliated by seeing another woman.

Once I found out about this affair, I knew the marriage was over. I had a therapist in Houston, Elizabeth, who had been offering me guidance for years and whom Mathew and I had also seen together for counseling. She had tried everything she could to help us, and now I called her to say I was finally ready to break the cycle for good. She organized a "retreat" for just me at my house in Houston, coming on Friday and staying until Monday. Elizabeth is Jewish and she brought her friend, a woman named Sydney who is a Christian, because she knew prayer would fortify me.

It was a spiritual intensive, rounds and rounds of therapy with these two women nurturing me but also being straight with me. They made me tea and wrapped me in blankets, asking me to detail what I had been through in the marriage. Not for them, but for *me*. Elizabeth held my hand as I talked about everything, even about the latest woman Mathew had brought into my house and onto the boat where he made me feel so special and safe. Through talk and prayer, Elizabeth and Sydney helped me face my pain around the decision I'd made to divorce. I had allowed my life outside my children's needs to become a blur, never really facing how horrible things got. Elizabeth helped me realize that was why I always forgave Mathew; how could I hold him accountable when I never absorbed how painful the shit had been?

"Tina, cry," Elizabeth said. "*Scream.* You got a right to take the time to feel the sadness and the hurt."

I did not know I needed permission to have that time, but I did. You do. As I prayed with Sydney, I read a passage from the beginning of Psalms 40: "I waited patiently for the Lord. He turned to me and heard my cry. He lifted me out of the slimy pit, out of the mud and mire; he set my feet on a rock and gave me a firm place to stand. He put a new song in my mouth, a hymn of praise to our God."

I was fifty-eight and about to upend my life. God gave me the power to lift myself from these depths, but I would have to do the work myself.

On Monday, I told Mathew I wanted a divorce.

CHAPTER 42

THE DISTANT BEAT
OF WINGS

August 2011

I WAS IN MATHEW'S office, and he'd uncapped his pen. The divorce papers were in front of him, ready to sign. He had gone through the motions of the lead-up to an amicable divorce, so amicable he believed in his heart it would never happen. We were civil as can be, each of us listing our assets, reminding each other of what we had. In January, we had sold the House of Deréon and Miss Tina brands, dividing the $66 million sale price equally. I continued working on the lines, going to the House of Deréon offices every day I was in New York City. Mathew and I were proud that we had so much to divvy up.

"Whatever you wanna give me is fine," he said. "Give me what you want."

"Well, what about the art?" I was willing to give him anything he paid for.

"Oh, you know I don't know nothing about art," he said. "Just give me whatever you don't want." We even laughed about a baby grand he bought me. He said he wanted it, but I loved it. "That was a gift," I said. "You go buy another one. You're good for it."

"I'm sentimental," he said, looking at me, trying to make this a moment.

"I know you are. Listen, I am gonna give you some art because it's expensive. I want to be fair."

"I'll do whatever it takes," he repeated, something he had said since I told him it was over. But I was done. He was living in my house, and

I made it clear he had to get out. But Mathew wouldn't really hear it, still trying to get back with me.

"Listen, sign these papers in good faith and I probably won't go through with it," I said. I hadn't the first time. "Just sign them for now to prove that you are really hearing me and understand this is over."

He signed the papers. "Okay," he said.

"Okay," I answered. And I did exactly what he thought I'd never do. I took those papers straight on and filed them.

THREE MONTHS LATER, IN NOVEMBER, I WAS IN A COURTROOM with my attorney and my friends Angie Phea and Cheryl Creuzot, who are both lawyers. I still had not told Mathew I had gone through with the filing, afraid that if I did, he would only work double-time to get me to change my mind.

My attorney asked the judge if we could do the proceedings in her chambers. Thank God, she agreed. She was younger than I imagined a judge would be, probably fifty. She had me put my hand on the Bible and swear to tell the truth and nothing but. My stomach was in knots as she went over the facts of what I'd stated: There could be no reasonable expectation of reconciliation.

"I declare this divorce final," she said.

There was no rush of relief. I did not feel some new freedom. I felt *sick*. Physically ill in my stomach, the core of me. I managed to thank my lawyer and then get to my car. I was deeply sad, not about him but about the marriage. I felt like I failed. I failed us, my kids—myself.

I didn't want to be in Houston when I told Mathew the divorce was final. I went to the airport to get a flight to New York. I had already talked him into us selling our apartment in the Bloomberg Tower, and had moved into Beyoncé's apartment two floors above. She was living with Jay in their Tribeca penthouse, so this place could be mine alone. Mathew would have no access.

I made my body move quickly, short efficient movements to hide that I was hollowed out. We'd been a couple for more than thirty years. I lost not just a husband, but a witness to each other's lives. It was as if I'd stored three decades of home movies and photo albums in a library, then watched it burn down. Memories only he knew of my mom, my dad, our siblings—all up in flames. The worst part is, I thought I was in those ashes too. I was about to turn fifty-eight years old. What kind of life was I going to have now? It was too late for me.

The plane touched down in New York, an abrupt landing that made the people around me lurch forward, then joke to show they weren't shaken.

I didn't react. I was too numb. But deep down, my heart beat without my knowing. This little bird in my chest that fascinated me as a kid. That I felt every time I ran faster than the boys or climbed out on the tallest limb of a tree, so high I could only hear the steady thump of its beat, pounding into my ears, louder than anyone yelling, "*Tenie. Get down!*" In those days, I thought my heart would someday beat so hard that this bird would fly away and leave me. And these past years, maybe I thought it had.

My heart was there, even if I didn't feel it yet. That little bird was there the whole time, waiting for me to follow its lead again.

ACT THREE

A Woman

CHAPTER 43

WHAT BECOMES
OF THE
BROKEN-HEARTED?

November 2011

I LOOKED OUT ON my view of Central Park from up high on the forty-fourth floor and waited to feel better.

In the past I had always given myself three days to get over something. Necessity and practice had gotten that down to two. I could jolt myself back, literally shake my head as if waking from a daydreamed nightmare. Say it out loud like a scold, naming the task in front of me. Or just remind myself that there were people much worse off than me, and I can't be here boohooing like someone who doesn't have work to do.

Two days into being divorced, and my little method—this thing I thought was "resilience"—would not take hold. I still had not told Mathew that I had gone ahead and finalized our divorce. Maybe on some level I hoped news would get out, that he would hear, and I would just have to confirm it was true, rather than break his heart myself. I still loved him that much.

I'd put this off long enough. I went to work because I felt stronger at my desk at House of Deréon. I called his office, and his assistant told me he wasn't there. "How is he?" I asked.

"He seems okay," she said. "He's in a good mood, but it's raining here a lot. Real gloomy. He's probably driving if you want to call his cell."

It was now or never, I told myself. When I called, I could even hear the horrible rain through the phone. I asked him to pull over, and I told him, direct but with love. My voice cracked and so did his, and we both cried at what we had lost.

This began a cycle of Mathew coming to New York to try to get me back. He returned many times wanting to talk it out, and time and again I told him, "There's nothing to talk about. Go home. Go back to Houston."

One afternoon at the office, I thought about the fact that Texas was still my home too. I was going through the motions in New York, showing up for work and never once crying to anyone or walking around sad-faced. I kept telling my kids I was doing okay, because I was so afraid of being a burden on them. But the sadness overwhelmed me.

I knew my therapist Elizabeth would be able to help me. I was afraid of doing the emotional work, but I was more afraid of continuing like this. Before I could rethink it, I decided to take a one-month leave from work. I would return to Texas with a new assignment: *Get yourself together.*

ONCE IN HOUSTON, I STOPPED EVERYTHING. FOR THE FIRST TIME in my entire life, I let myself lie in bed, day into night. I did this for a week, keeping up phone calls with Elizabeth. One morning we had a call before an in-person appointment for the next day, and she wanted a progress report. The only progress I'd made was through all the food in my fridge. But here came the tough love:

"Tina, while you're sitting there feeling sorry for yourself—"

"Oh, it's worse than you think, I'm lying down."

"However bad you're thinking your life is now, I want you to do something for me. I need you to make a list of all the worst times in your life. Name all your failures and everything you believe is wrong with you."

"Okay," I said, not hiding the dread.

"I'm not done," Elizabeth said, chuckling. "And I need you to make a list of all the *wins* that you've had. All the great things about you."

"Elizabeth, my life hasn't been all that."

"Just write it down and give it to me tomorrow."

Starting with the bad stuff, all my insecurities crowded to the front of my mind as I tried to give them some order. But then I gave up, just writing as they came: I was born poor, I wrote, surprising me. I never had money to do stuff. The nuns abused me. My mom never stuck up for me. I was never consistent in school, an A-student one minute and a D-student the next. I would sometimes get mental blocks, and if I was a kid in this modern age, I would probably be tested for ADHD.

I shook my head, skipping forward in time to why I was such a mess right then. I'd been married for thirty-three years and my husband consistently cheated on me. The obvious conclusion was always, I must not be good enough.

There were times I didn't feel attractive, but more important, I wrote: "People don't respect me as a designer. I'm not formally educated, so people make fun of me."

I sat with that last one and had a curious sensation: If you love water like I do, you know that there is the moment when you've dived down, down, down. Your body instinctively curls, rolls, until your feet touch the bottom. All the strength in your legs is called into action, and you are launched from the floor, that burst of strength and the air left in the lungs rockets you up, up, up. I felt it.

As I rose, the second list, the good things about me, played as a montage in my mind. "I designed some really beautiful clothes," I wrote, "and I don't need validation from those people." I saw them all—the knockout seventies dress I designed for *Dreamgirls,* peacock-inspired and glorious. Next was Beyoncé's tribute to Josephine Baker's iconic banana skirt, which won the love and approval of her son Jean-Claude. And also a dress I made for Beyoncé to wear to a movie premiere that was so beautiful people credited it to Givenchy and I never corrected them.

I wrote down the places that I had been to since my first passport, from Cairo to Milan to Paris to Cape Town, where I met Nelson Mandela. All these notable people I'd met, queens and kings, Elizabeth and her son-in-waiting, Charles. Foreign leaders and presidents at the White House—starstruck by President Obama and mesmerized by Michelle Obama and her beautiful mom. Starstruck in conversations with Tina Turner and Sade too.

I thought about how the ADHD had been a gift, allowing me to do so many things as I switched between hyperfocusing and multitasking. I was a businesswoman, at times the breadwinner who'd built Headliners from an idea. I started with a five-hundred-square-foot salon and turned it into a real little empire. I mentored at least fifteen women who opened their own salons, not to mention those who became doctors, lawyers, and real estate professionals. That all started at Headliners, the place where my daughters learned from my work ethic too. Mathew Knowles was a businessman ahead of his time, but I played a huge part in the success of Destiny's Child. I was the girls' day-to-day manager even though I didn't have the title, and a lot of creative ideas that they executed so beautifully came from me. It was never important to me that I get credit, but I had never given *myself* credit.

It would have meant so much to my childhood self to know that I owned my home, and I wasn't under financial pressure. "It's enough of this feeling sorry for yourself," I said, looking at that second list. "I am so blessed." I had left some space at the bottom. I wrote across the two lists: "This little girl from Galveston." And I said aloud again, proud of myself, "You're a badass."

And then I thought, *If I met me, I would want to date me. If I met me, I would want to be my friend. I would* like *me.*

Now I just had to meet me.

I got up off my ass, took me a shower, and got cute. If I was going to get to know me, I decided to take myself to the Museum of Fine Arts, Houston, which I hadn't been to in years. *When was the last time I'd even gone alone to a gallery or museum?* I wondered. When I was nineteen and comfortable with my own company, there were solo trips to art spaces in L.A. I'd bought a lithograph then, an abstract in a frame, just because I knew it would make me feel good. These days, I would hear about a show I wanted to see, and then not have time. I would just order the exhibition's art book and add it to the stack I'd collected. I probably had a hundred or so, none of them read.

It felt odd at first, being alone at the museum. I scolded myself for having no sense of direction but found MFAH's main exhibition, *Tutankhamun: The Golden King and the Great Pharaohs.* The piece everyone wanted to see was the little "coffinette," a gorgeous gold sar-cophagus just short of a foot high. Created to hold only Tutankhamun's stomach, it was the mummy's tomb we imagined as kids. I had a flash of memory from visiting Egypt when I was thirty-one, so this felt like another reminder of my blessings.

But as I walked around alone, the piece that resonated with me was a ten-foot portion of the Colossal Statue of King Tutankhamun. Fine pleats carved into his tunic, the stripes of his pharaoh head-covering falling onto his chest, and the broad collar of beads, teardrop and tubular. I admired the detail, and I found his face so familiar. Tut was seventeen when he died, and in this statue, I saw a young Black man, like the guys I knew in Galveston. Three thousand years between us, but here we were. Time and maybe malice had marred his face, but his strong eyes still regarded me as I regarded him.

I spent the day at the museum without a mission, stopping wherever my heart landed. Before I left, I went to the MFAH gift shop to buy another art book. But when I went home, I didn't just add it to the pile I already had. This time I read through it until the sun began to set.

As I closed the book, I made a decision. *I'd had a hell of a life as a mother and a wife, now it was time to start my* own *life*.

I looked at the stacks of art books in my house and decided to begin there. All the ones I'd ordered to support Black artists or purchased as a sort of IOU to be read someday when I could find some breathing room. That time was now. I started packing those books to ship them to New York City to really enjoy them. So I could enjoy *life*. I was back.

CHAPTER 44

SOUL SURVIVOR

Winter 2012

THERE WAS NEW life to inspire me as I began to fight my way back to mine. Beyoncé had her baby girl Blue Ivy on January 7, 2012, just after my fifty-eighth birthday. We were so looking forward to Beyoncé having her first child that at Solange's New Year's Eve party in New York, we were trying to dance that baby out of her.

This pregnancy was the greatest blessing to come to our family after a terrible time. Beyoncé had suffered through miscarriages before, and had recently been through yet another loss, one that was especially heartbreaking: Given her history, that time she had waited until she was at the twelve-week mark to even tell Jay's family and Kelly and Michelle. The very next day after opening up to her girls in person, she went to the doctor for a checkup, only to be told there was no heartbeat. I was at House of Deréon when she called me in tears, devastated, and I rushed over to be with her.

With this new pregnancy, Beyoncé understandably wanted to wait a long time before even telling close friends. This journey she was on was grueling emotionally and physically, and as her mother I vowed to help her keep it an absolute secret as long as possible. A tangible thing I could do for her was to continually find new ways to camouflage her growing pregnancy with all sorts of wardrobe tricks.

By mid-August, it was becoming a challenge to mask her pregnancy and keep her privacy. The most difficult was a four-night concert gig at New York's famed Roseland Ballroom, a smaller, more intimate space than the huge arenas she was accustomed to. People were so up close, yet we pulled it off. People study the footage now, freeze-framing on a turn in her gold dress, claiming they can see the bump now. But not then. For a little while longer, her secret remained safe.

My daughter waited two more weeks to announce the good news onstage at the MTV Video Music Awards at the very end of August. She only had four months to go, and we were all in the clear. And then in October she did a TV appearance in Australia, wearing a dress with a stiff fabric that folded when she sat. Media outlets helped spread a hateful rumor that she was faking being pregnant—there was even an ABC News bulletin calling it a "mystery." Mainstream news sources ran photos of Beyoncé from months of earlier events, when I'd used magic and fabric to hide her growing stomach, and in reporting on "the speculation" they fueled the nonsense that she couldn't possibly have been pregnant and had to be covering for a surrogate.

This sacred time, after such tragedy and pain, was marred by some of the stupidest shit I had ever seen. People could not understand how hurtful it was for the media to exploit a life that miraculous and doubt its existence and origin. The worst thing is that people had no idea how hard it was for Beyoncé to go through multiple miscarriages and then when finally blessed to carry a baby to term, the world starts heckling you as you both try to make it to the finish line.

This child was prayed for and prayed over—a wanted, cherished, *real* baby, and people were making a living off saying she was a lie. I wanted to curse some people out and scream at these losers to set the record straight. They had no idea what she and Jay, and our whole family, had been through. It was one of the worst times that Beyoncé would not allow me to speak publicly.

"Mama, you cannot address these ignorant people," she would tell me. "Let them talk, I don't care. It's gonna go away."

But it didn't. And people would ask me, right to my face, "Is Beyoncé really pregnant?" Which was saying to me, "Are you a liar? Is your daughter? Would you take this most sacred experience and lie on the life of this baby you pray will make it?"

This matrilineal line—generations who fought to be together, to literally hold on to our children and keep them safe from harm—was now the subject of a vicious lie. I would get incensed, so furious that I would beg again and again, "Can I say something to these idiots?"

"I gotta have a baby, and when she's older, she's gotta hear about this. So, no, Mama. Let it be." She was right. It would make me feel better in that moment, but anything I said would be plucked and chopped into endless articles until my name alone legitimized the discussion.

The hurt didn't end once Blue was born. One day she will still have to read that people said that her mother is not her "real" mother. These sad people have called Beyoncé things beneath mentioning, and the throughline is that they are lying on her name. As a mother, the constant rumors make me feel helpless, unable to protect my children. I can work on anything else that comes about, but rumors? It feels out of my control. Since my girls' stardom, I watched how megastars were harassed and targeted, tortured in one way or another until their lives were living hell—only to be celebrated once they were gone. Flowers given at the grave. I have said this before, and I say it again now: Y'all are not gonna kill my children with this madness.

But for now, we were all safe together in our little world in New York City. Mathew came to visit Blue not long after she was born, something I advocated for. There had been distance between Beyoncé and her father, but I asked if he could come see the baby. So at my apartment, Blue and her grandfather met for the first time. Unfortunately, Mathew arrived with a cold, so we all thought it was best that he not hold the baby. He was crushed.

"I miss y'all so much," he told me when Beyoncé finally left to head home with her newborn. "I would do anything to have my family back." I didn't answer. "Tina, please don't make me go back to the hotel," he said. "Let me stay here with you. I promise I won't bother you. I'll just sleep on the couch."

I relented like I always did and let him stay, but this time I felt empowered. Like the first time an alcoholic goes to an event where there will be drinks. It was a test, and I wanted to pass. We both did. Mathew was a perfect gentleman that night and he did not bother me. The next morning, before I went to work, I made some coffee and drank a cup with him. When he left, I wanted to say something profound at the door, but I wasn't there yet. "I hope," I started, "you know, I really hope you're doing okay."

Two weeks later, he called saying he wanted to come see Blue so he could hold her this time. Again, Beyoncé came over and they visited for a couple hours, Blue cooing in her grandfather's arms. When

Beyoncé left with the baby, Mathew repeated his request. "I'm just so sad, Tina," he said. "Can I just stay here on the couch again? I won't bother you." I believed him, so I said yes.

When I went to bed, I locked the door. Force of habit. A habit I was grateful for when Mathew, breaking his promise, started knocking. When I wouldn't open it, he started drinking. He returned to my door. "Please talk to me," he said. This went on half the night, and I refused to even speak.

The next morning, I made my ex-husband coffee as I had done before, but I let him know he could not stay over again.

"Take me back," he pleaded. I shook my head and answered a strong "No."

When Mathew walked out the door this time, it finally became real that the marriage was over. I had myself a good cry. I don't even know who I reached out to first, I was such a mess. But then somebody called somebody. When the distress call went out among my daughters, Solange, Kelly, Angie, and Beyoncé all showed up for me. "We're coming over" was all I heard, and it was all I needed to hear.

My daughters—girls I'd helped nurture into full-grown women—were now caring for me. I had a big bed, large enough for us all to get into and watch movies. That night, we had a few pints of Häagen-Dazs, too far from Texas for Blue Bell, and settled in cozy to watch a throwback, *Set It Off.* We drew strength from seeing four women who get fed up enough with the system to rob it blind.

Kelly paused the movie to get more salted caramel ice cream out of the freezer, and when she came back in the bedroom, I was overcome by emotion, the pure joy of seeing her and the comfort of being surrounded by the people I loved most in the world. It struck me I hadn't felt happy in a long time. "Just come here and let me hug you," I said.

I wrapped my arms around her, and then Solange enveloped us both in her arms. Before I knew it, Angie, and then Beyoncé, circled our embrace. My girls were loving me back whole. "I just feel blessed," I said. "I am so blessed to have you all right here." And I began to cry a river of cleansing tears.

"I'm good," I said.

That was the breakthrough they had been waiting for. My daughters had let me feel sorry for myself long enough, and now in this moment of emotional clarity they wanted me to know what they'd known the whole time: "Mama, you're a bad bitch," said Solange.

"A *bad* bitch," repeated Beyoncé and Angie in unison.

"The *baddest*," said Kelly, with attitude. "Period."

They reminded me I had too much going on for me to feel my life was over. God had something for me, bigger than I could dream, in the same way I couldn't imagine all the other blessings in my life. God's imagination is infinite—and despite my divorce, my incredible life was my proof. I just had to remember to trust.

I admitted to my girls that I hoped to find love again. At that point, I didn't know another way to feel fulfilled in life without having a partner to share it with. And I couldn't imagine finding a man when I was starting over at fifty-eight.

"Mom," said Solange, "I have *four* friends who have mothers or fathers that are divorced, and they're in their late fifties and sixties. And they have all remarried and they are so happy."

"I don't believe that," I said.

"Oh no, you're gonna meet somebody and you're gonna have a good life," said Angie.

"Where am I going to meet somebody? I'm not going to clubs. I'm not going to—"

"I don't know, maybe on a plane?" Solange said, trying to sound convincing. "Somebody you went to high school with? Who knows, but it's gonna happen."

Kelly started to say, "Ma, you are a beautiful wom—" when I cut her off with a face, and a reflexive "Oh, please."

"Don't do that," said Beyoncé. "Mama, you cannot take a compliment. If I say, 'Oh, you look pretty today,' you always say, 'Oh God, I didn't have time to really do my makeup right,' or 'My hair looks—'"

"Just say 'thank you' because it's true," Kelly said softly.

"No really, I had to learn to do that myself," said Beyoncé.

"And she had to teach me," said Kelly. "Beyoncé had to teach me to take the compliment, and just say 'thank you.'"

I had a moment of revelation: It's not as effective to just *talk* the lesson, you have to walk it. I had tried to teach my daughters to know their value so they would have confidence, but I hadn't truly modeled how to do it. Instead, I had clung to what I learned from my mother and the nuns of Holy Rosary—what so many women grow up learning—mistaking shame for humility. How to dumb yourself down a little bit, hide your light so people won't be offended or intimidated. Deny your own beauty. Beyoncé was breaking the cycle and had shown her sisters what she figured out on her own. And now she was showing her daughter. And, apparently, her mother too. Because I hadn't learned that myself.

"Okay," I said. "I *am* a badass. Thank you for the compliment."

We all cracked up with laughter, and then I hugged all my girls again, truly grateful for the lesson. Grounded by their maturity and fierce love. Sometimes, your children become the wise ones parenting the wounded child in you. And if you are open to it, sometimes your children will fight for you, advocate for you, in ways that you thought only a mother could.

I TOOK THIS NEW INSIGHT INTO THERAPY WITH ELIZABETH, AND together we made the connection that early on I learned that it felt good to care for others because it came with the accolades that proved my worth. My mom was sick as long as I'd been alive, so I cared for her, then I transferred all that work and worry to caring for my children and all the children I picked up and mothered along the way. Mothering someone is such an important job that you naturally put yourself on the back burner, wanting to do so well that you lose yourself. I was no doormat, but I was damn sure hardheaded about taking care of everybody except me. And yes, getting the praise for it.

I could recite this "diagnosis" as plainly as a Catholic school student can run through a "Hail Mary"—it's just about saying the right words. But to feel and understand what this had meant my whole life, and do something about it? To put myself not *even* first, but just on even keel with my family, my friends, or . . . anybody? At this age? That was where the work would be.

Elizabeth recommended that I try EMDR therapy. Eye Movement Desensitization and Reprocessing therapy sounds very technical, but it amounted to holding a memory in my mind while the therapist directed my eye movement left and right and presented a tapping stimulus on my leg. She asked me to think about a tough time from childhood, and I immediately went to Holy Rosary. I could see myself as a little girl with my candy curls and my school uniform, and I saw those nuns as witches, yelling at me and hitting me. I hadn't realized how much that had stayed with me, shaping my relationships and my instinct to run away. How many times had I bolted from situations with Mathew, just left him the family home to find some place on my own? More important, how many times had I run away from myself?

But the true discovery was in the EMDR session in which I saw myself as an adult, talking to my mom. My mother did not protect me from those nuns, continually choosing them over me. It taught me that I was not worthy, and that I should put everybody before myself.

We had touched on this life, when my mother and I had had that call from California, when I thanked her for being a wonderful mom but asked her why she hadn't trusted me. I know my mama died with the sureness of how much I honored and adored her. I wanted to be like her in so many ways, and yet I had said from my children's first breath, "I'm never going to be like my mom in this way." The defining theme of my parenting—"I want them to know I trust them"—was a rebuke to her. It was a shock to realize how mad I was at my mother. I didn't want to be.

Doing the session, I saw her and myself as clear as a movie in my mind. I held her beautiful hands, and I just talked to her. *I forgave her.* I forgave her for not trusting me and being afraid to let me dream, and I realized that was her way of protecting me from the disappointments that she had experienced in her own life. She had been run out of Louisiana with only the clothes she could carry. She had made do, her young family dependent on the fragile conversion of her ex-husband from sinner to savior. Our family's security depended on her ability to withstand the arthritis in her hands I held in memory, and yet I needed her to tell me to dream? To risk?

I let go of that resentment and gained a new understanding of my mother, and new perspective on her sacrifices—which helped me get to know me.

Next was a talk with my girls. I didn't regret living for them, following them around the world, and having their backs against anything and anyone, but I had missed out on a lot of life standing guard. It was clear that to be the great mother I always wanted to be, I needed to model a new kind of self-love. "Listen, I'll be there if you need me, but really it's gonna be about me now," I told them each individually. "This is my selfish era."

I'd dreaded this conversation, because of my codependency. I was afraid I would appear selfish. Instead, they were all *ecstatic* that I'd had this realization. My daughters had never put this burden on me; I'd placed it on myself. "Mom," each said in one way or another, "you've got to live your own life. We're gonna be okay."

CHAPTER 45

SINGLE IN THE CITY

Spring 2012

This girl in the office at House of Deréon was the one who told me about him. He was her OB/GYN, an accomplished doctor. "He saw your picture and he said, 'Oh, she is beautiful.'"

"You just suddenly had a picture of me at your appointment?" I joked. "Or were you trying to set us up?"

"Well, yes," she said. "He's such a nice man, Ms. Tina. He's been divorced for a while, and he wants to take you out for dinner. He thinks you're hot."

Hot? "Really?" I asked. "He said 'hot'?"

"He did," she said. "And you figure he's seen a lot of women."

I laughed. "True." I heard my daughters' voices in my ear, reminding me to take the compliment. "Well, okay."

We arranged for the Doctor to pick me up at my apartment after work for a Friday dinner at eight, and I changed outfits at least five times getting ready. I called Beyoncé to describe the first one. "Take a picture of that," she said. I texted the photo to her, and the phone rang right away.

"No, don't wear that," she said, right to it. "That's too old—wear something fly."

"Fly," I said. "Okay." We talked it out, going through four looks and looping in Solange until I decided on these tight straight-leg jeans, a really cool jacket, and all my jewelry. Which is funny, because that was my style every day.

The Doctor was in prep-mode too, and had been asking my friend about me. What type of food did I like, what music was I into, and how did I feel about flowers? When he came to the door, I was touched that he'd brought me roses.

We went to an Italian place he picked in SoHo, and at dinner, I quickly learned that the Doctor had recently broken up with a young woman, and he was still a little sad about that. But gradually, he started talking about all the cultural touchstones of being our age and Black. We remembered *Julia,* the first weekly series on TV to star a Black woman, the incredible Diahann Carroll, and he told me all about visiting the set of *Soul Train* when he was young. But besides these throwbacks, he didn't have any other conversation except his work. I thought, *That young woman was probably so bored with his ass.*

Near the end of dinner, he said, "I have had the best time. I just love talking to you."

"Well, you know, if you stop dating fetuses, maybe you could enjoy yourself on these dates. Because I'm sure it makes you feel old trying to explain the eighties to people, let alone the sixties."

He started laughing, "I never met anybody like you. You're crazy."

It was still early and I wanted the night to continue, so I asked the good doctor, "Do you ever go dancing?"

He looked like I'd suggested skydiving. Still, he called his daughter and she recommended a jazz place. But when we got there, he told me he never danced. It was a mid-tempo song, so I asked, "I mean, can you just move? Like, if I get up will you just sway?"

"No, I don't dance." And that was it. I worried this is what dating would be. Sitting down with men who'd settled in their ways. I gave him two more dates just to see if anything changed, but decided not to continue.

When sharing my story about the good doctor, at dinner out with Beyoncé and Jay, we laughed and my son-in-law told me that maybe I should try dating somebody young. "I don't know if these old men can keep up with you."

"I don't *like* younger men," I said. "I would never want some guy walking around feeling like I'm his sugar mama. Even if I wasn't—even if he makes ten times what I do—I don't like that scenario for me." This wasn't just vanity: I enjoyed a shared history to discuss, even if we'd experienced things separately. I didn't want to talk about where I first heard Marvin Gaye sing "What's Going On" and have him say, "Oh, my mom used to play him."

I sighed. "If y'all don't introduce me to somebody," I said, "I'm gonna resort to reading obituaries and going to funerals to meet widowers. Saying I was their wife's good friend."

We laughed, and I switched the topic back to my grandchildren. But I brought it up to my therapist. "Tina," she said. "You gotta kiss some more frogs before you find that prince. You just keep at it."

I would hear "You'll meet someone" so constantly that I felt like a failure. Suddenly, I was throwing myself back into the cause and effect of work and motherhood. This was what I loved and found rewarding without question. Who would have time for emotions if I just kept busy?

That summer, I went with Solange to shoot her video "Losing You" in South Africa. She had become an independent artist with a shoe-string budget, so she and director Melina Matsoukas shot "guerrilla style" in Cape Town. To help, I brought Ty Hunter, Vernell, and my friend Alvia Wardlaw, a renowned art historian with an expertise in African and African American culture. And we all just *worked*. Vernell and I, Alvia too, were the grips, the packers, the catering, art direction— whatever was needed.

In these neighborhoods everywhere my eye went, there was a rich-ness to the culture. Women went about their days in royal blues and lime greens, their makeup done to coordinate with the colors. I said, "Oh my God, look at that" at every clothesline, the fabrics and prints so bright—a beautiful red cape next to an orange and yellow duster. The colors complemented each other so well that the arrangement on the line seemed premeditated.

Solange and Melina were in heaven in Cape Town, this place where every new corner seemed already art directed. I had to watch them, because if I turned my back they would be running to a vacant lot where they had seen a bunch of old dirty mattresses to stack up really tall.

"You are not getting up there," I said to Solange.

"Mama, this is why I didn't want you to come. You just need to get out of here."

"Well, this is why I'm here." We both laughed.

The truth is, God put me there to reinvigorate me. Being in Africa, seeing the innate creativity of the people I share an ancestry with, reminded me how strong we are as a people. How resilient. This ability to appreciate beauty and create it in the everyday is passed down in our cells—life to life, story to story—no matter where fate takes us. I left with an even deeper appreciation of my people. And a new confidence in myself as a woman.

CHAPTER 46

GET YOUR GROOVE BACK

January 2013

IT STARTED AROUND my fifty-ninth birthday—these "Poor Miss Tina" looks I would get from acquaintances and strangers alike. I honestly didn't want the divorce to define my life—I was too badass for that—but it was hard not to feel the judgmental eyes of others on me. *Keep your head down and work,* I told myself. But the truth was that under my annoyance with those people, there was real depression. Even badasses get the blues.

Beyoncé was worried about me. We were sitting on the couch at her place, talking about her upcoming world tour, The Mrs. Carter Show, which would start in April. She was talking a mile a minute, full of ideas, and I found myself nodding. And then she asked me a simple question.

"Mama, what makes you happy?"

The question was so sudden, so pointed, I got defensive.

"Hunh?" I asked. "Why would you even ask that?" She was waiting for an answer. "Uh, you know, my grandchildren. Julez and Blue make me happy. I mean, y'all make me happy."

"Okay, well, what makes you *laugh*?"

I paused. "Monica," I said, surprising myself. Monica Stewart was a friend I'd had but had somehow lost touch with. Our main connection was our mutual friend Gwen, who died of breast cancer years earlier. "My friend Monica makes me laugh."

"Monica?" said Beyoncé. I hadn't mentioned her name in years. She and Gwen were like scandalous sisters, the kind of rule-breakers who fascinate me—I'm not going to do what y'all are doing, but I sure love witnessing it. They always said I was a goody two-shoes.

"Oh, she was so crazy," I said. "I mean, I'm sure she still is. She's one of those people that'll have you laughing because she has no filter. None! She can read people like nobody else, pure entertainment."

"Call her," said Beyoncé, looking at my phone on the coffee table.

"It's been so long, I don't even know if I have her right number," I said. "I think she was mad at me about something—I can't remember what." Monica and I had always had these little falling-outs, the way Lucy and Ethel did because those two really could go at it.

"Figure it out then," she said, handing me my phone.

I opened my contacts. I had changed my number so often I was sure Monica's was gone. But there she was, a number I recognized from dialing all those years on Houston landlines.

She picked up! "Monica?"

"Oh," she said, real proper and chilly. "Tina. Yes?"

"Well, why are you talking like that?"

She paused. "Tina, my mom died."

"I had no idea."

"No, you did not, because I haven't talked to you in forever."

"I am so sorry to hear that. I wish I could have been there for you." I was heartbroken for her, and as we talked about what she'd been through, I felt her softening to me.

"Well, what made you reach out?" she asked.

"The truth is I got a divorce and I'm really sad. Beyoncé just asked me who makes me laugh, and I immediately thought of you. Because you did. You do. And she said to call you and I was nervous because it's been a while but I'm calling you and you can be mad at me if you want, but you need to get over it because we love each other."

Part of the falling-out was that when my life changed and I got so busy I barely returned calls, she read my lack of communication as me leaving her behind. "You know I've always been proud of the girls, but you got a little big time for me." She thought I was somewhere in first class sipping champagne all the time—without her.

"I was working like a dog, Monica. I didn't even have time for myself." Gradually, she and I broke that bit of ice that had formed, just enough that she wanted to make plans.

"Well, I'm gonna come see you," she said, "but you are gonna pick me up from the airport—not a car service. You."

"Girl, I'm not coming out to no airport. JFK is an hour away and even to ride with somebody is a waste of my time. I just told you I barely have time to do anything."

"That is important to me," she said. I guessed anything otherwise would be me putting on airs, so when she arrived in New York, I went with the car service to get her.

Monica and I fell into the rhythm of friendship in New York, but it felt short-lived. Soon I would start work on Beyoncé's tour. The two of us were at Cabana, a Cuban lunch place near my apartment where I always got jerk chicken with yellow rice and black beans, and I reeled off the list of stops on the initial leg of the tour. "Pretty much all of Europe all spring."

"How are you not excited?"

"Well, you don't really see these places, Monica. It's always just a lot of work."

"Well, then *don't* work," she said. She saw me start to protest, but she was going to make her point. "That's right. You're gonna go with Beyoncé, and you're taking me, and we're not gonna work. We're gonna go to museums, and eat great food, and meet you a man."

I tried to say no, but Monica was clear: "Tina, we're gonna get your groove back."

THAT CONVERSATION CHANGED MY LIFE. THAT ENCHANTED SPRING started with Monica and me getting on the plane to travel with the band like groupies. It was hard for me at first to just be present, not prove I was useful every five seconds.

Monica and I spent mornings exercising, because our goal was to get really fine on this trip, which I have to say we did. Then we would go to museums and cafés. Jay wanted to help with this time of discovery, giving us the names of the best restaurants in each city for lunch. Lucy and Ethel had their fun. And every show, for the first time in years, I got to watch my daughter from down front, not backstage working. There's a section in all the concerts, about ten feet between the stage and the first seats, and I would hide out there. The back of my head is in so many videos of people taping the show.

On this tour, the people my daughter worked with—newcomers and old friends—got to know *me*. Not Ms. Tina, the person who can solve any wardrobe problem with superglue, or the lady who can go get an answer from Beyoncé on which boot she wants. Just me. There were moments of adjustment for me. The tour photographer Yosra El-Essawy, a gorgeous young British Egyptian woman, had been hired about a week before the first stop, and no matter how I hid from her, she would follow me around to take pictures. She saw me ducking from the frame. "Miss Tina, you're so beautiful."

"Girl, please," I said, thinking how I wasn't done up.

"You deserve to be captured," Yosra said. "One day you're going to be so happy you have these photos." I barely had any pictures of me from the Destiny's Child days, unable to appreciate my beauty.

Yosra gave me that gift, and during the time of the tour I grew to love her as she became family to me and a very close friend to my daughter. Unfortunately, just before the U.S. part of the tour, a couple of weeks before her thirty-second birthday, she was diagnosed with esophageal cancer. I talked to her every day, and near the end of Yosra's short life, Yvette Noel-Schure told us one of Yosra's last wishes was to have a slumber party with Beyoncé and me. We were able to do that for her, drinking tea and playing music. She even had the strength to get up to dance a little. I got to tell her how much it meant to me that she saw me, no matter how I'd tried to fade away.

CHAPTER 47

READY FOR LOVE

June 2013

I WAS IN L.A. on a Thursday near the end of June, walking into the restaurant at the Hotel Bel-Air with Monica. We were staying there, and I was in the beginning stages of paring down my life and cutting back on obligations, but I had agreed to plan the wedding for Vernell. You would think that her finding love again would have given me hope, but it didn't. My best friend was also surprising us all by becoming a Bridezilla. I didn't want to plan a dream wedding when I couldn't even get a date.

Making it worse, so much worse, was that Mathew was about to marry his girlfriend in Houston the week before my friend's wedding. I didn't want to get back with him at all, but it was still a blow to my ego.

That Thursday before the wedding, Monica was not interested in another lunch where she sat down to listen to me boohoo about being single. There was a couple at a table a little too close to us, and I saw her glance at them after we sat.

"Tina, how did that plan work out?" she asked me.

"What plan?"

"You wanted a man so bad you were gonna go under the bridge and get one," she said, knowing she had the attention of that couple.

"Girl, you better stop," I said.

"You said, and I quote, 'I'm gonna clean him up—give him a shave and dress him up. Take him out and he's gonna be my man.'"

"Monica," I said, forcing a laugh so this now dead-silent couple would know this was just my crazy friend running her mouth. They didn't laugh with me.

"How did that work out?"

"Not well if I'm here with your sorry ass," I said.

"Well, then what's the next plan?" she said, finally breaking character and laughing. "Let's go see some men."

"Girl, where are we gonna find some men at our age?" I said. "And where do they keep them? 'Cause I don't know where to find 'em."

Monica made a puzzled face. She didn't know either, but she is a fixer. She picked up her phone.

"Who are you calling?" I said.

"Richard, hi," she said. Richard Lawson was the older brother of Gwen, the good friend we had shared. An actor in L.A. who I'd known for about thirty years, meeting him shortly after I became close with his sister.

Monica spoke in a hurry. "Hey, you know Tina's in town, and you know . . ." She paused, seeming to remember manners—"What you doing?"—but then skipped past his response to an eager "Where can we find some *men?*"

In my dramatic eyeroll, I accidentally turned toward the couple at the next table. They were watching this show. Practically munching popcorn. "Monica, you are gonna make me sound like the most desperate person—"

"Okay, see you there," Monica said, hanging up. She said Richard suggested we stop by the acting class he was teaching that night in L.A. "He wants to know more about what you're looking for."

"What I'm looking for?"

"I mean, he doesn't know you just want a pulse." She smiled at the couple, who I couldn't even look at. "A weak pulse is fine. A little beat here and there."

We went to Richard's acting class, showing up a little late and sitting in the back. I noticed all the young female students giving him goo-goo eyes. "Where are the men in this class?" I asked Monica, who gave me a knowing look.

Afterward, we went to have drinks with Richard, and Monica started right in. "Okay, Richard, we need Tina to meet a nice guy," she said. "Just to get her feet wet and get back out there."

Richard looked at me. "Well, what are you looking for?"

I started talking before Monica made a joke. I had prayed on this, so I knew right away. "I want someone with integrity who believes in God. Someone who likes to dance and likes art and is just . . ." I heard myself say, "Free."

"Oh," Richard said quietly. "Well, what about me?"

Monica and I paused maybe a quarter of a second and didn't even have to look at each other. We both said, simultaneously: *"Hell no."*

Richard was just not on my radar. Monica and I had known him forever and thought of him only as Gwen's older brother. And I was not about to compete with all the women giving him goo-goo eyes. But that night out with those two was nice, so we agreed to all meet up to go dancing Friday, and then to go to a jazz club the night after.

I knew the next day, Mathew's wedding day, would be painful for me, so I asked Richard if he could recommend a church in L.A. for me and Monica to go to. The sermon, ironically, was about letting go. I had one of those Sundays where you feel the preacher is talking directly to you. I got on my knees and prayed, feeling a thousand-pound weight lift off my shoulders. At that very moment, I let Mathew go.

I left that church unburdened and unbothered. "Let's go eat and go to a movie," I told Monica. When I called Richard to thank him for the perfect recommendation for a church, he asked if we could have lunch the next day. "Without Monica," he said. "Just us."

The euphoria of letting go of Mathew distracted me from thinking this might be leading to something with Richard. At lunch, I shared how relieved I was. "I feel like my life is gonna start over," I said. "It's fresh, and I feel *good.*" The only thing I was worried about was that Beyoncé had a concert in Houston in two weeks. "I don't want people looking at me saying, 'Poor Ms. Tina.'" I made such a pitiful pity face Richard laughed, and I liked that laugh. I confessed I worried Mathew would show up with his new wife.

"Oh well, let's just fuck with him a bit," joked Richard. "I'll come down there and be your date. You know, as your friend. But people can think what they want."

So he did, and we had so much fun that we started to spend as much time together as we could. I hadn't had a companion in so long that I just wanted to share the things that brought me happiness. I took him to museums, cafés, to breakfast, lunch, and dinner—each finding reasons to call the other and say, "You know what we could do?" and go off to have some adventure.

One night before he left my house, I looked him in the eye. I said, "Thank you for being my friend." I meant it.

"I'm just so happy to be here for you to be your friend," he said, then paused. "But I'm also attracted to you."

I exhaled, then said it plain: "I'm too old for you," I said, even though he was seven years older than me. Before he could argue I added, "Because you like young women."

"Yeah, but you've got more energy than anybody I've ever met. You're the first woman that could really keep up with my energy."

And so it began. I was drawn to Richard's kindness and willingness to help people—and his energy. We never ran out of things to talk about, because there was always some new idea for how we could contribute to making the world a better place. Here was new love, yet it was comfortable after those decades of friendship.

KELLY CAME TO US WITH THE BEST NEWS IN EARLY 2014—SHE WAS pregnant. I was over the moon to have another grandchild. I have always told Kelly she can do anything, but I knew right then what she would do best would be as a mom. She is so sensitive to other people's needs and emotions, and she prioritizes family—when you combine that with her being such a constant learner, always reading some book, I got excited about how lucky this highly anticipated child would be.

She and Tim Weatherspoon were already engaged, my daughter evenly yoked with this kind, present man she had dated for years. Kelly planned a small wedding in Costa Rica herself, a family-only ceremony by a majestic waterfall. Because Doris was seriously ill, she could not travel to be there. It was a privilege and honor for me to walk Kelly down the aisle. Afterward, we danced the night away, and in six months, her mothers and sisters were by her side at St. John's Hospital in L.A. when she was ready to have the baby. Her mom Doris, me, Beyoncé, Solange, Angie—all of us there with Tim to support her. I had knee surgery scheduled for November, so I was zipping around St. John's on a little scooter, too excited to be still. We joined in prayer around her, family by blood and by God, as she welcomed their beautiful boy Titan.

I have never had the gift of a natural-born son, but God has given me my sons-in-law, Tim and Jay. They are true blessings, and I could not ask for better providers and protectors of my daughters and their children, and I am always touched that their sense of protection extends to me. Jay is an example for his children, starting with very humble beginnings and overcoming every obstacle in the world to be the successful businessman he is. Tim is humble and quiet but incredibly perceptive, managing Kelly's career for years before becoming an executive at Nickelodeon. Even with all the things they are involved in, their best performance is as fathers.

The sadness of that time is that just a month after Kelly became a mother herself, her mother Doris passed from a heart attack. Losing that vibrant, funny storyteller a month into Titan's life was devastating to all of us. Her funeral services would be held in Georgia. I had just had my knee surgery the week before, so my doctor told me I could not fly. But there was no way I was not going to be at Kelly's side at the hardest time of her life. In a way, I knew what it was like to be her, a new mother facing the unknown without your own mother there. She later let me know that she was grateful I made it: "I had a mother in heaven and a mother next to me." We will never leave her.

ONE DAY IN THAT YEAR OF LOVE AND LOSS, WHEN GOD HELPED US see what was essential, my granddaughter Blue, all of two years old, said to me and Richard, "When are y'all getting married?"

"Blue, would you approve if that happened?" Richard asked.

"Yes," she said.

She'd seen us stand together and was probably thinking, *Okay, what's going on here? 'Cause I know that when two people love each other they are supposed to be married.* Blue's question isn't what made us do it, but it opened up possibilities. *What if?*

We married April 12, 2015, with a beautiful ceremony on a boat at Newport Beach. It was important to me to walk in white. I was going to break any rule that tried to tell me what I couldn't do because of my age. This was my day.

It was a blessing to spend the day with my daughters, and also my brothers and sisters, on the water. Of course, we reminisced about our mother taking us on that free ferry from Galveston to Louisiana, back and forth telling us, "This is our own boat."

We were still the same kids though. I was the baby sister who couldn't see the punch lines of Skip's corny jokes coming, and I'd guffaw and shake my head while Flo and Selena groaned. I'd told handsome Butch that he couldn't take any pictures with our actor friends like Samuel L. Jackson and Glynn Turman, but there he went, holding up a phone to get a selfie as he told them some adventure story he had at the ready, an ex-military guy who did karate and rode motorcycles.

We women were all in white, except Selena in a muted gold tweed jacket and skirt, just as elegant and movie-star gorgeous as she'd always been. I wanted the photographer to take a picture of Selena, and it was hard for her to stand long so I had someone grab a slipcovered chair. Well, Blue, who wanted to be in every picture that day, sat right in it, ready for her portrait. I got another chair and decided it would just have to be Selena and Blue seated together—nearly ninety and just three—the oldest and youngest in their splendor.

I was doing my stage managing of the shot when I realized Selena and Blue each held their hands in their laps the same way my mother did when she had to be still for a photograph. And each had their lips pressed into my mom's flatline smile suggesting, "Okay, get your shot." I ran to be in the photo with them, not wanting to miss this moment. Standing proudly between them, I placed my hands on their shoulders, grateful to bridge these generations.

CHAPTER 48

LOUISIANA ROOTS

June 2016

SOLANGE HAD MOVED to Louisiana to write her masterpiece, *A Seat at the Table*. She found a place to record in a little town near New Iberia, just north of Weeks Island, an old house with lots of trees. She walked in the same air as her grandparents, the same ground beneath her feet. But the atmosphere at the property felt particularly heavy, and she had someone research the area. Her intuition was right: The house had been part of a slave plantation. The historical records also showed a strong possibility that the white man she was renting from was a relative. He was not happy to hear we might be kin of some sort. "Oh no, I doubt that," he said.

I had family on my mind. My brother Skip had passed that March, and we brothers and sisters felt his absence terribly. I did a film, a sort of visual obituary, for which I interviewed the people who knew our brother. At least five people had stories about driving around with Skip in his truck and having to move over because he stopped to pick up some homeless person. Wherever they were going had to wait, because Skip wanted to take them to get them something to eat. His wife Cynthia beat all that, talking about the times Skip came home with no shoes on because he'd stopped to give them to a barefoot person he saw on the road.

I compensated for this loss, periodically going on Instagram to announce it was "corny joke time." No one could know this was really for Skip, telling the absolute shaggiest dog of a joke and then overexplaining it just like him.

My daughters didn't want me on social media because they were trying to protect me. They were like, "Mama, people are so mean on Instagram and they will tear you apart."

"I'm ready for it," I said. "Because guess what? I don't really give a shit." When you get older, you become freer. I was making up for lost time.

So I said yes when Solange called to ask if she could interview me for the album near the end of her recording sessions. "I might like to use a few words on my record." By then, she had a recording studio in New Orleans and had asked Master P to come add his touch as a sort of narrator for the work. Solange had long admired his business mind and entrepreneurship, Mathew holding him up as an example of someone who owned his own label, No Limit. Because Master P built his own empire selling records off the back of his car, Mathew had explained, he never had to compromise as an artist.

Solange had two rooms going at the recording studio, and I noticed she kept stealing looks at the other studio door. A little kid anxious about how a plan was coming together. Finally, she just said, "Mama, my daddy is here."

"Oh really?" I said. Mathew and I had not been in the same room in almost five years. I had absolutely no contact with him—not a word spoken. She had parent-trapped us. "Why didn't you tell me?"

"Oh, because . . . you know . . . it just happened he was down here this week. He was supposed to come another time."

When Mathew came into the room I hugged him. "Careful," I said. "I hear your ex-wife is around here." We shared a small laugh, and it was the beginning of me coming to understand how to navigate being with Mathew. He was like a little fuck-up brother—you love him and can be happy to see him, but you can't be around him all the time. As we talked that day, I saw Mathew had grown so much— a changed man after facing his demons.

In Mathew's contribution to the album, the interlude "Dad Was Mad," Solange interviews him about being one of six kids integrating his school in Alabama and living with the threat of death every day as a child. Mine was "Tina Taught Me," in which Solange got me going about the beauty of being Black and having pride in our history. It had started earlier, in a conversation that I had with a white woman who wondered if Black History Month was even necessary anymore. I strongly disagreed with her, arguing that every day was White History

Day, even in February; whether it was me in Ball High, or my daughters in their schools, American history was taught as white history. I said to Solange what I have always known: "I've always been proud to be Black—never wanted to be nothing else. It's such beauty in Black people, and it really saddens me when we're not allowed to express that pride in being Black, and that if you do then it's considered anti-white. No! You're just pro-Black, and that's okay."

It was fascinating watching Solange work on *A Seat at the Table*. She made very specific choices as an artist, one who did not care about money or fame. In January 2017 she performed at the Peace Ball concert held at the National Museum of African American History and Culture in Washington, D.C. The entire show was an act of resistance during the inauguration of Donald Trump, and Solange was introduced onstage by Angela Davis—one of my idols and the woman I represented in my own act of resistance at Ball High.

I then watched Solange go into spaces that had long been closed off to Black artists and audiences who look like them. As she did, her actions were the embodiment of what I knew about "crossing over." A true artist doesn't change herself to pass through a barrier to get to some supposedly better place; she removes that barrier altogether, remaining herself as she creates, giving others the example and opportunity to do the same. After the Peace Ball, she spoke at Yale Law School, where tickets to her talk were gone in minutes. There, she spoke to the audience about the resistance she faced navigating the white space of the Brooklyn alternative music scene, and coming to the realization, "I belong in the space that I create myself." The message had to resonate with the law students, who had recently protested the lack of diversity at Yale Law after an American Bar Association report showed only 5 percent of first-year students at the law school for 2015–16 were Black, continuing a then steady drop from an already tiny number.

Just a few months later, Solange prepped for a show at the Guggenheim Museum in New York. Looking at the interior—an open space of spiraled tiers ascending to a glass dome of sky—she planned an installation and dance performance. And again, I saw she met resistance. She was told she could not add her sculptures to her set, beautiful white geometric shapes of rectangles and spheres. When she was initially refused, the Black woman from the South in me felt it was because nothing had really changed. She could sing and dance there, but her physical art would not have a place. It reminded me of when Black singers were allowed to sing at the hotel but not stay there. "You gotta stay down at somebody's house," I told Solange, "but we're gonna take your performance though because we wanna be entertained." That's how I took it anyway.

Solange got her way and brought her sculptures in, but I know she understood the stakes. As she tweeted the day before the show: "We aren't thanking anyone for 'allowing us' into these spaces . . . until we are truly given the access to tear the got damn walls down."

The installation was astonishing. One of the most beautiful things I have ever seen, and there was so much pride—Black pride—from the audience making that space hers. This was not the usual crowd for the Guggenheim, which a year later was criticized in a report that said 73 percent of museum visitors were white, while only 8 percent were Black. *The New York Times* called Solange's work "sublime" and pointed out the transgressive power of bringing her art to the Guggenheim (even if the paper used lowercase for Black): "To fill the museum with the sounds of an album that celebrates black womanhood and black manhood—sung, played and channeled into movement by black women and men—was its own symbolic retort to the art world's (and the dance world's) histories of exclusion."

Solange continued to tear down the walls, creating work and spaces for Black audiences around the world, from the Sydney Opera House to the Brooklyn Academy of Music, from the Getty Museum in L.A. to a site-specific performance at the Donald Judd sculptures in Marfa, Texas. She even became the first Black woman to compose music for the New York City Ballet. This is a girl who will say offhand, "I want to take a glassblowing class." Then suddenly we were getting these little crooked vases for Christmas with the bubbles in them. And of course she went off and just got *good* at it, crafting these stunning glassworks and then expanding that work to create a space for the best Black glass-blowers to present objects, as she put it, "designed with Black thought and created by Black hands."

There is so much of her grandmother in Solange, these two Cancers who became parents early and who raise the quality of every art they encounter. I often wonder what my mother could have crafted if she had more exposure, more education, and more opportunities. She showed such promise, and now Solange is the fulfillment.

CHAPTER 49

TINA'S ANGELS

Fall 2016

I HAD ALWAYS SAID that when I "retired," I wanted to mentor young girls. I often thought about how my brother's girlfriend Lydia changed my life that night when I was fourteen, taking me to see the Alvin Ailey American Dance Theater performance in Houston. She opened my eyes not just to culture but to possibility, and the idea that I could have a life in that possibility. I had been in L.A. with my husband Richard, and in my new life I wanted to start mentoring full time.

The dream was for a free program focusing on girls, taking them on field trips to plays and restaurants, exposing them to art and opportunities. My friend Melba Farquhar told me about her cousin, Kasiopia Moore, a teacher at the KIPP public middle school on Figueroa in South Central L.A. Kasi was open to me starting the mentorship program, and told me about the school, which was tuition-free with almost every student eligible for the free meal program. "What's your grading criteria for entrance to the program?" Kasi asked.

"Uh, that they want to do it, and I think it should be mandatory that a parent or caregiver show up for the first meeting," I said.

"Well, they don't have to be passing all their classes or have a certain grade point?"

"No, I just want to have kids I can help," I said. "I can help anybody."

Kasi passed out my flyers and talked to parents to explain what an opportunity this was. She came up with twenty-six girls, and that first

Monday, there they were. I was directing this first talk to the parents, and then having individual interviews with each girl.

The first child I met, Arielle, had a cautious feel to her. "If you could do or be anything in life," I asked her, "what would it be?"

"I'm just gonna move down the street from my mama," she said.

"Yeah, but what are you gonna *do*?"

"I don't know," she said, sounding so resigned at this young age.

"Listen," I said, lowering my voice. "You are deserving. And you can live *anywhere* you want to be. Become *anything* you want to be. It's okay not to know yet, but when you do, we are going to be right here to help you get through. I promise you."

One little tear formed, and I realized this girl believed me. Which meant she could believe in herself if I kept that promise. Which, I decided, there was no way I wasn't going to. I had not just found my calling; I had answered it.

As we all settled into this mentorship, I called it Tina's Angels. I talked my husband into getting involved, starting Richard's Warriors with about a dozen boys from the school. For field trips, I looked for anything to spark their imagination, like my mother when she scoured the newspaper to find anything free to bring us kids to. The first thing we did was take them to see the Alvin Ailey American Dance Theater perform, just as Lydia had done for me, then to museums to show them Black art that reflects their lifestyles. These kids could stand in front of Kerry James Marshall's works, these beautiful huge paintings, scenes of barbershops and beauty shops and liquor stores, and see the things that go on in their neighborhoods. But because it was in a museum, it showed them their own surroundings were beautiful, and worthy of art. Places like LACMA and MOCA had seemed closed off to them—but they belonged. I gave each child a journal so they could record and capture what they saw and felt in their own lives.

Years before, I had read *A Piece of Cake: A Memoir* by Cupcake Brown, which provided a you-are-there account of being a teenager in South Central L.A. I bought twenty-six copies, and every Monday we read the book together, and whenever we came to a curse word, we only said the first letter. The memoir reflected the lives of some of the kids that I was truly worried about, and also what they saw around them coming to school. KIPP was on a tough block, elementary school on one side, a junior high on the other, and in the middle was a *motel* that rented out by the hour. That meant there were pimps and prostitutes and drug dealers everywhere, all over the campus of these kids' school. They loved that book, and if I would have given them *Huckleberry Finn* or something like that, they would have been like, "I walk through prostitutes every day. What do you think I can get out of this?"

In addition to the book, I also gave one student, Nyarae, extra reading assignments. When she started, she had been reading at a second-grade level, but she loved books. She just needed the support to stick with them. The more I called on her, the more confident she became, and we all lavished praise on her for the poetic way she would put things.

Nyarae wrote a piece called "Tina's Angels" to share with the group: "Ms. Tina hands us red diaries. Tells me, 'Hold your head up.' We travel to museums of beauty, see our culture and neighborhood, and parking lots and beauty shops in a new light. We are the roses that grew from the concrete. Proving nature's law is wrong. Learning to fly when given wings. Funny it seems, but by keeping our dreams, we learned to breathe fresh air. Long live the legacy that grew from concrete. When someone cared."

As Tina's Angels grew—we were even able to take ten kids to visit Ghana in the 2019 Year of Return—I have kept track of all my "classes," but I am especially close to that first group. I am also happy to say that after years of trying, KIPP was finally able to buy that motel to tear it down, with L.A. mayor Karen Bass leading the charge.

One of the traditions I like at the end of the school year is a gathering for everyone at Zuma Beach in Malibu, a throwback to when I was growing up, seeing the segregated beaches with their lounge chairs and umbrellas. Now we have a big party with all the past Angels and Warriors and current ones. At the end, we give the high school graduates a whole set of luggage for the places they'll go. It's our way of manifesting.

I want to keep creating those opportunities for young people. It continues to astonish me that all kids need is somebody who really believes in them. And you can do that for somebody. You don't have to mentor twenty-six kids—you can mentor *one*.

CHAPTER 50

CAPRI MOON

Summer 2021

J AY WAITED UNTIL the coast was clear to tell me about his secret plan for Beyoncé's fortieth birthday in September. We were out on the patio after lunch at their summer house in the Hamptons, and she'd just gone for a walk.

"I wanna make her birthday the best birthday ever," he said, quiet even though it was just us. "I want everybody that she loves there. I'm gonna fly them all over to Italy."

I smiled. "That sounds really nice."

He moved his lower jaw, gearing up for something. "I have a really big favor to ask."

"What?"

"Can you get Beyoncé's dad there?"

"What?"

"I want you to be okay with it," he said. "I know it would be a real act of love for you. But I'm asking you, could you get him there?"

"Well, it's gonna be in Italy," I said, like that was the issue, then started to sputter a little. "I, I would never ask him to come to this party around me and Richard because I want to be sensitive to . . . He would need to bring someone with him."

Jay kind of cocked his head.

"Oh, yes, he would have his wife with him," I said, fully realizing how out of it I sounded. "Of course. Oh my God, I don't know if I'm ready for this."

"Well, just think about it," he said.

"For sure," I said. I took my time praying that afternoon. Doing an inventory of my soul, I realized that I didn't hold any grudges or animosity. We have these beautiful kids, and we built a life together. I never questioned whether Mathew loved me or his family, and that was what made his issues so hard for me. Here I was so protected by him—if you messed with me, you had to deal with him—and the only person he ever let hurt me was him with his demons.

By sunset, when the light shone gold on the pond, I found Jay. "At the end of the day, this is really about Beyoncé being happy," I said. "And I know she loves her dad. So of course, he can come and bring his wife. I will call to invite him. And I just have to deal with it."

When Beyoncé's birthday came, Jay got a boat large enough to accommodate her family and friends, and set it floating along the island of Capri. It was important to him that he honor her, show his love for her by planning the best birthday of her life. It began with five days of her inner circle staying on the boat, and we watched each chopper come in to drop people off on the heliport like *Fantasy Island*. Angie came with me, then Kelly and her husband, Tim. We saw those little feet of her son Titan get out of the chopper first and started yelling in excitement. We knew Solange would not be able to make it because of a huge commitment she had, but Beyoncé admitted to me that with each helicopter that landed, she had thought, "I hope it's Solange."

Then Jay's plan was to host a luncheon for a larger group of loved ones, each person coming in by boat. Michelle was the first to arrive, and I was then excited to see Jay Brown and Kawana come, along with Mai and James Lassiter, as well as Emory, Andrea, and Justice Jones.

More and more people came, but I was waiting for Mathew and his wife. I had butterflies, unable to really relax until the first moments of awkwardness were behind me.

When the last boat arrived and they didn't show, I was relieved. *Oh good,* I thought to myself, *maybe they missed their flight.* God must have laughed, because here came their boat, the real last one. Beyoncé greeted her dad, excited to see him because it had been a long time, too long, and this was a truly special day. She said hello to Mathew's wife, then she and her father went off to talk separately.

Tina, you gotta be a big girl. I went over to his wife to make her feel welcome, and she hugged me. Maybe a beat too long, but she was very nice. "Oh my God, it's so good to meet you," she said.

When I then went over to the side, I started chatting with Angie and Kelly. But I realized nobody else was talking to Mathew's wife. There was a sense of loyalty—"Team Tina"—that I had to make clear I didn't need. I went over again to make small talk about their flight and their summer. And I embraced both that it was awkward and the possibility that someday it wouldn't be. Mathew and I did not work out—sometimes when two people each have these dynamic, expansive lives and big careers, they are not evenly yoked for each other. I was too much for Mathew, and the balance was off. But I have never wished him any ill will and I am happy that he's happy. She is perfect for him.

Later, Beyoncé came to me, saying Jay had just told her that I had invited her dad and his wife myself. She was beaming with happiness, but teary-eyed. "Mama, that was the most unselfish thing to do," she said, hugging me so close I got teary too. *"Thank you."*

Jay rented a private island for the night's dinner as a surprise for everyone. As we approached the island on a small boat, we saw what looked to be at least a thousand white lanterns floating on the water to guide us to shore. I caught the vision of us all dressed in our flyest all-white outfits, headed to my daughter's celebration.

Drinks and hors d'oeuvres were served in a one-of-a-kind restaurant built into a cave, and afterward we went down to the beach to find the most beautiful table set out on the sand with waves lapping on the shore. We dined and then danced until five o'clock in the morning, not wanting the night to end even as we greeted the sun. One by one, we toasted Beyoncé, honoring her forty years of life. It was the most magical party I had ever attended—not merely because it was so lavish, but because as a mother, I got to witness the remarkable effort Jay put into showing her how special she was to him. I marveled that my daughter seemed to feel so valuable, so happy, and so surprised. And *seen*.

The next afternoon back on the ship, when the party was over and most everyone was gone, I sat on the deck with the birthday girl, Angie, Kelly, and Michelle. We simply took in the beauty of Capri: giant rock formations like stone castles carved by the sea and the calming, constant breeze; limestone cliffs embellished with villas of terracotta and marble. We were so far out, the blue waves danced endlessly around us. I kept adjusting my eyes to the splendor of God's creation, and in the distance, a helicopter appeared. First far away, then unmistakably making its way to us.

"Oh Lord," Beyoncé said. "Let a crazy little designer shoe step out that helicopter."

The chopper door opened, and out stepped the heel of a colorful strappy shoe. Solange! Beyoncé squealed, and the sisters ran to each other.

All my girls spent the rest of the trip jet skiing, nobody around but them, tearing through the water and laughing. It was a party every night, and we all dressed in blue silk monogrammed pajamas to sit on the deck as Beyoncé played us some of the album she was working on, *Renaissance*. As I dropped it low before a backdrop of Capri's twinkling light, my daughter sang for me from my jam "CHURCH GIRL": "I'm finally on the other side. I finally found the urge to smile."

CHAPTER 51

COVER IT WITH CRYSTALS

October 2022

WELL, NOW I had stepped in it, but it was for a good cause. When United Airlines donated two first-class tickets to the WACO Theater Center's fifth annual Wearable Art Gala fundraiser, I thought it would be a nice idea to make it part of a larger auction package. "I'll get tickets for one of Beyoncé's future concerts." Her album *Renaissance* had just come out that summer and I knew she had very early plans to tour again. I think I said something like, "I think it'll be this summer, but whenever it happens, just say I'll give them a tour backstage."

It was a last-minute addition, so I didn't look over how my team presented it until everyone saw it up on the screen. "United x WACO offers you a chance to see Beyoncé on her Renaissance Tour starting in the Summer of 2023. . . ."

I looked over at Beyoncé and her look said, "What did you do?" I ran out onstage. "First of all, there is no Renaissance Tour," I yelled. "It hasn't been named; it hasn't even been planned!" But do you think people cared? They knew this was going to be a *show*.

Weeks later, Beyoncé's team had a meeting about trying to figure out this tour. We were talking about things to do for the fans, and I suggested a contest. Beyoncé looked at Jay and said, "Well, we know that that can be done, don't we?"

"Yes, I did that," I said, laughing. "But I didn't do *all* that. I just said tickets in the future."

But the future was coming, and now Beyoncé was really planning the show that would indeed be called the Renaissance World Tour, with a start in Stockholm that May. Watching these times of preparation for tours has become an increasingly complex master class in artistry. A typical day goes like this: Once she drops her kids off at school, she goes straight to the Parkwood office. She is in fighter mode, wearing an oversized hoodie and sweats, and the days are super long. Rooms are filled with dry-erase boards as she has meeting after meeting. The first might be with the stage designers, the second can focus on lighting, the third choreography. Then costuming, production, props . . . When you attend the show, she has seen to every detail with no expense spared. Still, she is the only artist I know who will tighten the budget, maximizing every dollar not for her but for the fans to get their money's worth.

Now she discussed previous tours, and how she could go *bigger*. In the past, Beyoncé always changed ten times in a show, but now she wanted to have a brand-new outfit to open the show every single night. Nothing worn twice for the opening, and then for all the numbers, on any given night we would add new looks. There would be about fifty shows planned, probably more, and I talked about the stress on the stylist—this person already would have to eat, breathe, and sleep the tour. Now with continual wardrobe changes?

"Well, I want *two* stylists," Beyoncé said.

In the past, I designed a lot of the costumes for the dancers, with the incredible Tim White making them, and I didn't think two stylists would be enough to execute her vision. The pressure on them would be too much, with Beyoncé's plans for something like two dozen dancers changing ten times per show, and the way she was talking, I knew by the end of those fifty-six tour stops Beyoncé could have more than two hundred changes, and six hundred costumes.

She said she wanted two stylists, but when I left, my goal was to put together a team of *four* high-profile stylists, with one more for dancers only. Nothing like this had been done before. If we pulled this off, it would make fashion history.

The first call was to Shiona Turini, a friend of the family and stylist we have worked with for a while. Then I added Karen Langley, an English girl who worked with Beyoncé on the Ivy Park line. I reached out to Edward Enninful, then the head of British *Vogue,* who generously directed me to his own magazine's style director, Julia Samois-Jones.

And finally, KJ Moody, the great-grandson of my oldest brother, Slack Jr. KJ grew up in Dallas and went to design school. I'd known he was special since he was eight or nine, when I let him come backstage at a Destiny's Child concert to see the wardrobe room. He saw all the sparkles and costumes and he said, "I fell in love with it."

We issued him the same challenge we gave all the stylists: Yes, I see you. Now, show us what you can do.

Beyoncé was so involved in every little detail. "No, that needs glasses." "No, find this kind of boot and cut the heel down." "No, we need to put latex with that, and can we . . ." I watched her give valuable input on everything, and she took the time to not just challenge the stylists but teach them so they could rise to the occasion.

There are so many things that you've got to know to make things *stage ready*. When you get these clothes from a designer, that is only half the battle. It's got to stay up, so you don't have a wardrobe mishap, and you've got to be able to *move in it* and have the audience see movement. I learned a long time ago that when you put this couture stuff on Beyoncé, she is killing herself dancing under that thing, but you see no movement. And it's also got to look good onstage from all angles.

And when all else failed, our running joke was "cover it with crystals." A little sparkle and rhinestone go a long way.

THE RENAISSANCE WORLD TOUR WAS REAL. IT FELT LIKE THE whole world was draped in silver. Our formidable, world-class stylists had pulled off Beyoncé's outrageous dream. The crowd roared as she appeared like a ray of light belting out "Dangerously in Love" in a custom Alexander McQueen bodysuit. The futuristic set design and fashion were absolutely breathtaking. This was *bigger*, exactly what my girl imagined when manifesting a year earlier. I've seen my daughter transform on many stages, but she was a hypnotizing goddess on opening night of the Renaissance World Tour.

We were staying in Paris as the family's central base of operations during the tour, spending time together in our own house in the hotel. Beyoncé wanted us all to have a sense of normalcy, and I loved having this day-to-day time with my grandchildren, Blue, who was eleven, and the twins, Sir and Rumi, who turned six on the tour.

In April, Beyoncé had rented out Europe's largest arena, Paris

La Défense Arena in Nanterre, France, for rehearsals. Blue would go to class there, sitting in rehearsals most days when she didn't have school. People make jokes about Blue being Beyoncé's manager because she is so on top of things, adding her thoughts at meetings. She is a very responsible kid, and she attended dance rehearsals watching intently, the same way Solange used to watch Beyoncé and Kelly practice routines as kids. Sometimes, Blue would run through the routines with the Renaissance dancers, but nothing formal.

It was not long after the tour started that Blue said to me: "Grandma, I really want to go dance one time with my mom."

"Well, you should—" I stopped myself. A grandmother knows when she is being asked for assurance. "We should talk to her about it."

Beyoncé's immediate answer was "No."

It was a protective response I recognized. But Blue wasn't giving up. "I know all the choreography."

Being able to do it was not enough, Beyoncé explained. "You have to work hard. You can't just go out there and do it."

"I *will*," she said.

Beyoncé thought for a second. She was protective, not wanting her daughter to be exposed at her age. "I'll let you do it one time, and that's it."

Blue got right to work, with two weeks to learn this complicated choreography that these seasoned dancers had three months to master. She would debut in Paris in late May, and if it worked out, the plan was for her to do another city. Maybe. She would join the dancers during "Black Parade" and "My Power"—two songs that claim the sustaining strength of our roots. Blue worked her butt off over those two weeks. "I know it," she would tell me. "I know it."

I helped her do her hair before that first show in Paris. Before I knew it, Blue was out there with her mother, flanked by dancers, all of them in thrilling looks. I cried watching my granddaughter perform. This child who had been bullied by strangers since before she was born was willing to show her gifts in front of almost seventy thousand people. The response from the crowd was so amazing, all of these throngs of lovely people cheering her on.

Blue Ivy was born to famous parents, but she was still a child. Awful people have said her mother faked her pregnancy, and adults made fun of a baby's hair because Beyoncé chose not to slick Blue's hair back and let her have a beautiful little afro. The irony was that as a little one Blue started a whole new trend of people letting their kids go natural, seeing the beauty of their kids' hair. Something she can be proud of forever. And now here she was, all of eleven, transforming this Black girl pride into the extraordinary courage to dance before packed stadiums, night after night. She did that, and I want Blue to hold a pride in that for all her days.

Rumi and Sir turned six on the tour. Sir shying away from the entertainment part of his family's life, loving his books and spelling as much as he did cars and trucks. But Rumi told Beyoncé every day, "I'm ready. I'm ready for the stage." She knew all the choreography and the words to all the songs.

"Those little Carter girls," I found myself saying as I watched her move in time to the music, echoing "Those little Knowles girls" I used to hear around Miss Darlette's dance class in Houston.

ONE OF THE OTHER JOYS OF THAT TIME WAS SEEING KELLY RETURN to acting, a great love of hers. All my daughters have these incredible talents, and something I have noticed about her is how much the camera loves her. You push a button and Kelly can turn it on, making a connection with the viewer. She had just finished filming Tyler Perry's *Mea Culpa*, which would become the number-one streamed film on Netflix.

"You are just scratching the surface of what you can do," I told her, the same pep talks I would give her when she was an eleven-year-old. My dream for her is to play Donna Summer in a biopic, a role I know she'd be a knockout in. "You can't wait," I said. "You're going to have to create this yourself. Get the script, and then you'll find the backing."

I know she will, because Kelly has always continued to bloom, daring herself to face whatever scares her to be the woman she wants to be. In October 2018, she had found her biological father, Christopher Lovett, after thirty years of not seeing him. She had so many questions, but she said she first chose to listen to him so he could give his side of their complicated story. They became so close again from that first day, and I admire that after nearly four years of talking just about every day, in 2022, they chose to share their journey back together with a joint interview on *Today*. Nothing is impossible when it comes to family.

CHAPTER 52

CHOOSING ME

July 2023

T HERE WAS A morning that I woke up with a clarity. It's not that the light of a new day shone down on me and I had some revelation, it was that I allowed myself to *see* what had been clear for so long: My marriage to Richard needed to end. Though we were friends for many years before our ten-year relationship, and he has great qualities, we just didn't bring them out in each other.

I had talked to him about my feelings for some time, but that morning of my decision I woke up and I realized that talking would change nothing. I just *grew up* at sixty-nine, and realized I deserved so much more. I wanted to be happy. I wanted someone to be happy when I walked in the room. If I stayed in this relationship, I would never feel whole, loved, cherished, and respected. And *seen*. Nothing else in a marriage matters if you are not first priority with each other. There was also the pressure of being an example for so many people who hoped to find a second chance at love. But I had to choose.

And I chose me. In July 2023, I filed for divorce from Richard. The specifics don't matter as much as the fundamentals: those tenets of 1 Corinthians again. Love is patient, love is kind. Love is also not a competition or mired in jealousy. I made the decision to divorce with a heavy heart but totally without malice, and I have not lost a night of sleep over it. Which, for me, is growth. When I went through my first divorce at fifty-eight, I thought I was going to die. I was in terrible emotional pain before making that decision then, but I was physically sickened at the idea. My minister, Juanita Rasmus, says that when

you're going through something, it means you're going *through* it—
you're not going to get stuck there. You will come out the other side
and survive.

I not only survived, I *thrived*. Now, I'm not saying it was easy to go
through a divorce this time. I would have much preferred to be happily
married and planning a simple retirement into full-time philanthropy.
But I was not paralyzed by sadness or suffering the emptiness I felt
before. My mission now was to focus on the things that bring me joy
and security that are not about marriage. I'd like a companion in life,
even to get married again, but whether or not I was with somebody, I
would still be good. I would lead a fulfilled life, because I'd come to
truly value the woman in the mirror. I'd never felt I could claim that
with confidence before—and that in itself was an amazing gift to have,
even if it was at that late time in my life.

There were people who didn't think I should feel amazing. Strangers on the internet said mean things, including one that cracked me
up: "Tina Knowles can't keep a man." Well, I kept one for thirty-three
years and the next one for ten, but okay. There was an underlying message to a lot of the comments: Not only did I not deserve to be happy,
but my age made me ineligible to even bother. People clipped and
snipped a TV interview Richard and I did where I had just said all
these great things about him, but they focused on the part where I said
my husband wasn't perfect. I guess as a woman, even though I reeled
off a list of positive attributes before I said that he was human, this was
taken as criticism. In retrospect, maybe I should have said no one is
perfect—I'm certainly not. Seeing all the hate directed at me on Instagram, so much of it posted by women, I thought about how much we
ourselves promote sexist thinking, how often we buy into the narrative
that men are superior and that we should just adore them. Had I ever
been guilty of that? I reflected on the messages we all get from girlhood
to adulthood that tell us our value is only connected to the presence of
a man.

At the beautiful July wedding of Jay's mom, Gloria Carter, to her
longtime love Roxanne Wiltshire in New York City, I had a revealing
conversation with Tyler Perry. This was weeks before I made the divorce announcement, and even though Tyler was disappointed to hear
the news because he liked Richard and me together, he shared something that would give me strength in the time to come.

"Do you understand how proud I am of you?" he asked me. "For making this decision at sixty-nine years old—that your happiness and the protection of your spirit are more important than appearances?"

This was no shade on Richard, who Tyler actually likes. Tyler was only talking about me and also about the women he knew in his life, women he loved with all his heart, who stayed in marriages because they thought that was the right thing to do. He reminded me I was doing this not just for those women—the moms, the sisters, the aunts and daughters—but the sons who adore them. As women, we convince ourselves that if we sacrifice our happiness, it will lead to the happiness of our children. But they will never know happiness if we don't have it. They will never have power until we do.

"You made the move," Tyler told me, leaning down to look me in the eye. "You are making the move for all of our mothers."

JUST A COUPLE OF MONTHS AFTER MY ANNOUNCEMENT, BEYONCÉ and I were in the back of a car, watching Houston roll by. We were heading to my hotel after spending the morning at the Friday groundbreaking of the Knowles-Rowland house, which our family helped develop with St. John's Downtown Church. The space has always changed according to the needs of the community. First, it was built as a nonprofit youth center and event space for kids, then a warehouse to accommodate the increasing needs of the church's food bank. Now it was transforming into thirty-one apartments with an aim toward helping kids aging out of foster care at eighteen, unable to get a job with no address or phone number. The complex would also provide health services and a job assistance program.

We were in Houston for Beyoncé's Saturday and Sunday night shows on the Renaissance Tour, and Kelly was going to attend the groundbreaking to represent the family. But that morning Kelly called me in a panic to say her nanny had Covid and she couldn't come. Beyoncé overheard the call, then me hanging up and saying to no one, "I'm about to go there and do this by myself."

"I'll take you, Mama," she said. I was so touched because she'd just had a concert the night before and had to be exhausted. She stood just behind me as I gave a speech on the importance of the project and its roots in the Sunday services at St. John's. As I spoke to my beloved community, just when I started to get emotional, I felt my daughter's hand on my back.

Heading to our next stop, the driver made a turn to avoid traffic, taking a side street he could not know was from the map of Beyoncé's childhood and my first years as a mother.

"Mom, isn't this the street that takes us to the house?"

"Yes," I said. "On Rosedale."

I had a luncheon I needed to get to for BeyGOOD, Beyoncé's philanthropy arm, but I asked the driver to make another turn so we could see the old house. As we drove, she sat up, and I watched her remember these streets, the same ones she took home as a toddler. "You were like a year old when we moved to Rosedale," I said. "That's where I glassed in the carport to make my original hair salon. That's where it all started."

I asked the driver to stop in front of the house. The second I unbuckled my seatbelt, Beyoncé knew. "Mama, don't go."

But it was too late. The current owners weren't home, and somewhere there is Ring camera footage of me leaning in, saying, "Hi, I used to live here, and I was just wondering if we could look around. My daughter Beyoncé used to live here too. . . ." They were probably like, "Oh my God."

"Nobody home," I told Bey when I got in the car.

"They saw you coming," she joked. "Well, isn't . . . wait, my school is just down the street."

"Yes, it is," I said, watching my girl become that kindergartner again. "Straight this way a bit," I told the driver, flashing back to the morning drop-off at St. Mary of the Purification and then the race to Headliners.

Of course, I jumped out at the school, seeing these cute kids walking across the parking lot. With Beyoncé lingering back a little, I made a beeline to the children to say hi, which naturally terrified their teacher. I heard her say, "Hurry, kids" as I got closer, this strange woman in a white suit coming at them with open arms.

"No, no, no," I said. "You know my daughter used to go to school here and I—we—just wanted to say hi to the kids." The teacher still looked at me crazy, so I gestured behind me. "Well, it's Beyoncé," I said, quieter. Bey gave a wave, and the teacher relaxed, a bit stunned, as my daughter came forward to meet the little kids, telling the girls how she wore uniforms just like theirs. "My mama loves Beyoncé," one said, talking right to Bey in the third person. "She's going to see Beyoncé Saturday night."

"That's so cool," Beyoncé told her. "I'll see your mom there." Then this little boy started breakdancing, totally auditioning for her. We all laughed, cheering on this sweet kid.

The flood of memories continued as we drove on, Beyoncé pointing out the bushes on the side of the school. "I used to go and pick berries right there," she said. She held out her hand, and in that moment, she was my little girl in the Third Ward again, eating the berries as wild and free as she.

CHAPTER 53

READING THE MARGINS

Summer 2024

THERE WAS A different ending envisioned for this book. I had been looking for one for a while, living my life with a sort of double vision: remaining grounded in the moment I was in, but grasping the fullness of my life just lightly enough to hold it at arm's length for a better view. The moment had to be one meaningful enough to be worthy of sharing with you here, but also timeless, something profound I could offer you and know it would last the wear and tear of *your* life.

I thought I'd found an ending the week of July 4th, spending time with my grandchildren out at Beyoncé's house in the Hamptons. We live in the pool, and there was one moment I felt so alive as I played with Rumi, who at seven years old was telling me all about the world as she saw it. It was like those days on the beach with my family in Galveston. Between one of our turns showing how long we could hold our breath under the water, I came to the surface and felt eyes on me. I recognized a specific stillness to the air, the singular awareness of being watched with love.

I instinctively turned, half-expecting to see my mother. It was Beyoncé, watching her daughter laugh with her mother. I smiled, and she smiled back, both of us grateful to God.

Joy, for Black women, is transformative. My mother's history of illness and violence made her fearful in life, but her prayers were for me, for all the children she nurtured, to have something that would seem *this* miraculous. All of us somewhere together, swimming in the miracle of safety, freedom, and love.

That night I dictated the moment into my phone to save.

But God has His plan, and while my mother prayed for my joy, she also prayed for my strength. That same night, I made the decision to go back to Los Angeles earlier than I'd planned. I'd put off biopsies of two potentially cancerous masses in my breasts.

Three months earlier, when my doctor asked me when I'd had my last mammogram, I told her 2022. But when I made the actual appointment, I was told I had not had one for four years. I'd made an appointment in 2022 but was told they were not doing mammograms at the time because of Covid. Then my life got so busy that I gradually fell into the magical thinking that I had done it. So in April I did a full battery of tests, and the main result that concerned them and me was that the lining of my uterus had thickened to eleven millimeters, a potential sign of cancer. They wanted to schedule an endometrial biopsy right away. They also said the mammogram was a little funky, suggesting biopsies of two potential masses, one in each breast, but the endometrial biopsy was considered the priority.

I had the uterine biopsy right away, and when that turned out to be just a fibroid, I had a false sense of security about all of my health. I'd had bad mammograms before, all of which turned out to be false alarms, so I didn't tell my daughters. I repeatedly called to schedule the breast biopsies, but when they didn't have a slot or the doctor would be out of town, I didn't stay on top of it. This went on for *months* until I finally secured an actual date to come in. I'd lost so much time, but I convinced myself it couldn't be that bad if no one was really rushing me to get the biopsies.

I still hadn't told Beyoncé, and she urged me to simply stay in the Hamptons and relax, not knowing this would just delay things further. Some part of me wanted to give in to putting it off, but I left New York early to fly home for the Monday morning July 8 biopsies. I was fully awake for the procedure, just lidocaine to numb the area. For my right breast, they were guided by an ultrasound, but the biopsy for my left breast involved a mammogram, and I noted that the doctor kept coming back to retrieve more tissue.

This unsettled me, but I prayed on it and let it go. A week later, I was in an important meeting late in the day at Cécred, Beyoncé's hair care line that launched in February 2024. I had been a big part of developing the products, and I am the vice chair of the company and run it day to day along with the CEO, Grace Ray. When Grace's assistant came in to tell me my doctor was on the line, I reflexively said I would call her back.

"No, they want you to come *now*."

And I knew. I went into my office, closed the door. No one in the room but me and God.

My doctor told me I had breast cancer. A small tumor in my left breast that was cancerous; the larger tumor in my right breast was benign, but it would also have to go. She said I was Stage 1A, assuring me my prognosis was good. The next step was to talk to an oncologist and a breast surgeon. "We feel like we got this super early," she said. "You're going to be fine."

When I hung up, I sat there in a daze, rubbing my neck. I immediately thought of my father, all those times taking him to chemo and how much cancer took from him. I had been through all of this stuff in life getting to be seventy years old, and now I'm gonna get cancer?

The house felt lonelier now that I had this news to share. I did wish I had a companion to get through this. I had my daughters, but I didn't want to be fully vulnerable with them. I am their mother, and there will always be some part of me that protects them. I did not want to tell Beyoncé at night, because I knew she wouldn't be able to sleep, so I waited until the light of a new day. She took it well, staying positive, and I could already feel her mind racing, focusing on this as a task to tackle with precision. She would find me the top specialist, and I distinctly remember her telling me, "I want you to get a second opinion on whatever the course of treatment is."

Solange is my baby, and I knew it would be hard for me to tell her. "Mom, we are going to take care of this," she said. "We will figure out what to do." Kelly prayed with me, and Angie made sure I had that fighting spirit. My girls became my team.

Beyoncé lined up one of the top breast surgery specialists in the country for me to get a private consult. I already had an appointment with the hospital breast surgeon for the coming Monday and the hospital oncologist Tuesday, but this private doctor would be able to see me the Friday before. I decided I had been too passive. I'd waited to hear from the doctor to even get a mammogram, and it was on me for not following up. Then I waited to get my biopsies, convincing myself that if they thought it was a big deal, then they would be more on it. *I had to be my own advocate.*

So the two options were in my hands: the private-practice breast surgeon or the hospital surgeon. I liked the energy of the surgeon at the private practice right away—reassuring but open to my concerns. She told me about two tests she liked to give patients pre-op to plan on the best course of action: One was the MammaPrint, which would use breast tissue to show what type of cancer I had. "It will show if you are dealing with a poodle or a Rottweiler," she said, adding that the test could be run with the existing tissue from my biopsy. The other exam was relatively new, a Signatera blood test that would show if there were other cancer cells in my body.

At the Monday appointment with the hospital surgeon, I told her I wanted to have the two tests. "We do the MammaPrint *after* the surgery," she said, "because it has no bearing on the outcome on our decision to do surgery. We use the tissue that we take out during the surgery."

"Well, I want to," I said. "I want the test before *and* after, and I'll pay for it."

She conceded, but there was something about the way she said "If you insist" that rubbed me wrong.

The next day I went to the oncologist, but she did not agree to me having the Signatera blood test the specialist had suggested. In fact, she said most people wouldn't even want to know about the results of the blood test. "You'll just be stressed out waiting for the other shoe to drop."

"That's up to the individual, right? I want to know."

"Oh, you want to know if you're gonna die of cancer?"

Well, that did me in. She tried to recover, saying it would only lead patients to worry, but as I continued to ask questions, that insensitivity colored everything. She predicted that I would not need chemotherapy but would definitely need radiation—five to ten treatments if I was lucky. In fact, she said I would be on a hormone blocker for five years, nullifying any natural estrogen my body still produced. She wasn't receptive to my questions about what that would mean for my quality of life.

According to the hospital, they did this for everyone, which struck me as a cookie-cutter approach. It didn't sit right with me, and it's only as I write this now that I realize why I am so triggered by doctors who speak with the voice of God. When they shut me down or dismiss my valid questions, this brings up childhood feelings of being helpless with doctors. I feel vulnerable and at their mercy, not listened to, even at this age.

I left her office so depressed and confused. That night, I talked to the CEO of Cécred, explaining to her that I would be working around the surgery. Grace told me one of her friends had gone through the same thing, and that when she had the tumor removed, they also did a breast reduction. "Now she has some thirty-five-year-old perky boobs."

When Solange called to check on me, I tried to keep it light, repeating what I'd just heard. "Yeah, and now she's got these young perky boobs."

"Well, Mom, that's your silver lining," she said. "You always wanted smaller breasts." It was true—there were so many looks I couldn't wear because of my DDs.

I called the private-practice surgeon to make the suggestion. But she said that a breast reduction would be a good thing, because then they wouldn't have to be so precious about removing the cancerous tissue. I made my decision: I wasn't going with the hospital surgeon who talked down to me, I went with the private surgeon, the woman who gave me options and hope. She recommended a different oncologist at the hospital, one who she thought would be a better fit for me. That is the lesson I want to share: Even if I had gone with the hospital surgeon, I could have asked for another oncologist. A lot of people, especially Black people, feel they have to go with the doctor they are given even if we are not treated well. You deserve second opinions, and it's your opinion that sets the decision.

We scheduled the surgery for August 19, and in late July I flew to Houston to have the support of my family and friends as part of my pre-op prep. I wanted to tell my sister Flo about my diagnosis in person, and did so after we attended Sunday services at my home church, St. John's. That time was so great for my healing, and we shared a song of surrender, asking God to fix the problem within us.

I knew Flo would take this hard. Our handsome brother Butch had just passed in February at the age of seventy-seven, and losing our adventurer had hurt like hell. Butch stayed in the military forever before retiring in Austin with his wife of so many decades, Jeanette, and his devoted daughter Dana. He'd had a stroke in 2019, just after my sixty-fifth birthday party, and complications from a feeding tube left him unable to walk or even talk. In July that year, Selena passed, the girl who'd been left behind as a little one, only to become the woman who held us all together over ninety-two years. She died on our mother's birthday, and I picture them reunited with their Johnny in heaven to never ever part, revered in their glamour and anointed in His glory.

Slack Jr. had died in 2012, and Larry's increasing anxiety meant it was hard to communicate with him now. A tumor on his retina caused blindness, adding to his troubles. My mother had told me to take care of him and we did. Last year we moved him to Los Angeles so he could be with his daughter Angie and son Larry Jr. Now Flo was eighty, and acutely aware of her own mortality. Flo had tried so hard to look after all of us, even if she complained about how we drove her crazy. She was the nurse in the family, the one with the answers.

Flo stayed with me in my hotel suite but would be heading back to Galveston soon. I took a breath. "Well, I have something to tell you," I said. "I have breast cancer. It's not bad. It's early stages."

She looked shocked—a little scared—but she recovered herself to be the big sister. She hugged me and said, "Do you want me to come for the surgery?"

"No," I said. "I'm gonna have nurses and people staying there, in and out. I would rather you come after the surgery when I can enjoy the visit. That's what I'll need from you. Just you."

We were all that was left from our home in Galveston. Two sisters who always loved each other, but only grew to *know* each other later in life.

That night, the day had been so heavy that I just wanted to have fun. I called around, gathering some girlfriends, and we headed to an R&B club like it was the old days. This was part of fortifying me for the road ahead.

In that spirit, I flew to the Hamptons when I left Houston, for a concentrated week and a half with all my daughters and grandchildren before returning to L.A. for the surgery. Everybody rented places in the Hamptons, and Kelly, Solange, Angie, and even Michelle my belle came to hug on me at Beyoncé's. I wore no makeup the whole time, and played with my grandchildren all day. Julez came down for a couple of days, so busy in Manhattan working on his modeling career and his streetwear clothing brand. I drew strength from us talking about all he is doing. I have always been very close to Julez, this kind, loving, talented young man who has been so protective of me. "You look just like your great-grandfather," I told him, seeing my daddy in his beautiful eyes, that same cleft in their chins.

Sir and I both get up early while his sisters tend to sleep in, so I would get to walk to the swing set with him. Spend some time admiring the ducks, like I used to when his mother was little. Sir, Rumi, and Blue ride horses when they're in the Hamptons, and I would go watch them running free. Blue is, of course, good at that too, her posture so strong at twelve.

I would marvel at how special Kelly's sons Titan and Noah are, and I was continually amazed by the amount of facts nine-year-old Titan knew about the ocean. I would ask him, "Well, what's the fiercest creature in the ocean?" and as he answered I would make a big fuss—"Oh my God. Really?"—and ten minutes later realize everybody had slipped out while Titan still had more facts to share. But I was still gasping. "Are you serious?"

One day in the pool, the kids kept trying to dump me out of the floatie when I didn't want to get my hair wet. And Noah said in his cute three-year-old voice, so protective of me: "Him told you him not wanna get wet!" Noah always called me "him," and I brought him close as I then let the water carry me.

With their friends stopping by, it would be nothing for ten kids to be over there every day, bringing all that life. I would fall into prayer, not bargaining or begging, but thanking God for this time. I didn't think about endings—to this book or my life—I just stayed present with my beloveds.

I flew back for my pre-surgery exams, then Angie and I went to the surgical center first thing that Monday morning. When I walked in, Beyoncé, Solange, and Kelly were already there, surprising me. They surrounded me with love and prayer, and they sang to me. They chose "Walk with Me," the song Michelle did when she auditioned for Destiny's Child.

To lighten things, Solange got out her phone and pulled up a viral meme of a young trans woman saying, "See how I do my makeup for work? Very demure, very mindful."

"Mom, when you go through this surgery, you're gonna be demure and mindful. Cutesy." And they all started saying it, giggling. We quickly said one more prayer, and as I was being wheeled away, my daughters said to me: "Remember, *demure!*" I entered the surgical room laughing, thanks to them, God walking alongside me, with the joy and strength my mother prayed we would have.

BY THE GRACE OF GOD AND THE PRAYERS SAID FOR ME BEFORE I was even born, I emerged from that surgical room cancer-free. There were complications that weren't readily apparent: In September I had to have a second surgery to remove a hematoma—a blood clot that formed after the reduction. When I developed an infection some time after, Beyoncé decided she wanted to get the information firsthand instead of from me, and she insisted I put her on speaker during my consult in the exam room with the infectious disease specialist. The doctor was impressed with her questions; I was impressed by her care.

Beyoncé made me move into her house so she could supervise my recuperation, exactly as my mother or I would have done. My dear friend Rachelle Fields came to take round-the-clock care of me, which I know was a sacrifice because she would be the first to say she is a hermit, and the Carter household is always bustling with activity.

In my mind, I set October 8 as the time to be well enough to travel to New York. I was receiving a *Glamour* Women of the Year award, and being at the ceremony was important to me.

"Your *health* is more important," Beyoncé told me.

When I had recovered enough, the girls rearranged their schedules to be in New York with me for the night. When I rose to deliver my speech, it was a full-circle moment: me onstage looking at my daughters in the crowd. I spoke from my heart, opening up about the blessings of my life, raising four daughters, two who were born to me and two who were a gift to me from God. I looked out at my girls, their eyes shining too as I talked about what they have given me.

"They are my crew, my tribe, my rocks, my ride-or-dies," I said. "They have been right there by my side at the lowest points in my life"—my voice began to crack—"and they have cheered me on at the highest points of my life. Making me feel that I can conquer anything."

Kelly yelled out, "'Cause you *can,*" and the audience erupted in applause. Nobody in that room but my girls—and now you—could know what I was talking about. I was still finding the words then to discuss this experience of cancer, but they had been my witnesses. My daughters and my faith carried me through.

Afterward, Solange planned for a beautiful dinner in my honor at Wall & Water, a restaurant downtown. She invited my friends, going to all this trouble for me. We were way up high, with a beautiful view of New York City and its bright lights. Everybody made loving toasts, and I cried more tears of gratitude hearing the stories of how I had touched each person's life in some way. When the meal was over, the girls stayed behind with me to talk more, just us.

I didn't want the night to end, feeling like my daddy at one of those homecoming nights with his brothers at Weeks Island, or my mom at one of Holy Rosary's masquerade balls, laying eyes on all of the children who were hers or loved into being hers. She'd come to Galveston, taken life's sorrow, and planted a garden. Mama understood it's in the chill of February that is the best time to plant roses. She turned her tears to water for her garden and relied on the full sun of God's light to warm us.

Looking around the room at my family, I saw the roses my mother entrusted me to nurture, the vibrant blooms grown from seeds of knowledge and devotion passed down through a line of mothers. And it is this beautiful garden that I will leave my daughters to tend.

THE WAVES AT MALIBU

November 2024

I'M SITTING HERE on the balcony in Malibu, still healing but stronger each day. Some time ago, I rented this little bungalow to write my book. It's right out on the water, and when I am here, I can block out the world. In L.A., there is always someone to meet with about Tina's Angels, and at the Parkwood or Cécred offices the phone rings and rings and people line up needing answers. Here, the ocean overwhelms all distractions, so I can be present as I walk through my past.

The first week I had the bungalow, the forecast was not good. It doesn't rain often in Malibu, but when it does it's to make up for the eleven and a half months of sunshine. The morning I was set to go and start writing, my assistant Bria gave me an out. "We don't need to go today," she said. "It's going to be raining."

"That's my favorite time," I said.

I don't think she believed me. I am stubborn, I know, always determined to turn the lemons into lemonade. We got here at high tide, and I went out to the balcony, the waves so *big* and coming right up in this display of power. All that fury calmed me, and I let out a sigh.

"Ms. Tina, you *like* this?" Bria asked me.

"I *love* this." I sent her away to explore Malibu so I could be alone. I didn't have any furniture yet, so I brought a towel out here on the balcony to sit on. Looking out at the Pacific, I recorded the beginnings of my book into my phone.

I've been back out here to write again and again, and I've appreciated all the times that the weather has been nice, when the tide is low and the dolphins are jumping. But I love it when the waves are at their most ferocious. It's been in the roughest times of the ocean that I feel Galveston closest. Whenever there was a storm, me and Johnny would be headed to the beach. It wasn't that he loved it as much as me, but he loved *me*. So we'd go far out on the fishing pier to watch the water crash and splash against it. My mother told us not to go out on the pier—"The water will take you flying"—but we did it anyway because I loved it. And I still do. At seventy, I am still that girl, though there are years I forgot. My heart, that bird in my chest, still loves the swoop and glide of letting the wind carry me.

In January, I brought all my life's friends out here to Malibu to celebrate that milestone birthday of seventy. The guests were the women who provided the backbone of this story, keeping me strong from Galveston to Houston to L.A. My sister Flo who was also the birthday girl, Vernell, Cheryl, Angie Phea, Beverly, Toni Smith, Halcyon, Monica, Melba, Ada, Holly, Jo Ann, my favorite niece Denise . . . It was ambitious to bring together old friends with new ones, but it was a spiritual weekend. Beyoncé rented a house on the water that we all could fit in, and I gave Flo the best view. When she wanted to give it over to someone else, she stayed with me in my room, just like the January mornings in our home in Galveston, when Mama set the heat to keep us warm and safe. My daughters arranged for us all to have a big lunch at Nobu Malibu, and of course it got out of hand, so many vibrant women laughing hysterically, all these girlfriends vying to prove who knew me best by telling the craziest Tina story. The best surprise was that Michelle flew in from Atlanta, just so she, Kelly, and Beyoncé could serenade me, a Destiny's Child reunion to sing "Happy Birthday" in perfect harmony before going into Stevie Wonder's version with everybody joining in.

For this last writing session today, I filled the trunk of my car with boxes of photographs to go through. I am hunting for some I particularly want to share with you—a heart drawn in the sand, me and my nephews with my brothers as little kids—but each new photo evokes a memory, and I find myself pulling out the people to place them together here beside me. I set a photo of my mother next to a shot of Beyoncé as a girl, and then one of my father next to a favorite picture of Solange. People who were not on this earth for even one moment together yet seem to remain in conversation. A picture of my daughters Kelly and Angie eyes-closed hugging in New York City, one I took just last month, lies next to a photo of me and Johnny a lifetime ago in Texas. Somehow across space and time, this book gives me a glimpse of the sweet hereafter my mother prayed for and was promised.

That's been the gift of this time writing to bear witness to my own story—gathering all these people together so I can convey my gratitude as I take an inventory of blessings and hurdles that brought *more* blessings. That lemonade that is the story of my mother Agnes, and Odilia my grandmother; of Célestine and Rosalie. And my daughters and grandchildren too.

Sometimes that sip of lemonade just refreshes your perspective. As I continue to grow, I am working now to devote more of my everyday work to the support of young people nurturing dreams to reality. I hope I find love again, but if I feel the relationship is not mutually fulfilling and nurturing, or if we don't bring out the best in each other, then I don't want it. Because if I don't find companionship, I'm going to be okay. And that's a new revelation for me. I am *seventy* and I just learned that *I am enough*. I wish I would have realized this at forty or fifty, maybe even younger, but that is why I am telling you. I have tried to collect as much of that wisdom as I can to pass on here.

The sun is setting in the darkening sky of autumn, my favorite hue of orange mixing with gold and thinning wisps of blue. I have lingered out on this balcony watching the waves long enough, knowing I would finish the book today. This precious time of gathering memories is closing. It's not an end, I know, but my new beginning.

PHOTOGRAPH CAPTIONS

14. Me, fifth grade public school photo, c. 1964

15. My brother Butch, c. 1971

16. My sister Flo—my "birthday twin"—high school sophomore, c. 1960

17. Mervin "Slack" Jr. Marsh, my brother, c. 1949

18. Skip, my brother, high school senior prom, c. 1967

19. My sister Selena, c. 1954

20. My brother Larry, c. 1966

21. Me, Gail, and Polly at a rehearsal for the Veltones, c. 1969

22. Me in a self-designed outfit, c. 1971

23. Me at Selena's house, c. 1971

24. Me in an outfit Johnny made, c. 1972

25. Me in Galveston, Texas, c. 1974

26. Me and Denise, my fave niece, c. 1970

27. My mentor, Lydia, sitting on Larry's lap, c. 1964

28. Me and my niece Elouise, c. 1967

29. Me with my new asymmetrical haircut, high school senior year, c. 1972

30. Me on South Padre Island, six weeks after giving birth to Beyoncé

31. Me on South Padre Island, 1981

32. Me on a beach in Mykonos, Greece

33. Me with my new bob, c. 1977

34. Me with my cobra cut, Hawaii, c. 1984

35. Me again, with my bob, c. 1977

36. Me in Paris at the Hotel de Crillon, 1983

37. Me being fabulous at forty!

38. Mama Lou Helen (mother-in-law), Mathew, me, Mama Agnes (mother), wedding day, 1980

39. Me and Mathew, wedding day, 1980

40. Me and Mathew, wedding day, 1980

41. Me and Mathew cutting the wedding cake, 1980

42. Me expecting Beyoncé, 1981

43. Me with friends in Houston, 1981

INSERT 2

44. Baby Beyoncé Giselle at five months old; baby Tina (inset)

45. Me, new mother, South Padre Island beach, 1981

46. Beyoncé, last day at Park Plaza Hospital, 1981

47. Newborn Beyoncé and me, Park Plaza Hospital, 1981

48. Flo and Linda, my sister and niece, 1980

49. In my "Lena Horne look," with Johnny

50. Johnny in one of his famous silk shirts

51. Ada, Johnny, and me in a leather-and-lace dress I made

52. My eldest sister, Selena, with her son Johnny (who made her dress)

53. Flo (my sister) and Peanut, Johnny's boyfriend

54. Mathew and me, a few weeks after giving birth to Solange, 1986

55. Mathew and me; MUSR conference, c. 1980

56. Mathew and me posing for a local newspaper in front of Beyoncé's trophy collection, 1989

57. Me with Mathew in Paris, 1988

58. Me with Mathew, Egypt, 1985

59. Mathew and me on camels in front of an Egyptian pyramid, 1985

60. Mathew and me as Mark Antony and Cleopatra on a cruise down the Nile River, Egypt, 1985

61. Me with Mathew on a camel in Egypt, 1985

62. Me with the Egyptian children I gifted with my bracelets, Egypt, 1985

63. Me in Egypt on the Nile River (expecting Solange), 1985

64. Solange, age two, the perfect cheerleader

65. Solange at six in *Hair International* magazine

66. Little Solange at Chuck E. Cheese, her favorite place in the world

67. Solange; press shot for *Solo Star* album, 2002

68. Beyoncé, Solange, me, Angie Beyincé, and Bono in South Africa, 2003

69. Beyoncé at five playing her keyboard on top of the baby grand piano, Houston

70. Big girl Beyoncé at four years old

71. Beyoncé showing kindness to an unhoused man, 1988

72. Beyoncé posing at nine years old

73. Beyoncé on the day she bought her first car, a vintage Jaguar convertible

74. Beyoncé and Solange at Ms. Darlette's dance class

75. Solange (with flowers) and Beyoncé after Solange's dance recital, 1998

76. Beyoncé and Solange at seven and two on the front lawn, Houston

77. Beyoncé and Solange at Ms. Darlette's dance class

78. Beyoncé and Solange on set for the "Survivor" music video

79. My salon, Headliners, est. 1986, Houston

80. Lead Headliners stylist Toni Smith and young Beyoncé with braids, 1990

81. Me working the sewing machine, Destiny Fulfilled Tour, 2005

82. Me styling hair at the Bronner Bros. hair show, 1994

83. Kelly at five years old

84. Kelly at eight years old

85. Kelly at eleven years old

86. Doris Garrison (Kelly's mom) and Kelly

87. Christopher Lovett (Kelly's dad) and Kelly

88. Destiny's Child (original members), the day of their record deal signing, 1997

89. One of Destiny's Child's first shoots with *Honey* magazine, 1998

90. Michelle, Beyoncé, and Kelly at the 2000 Grammy Awards in gowns I created

91. Michelle, Beyoncé, and Kelly—Destiny's Child, the trio—at the Rockefeller Center tree lighting

92. Skip, Flo, me, Butch, Blue, and Selena (both of them sitting with their hands crossed, the way my mother used to do), 2015

93. Kelly, Solange, Bianca, Angie, Beyoncé, and me at my wedding to Richard Lawson, 2015

94. Beyoncé with my grandkids Sir, Blue, and Rumi, 2020

95. Solange with my grandson Julez, 2005

96. Kelly having family time with baby Noah, Titan, and husband, Tim, 2021

97. Angie, Julez, Solange, Beyoncé, and Kelly celebrate me at the 2024 *Glamour* Women of the Year gala

98. Angie, Beyoncé, Julez, Solange, and me at the dinner Solange gave me, 2024. Photo by Rafael Rios

99. Solange and I strike a pose at the *Glamour* Women of the Year gala, 2024. Photo by Rafael Rios

100. Julez (now a model) and me at the *Glamour* Women of the Year gala, 2024. Photo by Rafael Rios

ACKNOWLEDGMENTS

T**HERE IS NO *book without God* . . .**
> I first give all thanks and praises to my Heavenly Father, Jesus Christ, to whom I owe everything.

There is no book without foremothers . . .

Mothers, may I? I am the proud fruit of your ancestral tree: Rosalie, who begat Célestine, who begat Odilia, who begat Agnes.

There is no book without family . . .

Thank you, Mama, for being the shining example of selfless love, deep faith in God, and making a way out of no way. The lessons of loving sacrifice I learned under the pecan tree have been my own steadfast blueprint for motherhood.

Daddy, you were always there for me, the baby of the family. Every girl needs her father, and I am so blessed that you were mine. It is you who taught me the meaning of unconditional love.

My two incredible daughters that I birthed, Solange and Beyoncé. And my two who were a gift from God, Kelly and Angie. Your support of my writing process made all the difference. I cannot thank you enough for allowing—and encouraging—me to be so open about my life, about our lives. Y'all are my ready-made cheering squad, and I thank God daily for your love. The world will never know your tenderness as I do. You all are my greatest blessings. My *crew.*

To my siblings in heaven: Mervin, My Selena, My Butch, and My Beautiful Skip. How lucky was I to have you in my life story? Flo, my forever birthday twin, look at us now. It means so much to me that we wound up being so close. I love you, sister. Larry, I still love your genius mind. . . .

Julez, my first grandchild; my road dog since your birth. I am so proud of the man you've become! I love you with all my heart. To my other grandbabies: Blue, Rumi, and Sir, you've been a lifeline of joy for me when I needed it most! Titan and Noah, you boys bring me pure happiness!

Johnny, my brother, my sister, my soulmate. I still miss you.

Jay, thank you for always loving me, supporting me, including me, and advising me. Thank you for loving and protecting Bey and the kids. Your heart is huge. You are the best son-in-law I could ask for and I love you.

Tim Weatherspoon, I love you dearly and I truly admire the hubby and father you are.

There is no book without a team . . .

Kierna, my beautiful editor, the many times we connected over and over in life led us to this moment. It was meant to be.

Kevin, another Johnny in my life and my writing soulmate, you found facts about my family and history that I didn't even know, and you made me feel safe enough to open up about things that I never would have. The best collaborator I could ask for. We did the damn thing!

Albert at UTA and Andrea, you both saw the vision and made me believe I could do this. I truly value your steadfast support.

Special love to the dedicated force behind the scenes: Yvette, you are family forever. Justina, Tyler, Leah, Bria, and Siena, thank you for seeing to all the little details. I appreciate you all more than I can ever say.

Thank you to the One World family who helped bring *Matriarch* to life: Chris Jackson, Sun Robinson-Smith, Carla Bruce, Susan Corcoran, Lulu Martinez, Tiffani Ren, Rebecca Berlant, Elizabeth Rendfleisch, Greg Mollica, Dennis Ambrose, Michael Burke, Avideh Bashirrad, Raaga Rajagopala, Casey Blue James, and Hiab Debessai.

To Kelani Fatai, thank you for this stunning work of art, you are so incredibly talented, but also so very kind. You helped make this book a beautiful visual object to behold. I cannot wait to see your career blossom.

To all of the Parkwood, Cécred, WACO, and BeyGOOD staff, I just adore your creative minds, thank you for sharing your brilliance.

There is no book without community . . .

My mentor, Lydia, you completely changed the trajectory of my life the day you took me to see Alvin Ailey. No words will ever capture the depth of my gratitude.

I've been blessed with the best girlfriends ever. They laugh and cry with me, they boot me up and always keep me grounded: Cheryl, Angie P., Rachelle, Wanda, Monica, Melba, Joanne, Halcyon, Ada, Denise, Toni, Beverly, Holly, Alvia, Lorraine, and my beautiful BFF since sixth grade, Vernell.

Also, the Road Dawgs, and Rudy and Juanita Rasmus. I love you and I am grateful for you.

Tyler Perry, you are a guardian angel; I will never forget your gifts of grace and understanding. Michelle Williams, with you as my prayer warrior, I will always triumph.

I must also shout out: Tina's Angels and Richard's Warriors, Melina, Kasi, Amanda, Johnny C., Ricky, Shiona, Jay and Kawana Brown, Emory, Andrea and Justice Brown, Neal F., Somer, Mellisa, Nakia, Kole, Trell, Terrance, Amanda, Neil B., Daniel S. Lese, Barbara L., Charlie, Cornelius, and Reign. Love, love, love y'all!

So much love to you, Gio.

Thank you to my brother Tim White, Miss Enid and Linda, Hymie, and Ty—the creative geniuses who made all the fashions I designed over the decades come to life.

Mathew, my babies' daddy, you will always be our family.

Richard, thanks for the good years.

A forever thank-you to the BeyHive for consistently having my back and for leading with love. Y'all are my babies, too.

There is no book without . . . Celestine Ann, Badass Tenie B, Lucy, Tina Beyoncé from Galveston, Almost-Grown Tina in L.A., Mrs. Knowles, Headliners Tina from Houston, Mrs. Knowles-Lawson, Mama Tina, and now, finally, Ms. Tina.

I am grateful for every single version of me. It took me a lifetime to get here. Without self-love there is no *Matriarch*.

ABOUT THE AUTHOR

TINA KNOWLES is an American businesswoman, fashion designer, art collector, and activist. Born Celestine Ann Beyoncé in Galveston, Texas, to a longshoreman father and seamstress mother, she learned dressmaking at an early age. In 1986, she opened Headliners, a groundbreaking hair salon that became a multimillion-dollar phenomenon in Houston. As a stylist, designer, and mother, she helped guide the day-to-day path of Destiny's Child—the music group comprised of Beyoncé Knowles, Kelly Rowland, and Michelle Williams, and former members LaTavia Roberson and LeToya Luckett—to global commercial success. With her daughter Beyoncé, she cofounded and ran the House of Deréon, a clothing line named for her mother, later adding the Miss Tina line, which revolutionized size inclusivity. In 2024, she helped to create Cécred, her daughter Beyoncé's hair care line. Her philanthropic portfolio includes the nonprofit performing arts organization WACO Theater Center, the Knowles-Rowland Center for Youth in Houston, and Tina's Angels, her thriving mentoring program for at-risk youth in South Central Los Angeles. She serves as chairwoman of BeyGOOD, a nonprofit dedicated to establishing economic equity through a wide array of initiatives. Tina Knowles is a grandmother of six and a Matriarch to many.